POWERFUL IDEAS

An Introduction to Philosophy

OCTAVIO ROCA

MATTHEW SCHUH

Miami Dade College

Kendall Hunt
publishing company

Kendall Hunt
publishing company

www.kendallhunt.com
Send all inquiries to:
4050 Westmark Drive
Dubuque, IA 52004-1840

Copyright © 2015 by Octavio Roca and Matthew Schuh

ISBN 978-1-4652-7468-7

Printed in the United States of America

CONTENTS

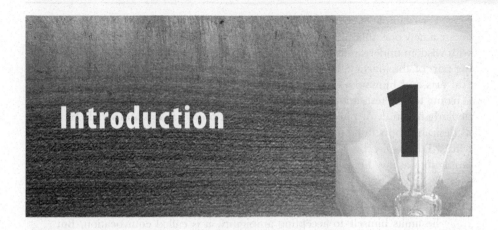

Introduction

1

Upon completing this chapter, students should be able to meet the following Learning Outcomes:

1.1 Articulate the benefits that a student may gain by studying philosophy.

1.2 Explain the Socratic Method of teaching.

1.3 Explain how critical thinking can be used to analyze a philosophical issue.

1.4 Compare and contrast induction, abduction, and deduction.

1.5 Evaluate philosophical arguments.

1.6 Synthesize or create a philosophical argument.

Importance of Philosophical Study

The word **philosophy** as many of the most interesting words in the English language do comes from Greek. The word is often translated as "the love of wisdom." This statement although true presupposes a distinction that Aristotle made in his study of knowledge—between "knowing how" to do something and "understanding how" the something you are doing actually takes place. For Aristotle, true knowledge was the deeper understanding of processes.

For example, a chemistry student may know how to mix certain chemicals to create a new one: mix two parts of X to one part of Y and get Z . . ., but the student with wisdom understands why the result unfolds. This unfolding is the most interesting part of the journey. That journey is alarmingly difficult these days, with the liberal arts and humanities under constant attack and learning too often defined as learning to take tests and learning how to get a job. And yet a liberal education, particularly the study of philosophy, may help in a project that is and should be at least as desirable: how to be happy, how to have a meaningful life, and how to know the truth. Truth may be objective and universal, but finding the truth can be as ambiguous as it is difficult. That is not a bad thing.

> "The philosopher is marked by the distinguishing trait that he possesses inseparably the taste for evidence and the feeling for ambiguity. When he limits himself to accepting ambiguity, it is called equivocation. But among the great it becomes a theme; it contributes to establishing certitudes rather than menacing them. Therefore it is necessary to distinguish good and bad ambiguity. It is useless to deny that philosophy limps. It dwells in history and in life, but it wishes to dwell at their center, at the point where they come into being with the birth of meaning"
>
> —*Maurice Merleau-Ponty, In Praise of Philosophy*

We tell our students that it is our hope that by the end of the course in introduction to philosophy they will know *less* than when they entered. This is not because we do not want them to learn about the various important ideas and thinkers that have grappled with deep philosophical questions, but rather it is because by the end of the course we want them to be in a position to examine their own beliefs and realize that most of what they are certain is true, is not. Our hope is that they develop the ability to think, reason, and evaluate ideas during the course. The study of philosophy involves critical thinking, which will be discussed below.

> "There is innate in the human heart a metaphysical hunger to know and understand what lies beyond the mysterious veil of nature . . . Philosophy is one of life's noblest pursuits; although its wisdom is the reward of few"
>
> —*Theos Bernard, 1947, Hindu Philosophy.*

Structure of the Textbook

This book is structured around various themes and ideas in philosophy. There is some overlap between chapters and many important philosophers will show in more than one place. Although the book is centered around important themes or questions, due respect is given to history and to the philosophers who have made contributions to the topics discussed, regardless of their historical era.

The Socratic Method

Another aspect of the book is its reliance upon the **Socratic Method**. Socrates was famous for asking broad questions in hopes of finding precise answers—he famously failed in this endeavor on more than one occasion—oftentimes pointing out to his interlocutors that they did not know the answers either. The Socratic Method is one of the oldest and powerful methods of teaching. The method develops critical thinking and involves giving students questions but not answers. It involves inquiry, analysis, evaluation, and synthesis of thoughts and ideas. Engaging in this process of questioning and probing can put our thoughts in order. Asking questions such as what is real? how we acquire knowledge? or how can we make value judgments? Our aim here is to help bring these questions into sharper focus and provide a foundation for the answers we are looking for.

Powerful Thinkers: Socrates

Socrates (469–399 BCE) asked probing questions of the intellectual elite in Athens. A stonecutter (or mason) by day, when he was not working, he was engaged in philosophical discourse with his students—or with just about anyone who would engage with him in the streets of ancient Athens. All sources agree that Socrates was exceedingly ugly, had an unorthodox (lowly) manner of dress, and often wandered around barefoot and seeming confused.

Socrates' students once made an offering to the Oracle at Delphi, the most holy temple not far from Athens dedicated to the god Apollo. They asked the Oracle who the wisest man in the world was. She declared that Socrates was the wisest of men. When he heard this, he said he was wise because he admitted his ignorance! Socrates taught orally and did not put his doctrines into writing. He did not write books. His student, Plato (439–347 BCE), wrote dialogues that reflect his views. The Socrates we know is a literary creation of Plato. He is the most famous philosopher who never wrote anything. The dialogues written by Plato are accounts of debates that Socrates had with other philosophers or sophists—a group of philosophers who taught rhetoric and denied the existence of a permanent truth. Unlike the sophists, who were paid for teaching wealthy aristocrats the skills of oration and persuasive argument, Socrates charged no fees and taught students, including women, from all walks of life. In one dialog, Plato's *Meno*, Socrates is shown in conversation with a slave boy that the slave in question and his owner were equal in terms of capacity to learn.

Unfortunately, in 399 BCE, Socrates' luck ran out and he was put on trial on trumped-up charges. It was the democratic government of Athens, not the oligarchy that preceded it, that put Socrates to death. This fact did not escape the notice of Plato, Socrates' young friend and pupil, who would harbor a distrust of democracy for the rest of his life—Plato's *Republic* embodies that mistrust, and his suggestion that perhaps idiots shouldn't be allowed to vote is just one of the many political principles that Plato suggests.

Socrates was accused of impiety, that is, of being unreligious, and of corrupting the youth of Athens. This was a time of uncertainty in the first democracy, following a humiliating military defeat by Sparta in the Peloponnesian War. Socrates, who was neither wealthy nor liked very much by the wealthy, was an easy target. A jury of 500 found Socrates guilty of his crimes, and he was sentenced to death. It is believed that he could have escaped into exile, but that would have meant violating Athenian laws that he had respected and followed his whole life. "It is better to suffer evil than to do evil," he said after his trial.

Areas of Philosophy

There are various areas of philosophy that are discussed within the textbook. **Critical thinking** is infused throughout the textbook. It deals with the evaluation of philosophical arguments. Such arguments normally consist of a number of premises and a conclusion. The premises provide reasons in support of the conclusion or position taken by the argument.

> "Thus, all Philosophy is like a tree, of which Metaphysics is the root, Physics the trunk, and all the other sciences the branches that grow out of this trunk, which are reduced to three principals, namely, Medicine,

Mechanics, and Ethics. By the science of Morals, I understand the highest and most perfect which, presupposing an entire knowledge of the other sciences, is the last degree of wisdom"

—*René Descartes, personal correspondence*

Metaphysics deals with the nature of existence, asking the question "What is real?" Metaphysics is a very broad field, and metaphysicians attempt to answer questions about *how the world is*. Ontology is a related subfield, partially within metaphysics, that answers questions of *what things exist in the world*. An ontology posits which entities exist in the world. So, while a particular metaphysics may include an implicit ontology (which means, *how* your theory describes the world may imply specific *things* in the world), they are not necessarily the same field of study.

Epistemology is closely tied to metaphysics and ontology, no longer asking what is real but asking "How do you know?" It deals with the nature and foundations of knowledge. Epistemologists employ various methods such as rationalism (knowledge based on logical analysis of ideas and terms) or empiricism (knowledge based on observation and experience) to formulate arguments to justify or support belief and knowledge claims.

Aesthetics deals with contemplating and making judgments about beauty. Our enjoyment, appreciation, and judgment of art—together with the question of what defines art to begin with—are the key elements to consider in aesthetics. The word itself is derived from the Greek Αισθητική, *aisthetikos*, meaning "coming from the senses." More than any other branch of axiology, that is, of the philosophy of making value judgments, aesthetics has sensuality built into it as much as it has seductive, ineffable quality in its critical analysis. Still, though some philosophers disagree, it is not just a matter of taste.

Ethics studies questions about right and wrong. Ethical theories provide a framework for answering those questions and for evaluating human actions. There are various views on what constitutes good and bad, as well as what have value. Ethics can be broadly broken down into deontological theories, which evaluate morality on the basis of actions, and teleological theories, which evaluate morality on the basis of the consequences. Other major ethical theories focus on virtues, sentiments, or even intuitions.

Political philosophy deals with questions pertaining to the foundations, nature, and purpose of government. It is closely related to the philosophy of law, which focuses on the foundation and nature of laws and legal systems. Social structures can be analyzed philosophically from both an economic perspective and a political one.

And finally, a particular field within metaphysics, **philosophy of religion,** is considered from both an Eastern and a Western perspective. From a Western perspective, the topics include proofs of the existence of a three omni (omni-benevolent, omniscience, and omnipotent) God, the rationality of religious belief, and the problem of evil. A number of Eastern religions and philosophical systems are discussed as well. These include Hinduism, Buddhism, Taoism, and Confucianism. Topics in Eastern philosophy also include reincarnation, karma, and the connection between Taoist principles and traditional Feng Shui.

POWERFUL IDEAS: DIVISIONS OF PHILOSOPHY

- Logic
- Metaphysics: Nature of Existence
- Epistemology: Theory of Knowledge
- Philosophy of Religion
- Eastern Philosophy
- Aesthetics
- Ethics: Study of Right and Wrong
- Political Philosophy

Although we focus on the main branches of philosophy within this introductory book on the topic, there are various other areas of philosophy. In fact, there can be a philosophical analysis of just about any topic in academia. For example, there are courses in philosophy of Education, Law, Science, Physics, Biology, Mathematics, Psychology, and Bioethics, just to name a few.

Ultimately, these topics are deep and have profound questions, and many of them will have bearing upon your life now or in the future. Each and every one of us is born into a political society. Further, we each make ethical decision every day. We may not always consider the meaning of life, but when things get tough or bad things happen, we often do reflect on these issues.

POWERFUL ANALYSIS: WHY ARE YOU HERE?

We often ask our students on the first day or during the first week, why are you here? For the most part, we know the answer: a philosophy class fulfills a general education requirement. But that is not the question I am asking. I am asking, why are you in college? What is your goal? Are you here because your parents said "go to school or get a job!" or are you here because "you have a job but want a career?" Socrates said, "The unexamined life is not worth living"; take some time to consider yours now and where you want it to be 5 years from now.

Logic and Critical Thinking

Logic is the study of rational thought. Logic is highly systematized and there are various logics that are almost mathematical in nature. In logic, there are various formal and informal fallacies. Formal fallacies denote a flaw in the structure of an argument. These are discussed in detail in logic courses. Informal fallacies are a flaw in reasoning that we make when we construct an argument. For example, when we make assumptions that are not supported by the evidence (or premise), then we are committing some version of an informal fallacy. So generally, the term "fallacy" is used to denote an unacceptable way of thinking or reasoning.

"We never come to thoughts. They come to us"

—*Martin Heidegger*

Critical thinking, on the other hand, is less systematized and somewhat more abstract. Critical thinking is the engagement of the thinker in rational deliberation, investigation of facts and reasons, and the evaluation of arguments. In this book, these ideas appear in the form of essays, readings, and philosophical arguments. As students of philosophy, one must be willing to employ rationality. Students must be able to justify their views in a coherent way. The skills that are developed by engaging in philosophical thought and analysis are essential for any college student or citizen in a democratic society.

Deduction

Deduction is the process of reasoning from one or more statements known as **premises** to reach a logically certain **conclusion**. Premises are statements made in support of a conclusion of an argument. The conclusion is the main position defended in an argument that is supported by the premises. Taken together, the premises and conclusion create an **argument**.

In deduction or deductive logic, an argument (which is what the premise and conclusion are called, collectively) must employ a **valid** (or correct formal) structure. A valid structure ensures that if the premises are true, then the conclusion must be true. There are various recognized valid structures, everything from the syllogism created by Aristotle to modus tollens.

POWERFUL IDEAS: DEDUCTIVE ARGUMENT STRUCTURE- MODUS TOLLENS

Modus tollens, which is Latin and means "the way that denies by denying," has a deductive structure as follows:

PàQ

~Q

Therefore, ~P

In the above argument, P and Q are variables that can stand for any term, and ~P and ~Q are the negations. The à means "if and only if." For example,

P could stand for the statement "pigs can fly," Q could stand for the statement, "it is raining." ~P would then mean, "pigs cannot fly" and ~Q would state, "it is not raining."

So, the argument would look as follows with the variables replaced by the statements:

1) pigs can fly and it is raining

2) it is not raining

3)Therefore, pigs cannot fly

As noted above, the argument about pigs flying has a valid structure, yet the conclusion is only true if the premises are true. Yet, the argument is lacking an important feature, it is not **sound.** A sound argument is one where the premises have some true relation between them. There is no correlation between the rain and pigs flying. The above argument, although it has a valid structure, is unsound and therefore false. If an argument is both valid and sound, then the conclusion must be true.

An example of an argument that is both valid and sound is as follows:

If your father is Prince William, then you are either Charlotte or George. Your father is in fact Prince William, therefore you are either Charlotte or George. These statements are all true (until Prince William and Duchess Kate have more children).

POWERFUL ANALYSIS: VALID AND SOUND

By employing some basic logically valid forms, determine if the arguments are both valid and sound.

1) If the traffic light turns red, I should stop. The traffic light has turned red, therefore I should stop.

2) If Florida is south of New York, then everyone is happy. Florida is south of New York, therefore everyone is happy.

3) If she is crying, she must be sad. She is crying, therefore she must be sad.

4) All dogs go to heaven when they die. Lassie is a dog that has died, therefore she went to heaven.

5) All people live on Earth. Sam is a person, therefore he lives on earth.

Induction

Although deduction is a powerful method of reasoning, it is not the one we normally employ on a daily basis. Rather for the most part, we draw our beliefs from a form of logic known as induction. Induction is a type of reasoning where the premises provide strong evidence for (not absolute proof of) the truth of the conclusion. For example, when we flip a light switch, we assume the lights will turn on. We believe this because of our past experience and observations of the world. Although it would be wonderful if the lights always turn on, we all know there are times they do not. So, the conclusion of an induction is not 100% certain.

Powerful Thinkers: David Hume (1711–1776)

David Hume (1711–1776) was a staunch opponent of inductive reasoning. He argued that most of our beliefs (and any that rely upon induction) are simply custom or habit. He was known as the Great Infidel in his lifetime, but today, he is widely considered the key figure in the Scottish Enlightenment and the greatest philosopher in the English language.

David Hume believed that we assume too much, not only about ourselves but also about the world around us. He believed, in fact, that we have no proof of any causal necessity in the order of events. There is no reason why the future will follow from the present, or at least we cannot prove the connection since all we perceive are the events themselves. We know only as much as we can gather from experience. The very concept of cause and effect is a projection of our understanding, not a fact. The laws of science are generalizations from inductive reasoning. And inductive reasoning, Hume believed, simply cannot lead us to the truth.

He considered emotions to be significant, both in aesthetics and in ethics, given that there was no evidence for either aesthetic or moral facts. Our taste determines what we mean by good or bad art, just as our approval or disapproval is all we can mean by right or wrong.

His skepticism went still farther. We never experience our own self directly, only the continuing chain of experiences in our lives. All knowledge in fact is based on sense impressions and on experiences. It follows that we don't even have any factual knowledge of the self since any conception of identity must be based on impressions. "It must be some impression that gives rise to every real idea," he wrote in his *Treatise on Human Nature* when he was only 24. The self is not any one impression, but that to which our several impressions are supposed to have a reference. Therefore, as far as our idea of the self, Hume believed "there is no such idea."

He was born and died in Edinburgh, Scotland. An empiricist of considerable influence on future philosophy, Hume anticipated the science of psychology by more than a century in his precocious *Treatise*. But describing emotions accurately, while pointing out the impossibility of using reason as a guide to aesthetics or ethics, is not the same thing as prescribing a course of action. It may very well be true that "morals excite passions, and produce or prevent actions," Hume wrote, adding that "reason itself is utterly impotent in this particular."

As Hume developed his ideas, he also was led to discovering the faulty logic of what is today called an "intelligent design" argument for the existence of God. Hume was an atheist, a skeptic, and a confirmed bachelor to boot—none of which endeared to the church. Like his intimate friend and fellow philosopher Adam Smith, Hume longed for a teaching position in the University of Edinburgh. He did not get his wish; an influential clergy made sure that he never would teach. In fact, Hume narrowly escaped being tried for heresy. Smith did land a position late in life in his own alma mater, the University of Glasgow.

Hume died of cancer in 1776, shortly after completing his autobiography. The younger Adam Smith died in Edinburgh in 1790. Adam Smith is buried in the Canongate churchyard in Edinburgh's Royal Mile, not far from a monument honoring David Hume, itself not far from the venerable university that would not have either of them.

Abduction

The concept of abduction was first introduced by Charles Sanders Peirce. He meant it to mean a type of non-deductive inference that was different than induction. Abduction is also known as "Inference to the Best Explanation." Abduction is the process of reasoning that is a type of non-deductive inference where based on the evidence at hand we draw an inference to the best explanation. It is believed to be commonly employed by people on a regular basis. Peirce thought that it was the only way to generate new ideas in the realm of science. He also thought that we make observations and developed new ideas based on what we see. For example, if we know there was a football game today, but we did not see the score, but we see a picture of all of the fans belonging to one of the teams sad and crying, it is safe for us to conclude that the team has lost and the other team has won.

"Abduction consists in studying facts and devising a theory to explain them. Its only justification is that, if we are ever to understand things at all, it must be in that way"

—*C. S. Peirce, 1932, Collected Papers*

Putting It All Together: Evaluating Philosophical Readings and Arguments

When evaluating a reading in philosophy, it is essential to clearly articulate your view. You must not assume that your audience knows what you are thinking, but you should clearly state each premise and the reasoning behind it. You will note that many of the readings by philosophers in this textbook break this first rule. There are times when the ideas of philosophers seem tangential or even incomprehensible. This should not be discouraging—you will grow in your understanding and comprehension of the readings as you read more philosophy. The readings selected for this book have been shortened in many cases, and attempts have been made by the authors of this book to focus on some of the main points of the various philosophers represented in the book. As a student, when you read philosophy, you should focus on those essential points. If you were asked to summarize a reading, you could think of it as a book report where you find the main ideas and explain what those ideas are by citing the evidence from the text.

"We never come to thoughts. They come to us"

—*Martin Heidegger*

POWERFUL IDEAS: ANALYZING A PHILOSOPHICAL ARGUMENT

Let's consider an example of a philosophical argument from the philosopher René Descartes. Descartes argues that he can doubt his body but not his mind. He goes on to argue that since his body can be doubted, but his mind cannot, they must be different things. These statements are structured in a systematic way, but they could be. His main point is that the body has a property or quality that the mind does not; since they have different qualities, they must be different things.

To clarify Descartes' argument, consider the following: if you're a member of a tribe cut off from the modern world and have never seen a smartphone, but one day you see a smartphone next to a book—regardless of what you thought of the two objects, logic would dictate that they could not be the same type of object because they have different qualities.

Books are made of paper, and smartphones are made of metal and plastic. Books have pages, smartphones have apps. These differences lead to the conclusion that they are not the same object. None of this is profound, but in Descartes' case, he is attempting to argue that the mind and body are different. His views will be examined later, but the crux of the argument in his view is that one can be doubted and the other cannot.

Ultimately, however, the argument fails because Descartes' doubt is not an actual property of his body. Descartes' internal psychological state or perception of reality has no bearing upon his body. In other words, your perception of an object does not change its qualities. A better argument for Descartes' views on the mind and body will be considered in another chapter.

In short, philosophy is a study in the analysis of ideas. We analyze ideas each and every day. We do so at work and at home. We deal with complex issues and problems and try to develop solutions. The study of philosophy will enhance your ability to analyze the trials and tribulations of life.

What, Then, Does Philosophy Do, Exactly?

Philosophy aims at the kind of knowledge which gives unity to the body of the sciences, and the kind which results from a critical examination of the grounds of our convictions, prejudices, and beliefs. But it cannot be maintained that philosophy has had any very great measure of success in its attempts to provide definite answers to its questions. If you ask a mathematician, a historian, or any other man of learning, what definite body of truths has been ascertained by his science, his answer will last as long as you are willing to listen. But if you put the same question to a philosopher, he will have to confess that his study has not achieved positive results such as have been achieved by other sciences. It is true that this is partly accounted for by the fact that, as soon as definite knowledge concerning any subject becomes possible, this subject ceases to be called philosophy. The whole study of the heavens, which now belongs to astronomy, was once included in philosophy; Newton's great work was called "the mathematical principles of natural philosophy." The study of the human mind, which was a part of philosophy, has now been separated from philosophy and has become the science of psychology. Those questions which are already capable of definite answers are placed in the sciences, while those only to which, at present, no definite answer can be given, remain to form the residue which is called philosophy. Bertrand Russell, *The Problems of Philosophy*.

POWERFUL ANALYSIS

Can you see ways that the study of philosophy might benefit you in other facets of your life?

READINGS

What is it we do when we think, and is it something we can learn? Martin Heidegger (1889–1976) in this excerpt from his book *What Is Called Thinking?* suggests that in order to be capable of thinking, we need to learn it. And we learn to think by paying attention to what there is to think about.

WHAT CALLS FOR THINKING?

We come to know what it means to think when we ourselves are thinking. If our attempt is to be successful, we must be ready to learn thinking.

As soon as we allow ourselves to become involved in such learning we have admitted that we are not yet capable of thinking.

Yet man is called the being who can think, and rightly so. Man is the rational animal. Reason, *ratio*, evolves in thinking. Being the rational animal, man must be capable of thinking if he really wants to. Still, it may be that man wants to think, but can't. Ultimately he wants too much when he wants to think, and so can do too little. Man can think in the sense that he possesses the possibility to do so. This possibility alone, however, is no guarantee to us that we are capable of thinking. For we are capable of doing only what we are inclined to do. And again, we truly incline toward something only when it in turn inclines toward us, toward our essential being, by appealing to our essential being as what holds us there. To hold genuinely means to heed protectively, for example, by letting a herd graze at pasture. What keeps us in our essential being holds us only so long, however, as we for our part keep holding on to what holds us. And we keep holding on to it by not letting it out of our memory. Memory is the gathering of thought. To what? To what holds us, in that we give it thought precisely because it remains what must be thought about. What is thought is the gift given in thinking back, given because we incline toward it. Only when we are so inclined toward what in itself is to be thought about, only then are we capable of thinking.

In order to be capable of thinking, we need to learn it. What is learning? Man learns when he disposes everything he does so that it answers to whatever addresses him as essential. We learn to think by giving heed to what there is to think about.

For example, what is essential in a friend is what we call "friendliness." In the same sense we now call what in itself is to be thought about "the thought-provoking." Everything thought-provoking *gives* us to think. But it always gives that gift just so far as the thought-provoking matter already *is* intrinsically what must be thought about. From now on, we will call "most thought-provoking" what remains to be thought about always, because it is so at the beginning and before all else. What is most thought-provoking? How does it show itself in our thought-provoking time?

Most thought-provoking is that we are still not thinking—not even yet, although the state of the world is becoming constantly more thought-provoking. True, this course of events seems to demand rather that man should act without delay, instead of making speeches at conferences and international conventions and never getting beyond proposing ideas on what ought to be, and how it ought to be done. What is lacking, then, is action, not thought.

It is no evidence of any readiness to think that people show an interest in philosophy. There is, of course, serious preoccupation everywhere with philosophy and its questions. The learned world is expending commendable efforts in the investigation of the history of philosophy. These are useful and worthy tasks, and only the best talents are good enough for them, especially when they present to us models of great thinking. But even if we have devoted many years to the intensive study of the treatises and writings of the great thinkers, that fact is still no guarantee that we ourselves are thinking, or even are ready to learn thinking. On the contrary—preoccupation with philosophy more than anything else may give us the stubborn illusion that we are thinking just because we are incessantly "philosophizing."

Even so, it remains strange, and seems presumptuous, to assert that what is most thought-provoking in our thought-provoking time is that we are still not thinking. Accordingly, we must prove the assertion. Even more advisable is first to explain it. For it could be that the demand for a proof collapses as soon as enough light is shed on what the assertion says. It runs:

Most thought-provoking in our thought-provoking time is that we are still not thinking.

It has been suggested earlier how the term "thought-provoking" is to be understood. Thought-provoking is what gives us to think. Let us look at it closely, and from the start allow each word its proper weight. Some things are food for thought in themselves, intrinsically, so to speak, innately. And some things make an appeal to us to give them thought, to turn toward them in thought: to think them.

What is thought-provoking, what gives us to think, is then not anything that we determine, not anything that only we are instituting, only we are proposing. According to our assertion, what of itself gives us most to think about, what is most thought-provoking, is this—that we are still not thinking.

This now means: We have still not come face to face with, have not yet come under the sway of, what intrinsically desires to be thought about in an essential sense. Presumably the reason is that we human beings do not yet sufficiently reach out and turn toward what desires to be thought. If so, the fact that we are still not thinking would merely be a slowness, a delay in thinking or at most a neglect on man's part. Such human tardiness could then be remedied in human ways by the appropriate measures. Human neglect would give us food for thought—but only in passing. The fact that we are still not thinking would be thought-provoking, of course, but being a momentary and curable condition of modern man, it could never be called the one most thought-provoking matter. Yet that is what we call it, and we suggest thereby the following: that we are still not thinking is by no means only because man does not yet turn sufficiently toward that which, by origin and innately, wants to be thought about since in its essence it remains what must be thought about. Rather, that we are still not thinking stems from the fact that what is to be thought about turns away from man, has turned away long ago.

We will want to know at once when that event took place. Even before that, we will ask still more urgently how we could possibly know of any such event. And finally, the problems which here lie in wait come rushing at us when we add still further: that which really gives us food for thought did not turn away from man at some time or other which can be fixed in history— no, what really must be thought keeps itself turned away from man since the beginning.

On the other hand, in our era man has always thought in some way; in fact, man has thought the profoundest thoughts, and entrusted them to memory. By thinking in that way he did and does remain related to what must be thought. And yet man is not capable of really thinking as long as that which must be thought about withdraws.

If we, as we are here and now, will not be taken in by empty talk, we must retort that everything said so far is an unbroken chain of hollow assertions, and state besides that what has been presented here has nothing to do with scientific knowledge.

We can learn thinking only if we radically unlearn what thinking has been traditionally. To do that, we must at the same time come to know it.

We said: man still does not think, and this because what must be thought about turns away from him; by no means only because man does not sufficiently reach out and turn to what is to be thought.

What must be thought about turns away from man. It withdraws from him. But how can we have the least knowledge of something that withdraws from the beginning, how can we even give it a name? Whatever withdraws, refuses arrival. But—withdrawing is not nothing. Withdrawal is an event. In fact, what withdraws may even concern and claim man more essentially than anything present that strikes and touches him. Being struck by actuality is what we like to regard as constitutive of the actuality of the actual. However, in being struck by what is actual, man may be debarred precisely from what concerns and touches him—touches him in the surely mysterious way of escaping him by its withdrawal. The event of withdrawal could be what is most present in all our present, and so infinitely exceed the actuality of everything actual.

What withdraws from us draws us along by its very withdrawal, whether or not we become aware of it immediately, or at all. Once we are drawn into the withdrawal, we are, somewhat like migratory birds, but in an entirely different way, caught in the pull of what draws, attracts us by its withdrawal. And once we, being so attracted, are drawing toward what draws us, our essential being already bears the stamp of that "pull." As we are drawing toward what withdraws, we ourselves point toward it. We are who we are by pointing in that direction—not like an incidental adjunct but as follows: this "being in the pull of" is in itself an essential and therefore constant pointing toward what withdraws. To say "being in the pull of" is to say "pointing toward what withdraws."

To the extent that man *is* in this pull, he *points* toward what withdraws. *As* he is pointing that way, man *is* the pointer. Man here is not first of all man, and then also occasionally someone who points. No: drawn into what withdraws, pulled toward it and thus pointing into the withdrawal, man first *is* man. His essential being lies in being such a pointer. Something which in itself, by its essential being, is pointing, we call a sign. As he draws toward what withdraws, man is a sign. But since this sign points toward what draws *away*, it points not so much at *what* draws away as into the withdrawal. The sign remains without interpretation.

In universities especially the danger is still very great that we misunderstand what we hear of thinking, particularly if the immediate subject of the discussion is scientific. Is there any place compelling us more forcibly to rack our brains than the research and training institutions pursuing scientific work? Now everyone admits unreservedly that the arts and the sciences are totally different from each other, though in official oratory they are still mentioned jointly. But if a distinction is made between thinking and the sciences, and the two are contrasted, that is immediately considered a disparagement of science. There is the fear even that thinking might open hostilities against the sciences, and becloud the seriousness and spoil the joy of scientific work.

But even if those fears were justified, which is emphatically not the case, it would still be both tactless and tasteless to take a stand against science upon the very rostrum that serves scientific education. Tact alone ought to prevent all polemics here. But there is another consideration as well. Any kind of polemics fails from the outset to assume the attitude of thinking. The role of thinking is not that of an opponent. Thinking is thinking only when it pursues whatever speaks *for* a matter. Everything said here defensively is always intended exclusively to protect the matter. When we speak of the sciences as we pursue our way, we shall be speaking not against but for them, for clarity concerning their essential nature. This alone implies our conviction that the sciences are in themselves positively essential. However, their essence is frankly of a different sort from what our universities today still fondly imagine it to be. In any case, we still seem afraid of facing the exciting fact that today's sciences belong in the realm of the essence of modern technology, and nowhere else. Note that I am saying "in the realm of the *essence* of technology," and not simply "in technology." A fog still surrounds the essence of modern science. That fog, however, is not produced by individual investigators and scholars in the sciences. It is not produced by man at all. It arises from the region of what is most thought-provoking— that we are still not thinking; none of us, including me who speaks to you, me first of all.

This is why we are here attempting to learn thinking. We are all on the way together, and are not reproving each other. To learn means to make everything we do answer to whatever addresses us as essential. Depending on the kind of essentials, depending on the realm from which they address us, the answer and with it the kind of learning differs.

A cabinetmaker's apprentice, someone who is learning to build cabinets and the like, will serve as an example. His learning is not mere practice, to gain facility in the use of tools. Nor does he merely gather knowledge about the customary forms of the things he is to build. If he is to become a true cabinetmaker, he makes himself answer and respond above all to the different kinds of wood and to the shapes slumbering within wood—to wood as it enters into man's dwelling with all the hidden riches of its nature. In fact, this relatedness to wood is what maintains the whole craft. Without that relatedness, the craft will never be anything but empty busywork, any occupation with it will be determined exclusively by business concerns. Every handicraft, all human dealings, are constantly in that danger. The writing of poetry is no more exempt from it than is thinking.

Whether or not a cabinetmaker's apprentice, while he is learning, will come to respond to wood and wooden things depends obviously on the presence of some teacher who can teach the apprentice such matters.

True. Teaching is even more difficult than learning. We know that; but we rarely think about it. And why is teaching more difficult than learning? Not because the teacher must have a larger store of information, and have it always ready. Teaching is more difficult than learning because what teaching calls for is this: to let learn. The real teacher, in fact, lets nothing else be learned than—learning. His conduct, therefore, often produces the impression that we really learn nothing from him, if by "learning" we now automatically understand merely the procurement of useful information. The teacher is ahead of his apprentices in this alone, that he has still far more to learn than they—he has to learn to let them learn. The teacher must be capable of being more teachable than the apprentices. The teacher is far less sure of his material than those who learn are of theirs. If the relation between the teacher and the learners is genuine, therefore, there is never a place in it for the authority of the know-it-all or the authoritative sway of the official. It still is an exalted matter, then, to become a teacher—which is something else entirely than becoming a famous professor. That nobody wants any longer to become a teacher today, when all things are downgraded and graded from below (for instance, from business), is presumably because the matter is exalted, because of its altitude. And presumably this disinclination is linked to that most thought-provoking matter which gives us to think. We must keep our eyes fixed firmly on the true relation between teacher and taught—if indeed learning is to arise in the course of these lectures.

We are trying to learn thinking. Perhaps thinking, too, is just something like building a cabinet.

(. . .)*What is called thinking?* The question sounds definite. It seems unequivocal. But even a slight reflection shows it to have more than one meaning. No sooner do we ask the question than we begin to vacillate. Indeed, the ambiguity of the question foils every attempt to push toward the answer without some further preparation.

We must, then, clarify the ambiguity. The ambiguousness of the question "What is called thinking?" conceals several possible ways of dealing with it. Looking ahead, we may stress *four* ways in which the question can be posed.

"What is called thinking?" says for one thing, and in the first place: what is it we call "thought" and "thinking," what do these words signify? What is it to which we give the name "thinking"?

"What is called thinking?" says also, in the second place: how does traditional doctrine conceive and define what we have named thinking? What is it that for two and a half thousand years has been regarded as the basic characteristic of thinking? Why does the traditional doctrine of thinking bear the curious title "logic"?

"What is called thinking?" says further, in the third place: what are the prerequisites we need so that we may be able to think with essential rightness? What is called for on our part in order that we may each time achieve good thinking?

"What is called thinking?" says finally, in the fourth place: what is it that calls us, as it were, commands us to think? What is it that calls us into thinking?

These are four ways in which we can ask the question and bring it closer to an answer by corresponding analyses. These four ways of asking the question are not just superficially strung together. They are all interrelated. What is disturbing about the question therefore lies less in the multiplicity of its possible meanings than in the single meaning toward which all four ways are pointing. We must consider whether only one of the four ways is the right one, while the others prove to be incidental and untenable; or whether all four of them are equally necessary because they are unified and of a piece. But how are they unified, and by what unity? Is oneness added to the multiplicity of the four ways as a fifth piece, like a roof to four walls? Or does one of the four ways of asking the question take precedence? Does this precedence establish a hierarchy within the group of questions? Does the hierarchy exhibit a structure by which the four ways are coordinated and yet subordinated to the one that is decisive?

The four ways we have mentioned, in which the question "What is called thinking?" may be asked, do not stand side by side, separate and unrelated. They belong together by virtue of a union that is enjoined by one of the four ways. However, we must go slow, one step at a time, if we are to become aware how this is so. We must therefore begin our attempt with a statement which will at first remain a mere assertion. It runs:

The meaning of the question which we noted in the fourth place tells us how the question would want to be asked first in the decisive way: "What calls for thinking?" Properly understood, the question asks what it is that commands us to enter into thought, that calls on us to think. The turn of phrase, "What calls for thinking on our part?," could of course intend no more than "What does the term 'thinking' signify to us?" But the question as it is really asked, "What calls for thinking on our part?," means something else. . . . It means: What is it that directs us into thought and gives us directions for thinking?

Accordingly, does the question ask what it is that gives us the impetus to think on each occasion and with regard to a particular matter? No. The directions that come from what directs us into thought are much more than merely the given impetus to do some thinking.

That which directs us to think gives us directions in such a way that we first become capable of thinking, and thus *are* as thinkers, only by virtue of its directive. It is true, of course, that the question "What calls for thinking?," in the sense of "What calls on us to think?," is foreign to the common understanding. But we are all the less entitled simply to overlook the fact that the question "What is called thinking?" presents itself at first quite innocently. It sounds as if, and we unknowingly take it as if, the question merely asked for more precise information about what is supposedly meant when we speak of such a thing as thinking. Thinking here appears as a theme with which one might deal as with any other. Thus thinking becomes the object of an investigation. The investigation considers a process that occurs in man. Man takes a special part in the process, in that he performs the thinking. Yet this fact, that man is naturally the performer of thinking, need not further concern the investigation of thinking. The fact goes without saying. Being irrelevant, it may be left out of our reflection on thinking. Indeed, it must be left out. For the laws of thought are after all valid independently of the man who performs the individual acts of thinking.

But if the question "What calls for thinking?" is asking what it is that first of all directs us to think, then we are asking for something that concerns ourselves because it calls upon us, upon our very being. It is we ourselves to whom the question "What is called thinking—what calls for thinking?" is addressed directly. We ourselves are in the text and texture of the question. The question "What calls on us to think?" has already drawn us into the issue in question. We ourselves are, in the strict sense of the word, put in question by the question. The question "What calls on us to think?" strikes us directly, like a lightning bolt. Asked in this way, the question "What calls for thinking?" does more than merely struggle with an object, in the manner of a scientific problem. . . .

(. . .) The place of language properly inhabited, and of its habitual words, is usurped by common terms. The common speech becomes the current speech. We meet it on all sides, and since it is common to all, we now accept it as the only standard. Anything that departs from this commonness, in order to inhabit the formerly habitual proper speaking of language, is at once considered a violation of the standard. It is branded as a frivolous whim. All this is in fact quite in order, as soon as we regard the common as the only legitimate standard, and become generally incapable of fathoming the commonness of the common. This floundering in a commonness which we have placed under the protection of so-called natural common sense is not accidental, nor are we free to deprecate it. This floundering in commonness is part of the high and dangerous game and gamble in which, by the essence of language, we are the stakes.

Is it playing with words when we attempt to give heed to this play of language and to hear what language really says when it speaks? If we succeed in hearing that, then it may happen—provided we proceed carefully—that we get more truly to the matter that is expressed in any telling and asking. (. . .)

When we name a thing, we furnish it with a name. But what about this furnishing? After all, the name is not just draped over the thing. On the other hand, no one will deny that the name is coordinated with the thing as an object. If we conceive the situation in this way, we turn the name, too, into an object. We represent the relation between name and thing as the coordination of two objects. The coordination in turn is by way of an object, which we can see and conceive and deal with and describe according to its various possibilities. The relation between what is named and its name can always be conceived as a coordination. The only question is whether this correctly conceived coordination will ever allow us, will allow us at all, to give heed to what constitutes the peculiar character of the name.

To name something—that is to call it by name. More fundamentally, to name is to call something into its word. What is so called is then at the call of the word. What is called appears as what is present, and in its presence it is secured, commanded, called into the calling word. So called by name, called into a presence, it in turn calls. It is named, has the name. By naming, we call on what is present to arrive. Arrive where? That remains to be thought about. In any case, all naming and all being named is the familiar "to call" only because naming itself consists by nature in the real calling, in the call to come, in a commending and a command.

What is called thinking? At the outset we mentioned four ways to ask the question. We said that the way listed in the fourth place is the first, first in the sense of being highest in rank since it sets the standard. When we understand the question "What is called thinking?" in the sense that it is a question about what calls upon us to think, we then have understood the word "to call" in its proper significance. That is to say also: we now ask the question as it properly wants to be asked. Presumably we shall now almost automatically get to the three remaining ways to ask the question. It will therefore be advisable to explicate the proper question a little more clearly. It runs: "What is it that calls on us to think?" What makes a call upon us that we should think and, by thinking, be who we are?

That which calls us to think in this way presumably can do so only insofar as the calling itself, on its own, needs thought. What calls us to think, and thus commands, that is, brings our essential being into the keeping of thought, needs thinking because what calls us wants itself to be thought about according to its essence. What calls on us to think demands for itself that it be tended, cared for, husbanded in its own essential being, by thought. What calls on us to think gives us food for thought.

What gives us food for thought we call thought-provoking. But what is thought-provoking not just occasionally, and not just in some given limited respect, but rather gives food for thought inherently and hence from the start and always—is that which is thought-provoking perse. This is what we call most thought-provoking. And what it gives us to think about, the gift it gives to us, is nothing less than itself—itself which calls on us to enter thought.

The question "What calls for thinking?" asks for what wants to be thought about in the pre-eminent sense: it does not just give us something to think about, nor only itself, but it first gives thought and thinking to us, it entrusts thought to us as our essential destiny, and thus first joins and appropriates us to thought.

Charles Saunders Peirce argues in his essay *How to Make Our Ideas Clear* (1878) about the importance of clarity in our thoughts. He notes how lack of clarity can cause great problems and lead to difficulties. He makes notes of various methods, including Descartes' philosophy.

How to Make Our Ideas Clear (1878)

I

Whoever has looked into a modern treatise on logic of the common sort, will doubtless remember the two distinctions between *clear* and *obscure* conceptions, and between *distinct* and *confused* conceptions. . . . A clear idea is defined as one which is so apprehended that it will be recognized wherever it is met with, and so that no other will be mistaken for it. If it fails of this clearness, it is said to be obscure.

This is rather a neat bit of philosophical terminology; yet, since it is clearness that they were defining, I wish the logicians had made their definition a little more plain. Never to fail to recognize an idea, and under no circumstances to mistake another for it, let it come in how recondite a form it may, would indeed imply such prodigious force and clearness of intellect as is seldom met with in this world.

On the other hand, merely to have such an acquaintance with the idea as to have become familiar with it, and to have lost all hesitancy in recognizing it in ordinary cases, hardly seems to deserve the name of clearness of apprehension, since after all it only amounts to a subjective feeling of mastery which may be entirely mistaken. I take it, however, that when the logicians speak of "clearness," they mean nothing more than such a familiarity with an idea, since they regard the quality as but a small merit, which needs to be supplemented by another, which they call *distinctness.*

A distinct idea is defined as one which contains nothing which is not clear. This is technical language; by the *contents* of an idea logicians understand whatever is contained in its definition. So that an idea is *distinctly* apprehended, according to them, when we can give a precise definition of it, in abstract terms. . . .

. . . When Descartes set about the reconstruction of philosophy, his first step was to (theoretically) permit skepticism and to discard the practice of the schoolmen of looking to authority as the ultimate source of truth. That done, he sought a more natural fountain of true principles, and thought he found it in the human mind; thus passing, in the most direct way, from the method of authority to that of apriority, as described in my first paper. Self-consciousness was to furnish us with our fundamental truths, and to decide what was agreeable to reason. But since, evidently, not all ideas are true, he was led to note, as the first condition of infallibility, that they must be clear. The distinction between an idea *seeming* clear and really being so, never occurred to him. . . .

... Descartes labored under the difficulty that we may seem to ourselves to have clear apprehensions of ideas which in truth are very hazy, no better remedy occurred to him than to require an abstract definition of every important term. Accordingly, in adopting the distinction of *clear* and *distinct* notions, he described the latter quality as the clear apprehension of everything contained in the definition; and the books have ever since copied his words. There is no danger that his chimerical scheme will ever again be over-valued. Nothing new can ever be learned by analyzing definitions. Nevertheless, our existing beliefs can be set in order by this process, and order is an essential element of intellectual economy, as of every other. It may be acknowledged, therefore, that the books are right in making familiarity with a notion the first step toward clearness of apprehension, and the defining of it the second. But in omitting all mention of any higher perspicuity of thought, they simply mirror a philosophy which was exploded a hundred years ago....

The very first lesson that we have a right to demand that logic shall teach us is, how to make our ideas clear; and a most important one it is, depreciated only by minds who stand in need of it.... It is terrible to see how a single unclear idea, a single formula without meaning, lurking in a young man's head, will sometimes act like an obstruction of inert matter in an artery, hindering the nutrition of the brain, and condemning its victim to pine away in the fullness of his intellectual vigor and in the midst of intellectual plenty.

Many a man has cherished for years as his hobby some vague shadow of an idea, too meaningless to be positively false; he has, nevertheless, passionately loved it, has made it his companion by day and by night, and has given to it his strength and his life, leaving all other occupations for its sake, and in short has lived with it and for it, until it has become, as it were, flesh of his flesh and bone of his bone; and then he has woken up some bright morning to find it gone, clean vanished away like the beautiful Melusina of the fable, and the essence of his life gone with it....

II

The principles set forth in the first part of this essay lead, at once, to a method of reaching a clearness of thought of higher grade than the "distinctness" of the logicians. It was there noticed that the action of thought is excited by the irritation of doubt, and ceases when belief is attained; so that the production of belief is the sole function of thought. All these words, however, are too strong for my purpose. It is as if I had described the phenomena as they appear under a mental microscope.

Doubt and Belief, as the words are commonly employed, relate to religious or other grave discussions. But here I use them to designate the starting of any question, no matter how small or how great, and the resolution of it. If, for instance, in a horse-car, I pull out my purse and find a five-cent nickel and five coppers, I decide, while my hand is going to the purse, in which way

I will pay my fare. To call such a question Doubt, and my decision Belief, is certainly to use words very disproportionate to the occasion.

To speak of such a doubt as causing an irritation which needs to be appeased, suggests a temper which is uncomfortable to the verge of insanity. Yet, looking at the matter minutely, it must be admitted that, if there is the least hesitation as to whether I shall pay the five coppers or the nickel (as there will be sure to be, unless I act from some previously contracted habit in the matter), though irritation is too strong a word, yet I am excited to such small mental activity as may be necessary to deciding how I shall act. Most frequently doubts arise from some indecision, however momentary, in our action. Sometimes it is not so. I have, for example, to wait in a railway-station, and to pass the time I read the advertisements on the walls. I compare the advantages of different trains and different routes which I never expect to take, merely fancying myself to be in a state of hesitancy, because I am bored with having nothing to trouble me. Feigned hesitancy, whether feigned for mere amusement or with a lofty purpose, plays a great part in the production of scientific inquiry. However the doubt may originate, it stimulates the mind to an activity which may be slight or energetic, calm or turbulent. Images pass rapidly through consciousness, one incessantly melting into another, until at last, when all is over—it may be in a fraction of a second, in an hour, or after long years—we find ourselves decided as to how we should act under such circumstances as those which occasioned our hesitation. In other words, we have attained belief....

... The essence of belief is the establishment of a habit; and different beliefs are distinguished by the different modes of action to which they give rise. If beliefs do not differ in this respect, if they appease the same doubt by producing the same rule of action, then no mere differences in the manner of consciousness of them can make them different beliefs, any more than playing a tune in different keys is playing different tunes. Imaginary distinctions are often drawn between beliefs which differ only in their mode of expression.... Instead of perceiving that the obscurity is purely subjective, we fancy that we contemplate a quality of the object which is essentially mysterious; and if our conception be afterward presented to us in a clear form we do not recognize it as the same, owing to the absence of the feeling of unintelligibility. So long as this deception lasts, it obviously puts an impassable barrier in the way of perspicuous thinking; so that it equally interests the opponents of rational thought to perpetuate it, and its adherents to guard against it...

Another such deception is to mistake a mere difference in the grammatical construction of two words for a distinction between the ideas they express. In this pedantic age, when the general mob of writers attended so much more to words than to things, this error is common enough. When I just said that thought is an *action*, and that it consists in a *relation*, although a person performs an action but not a relation, which can only be the result of an action, yet there was no inconsistency in what I said, but only a grammatical vagueness.

From all these sophisms we shall be perfectly safe so long as we reflect that the whole function of thought is to produce habits of action; and that whatever there is connected with a thought, but irrelevant to its purpose, is an accretion to it, but no part of it. If there be a unity among our sensations which has no reference to how we shall act on a given occasion, as when we listen to a piece of music, why we do not call that thinking.

To develop its meaning, we have, therefore, simply to determine what habits it produces, for what a thing means is simply what habits it involves. Now, the identity of a habit depends on how it might lead us to act, not merely under such circumstances as are likely to arise, but under such as might possibly occur, no matter how improbable they may be. What the habit is depends on *when* and *how* it causes us to act. As for the *when*, every stimulus to action is derived from perception; as for the *how*, every purpose of action is to produce some sensible result. Thus, we come down to what is tangible and conceivably practical, as the root of every real distinction of thought, no matter how subtle it may be; and there is no distinction of meaning so fine as to consist in anything but a possible difference of practice. . . .

IV

Let us now approach the subject of logic, and consider a conception which particularly concerns it, that of *reality*. Taking clearness in the sense of familiarity, no idea could be clearer than this. Every child uses it with perfect confidence, never dreaming that he does not understand it. As for clearness in its second grade, however, it would probably puzzle most men, even among those of a reflective turn of mind, to give an abstract definition of the real.

Yet such a definition may perhaps be reached by considering the points of difference between reality and its opposite, fiction. A figment is a product of somebody's imagination; it has such characters as his thought impresses upon it. That those characters are independent of how you or I think is an external reality. There are, however, phenomena within our own minds, dependent upon our thought, which are at the same time real in the sense that we really think them. But though their characters depend on how we think, they do not depend on what we think those characters to be. Thus, a dream has a real existence as a mental phenomenon, if somebody has really dreamt it; that he dreamt so and so, does not depend on what anybody thinks was dreamt, but is completely independent of all opinion on the subject. On the other hand, considering, not the fact of dreaming, but the thing dreamt, it retains its peculiarities by virtue of no other fact than that it was dreamt to possess them. Thus we may define the real as that whose characters are independent of what anybody may think them to be....

.... [R]eality is independent, not necessarily of thought in general, but only of what you or I or any finite number of men may think about it; and that, on the other hand, though the object of the final opinion depends on what that opinion is, yet what that opinion is does not depend on what you or I or any man thinks. Our perversity and that of others may indefinitely postpone the settlement of opinion; it might even conceivably cause an arbitrary proposition to be universally accepted as long as the human race should last. Yet even that would not change the nature of the belief, which alone could be the result of investigation carried sufficiently far; and if, after the extinction of our race, another should arise with faculties and disposition for investigation, that true opinion must be the one which they would ultimately come to. "Truth crushed to earth shall rise again," and the opinion which would finally result from investigation does not depend on how anybody may actually think. But the reality of that which is real does depend on the real fact that investigation is destined to lead, at last, if continued long enough, to a belief in it....

...We have, hitherto, not crossed the threshold of scientific logic. It is certainly important to know how to make our ideas clear, but they may be ever so clear without being true. How to make them so, we have next to study. How to give birth to those vital and procreative ideas which multiply into a thousand forms and diffuse themselves everywhere, advancing civilization and making the dignity of man, is an art not yet reduced to rules, but of the secret of which the history of science affords some hints.

KEY TERMS

Abduction is the process of reasoning that is a type of nondeductive inference where based on the evidence at hand we draw an inference to the best explanation.

Argument is a set of statements made in support of a position along with the conclusion.

Conclusion is the main position defended in an argument, which is supported by the premises.

Critical thinking is the engagement of the thinker in rational deliberation, investigation of facts and reasons, and evaluation of arguments.

Deduction is the process of reasoning from one or more statements known as premises to reach a logically certain conclusion.

Epistemology is a branch of philosophy that deals with the nature and foundations of knowledge.

Ethics is a branch of philosophy that studies questions about right and wrong. Ethical theories provide a framework for answering those questions and for evaluating human actions.

Fallacy is used to denote an unacceptable way of thinking or reasoning.

Induction is the process of reasoning where the premises provide strong evidence for (not absolute proof of) the truth of the conclusion.

Logic is a branch of philosophy that deals with rational thought and the art and science of reasoning.

Metaphysics is a branch of philosophy that deals with the nature of existence. It is a very broad field, and metaphysicians attempt to answer questions about *how the world is*.

Philosophy of religion is a branch of philosophy that deals with questions related to religion and the nature of god. It may also deal with questions of the afterlife, soul, and existence before or after death.

Political philosophy is a branch of philosophy that deals with questions pertaining to the foundations, nature, and purpose of government.

Premises are statements made in support of a conclusion of an argument.

Socratic Method is one of the oldest and powerful methods of teaching. The method develops critical thinking. The method involves giving students questions but not answers. It involves inquiry, analysis, evaluation, and synthesis of thoughts and ideas.

Valid is a term applied to a deductive argument. An argument is valid if it employs a correct logical structure, which will yield a true conclusion from true premises.

Sound is a term applied to a deductive argument. An argument is sound if it employs true premises.

QUESTIONS FOR DISCUSSION AND REVIEW

1. Explain some of the benefits a student may gain by studying philosophy.
2. Explain the Socratic Method of Teaching. Is this a useful way for students to learn?
3. Explain how critical thinking can be used to analyze a philosophical issue.
4. Compare and contrast induction, abduction, and deduction.
5. Explain some of different areas of philosophy which will be discussed in this course.

BIBLIOGRAPHY AND SUGGESTED READINGS

Heidegger, M. (1977). "What Calls for Thinking?" In *Basic Writings*.

Internet Encyclopedia of Philosophy. A peer-reviewed academic resource. Available from http://www.iep.utm.edu/

Merleau-Ponty, M. (1963). *In Praise of Philosophy*. (H. L. Dreyfus and P. A. Dreyfus, transl.).

Peirce, C. S. (1881). *How to Make our Ideas Clear*.

Russell, B. (2007). *The Problems of Philosophy*.

Sartre, J-P. (1963). *Search for a Method*. (Knopf, A. transl.).

Stanford Encyclopedia of Philosophy. Available from http://plato.stanford.edu/

Metaphysics— What is Real?

2

Upon completing this chapter, students should be able to complete the following Learning Outcomes:

2.1 Articulate the different views as to the nature of reality.

2.2 Compare and contrast the various views on substance such as materialism, dualism, and idealism.

2.3 Evaluate views as to the nature of universals and particulars.

2.4 Articulate the various views proposed by the early Greeks regarding substance.

What Do We Mean By Reality?

Humans have been asking the questions such as "what is real?" "what is the nature of being?" and "what is the primary substance?" since time immemorial. **Metaphysics**, sometimes referred to as ontology, since the twentieth century, is the branch of philosophy that addresses these issues about the nature of reality.

Ancient civilizations, such as the Greeks and the Chinese, focused on what they believed to be the basic elements or building blocks of matter, such as air, fire, water, and earth. These elements, like the ones we know today, are considered to be material elements. Most scientists today consider the question resolved and will simply point to the current periodic table of chemical elements as a solution to the question of what is everything made out of. For others, on the other hand, there has to be more to life than that. How we know these things is the next obvious question, one explored in the next chapter.

The Nature of Being

Is "Being" a thing in itself or merely a property of things? Is it permanent and eternal or changing? Is it one or many? What is it, really? These are basic metaphysical questions that, even if you don't often realize it, are very much with us today. For example, many of you reading this perhaps hope to go to heaven. What is it that will go? Not your body, presumably, or your clothes, your voice, or your smile; we can verify what happens to a body after death, and it's not pretty. So what is it that goes to heaven? If you answer your soul, what does that mean? Is that the real you? In what sense is it you? Or is this it? In other words, maybe there is nothing more after you die. Both possibilities are part of the quest for meaning in metaphysics.

Although the elements mentioned by our ancestors are real, deeper metaphysical questions regarding the nature of substance or being persist. Metaphysics, the critical questioning of what is real and what we are doing here, remain as a big concern in philosophy today. The pre-Socratics in Ancient Greece offered clever theories, all of them asking the right questions in new ways. Most of them believed that reality might not be what we experience in our everyday lives but rather something else, something more basic. In other words, given that the world we know is changing, transient, and imperfect, there must be something permanent you can count on.

Philosophy and Science in the Ancient World

Philosophy and science were not originally separate. They were in fact born together in the beginning of the sixth-century BCE—not coincidentally, also the birth of democracy—and they both involved a transition from a purely theistic toward a natural way of thinking about the world. If you could imagine yourself in college in the sixth-century BCE—a stretch, given that the first college, Plato' Academy was founded around 387 BCE—you would be a philosophy major since that was basically the only major available: math, logic, science, physics, politics, ethics, and every other subject was within the corpus of philosophy.

POWERFUL IDEAS BOX: MATERIALISM, IDEALISM, AND SUBSTANCE DUALISM

Materialism claims that reality, or Being, consists of physical objects and their components. **Idealism** claims that reality is immaterial, something other than matter. **Substance dualism** claims that both the immaterial and the material objects exist. From the Ancient Greeks through today, this dualism remains a challenging problem. Even if the elements are the basic building blocks of objects, idealist still maintain that they are ultimately immaterial. Substance dualists argue that the objects we encounter in everyday experience are material, but that there also exist immaterial objects such as thoughts, feelings, and ideas that are contained in our minds, which are immaterial as well.

Universals and Particulars

There are various other problems inherent to metaphysics. Another fundamental question is the relationship between ideas and objects. This is sometimes termed the problem of **Universals.** The term "universal" is another name for ideas or general concepts or terms that can be applied to various particular objects. "**Particular**" is another name for objects or individual things that we encounter in the world.

Universals or general terms are words or concepts such as blue, red, book, or car. These words and millions more words apply not only to one individual or particular object. Plato, for example, argues that reality consists of the **Forms** and that the Forms exist in a separate realm. This view is known as **extreme or Platonic realism**. For him, ideas are real. They have independent existence, apart from our thoughts. They have transcendental existence apart from the particulars that participate in them. The Form, according to Plato, is the essence of a thing, and, on his view, the particulars are said to imitate or copy them in an imperfect way.

For example, a blue book and blue car both share in the Form "blue" Plato, himself, was not very concerned with mundane or basic Forms such as books, tables, or chairs. But he was more concerned with what he called higher Forms such as justice, beauty, and love. These Forms are abstract in nature and more difficult for us to recognize. Plato claimed that all physical objects copy the original, unchanging Form or Forms. Physical objects are imperfect copies of the Forms. Like Heraclitus (another pre-Socratic philosopher who famously said we can never step into the same river twice), he held that this reality is constantly changing and shifting. What is true today may be false tomorrow in this world. In order to find an eternal truth, we must look to the realm of the Forms, where truth is constant and eternal.

Aristotle argued for a view known as **exaggerated realism**. This holds that universals exist in the particulars as part of what makes them similar. In other words, the form blue is in the object, not a separate reality as Plato claimed. On this view, the particulars have the universal within them. Ideas exist in the physical objects (and our minds), not in a separate reality. The particulars are a mixture or composite of form (idea) and matter.

Another view on this topic is known as **conceptualism**. This view holds that ideas are real, but they are dependent upon a mind or thought. The function of a universal term is to denote a special relationship between particular objects. Universals or forms are object concepts that we create in our minds by examining particulars.

A final view known as **extreme nominalism** claims that universals do not exist. On this view, ideas (universals or forms) are not real objects. They do not have real existence. Only particulars or individual objects exist. A general term (universal) is a word that does not refer to anything. This view is a result of what the nominalist feels is a logical problem in discussing universals.

Although this may seem to be much to do about nothing, on closer analysis the issue is not as simple as it may seem. Consider the following mathematical formula: $C^2 = A^2 + B^2$. This formula is known as the Pythagorean Theorem. It is named after the famous ancient Greek philosopher and mathematician Pythagoras, who was part of a secret math cult. Although Pythagoras is given credit for the formula, it was used by various ancient cultures such as the Egyptians, Mesopotamians, and Chinese. Was this theorem (a universal truth of mathematics) created or discovered? If you say it was created by mankind, then it seems to be relative to us, and if you say it is discovered, then where was it before mankind found it? Plato's answer to the questions of universals is that such a theorem is eternally true and it always existed in the realm of the Forms.

Powerful Thinkers: The Atomists

Democritus (ca. 460–370 BCE) and Epicurus (341–270 BCE) had reality figured out Over two thousand years ago, Democritus, a visionary philosopher and mathematician born in Thrace. He developed the atomic theory of the universe while looking for the meaning of reality. Much like his fellow pre-Socratics, he worked out ideas first developed by his teacher Leucippus and detailed that reality must consist of small, invisible components that come together in different combinations. He called them atoms. The implications of this insight were and are huge.

The mind is made of atoms, just like the book you are holding. This materialist position, as it came to be known, understandably was not as influential as the ideas of Plato or Aristotle. We have lost most of his writings and, it is believed, that his philosophy was not as thoroughly or systematically elaborated as those of Plato and Aristotle. Also, a materialist view of the universe makes belief in god or any other supernatural being at the very least tough to justify: gods, or later the Abrahamic God, cannot be material.

Still, there was something new here.

Lefteris Papaulakis/Shutterstock.com

After Aristotle, **Epicurus** (341–270 BCE) was a materialist philosopher who followed the lead of Democritus and developed an ethics from that materialist metaphysics. Epicurus also believed reality was composed of atoms, and he worked out a sophisticated moral philosophy that values happiness as the ultimate goal in life: happiness is achievable by not fearing death and by enjoying life's small pleasures and by finding guidance in the pursuit of wisdom. He called this freedom from worry as *ataraxia*. According to Epicurus, This was the way to be happy.

Neglected at first, and certainly banned after the conversion of the Roman Empire to Christianity, Democritus and Epicurus exerted an unexpected influence in future philosophy. The belief that everything was made of atoms in motion anticipated **Thomas Hobbes** (1588–1679) and his own revolutionary claim that all there can be is atoms in motion. The nature of that motion, the Epicurean theory that atoms swerved from their parallel path, anticipated modern physics' explanation of the formation of different elements and their combinations including **Albert Einstein's** (1879–1975) Theory of Relativity.

The Roman poet and philosopher Lucretius (99–55 BCE), in his ravishing epic *De rerum natura (On the Nature of Things)*, gave us the most complete picture of Epicurean metaphysics, with a materialist explanation of everything in our lives.

The Epicurean insights into human psychology, as well as Lucretius' detailed exposition in his poem, found disfavor and censorship in the coming millennium. This materialism was rediscovered first briefly in the Renaissance by Niccolò di Bernardo dei Machiavelli (1469–1527) and others, and much later by **Karl Marx** (1818–1883), who found inspiration in Epicurus' view of reality being composed of atoms that moved freely for no good reason, taking that swerve of the atoms as a paradigm for human freedom. In 1841, the budding German philosopher wrote his doctoral dissertation *On The Difference Between the Democritean and Epicurean Philosophy of Nature*, thus placing Atomism at the foundations of Marxism.

Back to Those Questioning Pre-Socratics

The story of philosophy begins, in the city of Miletus, in what today is modern day Turkey, where the first three Western philosophers were born and lived: **Thales** (620–540 BCE) is often called the first philosopher because his pithy, enigmatic statement "All is water" cannot be taken literally but must be taken seriously. He was the first to suggest that there is some basic substance at the heart of reality, not the reality we experience but something else—in his case, water.

Together with fellow pre-Socratics **Anaximenes** (585–528 BCE) and **Anaximander** (610–546 BCE), Thales sought to discover the primary substance of reality. Others followed, all of them offering different, variously challenging ideas about reality. Anaximenes claimed that the primary substance is air. He believed that all objects are composed of air. He claimed that different densities of air explain the different types of object we encounter in our daily lives. The air we breathe is very light, whereas the air in a rock is very dense. Air, of course, is central for human life. Anaximander stated that the Primary Substance is in fact boundless, or infinite. He doubted whether any fundamental or primary substance would exist in an observable *pure* form. In a sense he was correct, as we today know that we don't observe a primary substance anywhere in the world.

The truth about reality must be in numbers, which never lie, thought **Pythagoras** (ca. 570–480 BCE), best known today for his famous theorem. That the square of the hypotenuse of a right-angled triangle is always equal to the sum of the square of the two other sides is always true. It is verifiable, impossible to falsify, much like the statement "2 + 2 = 4." To get to the nature of Being, understand numbers.

"You can never step into the same river twice"

—*Heraclitus*

Or perhaps reality is something else entirely, perhaps it is far from permanent and is rather always changing. **Heraclitus** (ca. 540–480 BCE) thought precisely that, putting it poetically by saying "life is like a river, and you can never step into the same river twice." Is that true? If so, then truth is impossible, since whatever you find or whatever you say will change and change again. The only metaphysical truth is change itself.

In contrast, the visionary **Parmenides** (ca. 510–440 BCE) thought that reality was permanent, that it could not be changing that it had to be "One" and could not be many. Being does not, cannot change. Reality in fact is the One. That One is the true object of knowledge since it is impossible to know that which is not. Both Parmenides and Pythagoras had a major influence on the most powerful thinkers to come.

Socrates and His Kin

Anaximander's idea of a boundless universe lent an optimistic tone to the possibility of knowledge, but then everything changed with **Socrates** (ca. 610–546 BCE), the most famous philosopher who never wrote anything. "The only thing I know is that I know nothing," Socrates said. And we know he said that because his most famous pupil said so. Though a real historical figure, the Socrates we know today is a literary creation of **Plato** (427–347 BCE). When we say that Socrates said "The unexamined life is not worth living," we mean it in the same sense that Hamlet said "To be or not to be, that is the question." Hamlet said it, but it was William Shakespeare who wrote it.

Plato knew and loved Socrates, studied with him, and he was disillusioned with democracy after his beloved Socrates was condemned to death in trumped-up charges of heresy and corrupting youth. Plato's pupil Aristotle (324–322 BCE), together with his teacher, set philosophy on an adventure that would last millennia.

"The only thing I know is that I know nothing"

—Socrates

Plato and Aristotle on Reality

There is a beautiful, monumental fresco in the Vatican that goes a long way to explain what is at stake in the matter of Plato and Aristotle. Pope Julius II commissioned Raphael to paint it in 1509. What the great genius created is *School of Athens*, a vast and inclusive portrait of everyone who was known to matter intellectually in the ancient world, giving us a glimpse into how Renaissance civilization understood the profound philosophical debates that raged until the Dark Ages brought all debate to a close. They, and Raphael, got it right. A whole heritage of knowledge and wisdom are illustrated here.

© Ted Spiegel/CORBIS

At the center of the fresco—the central vanishing point of the picture—are the figures of two bearded men in colorful togas. They are, as Raphael saw it, the ones who matter most. The older Plato is on the left, holding his arms upward pointing at the heavens. His student Aristotle is on the right, younger and better looking, with other men in the picture looking his way. Aristotle holds out his left arm, palms down, as if saying "Right here." Both are holding anachronistically bound books in their hands, Plato his *Timaeus* and Aristotle his *Nicomachean Ethics*. Many other famous philosophers are in the fresco, improbably from different centuries, including Socrates but also everyone from Anaximander to Zeno, with Epicurus, Heraclitus, Anaximander, Pythagoras, Euclid, Averroes, and even Alexander the Great—himself a pupil of Aristotle—thrown in for good measure. But it is the two at the center that counted the most then, and they still do.

Reality is Somewhere Else

For **Plato** (427–347 BCE), reality is eternal and perfect, but it is elsewhere, not here; appearances can deceive us, and reality is elusive. Plato's reality was in what he called the world of **Forms**, universals that are perfect and inform the meaning of our lives—we are all reflections, copies of reality. Our life is like that of someone living in a cave knowing only shadows, never seeing the sun or the real world outside, Plato suggests in the *Myth of the Cave* that is a key section of his *Republic*. The nature of truth and the possibilities of knowledge are illustrated by a tale of prisoners in a cave where all they can see is the shadows made by figures moving in front of an unseen fire behind them. What the prisoners think is real in fact is not, rather it is merely shadows. The prisoners must, if they can, turn around, leave the cave, know the world outside and maybe then come close to reality. We are all prisoners in the shadows, Plato suggests, and we must move toward the light of wisdom and truth—toward the Forms.

The sun outside the cave will inform our experiences, let our eyes do what they can do, according to Plato. But our eyes will never see anything true unless and until we get out of the cave. Even then, clarity might be elusive.

POWERFUL ANALYSIS

Plato does not trust appearances, since everything in this world is just a copy or an imitation of the Forms, or reality.

Aristotle trusts appearances, since there is no form without matter and no matter without form. Appearances actually can help you find the truth.

Who's right?

© AkeSak/Shutterstock.com

We might eventually come close to the truth about reality, but we might not. Very likely, the most we can do is come as close as possible in the knowledge that we will never reach it. There might be more than one way of knowing—and this Platonic insight returned unexpectedly in the twentieth century with the mathematician and philosopher **Kurt Gödel** (1906–1978). If you want certainty, however, you are not going to have it in this world.

Plato would be the leading influence in the philosophy of **St. Augustine** (354–430 BCE), who made reason the servant of faith and in the process transformed Platonism into Christian theology—quite a feat, considering that the Greek philosophers were pagans who believed in different gods, and that heretics were routinely burned at the stake. From Plato, St. Augustine got the notion that there are two realms of reality, the intelligible realm where God and the truth dwell, and the sensible world we experience in our lives. That perhaps we are not built in such a way that we can ever understand God's realm, but that being close to the light is better than remaining in the dark, was a Platonic insight of reality that remains influential to this day.

Reality Is Right Here

Plato's brilliant student **Aristotle** (324–322 BCE), on the other hand, also believed reality must be the forms, perfect and eternal; but he thought that at least in part that reality was right here. There is no form without matter, and no matter without form according to Aristotle. Given that we have no access to the perfection of the forms, we can use the matter that is part of our experience to get to their meaning. In other words, reason, which makes us better than animals according to Aristotle, can take us closer to reality if we simply ask the right questions. These questions were what Aristotle called the **Four Causes**: "What is it? What is it made of? "How was it made or who made it?" and most important "What is it for?"

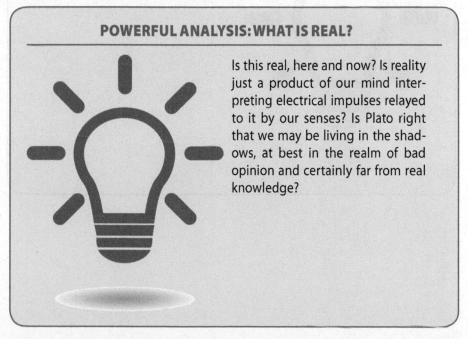

POWERFUL ANALYSIS: WHAT IS REAL?

Is this real, here and now? Is reality just a product of our mind interpreting electrical impulses relayed to it by our senses? Is Plato right that we may be living in the shadows, at best in the realm of bad opinion and certainly far from real knowledge?

Those questions, and the fact that we can use our reason to find the answers, became the blueprint for **St. Thomas Aquinas** (1225–1274), a much later philosopher and theologian, who tried to follow Aristotle and based both his theology and his ethics on a Christian interpretation of Aristotle that departed sharply from St. Augustine's Platonic views.

Aristotle's four causes are the basis of today's scientific method. We may not agree with Aristotle's metaphysics, that is, with his certainty that there must be Forms, or that there must be a universal, eternal truth beyond the particulars of our experience. But we still ask the same questions Aristotle asked, whether looking down on a Petri dish in chemistry class or wondering about what is the right way to live. Plato and his pupil Aristotle both agreed that truth was the only meaning of reality, and that truth must be unchanging, eternal, and perfect. It must be something you can count on in the midst of the change all around you. But their two ways of approaching the search for truth developed into two very different trends in Western thought: whether or not to trust appearances. Bertrand Russell, in his idiosyncratic and highly entertaining *History of Western Philosophy*, quipped that "Aristotle is Plato diluted by common sense."

POWERFUL ANALYSIS

What do you mean by reality? Is reality a matter of, well, just matter? Or is there more to it? What is real to you?

READINGS

Plato: *The Myth of the Cave*

> *The Myth of the Cave*, a justly famous section of Plato's larger political dialog *The Republic*, the nature of truth and the possibilities of knowledge are illustrated by a tale of prisoners in a cave who can see only shadows and have no knowledge of the reality outside. We are all prisoners in the shadows, Plato suggests, and we must move toward the light of wisdom and truth. Plato is speaking with Glaucon in this excerpt.

Behold! human beings living in a cave, which has a mouth open towards the light Here they have been since childhood, and have their legs and necks chained so that they cannot move, and can only see before them, being prevented by the chains from turning round their heads. Above and behind them a fire is blazing at a distance, and between the fire and the prisoners there is a raised way; and you will see, if you look, a low wall, like the screen puppet-masters have in front of them, over which they show the puppets.

I see.

And do you see, I said, men passing along the wall carrying all sorts of vessels, and statues and figures of animals, which appear over the wall? Some of them are talking, others silent.

You have shown me a strange image, and they are strange prisoners.

Like ourselves, I replied; and they see only their own shadows, or the shadows of one another, which the fire throws on the opposite wall of the cave?

True, he said; how could they see anything but the shadows if they were never allowed to move their heads?

And of the objects which are being carried in like manner they would only see the shadows?

Yes, he said. And if they were able to converse with one another, would they not suppose that they were naming what was actually before them?

Very true.

And suppose further that the prison had an echo which came from the other side, would they not be sure to fancy when one of the passers-by spoke that the voice which they heard came from the passing shadow?

No question, he replied.

To them, I said, the truth would be literally nothing but the shadows of the images.

That is certain.

And now look again, and see what will naturally follow if' the prisoners are released and disabused of their error. At first, when any of them is liberated and compelled suddenly to stand up and turn his neck round and walk and look towards the light, he will suffer sharp pains; the glare will hurt, and he will be unable to see the realities that in his former state had been mere shadows; and then conceive someone saying to him, that what he saw before was an illusion, but that now, when he is approaching nearer to being and his eye is turned towards more real existence, he has a clearer vision—what will be his reply? And you may further imagine that his instructor is pointing to the objects as they pass and requiring him to name them—will he not be confused? Will he not imagine that the shadows which he formerly saw are truer than the objects which are now shown to him?

Far truer.

And if he is compelled to look straight at the light, will he not have a pain in his eyes which will make him turn away to take and take in the objects of vision which he can see, and which he will conceive to be in reality clearer than the things which are now being shown to him?

True.

And suppose that he is reluctantly dragged up a steep ascent, and held fast until he's forced into the presence of the sun, is he not likely to be pained and irritated? When he approaches the light his eyes will be dazzled, and he will not be able to see anything at all of what are now called realities.

Not all in a moment, he said.

He will require to grow accustomed to the sight of the upper world. And first he will see the shadows best, next the reflections of men and other objects in the water, and then the objects themselves; then he will gaze upon the light of the moon and the stars and the spangled heaven; and he will see the sky and the stars by night better than the sun or the light of the sun by day?

Certainly.

Last of he will be able to see the sun, and not mere reflections of him in the water, but he will see him in his own proper place, and not in another; and he will contemplate him as he is.

Certainly.

He will then proceed to argue that this is he who gives the season and the years, and is the guardian of all that is in the visible world, and in a certain way the cause of all things which he and his fellows have been accustomed to behold?

Clearly, he said, he would first see the sun and then reason about him.

And when he remembered his old habitation, and the wisdom of the den and his fellow-prisoners, do you not suppose that he would felicitate himself on the change, and pity them?

Certainly, he would.

Yes, he said, I think that he would rather suffer anything than entertain these false notions and live in this miserable manner.

"To them, the truth would be literally nothing but the shadows of the images."

Plato

Imagine once more, I said, such a one coming suddenly out of the sun to be placed again in his old situation; would he not be certain to have his eyes full of darkness?

No question, he said.

This entire allegory, I said, you may now append, dear Glaucon, to the previous argument; the prison-house is the world of sight, the light of the fire is the sun, and you will not misapprehend me if you interpret the journey upwards to be the ascent of the soul into the intellectual world according to my poor belief, which, at your desire, I have expressed whether rightly or wrongly God knows. But, whether true or false, my opinion is that in the world of knowledge the idea of good appears last of all, and is seen only with an effort; and, when seen, is also inferred to be the universal author of all things beautiful and right, parent of light and of the lord of light in this visible world, and the immediate source of reason and truth in the intellectual; and that this is the power upon which he who would act rationally, either in public or private life must have his eye fixed.

I agree, he said, as far as I am able to understand you.

Moreover, I said, you must not wonder that those who attain to this beatific vision are unwilling to descend to human affairs; for their souls are ever hastening into the upper world where they desire to dwell; which desire of theirs is very natural, if our allegory may be trusted.

Yes, very natural.

And Is there anything surprising in one who passes from divine contemplations to the evil state of man, misbehaving himself in a ridiculous manner; if, while his eyes are blinking and before he has become accustomed to the surrounding darkness, he is compelled to fight in courts of law, or in other places, about the images or the shadows of images of justice, and is endeavoring to meet the conceptions of those who have never yet seen absolute justice?

Anything but surprising, he replied.

Anyone who has common sense will remember that the bewilderments of the eyes are of two kinds, and arise from two causes, either from coming out of the light or from going into the light, which is true of the mind's eye, quite as much as of the bodily eye; and he who remembers this when he sees any one whose vision is perplexed and weak, will not be too ready to laugh; he will first ask whether that soul of man has come out of the brighter light, and is unable to see because unaccustomed to the dark, or having turned from darkness to the day is dazzled by excess of light. And he will count the one happy in his condition and state of being, and he will pity the other; or, if he have a mind to laugh at the soul which comes from below into the light, there will be more reason in this than in the laugh which greets him who returns from above out of the light into the den.

That, he said, is a very just distinction.

But then, if I am right, certain professors of education must be wrong when they say that they can put a knowledge into the soul which was not there before, like sight into blind eyes. They undoubtedly say this, he replied.

Whereas, our argument shows that the power and capacity of learning exists in the soul already; and that just as the eye was unable to turn from darkness to light without the whole body, so too the instrument of knowledge can only by the movement of the whole soul be turned from the world of becoming into that of being, and learn by degrees to endure the sight of being, and of the brightest and best of being, or in other words, of the good.

Aristotle: *Metaphysics*

According to Aristotle, we have something animals and plants don't have: reason. We can use reason to get close to knowledge of reality, by asking about the four causes of everything in our experience: "What is it? "What is it made of? "How was it made or who made it?" and most important "What is it for?" While Plato thought truth was elsewhere, in the world of Forms, Aristotle thought that Forms were in fact within the matter, and since we have access to matter in our experience, we can ask questions and reason will reveal the truth to us.

Aristotle: The Four Causes

"Beginning" means (1) that part of a thing from which one would start first, e.g a line or a road has a beginning in either of the contrary directions. (2) That from which each thing would best be originated, e.g. even in learning we must sometimes begin not from the first point and the beginning of the subject, but from the point from which we should learn most easily. (4) That from which, as an immanent part, a thing first comes to be, e,g, as the keel of a ship and the foundation of a house, while in animals some suppose the heart, others the brain, others some other part, to be of this nature. (4) That from which, not as an immanent part, a thing first comes to be, and from which the movement or the change naturally first begins, as a child comes from its father and its mother, and a fight from abusive language. (5) That at whose will that which is moved is moved and that which changes, for example, oligarchies, monarchies, and tyrannies, are called *arhchai*. So are the arts, and of these especially the architectonic arts. (6) That from which a thing can first be known,-this also is called the beginning of the thing, e.g. the hypotheses are the beginnings of demonstrations. Causes are spoken of in an equal number of senses; for all causes are beginnings.

It is common, then, to all beginnings to be the first point from which a thing either is or comes to be or is known; but of these some are immanent in the thing and others are outside. Hence the nature of a thing is a beginning, and so is the element of a thing, and thought and will, and essence, and the final cause-for the good and the beautiful are the beginning both of the knowledge and of the movement of many things.

"Cause" means (1) that from which, as immanent material, a thing comes into being, for example, the bronze is the cause of the statue and the silver of the saucer, and so are the classes which include these. (2) The form or pattern, that is, the definition of the essence, and the classes which include this—for example, the ratio 2:1 and number in general are causes of the octave-- and the parts included in the definition. (3) That from which the change or the resting from change first begins; such as the advisor is a cause of the action, and the father a cause of the child, and in general the maker a cause of the thing made and the change-producing of the changing. (4) The end, that for the sake of which a thing is. For example, health is the cause of walking. For "Why does one walk?" we say; "so that one may be healthy." In speaking thus we think we have given the cause. The same is true of all the means that intervene before the end, when something else has put the process in motion, as e.g. thinning or purging or drugs or instruments intervene before health is reached; for all these are for the sake of the end, though they differ from one another in that some are instruments and others are actions.

These, then, are practically all the senses in which causes are spoken of, and as they are spoken of in several senses it follows both that there are several causes of the same thing, and in no accidental sense: both the art of sculpture and the bronze are causes of the statue not in respect of anything else but as a statue. Things can be causes of one another (for example, exercise of good condition, and the latter of exercise; not, however, in the same way, but the one as end and the other as source of movement).Again, the same thing is the cause of contraries; for that which when present causes a particular thing, we sometimes charge, when absent, with the contrary.We impute the shipwreck to the absence of the steersman, whose presence was the cause of safety; and both the presence and the privation-are causes as sources of movement.

All the causes now mentioned fall under four senses which are the most obvious. For the letters are the cause of syllables, and the material is the cause of manufactured things, and fire and earth and all such things are the causes of bodies, and the parts are causes of the whole, and the hypotheses are causes of the conclusion, in the sense that they are that out of which these respectively are made; but of these some are cause as the substratum (e.g. the parts), others as the essence (the whole, the synthesis, and the form). The semen, the physician, the adviser, and in general the agent, are all sources of change or of rest. The remainder are causes as the end and the good of the other things; for that for the sake of which other things are tends to be the best and the end of the other things; let us take it as making no difference whether we call it good or apparent good.

These, then, are the causes, and this is the number of their kinds, but the varieties of causes are many in number, though when summarized these also are comparatively few. Causes are spoken of in many senses, and even of those which are of the same kind some are causes in a prior and others in a posterior sense, for example both "the doctor" physician' and '"the professional man" are causes of health, and both "the ratio 2:1" and 'number' are causes of the octave, and the classes that include any particular cause are always causes of the particular effect. Again, there are accidental causes and the classes which include these; e.g. while in one sense "the sculptor" causes the statue, in another sense "Polyclitus" causes it, because the sculptor happens to be Polyclitus; and the classes that include the accidental cause are also causes, for example man or "animal" is the cause of the statue, because Polyclitus is a man, and man is an animal. Again, both accidental and proper causes may be spoken of in combination. We may say not "Polyclitus" nor "the sculptor" but "Polyclitus the sculptor." Yet all these are but six in number, while each is spoken of in two ways; for (A) they are causes either as the individual, or as the genus, or as the accidental, or as the genus that includes the accidental, and these either as combined, or as taken simply; and (B) all may be taken as acting or as having a capacity. But they differ inasmuch as the acting causes, i.e. the individuals, exist, or do not exist, simultaneously with the things of which they are causes, e.g. this particular man who is healing, with this particular man who is recovering health, and this particular builder with this particular thing that is being built; but the potential causes are not always in this case; for the house does not perish at the same time as the builder.

On What There Is by Willard Van Orman Quine. From Review of Metaphysics (1948). Reprinted in 1953 From A Logical point of View, Harvard University Press [excerpts from pp. 1–11].

Reality is what there is, and in this essay W. V. O. Quine (1908–2000) distinguishes reality from the conceptual schemes we use to define it. Only science, Quine believes, can reveal the truth about reality.

On What There Is

Willard Van Orman Quine

A curious thing about the ontological problem is its simplicity. It can be put in three Anglo-Saxon monosyllables: 'What is there?' It can be answered, moreover, in a word— 'Everything'—and everyone will accept this answer as true. However, this is merely to say that there is what there is. There remains room for disagreement over cases; and so the issue has stayed alive down the centuries.

Suppose now that two philosophers, McX and I, differ over ontology. Suppose McX maintains there is something which I maintain there is not. McX can, quite consistently with his own point of view, describe our difference of opinion by saying that I refuse to recognize certain entities. I should protest, of course, that he is wrong in his formulation of our disagreement, for I maintain that there are no entities, of the kind which he alleges, for me to recognize; but my finding him wrong in his formulation of our disagreement is unimportant, for I am committed to considering him wrong in his ontology anyway.

When *I* try to formulate our difference of opinion, on the other hand, I seem to be in a predicament. I cannot admit that there are some things which McX countenances and I do not, for in admitting that there are such things I should be contradicting my own rejection of them.

It would appear, if this reasoning were sound, that in any ontological dispute the proponent of the negative side suffers the disadvantage of not being able to admit that his opponent disagrees with him.

This is the old Platonic riddle of nonbeing. Nonbeing must in some sense be, otherwise what is it that there is not? This tangled doctrine might be nicknamed *Plato's beard*; historically it has proved tough, frequently dulling the edge of Occam's razor.

It is some such line of thought that leads philosophers like McX to impute being where they might otherwise be quite content to recognize that there is nothing. Thus, take Pegasus. If Pegasus *were* not, McX argues, we should not be talking about anything when we use the word; therefore it would be nonsense to say even that Pegasus is not. Thinking to show thus that the denial of Pegasus cannot be coherently maintained, he concludes that Pegasus is.

McX cannot, indeed, quite persuade himself that any region of space-time, near or remote, contains a flying horse of flesh and blood. Pressed for further details on Pegasus, then, he says that Pegasus is an idea in men's minds. Here, however, a confusion begins to be apparent. We may for the sake of argument concede that there is an entity, and even a unique entity (though this is rather implausible), which is the mental Pegasus-idea; but this mental entity is not what people are talking about when they deny Pegasus.

McX never confuses the Parthenon with the Parthenon-idea. The Parthenon is physical; the Parthenon-idea is mental (according anyway to McX's version of ideas, and I have no better to offer). The Parthenon is visible; the Parthenon-idea is invisible. We cannot easily imagine two things more unlike, and less liable to confusion, than the Parthenon and the Parthenon-idea. But when we shift from the Parthenon to Pegasus, the confusion sets in—for no other reason than that McX would sooner be deceived by the crudest and most flagrant counterfeit than grant the nonbeing of Pegasus.

The notion that Pegasus must be, because it would otherwise be nonsense to say even that Pegasus is not, has been seen to lead McX into an elementary confusion. Subtler minds, taking the same precept as their starting point, come out with theories of Pegasus which are less patently misguided than McX's, and correspondingly more difficult to eradicate. One of these subtler minds is named, let us say, Wyman. Pegasus, Wyman maintains, has his being as an unactualized possible. When we say of Pegasus that there is no such thing, we are saying, more precisely, that Pegasus does not have the special attribute of actuality. Saying that Pegasus is not actual is on a par, logically, with saying that the Parthenon is not red; in either case we are saying something about an entity whose being is unquestioned.

. . . Possibility, along with the other modalities of necessity and impossibility and contingency, raises problems upon which I do not mean to imply that we should turn our backs. But we can at least limit modalities to whole statements. We may impose the adverb 'possibly' upon a statement as a whole, and we may well worry about the semantical analysis of such usage; but little real advance in such analysis is to be hoped for in expanding our universe to include so-called *possible entities*. I suspect that the main motive for this expansion is simply the old notion that Pegasus, for example, must be because otherwise it would be nonsense to say even that he is not.

I have spoken disparagingly of Plato's beard, and hinted that it is tangled. I have dwelt at length on the inconveniences of putting up with it. It is time to think about taking steps.

Russell, in his theory of so-called singular descriptions, showed clearly how we might meaningfully use seeming names without supposing that there be the entities allegedly named. The names to which Russell's theory directly applies are complex descriptive names such as 'the author of *Waverley*', 'the present King of France', 'the round square cupola on Berkeley College'. Russell analyzes such phrases systematically as fragments of the whole sentences in which they occur. The sentence "The author of *Waverley* was a poet", for example, is explained as a whole as meaning 'Someone (better: something) wrote *Waverley* and was a poet, and nothing else wrote *Waverley*'. (The point of this added clause is to affirm the uniqueness which is implicit in the word 'the', in '*the* author of *Waverley*'.) The sentence 'The round square cupola on Berkeley College is pink' is explained as 'Something is round and square and is a cupola on Berkeley College and is pink, and nothing else is round and square and a cupola on Berkeley College'.

The virtue of this analysis is that the seeming name, a descriptive phrase, is paraphrased *in context* as a so-called incomplete symbol. No unified expression is offered as an analysis of the descriptive phrase, but the statement as a whole which was the context of that phrase still gets its full quota of meaning—whether true or false.

The unanalyzed statement 'The author of *Waverley* was a poet' contains a part, 'the author of *Waverley*', which is wrongly supposed by McX and Wyman to demand objective reference in order to be meaningful at all. But in Russell's translation, 'Something wrote *Waverley* and was a poet and nothing else wrote *Waverley*', the burden of objective reference which had been put upon the descriptive phrase is now taken over by words of the kind that logicians call bound variables, variables of quantification, namely, words like 'something', 'nothing', 'everything'. These words, far from purporting to be names specifically of the author of *Waverley*, do not purport to be names at all; they refer to entities generally, with a kind of studied ambiguity peculiar to themselves. These quantificational words or bound variables are, of course a basic part of language, and their meaningfulness, at least in context, is not to be challenged. But their meaningfulness in no way presupposes there being either the author of *Waverley* or the round square cupola on Berkeley College or any other specifically preassigned objects.

Where descriptions are concerned, there is no longer any difficulty in affirming or denying being. 'There *is* the author of *Waverley*' is explained by Russell as meaning 'Someone (or, more strictly, something) wrote *Waverley* and nothing else wrote *Waverley*'. 'The author of *Waverley* is not' is explained, correspondingly, as the alternation 'Either each thing failed to write *Waverley* or two or more things wrote *Waverley*'. This alternation is false, but meaningful; and it contains no expression purporting to name the author of *Waverley*. The statement 'The round square cupola on Berkeley College is not' is analyzed in similar fashion. So the old notion that statements of nonbeing defeat themselves goes by the board. When a statement of being or nonbeing is analyzed by Russell's theory of descriptions, it ceases to contain any expression which even purports to name the alleged entity whose being is in question, so that the meaningfulness of the statement no longer can be thought to presuppose that there be such an entity.

Now what of 'Pegasus'? This being a word rather than a descriptive phrase, Russell's argument does not immediately apply to it. However, it can easily be made to apply. We have only to rephrase 'Pegasus' as a description, in any way that seems adequately to single out our idea; say, 'the winged horse that was captured by Bellerophon'. Substituting such a phrase for 'Pegasus', we can then proceed to analyze the statement 'Pegasus is', or 'Pegasus is not', precisely on the analogy of Russell's analysis of 'The author of *Waverley* is' and 'The author of *Waverley* is not'.

In order thus to subsume a one-word name or alleged name such as 'Pegasus' under Russell's theory of description, we must, of course, be able first to translate the word into a description. But this is no real restriction. If the notion of Pegasus had been so obscure or so basic a one that no pat translation into a descriptive phrase had offered itself along familiar lines, we could still have availed ourselves of the following artificial and trivial-seeming device: we could have appealed to the *ex hypothesi* unanalyzable, irreducible attribute of *being Pegasus*, adopting, for its expression, the verb 'is-Pegasus', or 'pegasizes'. The noun 'Pegasus' itself could then be treated as derivative, and identified after all with a description: 'the thing that is-Pegasus', 'the thing that pegasizes'.

If the importing of such a predicate as 'pegasizes' seems to commit us to recognizing that there is a corresponding attribute, pegasizing, in Plato's heaven or in the minds of men, well and good. Neither we nor Wyman nor McX have been contending, thus far, about the being or nonbeing of universals, but rather about that of Pegasus. If in terms of pegasizing we can interpret the noun 'Pegasus' as a description subject to Russell's theory of descriptions, then we have disposed of the old notion that Pegasus cannot be said not to be without presupposing that in some sense Pegasus is.

Our argument is now quite general. McX and Wyman supposed that we could not meaningfully affirm a statement of the form 'So-and-so is not', with a simple or descriptive singular noun in place of 'so-and-so', unless so-and-so is. This supposition is now seen to be quite generally groundless, since the singular noun in question can always be expanded into a singular description, trivially or otherwise, and then analyzed out à la Russell.

We commit ourselves to an ontology containing numbers when we say there are prime numbers larger than a million; we commit ourselves to an ontology containing centaurs when we say there are centaurs; and we commit ourselves to an ontology containing Pegasus when we say Pegasus is. But we do not commit ourselves to an ontology containing Pegasus or the author of *Waverley* or the round square cupola on Berkeley College when we say that Pegasus or the author of *Waverley* or the cupola in question is *not*. We need no longer labor under the delusion that the meaningfulness of a statement containing a singular term presupposes an entity named by the term. A singular term need not name to be significant.

An inkling of this might have dawned on Wyman and McX even without benefit of Russell if they had only noticed—as so few of us do—that there is a gulf between *meaning* and *naming* even in the case of a singular term which is genuinely a name of an object. The following example from Frege [3] will serve. The phrase 'Evening Star' names a certain large physical object of spherical form, which is hurtling through space some scores of millions of miles from here. The phrase 'Morning Star' names the same thing, as was probably first established by some observant Babylonian. But the two phrases cannot be regarded as having the same meaning; otherwise that Babylonian could have dispensed with his observations and contented himself with reflecting on the meanings of his words. The meanings, then, being different from one another, must be other than the named object, which is one and the same in both cases.

Confusion of meaning with naming not only made McX think he could not meaningfully repudiate Pegasus; a continuing confusion of meaning with naming no doubt helped engender his absurd notion that Pegasus is an idea, a mental entity. The structure of his confusion is as follows. He confused the alleged *named object* Pegasus with the *meaning* of the word 'Pegasus', therefore concluding that Pegasus must be in order that the word have meaning. But what sorts of things are meanings? This is a moot point; however, one might quite plausibly explain meanings as ideas in the mind, supposing we can make clear sense in turn of the idea of ideas in the mind. Therefore Pegasus, initially confused with a meaning, ends up as an idea in the mind. It is the more remarkable that Wyman, subject to the same initial motivation as McX, should have avoided this particular blunder and wound up with unactualized possibles instead.

Now let us turn to the ontological problem of universals: the question whether there are such entities as attributes, relations, classes, numbers, functions. McX, characteristically enough, thinks there are. Speaking of attributes, he says: "There are red houses, red roses, red sunsets; this much is prephilosophical common sense in which we must all agree. These houses, roses, and sunsets, then, have something in common; and this which they have in common is all I mean by the attribute of redness." For McX, thus, there being attributes is even more obvious and trivial than the obvious and trivial fact of there being red houses, roses, and sunsets. This, I think, is characteristic of metaphysics, or at least of that part of metaphysics called ontology: one who regards a statement on this subject as true at all must regard it as trivially true. One's ontology is basic to the conceptual scheme by which he interprets all experiences, even the most commonplace ones. Judged within some particular conceptual scheme—and how else is judgment possible?— an ontological statement goes without saying, standing in

need of no separate justification at all. Ontological statements follow immediately from all manner of casual statements of commonplace fact, just as—
from the point of view, anyway, of McX's conceptual scheme—'There is an
attribute' follows from 'There are red houses, red roses, red sunsets'.

... The useful ways in which people ordinarily talk or seem to talk about
meanings boil down to two: the *having* of meanings, which is significance,
and *sameness* of meaning, or synonymy. What is called *giving* the meaning
of an utterance is simply the uttering of a synonym, couched, ordinarily, in
clearer language than the original. If we are allergic to meanings as such, we
can speak directly of utterances as significant or insignificant, and as synonymous or heteronymous one with another. The problem of explaining these
adjectives 'significant' and 'synonymous' with some degree of clarity and
rigor—preferably, as I see it, in terms of behavior—is as difficult as it is
important. But the explanatory value of special and irreducible intermedi-
ary entities called meanings is surely illusory.

Up to now I have argued that we can use singular terms significantly in
sentences without presupposing that there are the entities which those
terms purport to name. I have argued further that we can use general terms,
for example, predicates, without conceding them to be names of abstract
entities. I have argued further that we can view utterances as significant,
and as synonymous or heteronymous with one another, without counte-
nancing a realm of entities called meanings. At this point McX begins; to
wonder whether there is any limit at all to our ontological immunity. Does
nothing we may say commit us to the assumption of universals or other entities which we may find unwelcome?

I have already suggested a negative answer to this question, in speaking
of bound variables, or variables of quantification, in connection with
Russell's theory of descriptions. We can very easily involve ourselves in ontological commitments by saying, for example, that *there is something* (bound
variable) which red houses and sunsets have in common; or that *there is
something* which is a prime number larger than a million. But, this is, essentially, the *only* way we can involve ourselves in ontological commitments: by
our use of bound variables. The use of alleged names is no criterion, for we
can repudiate their namehood at the drop of a hat unless the assumption of
a corresponding entity can be spotted in the things we affirm in terms of
bound variables. Names are, in fact, altogether immaterial to the ontological issue, for I have shown, in connection with 'Pegasus' and 'pegasize', that
names can be converted to descriptions, and Russell has shown that
descriptions can be eliminated.

Whatever we say with the help of names can be said in a language which
shuns names altogether. To be assumed as an entity is, purely and simply, to
be reckoned as the value of a variable. In terms of the categories of traditional grammar, this amounts roughly to saying that to be is to be in the

range of reference of a pronoun. Pronouns are the basic media of reference; nouns might better have been named propronouns. The variables of quantification, 'something', 'nothing', 'everything', range over our whole ontology, whatever it may be; and we are convicted of a particular ontological presupposition if, and only if, the alleged presuppositum has to be reckoned among the entities over which our variables range in order to render one of our affirmations true.

We may say, for example, that some dogs are white and not thereby commit ourselves to recognizing either doghood or whiteness as entities. 'Some dogs are white' says that some things that are dogs are white; and, in order that this statement be true, the things over which the bound variable 'something' ranges must include some white dogs, but need not include doghood or whiteness. On the other hand, when we say that some zoological species are cross-fertile we are committing ourselves to recognizing as entities the several species themselves, abstract though they are. We remain so committed at least until we devise some way of so paraphrasing the statement as to show that the seeming reference to species on the part of our bound variable was an avoidable manner of speaking.

Classical mathematics, as the example of primes larger than a million clearly illustrates, is up to its neck in commitments to an ontology of abstract entities. Thus it is that the great mediaeval controversy over universals has flared up anew in the modern philosophy of mathematics. The issue is clearer now than of old, because we now have a more explicit standard whereby to decide what ontology a given theory or form of discourse is committed to: a theory is committed to those and only those entities to which the bound variables of the theory must be capable of referring in order that the affirmations made in the theory be true.

Because this standard of ontological presupposition did not emerge clearly in the philosophical tradition, the modern philosophical mathematicians have not on the whole recognized that they were debating the same old problem of universals in a newly clarified form. But the fundamental cleavages among modern points of view on foundations of mathematics do come down pretty explicitly to disagreements as to the range of entities to which the bound variables should be permitted to refer.

The three main mediaeval points of view regarding universals are designated by historians as *realism*, *conceptualism*, and *nominalism*. Essentially these same three doctrines reappear in twentieth-century surveys of the philosophy of mathematics under the new names *logicism*, *intuitionism*, and *formalism*.

Realism, as the word is used in connection with the mediaeval controversy over universals, is the Platonic doctrine that universals or abstract entities have being independently of the mind; the mind may discover them but cannot create them. *Logicism*, represented by Frege, Russell,

Whitehead, Church, and Carnap, condones the use of bound variables to refer to abstract entities known and unknown, specifiable and unspecifiable, indiscriminately.

Conceptualism holds that there are universals but they are mind-made. *Intuitionism*, espoused in modern times in one form or another by Poincaré, Brouwer, Weyl, and others, countenances the use of bound variables to refer to abstract entities only when those entities are capable of being cooked up individually from ingredients specified in advance. As Fraenkel has put it, logicism holds that classes are discovered while intuitionism holds that they are invented—a fair statement indeed of the old opposition between realism and conceptualism. This opposition is no mere quibble; it makes an essential difference in the amount of classical mathematics to which one is willing to subscribe. Logicists, or realists, are able on their assumptions to get Cantor's ascending orders of infinity; intuitionists are compelled to stop with the lowest order of infinity, and, as an indirect consequence, to abandon even some of the classical laws of real numbers. The modern controversy between logicism and intuitionism arose, in fact, from disagreements over infinity.

Formalism, associated with the name of Hilbert, echoes intuitionism in deploring the logicist's unbridled recourse to universals. But formalism also finds intuitionism unsatisfactory. This could happen for either of two opposite reasons. The formalist might, like the logicist, object to the crippling of classical mathematics; or he might, like the *nominalists* of old, object to admitting abstract entities at all, even in the restrained sense of mind-made entities. The upshot is the same: the formalist keeps classical mathematics as a play of insignificant notations. This play of notations can still be of utility—whatever utility it has already shown itself to have as a crutch for physicists and technologists. But utility need not imply significance, in any literal linguistic sense. Nor need the marked success of mathematicians in spinning out theorems, and in finding objective bases for agreement with one another's results, imply significance. For an adequate basis for agreement among mathematicians can be found simply in the rules which govern the manipulation of the notations—these syntactical rules being, unlike the notations themselves, quite significant and intelligible.

I have argued that the sort of ontology we adopt can be consequential—notably in connection with mathematics, although this is only an example. Now how are we to adjudicate among rival ontologies? Certainly the answer is not provided by the semantical formula "To be is to be the value of a variable"; this formula serves rather, conversely, in testing the conformity of a given remark or doctrine to a prior ontological standard. We look to bound variables in connection with ontology not in order to know what there is, but in order to know what a given remark or doctrine, ours or someone else's, *says* there is; and this much is quite properly a problem involving language. But what there is is another question.

In debating over what there is, there are still reasons for operating on a semantical plane. One reason is to escape from the predicament noted at the beginning of this essay: the predicament of my not being able to admit that there are things which McX countenances and I do not. So long as I adhere to my ontology, as opposed to McX's, I cannot allow my bound variables to refer to entities which belong to McX's ontology and not to mine. I can, however, consistently describe our disagreement by characterizing the statements which McX affirms. Provided merely that my ontology countenances linguistic forms, or at least concrete inscriptions and utterances, I can talk about McX's sentences.

Another reason for withdrawing to a semantical plane is to find common ground on which to argue. Disagreement, in ontology involves basic disagreement in conceptual schemes; yet McX and I, despite these basic disagreements, find that our conceptual schemes converge sufficiently in their intermediate and upper ramifications to enable us to communicate successfully on such topics as politics, weather, and, in particular, language. In so far as our basic controversy over ontology can be translated upward into a semantical controversy about words and what to do with them, the collapse of the controversy into question-begging may be delayed.

It is no wonder, then, that ontological controversy should tend into controversy over language. But we must not jump to the conclusion that what there is depends on words. Translatability of a question into semantical terms is no indication that the question is linguistic. To see Naples is to bear a name which, when prefixed to the words 'sees Naples', yields a true sentence; still there is nothing linguistic about seeing Naples.

Our acceptance of an ontology is, I think, similar in principle to our acceptance of a scientific theory, say a system of physics: we adopt, at least insofar as we are reasonable, the simplest conceptual scheme into which the disordered fragments of raw experience can be fitted and arranged. Our ontology is determined once we have fixed upon the over-all conceptual scheme which is to accommodate science in the broadest sense; and the considerations which determine a reasonable construction of any part of that conceptual scheme, for example, the biological or the physical part, are not different in kind from the considerations which determine a reasonable construction of the whole. To whatever extent the adoption of any system of scientific theory may be said to be a matter of language, the same—but no more— may be said of the adoption of an ontology.

But simplicity, as a guiding principle in constructing conceptual schemes, is not a clear and unambiguous idea; and it is quite capable of presenting a double or multiple standard. Imagine, for example, that we have devised the most economical set of concepts adequate to the play-by-play reporting of immediate experience. The entities under this scheme—the values of bound variables—are, let us suppose, individual subjective events of sensation or reflection. We should still find, no doubt, that a physicalistic conceptual scheme, purporting to talk about external objects, offers great advantages in simplifying our over-all reports. By bringing together scattered sense events and treating them as perceptions of one object, we reduce the complexity of our stream of experience to a manageable conceptual simplicity. The rule of simplicity is indeed our guiding maxim in assigning sense data to objects: we associate an earlier and a later round sensum with the same so-called penny, or with two different so-called pennies, in obedience to the demands of maximum simplicity in our total world-picture.

Here we have two competing conceptual schemes, a phenomenalistic one and a physicalistic one. Which should prevail? Each has its advantages; each has its special simplicity in its own way. Each, I suggest, deserves to be developed. Each may be said, indeed, to be the more fundamental, though in different senses: the one is epistemologically, the other physically, fundamental.

The physical conceptual scheme simplifies our account of experience because of the way myriad scattered sense events come to be associated with single so-called objects; still there is no likelihood that each sentence about physical objects can actually be translated, however deviously and complexly, into the phenomenalistic language. Physical objects are postulated entities which round out, and simplify our account of the flux of experience, just, as the introduction of irrational numbers simplifies laws of arithmetic. From the point of view of the conceptual scheme of the elementary arithmetic of rational numbers alone, the broader arithmetic of rational and irrational numbers would have the status of a convenient myth, simpler than the literal truth (namely, the arithmetic of rationals) and yet, containing that literal truth as a scattered part. Similarly, from a phenomenalistic point, of view, the conceptual scheme of physical objects is a convenient myth, simpler than the literal truth and yet containing that literal truth as a scattered part.

Now what of classes or attributes of physical objects, in turn? A platonistic ontology of this sort is, from the point of view of a strictly physicalistic conceptual scheme, as much a myth as that physicalistic conceptual scheme itself is for phenomenalism. This higher myth is a good and useful one, in turn, in so far as it simplifies our account of physics. Since mathematics is an integral part of this higher myth, the utility of this myth for physical science is evident enough. In speaking of it nevertheless as a myth, I echo that philosophy of mathematics to which I alluded earlier under the name of formalism. But an attitude of formalism may with equal justice be adopted toward the physical conceptual scheme, in turn, by the pure aesthete or phenomenalist.

The analogy between the myth of mathematics and the myth of physics is, in some additional and perhaps fortuitous ways, strikingly close.

Consider, for example, the crisis which was precipitated in the foundations of mathematics, at the turn of the century, by the discovery of Russell's paradox and other antinomies of set theory. These contradictions had to be obviated by unintuitive, *ad hoc* devices; our mathematical myth-making became deliberate and evident to all. But what of physics? An antinomy arose between the undular and the corpuscular accounts of light; and if this was not as out-and-out a contradiction as Russell's paradox, I suspect that the reason is that physics is not as out-and-out as mathematics. Again, the second great modern crisis in the foundations of mathematics—precipitated in 1931 by Gödel's proof [2] that there are bound to be undecidable statements in arithmetic—has its companion piece in physics in Heisenberg's indeterminacy principle.

In earlier pages I undertook to show that some common arguments in favor of certain ontologies are fallacious. Further, I advanced an explicit standard whereby to decide what the ontological commitments of a theory are. But the question what ontology actually to adopt still stands open, and the obvious counsel is tolerance and an experimental spirit. Let us by all means see how much of the physicalistic conceptual scheme can be reduced to a phenomenalistic one; still, physics also naturally demands pursuing, irreducible *in toto* though it be. Let us see how, or to what degree, natural science may be rendered independent of platonistic mathematics; but let us also pursue mathematics and delve into its platonistic foundations.

From among the various conceptual schemes best suited to these various pursuits, one—the phenomenalistic—claims epistemological priority. Viewed from within the phenomenalistic conceptual scheme, the ontologies of physical objects and mathematical objects are myths. The quality of myth, however, is relative; relative, in this case, to the epistemological point of view. This point of view is one among various, corresponding to one among our various interests and purposes.

KEY TERMS

Conceptualism   holds that ideas are real, but they are dependent upon a mind or thought. The function of a universal term is to denote a special relationship between particular objects. Universals or forms are object concepts that we create in our minds by examining particulars.

Exaggerated Realism   holds that universals exist in the particulars as part of what makes them similar. Ideas exist in the physical objects (and our minds), not in a separate reality. The particulars are a mixture or composite of form (idea) and matter.

Extreme Nominalism   claims that universals or forms do not exist. On this view, ideas (universals or forms) are not real objects. They do not have real existence.

Extreme or Platonic Realism   is the view that the Forms (or universals) exist in a separate realm and that objects in this reality copy the immaterial Forms.

Form   is the word used by Plato (always with a big or capital F) to describe the immaterial essence of objects that he claims exists in a separate reality. Objects in this realm copy the Forms.

form   is the word used by Aristotle (always with a small or lower case letter f) to describe the essence of objects that he claims exists within material things.

Idealism   claims that reality is immaterial, something other than matter.

Materialism   claims that reality, or Being, consists of physical objects and their components.

Metaphysics   is the branch of philosophy that addresses these issues about the nature of reality.

Particular   is another name for objects or individual things that we encounter in the world.

Substance dualism   claims that both the immaterial and the material objects exist.

Universal   is another name for ideas or general concepts or terms that can be applied to various particular objects.

QUESTIONS FOR DISCUSSION AND REVIEW

1. Compare and contrast various views on substance such as materialism, dualism and idealism.
2. Evaluate the 4 views as to the nature of universals and particulars.
3. Explain and evaluate the views of Anaximander regarding the nature of substance.
4. Explain and evaluate the views of Pythagoras regarding the nature of substance.
5. Explain Aristotle's 4 causes.

BIBLIOGRAPHY, SUGGESTED READINGS, AND USEFUL LINKS

Aristotle. (1908) *Metaphysics*. (Ross. W. transl.).

Internet Encyclopedia of Philosophy. A peer-reviewed academic resource. Available from http://www.iep.utm.edu/

Plato. (1892). *Republic*. (Jowett, B, transl.).

Stanford Encyclopedia of Philosophy. Available from http://plato.stanford.edu/

Willard Van Orman Quine. (1948). "On What There Is". From *Review of Metaphysics*.

Epistemology— How do we Know That?

3

Upon completing this chapter, students should be able to meet the following Learning Outcomes:

3.1 Articulate the various methods of epistemology.

3.2 Explain the difference between a priori and a posteriori knowledge.

3.3 Explain and evaluate various theories of knowledge.

3.4 Compare and contrast pragmatic theories of truth with the correspondence theory of truth.

Methods of Epistemology

Although we feel we know a great many things, the reality is that most of what we "know" we do not know at all. **Epistemology** is the study of theories of knowledge. Epistemic theories attempt to explain the various ways we can arrive at knowledge. Primarily, there are two methods—**rationalism** and **empiricism**. Rationalism is a method of acquiring knowledge by means of logic and reason. Empiricism is a method of acquiring knowledge by means of observation, inquiry, and experience. Rationalism claims that knowledge is arrived at by means of our minds. We do not necessarily need experience to have knowledge. Rationalist claim that there exist analytic or a priori knowledge is real. **A priori knowledge** is knowledge that is arrived at without experience and is necessary and certain (must be true).

POWERFUL IDEAS BOX: A PRIORI AND A POSTERIORI KNOWLEDGE

A posteriori knowledge is knowledge that is acquired after some experience. For example, I know that the book will fall down after I release it, by experience. I know that the sun sets in the west, by experience. These are examples of a posteriori knowledge. They are sometime called examples of synthetic knowledge.

A priori knowledge is knowledge that is arrived at without experience and is necessary and certain. The statement: "a cat is a feline" is an example of a necessary, a priori statement. If you understand the concepts of feline and cat, then you understand that a cat is necessarily a feline. Most definitions are examples of a priori knowledge. They don't say what exist in the world, just what could exist. They are sometimes called examples of analytic knowledge.

Defining Knowledge

There are various ways to define knowledge. One of the most prominent theories is known as the **JTB** (Justified True Belief) theory of knowledge. In an attempt to define knowledge, the JTB theory claims that the following three conditions should be met: justification, truth, and belief.

According to JTB theory, a justified true belief is a definition of knowledge. In other words, K = JTB, where Knowledge = Justified + True + Belief. It is argued that all three conditions must be satisfied in order for one to possess knowledge. This theory seems to have some merit, but on closer examination, it is difficult to determine if all three conditions are met. The belief condition is the easiest as people believe a myriad of things (some of which that make sense and have a rational basis and many that do not make sense or seem to have rational support). The justification condition is more difficult, but it can be met if we can provide sound reasons for our beliefs. The quintessential problem is the truth condition. What constitutes truth? Various definitions of truth will be considered later.

Theories of Knowledge

There are various theories of how we can arrive at knowledge. The classic view was put forth by René Descartes (1596–1650) and is known as **Foundationalism**. Other theories include Coherentism and the reliability theory of knowledge.

> ### POWERFUL ANALYSIS: WHAT IS REAL?
>
> What is real? Is seeing, tasting, or touching something real? If that is the case, then "what is real" is simply an electrical impulse interpreted by our brain. Do you agree?

Foundationalism

Foundationalism is an epistemic theory that argues our knowledge claims must be based on basic true beliefs and that these basic believes provide a foundation for all knowledge. René Descartes is one of the most well-known proponents of Foundationalism and the father of modern philosophy. He argues that a rational method is required to have knowledge.

In 1641, he wrote the *Meditations on First Philosophy* in which he articulates his views on knowledge. In this work, he argues that we must find an absolutely certain (beyond doubt) true to serve as a foundational belief. The belief or beliefs that are found to be indubitable serve as a foundation for all of our other knowledge.

He wants to determine which, if any beliefs, he has that are certain. To accomplish this task, he employs a skeptical method often termed the method of doubt. He hopes that by employing this method of doubt, he will be able to examine his beliefs with great scrutiny and cast out the ones that has fault and that he will be to find at least one foundational belief.

He asks himself "Do I have any indubitable beliefs?" To answer this question, he placed his beliefs into three categories: (1) beliefs about the world, (2) beliefs about mathematics, and (3) beliefs about himself. He finds fault with beliefs in each category.

He claims that there are skeptical possibilities that call into question each category. He says that beliefs about the world are called into question by errors produced by our senses such as optical illusions. He claims that beliefs about ourselves can be called into question as we might be dreaming. And finally, beliefs about math and science are called into question by the possibility of an evil demon that is deceiving us.

In truth, optical illusions and the fact that we might be dreaming are not very powerful arguments against either knowing ourselves or the world around us, but the third skeptical hypothesis is more problematic. As Descartes says in the *Meditations*, let us imagine that "some malicious demon of the utmost power and cunning has employed all his energies in order to deceive me. I shall think that the sky, the air, the earth, colors, shapes, sounds and all external things are merely the delusions of dreams which he has devised to ensnare my judgment."

In other words, every perception, every sensation, and every feeling may very well be a lie created and perpetuated by some malicious force. To consider a contemporary cinematic example of this type of skepticism think of the film the *Matrix* (1999), which depicts just the type of skeptical situation as Descartes is describing in his book. In the film, people think they are living in the real world when in fact they are plugged into computers and living in an artificial virtual reality known as the matrix.

With the possibility of an evil demon in control, Descartes is left with very little to believe in, but as he ponders his situation, he comes to the conclusion that there is one thing, one believes that he still knows: ***Cogito ergo sum*** (in Latin) or literally in English: I think, I am. This is more often translated as: I think therefore I am. So, on Descartes view, even if the world around you is a lie created by an evil demon or an evil computer, the fact that you are able to perceive and think means that you exist in some shape or form. This does not mean your body, life, or world are real, but rather that you have some form of existence. Descartes then uses his foundational belief to construct an elaborate to prove that the rest of reality is real and true.

POWERFUL IDEAS BOX: DESCARTES PROOF FOR EVERYTHING?

1) I think therefore I am.
2) I have a clear and distinct conception of God.
3) In order for a lesser being to have an idea of a greater being, that idea must originate with the greater being
4) Therefore, God exist.
5) God exist and is Good therefore he would not let the evil demon deceive us about the world.
6) Therefore, the world exists as we perceive it so long as we have a clear and distinct conception of it.

This argument has been scrutinized for nearly 400 years. In the time since the argument was presented, a number of logical flaws have been found in Descartes reasoning. The central problem with the argument is known as the "Cartesian Circle," and it is this he claims in premise 2 to know that God exist because he has a clear and distinct conception of him. Yet, it is God's existence in premise 4 and the fact that he makes clear and distinct perception true in premise 6 that allow you to trust in such perceptions. In other words, he presupposes a concept that he uses to prove that God exists.

To put it another way, Descartes argues that clear and distinct perceptions provide the foundation or basis for the truth of our beliefs and that is so because God, who is not a deceiver, would not allow Descartes to be mistaken about that which he clearly and distinctly perceives. Yet, this notion of clear and distinct perceptions and their truth requires God's existence, which he has yet to establish. As such Descartes cannot know that his proof of God's existence is true or does not contain an error unless he assumes that his clear and distinct perception of the steps of his reasoning is correct. Thus, the criterion of clear and distinct perception depends on the assumption that God exists, which in turn depends on the criterion of clear and distinct perception.

"The Matrix Hypothesis threatens to undercut almost everything I know. It seems to be a *skeptical hypothesis*: a hypothesis that I cannot rule out, and one that would falsify most of my beliefs if it were true. Where there is a skeptical hypothesis, it looks like none of these beliefs count as genuine knowledge. Of course the beliefs *might* be true -I might be lucky, and not be envatted -but I can't rule out the possibility that they are false. So a skeptical hypothesis leads to *skepticism* about these beliefs: I believe these things, but I do not know them"

—*David Chalmers, (2003), The Matrix as Metaphysics.*

POWERFUL ANALYSIS: COULD GOD HAVE A REASON TO DECEIVE HUMANITY?

For a moment assume that Descartes' argument works in proving God's existence, does the ultimate conclusion follow as stated in premise 6? Can Descartes be certain that God would not allow an evil demon or computer to systematically deceive humanity? Maybe God has a reason, or needs to teach humanity a lesson.

Coherentism

Coherentism is an alternative theory of justification to Foundationalism and Reliabilism. Unlike Foundationalism, Coherentism denies the notion that there are basic foundational beliefs and instead argue that many of our beliefs are justified by other believes. To think of it metaphorically instead of a pillar of knowledge with a foundational belief at the base, there is a web of believes that in turn justify each other. According to Coherentism, whole systems of beliefs are justified by their coherence. This view also states that all of our beliefs must be compatible with one another. For example, if I believe X, Y, and Z, but if X contradicts Y and Z, then I cannot reasonably hold all three beliefs. One concern with the theory is that all of your beliefs could be compatible with one another and still all false. There could exists a coherent set of beliefs that all fit together but are ultimately false.

Reliability Theory of Knowledge

The **reliability theory of knowledge** (also known as reliabilism) states that knowledge should be acquired by means of a reliable process. According to reliabilism, a belief is justified based on the method by which it was acquired. On this view (as we know from everyday experience), there are good and bad ways to go about forming beliefs. Beliefs based on reliable belief-forming mechanisms are likely to be true; in other words, believe that we acquire, which are based on methods that have been reliable in the past, are beliefs we can have in and belief are true. Examples of reliable processes are our perceptions—sight, hearing, sound, taste, and touch as well as logical methods such as deduction, induction, and abduction. Unreliable processes might be things such as extra-sensory perception (ESP) and random guesses. In the end, this theory states that we "know" those beliefs that we obtain from reliable methods.

Powerful Thinkers: Kurt Gödel

© Bettmann/CORBIS

A mathematician who had an enormous influence on philosophy as well as on science, Kurt Gödel (1906–1978) was born an Austro-Hungarian in Brno, in what is now the Czech Republic; and he died as an American in Princeton, NJ. His journey was extraordinary, calling into question the rules of logic and rocking the foundations of mathematics in the twentieth century as well as signaling an unexpected return to Platonic views on the possibility of knowledge.

Human mind is superior to any machine and can work out truths that no artificial intelligence ever will reach is one of the many results of Gödel's work and particularly of his famous Incompleteness

Theorem—actually two related theorems—which showed that there are certain truths within any closed mathematical system that cannot be proved within that system. Gödel published his revolutionary essay "On Formally Undecidable Propositions of *Principia Mathematica* and Related Systems" in 1931, challenging what at the time were accepted tenets of mathematics and logic. It turns out that certainty has its limits.

There is, in fact, profound uncertainty about the universe, about reality. A difficult feat of logic that, once understood, boasts breathtaking simplicity, Gödel's Theorem shows that if a system is internally consistent—that is, without any contradictions—then it cannot be complete; and further that the consistency of axioms cannot be proved within that system. In other words, there always will be at least one truth that cannot be proved but is nevertheless true. There may be other ways of knowing truth beyond what had been previously accepted as mathematical evidence is what has been identified as a return to Plato, who believed that truth was elusive and we could at best get close to it. Gödel's Theorem also precludes the possibility that a machine, whether the rudimentary computers that were being developed when he came up with his discovery, or the so-called artificial intelligence foreseen by Alan Turing (1912–1954), cannot be up to the tasks that only the human mind might be able to perform. The most a computer can do is imitate the human mind—that is Turing's Imitation Game that helped win World War II. But there always be something true that even a computer with unlimited capabilities cannot prove.

Pragmatic Theories of Truth

Pragmatic theories of truth claim that, in a sense, truth is relative. Truth may be in a sense relative to: the individual, science, or society. William James (1842–1910) argued that truth could be defined as what was useful to believe by the individual. As radical as this might sound James defends this notion of truth in cases where the truth or falsity of a belief are primarily unproven or open to possibility. He thinks that religious beliefs or beliefs about our free will are things that can be true for some people and false for others. He also thinks we do not require evidence when engaging in the process of hypothesis venturing, which, in his view, creates beliefs whose evidence becomes available only after they are believed. James also claims that self-fulfilling beliefs (beliefs that by existing make themselves true) are true for the individual. Such a notion of truth means that if you believe in God, then it is true and I do not believe in God, then it is false. How a belief can be both true and false at the same time seems to fly in the face of convention and common sense. The correspondence theory of truth seems to make this case. It is will be discussed below.

A less radical notion of truth was developed by Charles Sanders Peirce (1839–1914) and endorsed by John Dewey (1859–1952). In his view, truth is whatever science determines to be true at the end of scientific inquiry. Truth is relative to the progress of science. In the past, given that different societies had different levels of scientific knowledge, truth was, in a sense relative to societies. At present, science is practiced in the same way everywhere in the developed world, there is only one science (unless we consider tribal peoples in remote regions of the world, that do not share our scientific concepts).

> "The opinion which is fated to be ultimately agreed to by all who investigate is what we mean by the truth, and the object represented in this opinion is the real."
>
> —*C. S. Peirce*

According to Peirce, at this moment, since we are not at the end of scientific investigation and inquiry, we only have some truths or an approximate version of truth. One day humanity will figure everything out, and at that moment, we will have knowledge.

John Dewey agreed with Peirce regarding the nature of truth and the importance of inquiry and investigation. Dewey in his book, *The Theory of Inquiry* (1938), gave the following definition of inquiry: inquiry is the controlled or directed transformation of an indeterminate situation into one that is so determinate in its constituent distinctions and relations as to convert the elements of the original situation into a unified whole. In the same work, Dewey, in the index has placed one footnote regarding the notion of truth, for which he cites the quote of Peirce given above and says "The best definition of *truth* from the logical standpoint which is known to me is that by Peirce": "The opinion which is fated to be ultimately agreed to by all who investigate is what we mean by the truth, and the object represented in this opinion is the real."

Correspondence Theory of Truth

The **correspondence theory of truth** basically says a belief is true if and only if, it corresponds with something that exists in the world. Alfred Tarski (1901–1983) developed a theory of truth for formalized languages, which can be seen as a statement of the correspondence theory of truth, although there is debate amongst philosophers if this is actually now the case. The classical interpretation of Tarski is that his work can be read as supporting the correspondence theory of truth. According to the theory, my belief that a table is in the room is true, if and only if there actually is a table in the room. As Tarski famously said, the statement "Snow is white" is true if and only if snow is white. He is not saying there is white snow, but if there is somewhere in the universe white snow, then the statement is true.

The interconnection of belief, justification, evidence, truth, and knowledge is very complex. Many philosophers have abandoned Descartes project of looking for certainly and have accepted either a pragmatic or a deflationary theory of knowledge. If knowledge requires certainty, then perhaps we should concede that many of our beliefs are not certain. If we need certainty in order to have knowledge, then we perhaps cannot have much knowledge at all.

POWERFUL ANALYSIS: TRUTH AND CERTAINTY

Does knowledge require certainty? Can you claim to know something that ultimately turns out to be false?

READINGS

In this reading, David Hume, the "great Skeptic" calls into question the human capacity to understand reality. Hume denies the rationality of induction and causality. As a result of this, he denies most science. (Since it is based on induction and causality.) Most "knowledge" is just custom or habit that is not actually justified by reason.

> AN ENQUIRY CONCERNING HUMAN UNDERSTANDING.
> BY DAVID HUME (1777)
> SECTION IV. SCEPTICAL DOUBTS CONCERNING THE OPERATIONS OF THE UNDERSTANDING.

PART I

20. All the objects of human reason or enquiry may naturally be divided into two kinds, to wit, "Relations of Ideas", and "Matters of Fact". Of the first kind are the sciences of Geometry, Algebra, and Arithmetic; and in short, every affirmation which is either intuitively or demonstratively certain. "That the square of the hypotenuse is equal to the square of the two sides", is a proposition which expresses a relation between these figures. "That three times five is equal to the half of thirty", expresses a relation between these numbers. Propositions of this kind are discoverable by the mere operation of thought, without dependence on what is anywhere existent in the universe. Though there never were a circle or triangle in nature, the truths demonstrated by Euclid would forever retain their certainty and evidence.

21. Matters of fact, which are the second objects of human reason, are not ascertained in the same manner; nor is our evidence of their truth, however great, of a like nature with the foregoing. The contrary of every matter of fact is still possible; because it can never imply a contradiction, and is conceived by the mind with the same facility and distinctness, as if ever so conformable to reality. "That the sun will not rise tomorrow" is no less intelligible a proposition, and implies no more contradiction than the affirmation, "that it will rise". We should in vain, therefore, attempt to demonstrate its falsehood. Were it demonstratively false, it would imply a contradiction, and could never be distinctly conceived by the mind.

It may, therefore, be a subject worthy of curiosity, to enquire what is the nature of that evidence which assures us of any real existence and matter of fact, beyond the present testimony of our senses, or the records of our memory. This part of philosophy, it is observable, has been little cultivated, either by the ancients or moderns; and therefore our doubts and errors, in the prosecution of so important an enquiry, may be the more excusable; while we march through such difficult paths without any guide or direction. They may even prove useful, by exciting curiosity, and destroying that implicit faith and security, which is the bane of all reasoning and free enquiry. The discovery of defects in the common philosophy, if any such there be, will not, I presume, be a discouragement, but rather an incitement, as is usual, to attempt something more full and satisfactory than has yet been proposed to the public.

22. All reasoning concerning matter of fact seem to be founded on the relation of "Cause and Effect". By means of that relation alone we can go beyond the evidence of our memory and senses. If you were to ask a man, why he believes any matter of fact, which is absent; for instance, that his friend is in the country, or in France; he would give you a reason; and this reason would be some other fact; as a letter received from him, or the knowledge of his former resolutions and promises. A man finding a watch or any other machine in a desert island, would conclude that there had once been men in that island. All our reasoning concerning fact are of the same nature. And here it is constantly supposed that there is a connection between the present fact and that which is inferred from it. Were there nothing to bind them together, the inference would be entirely precarious. The hearing of an articulate voice and rational discourse in the dark assures us of the presence of some person: Why? because these are the effects of the human make and fabric, and closely connected with it. If we anatomize all the other reasoning of this nature, we shall find that they are founded on the relation of cause and effect, and that this relation is either near or remote, direct or collateral. Heat and light are collateral effects of fire, and the one effect may justly be inferred from the other.

23. If we would satisfy ourselves, therefore, concerning the nature of that evidence, which assures us of matters of fact, we must enquire how we arrive at the knowledge of cause and effect.

I shall venture to affirm, as a general proposition, which admits of no exception, that the knowledge of this relation is not, in any instance, attained by reasoning "a priori"; but arises entirely from experience, when we find that any particular objects are constantly conjoined with each other. Let an object be presented to a man of ever so strong natural reason and abilities; if that object be entirely new to him, he will not be able, by the most accurate examination of its sensible qualities, to discover any of its causes or effects. Adam, though his rational faculties be supposed, at the very first, entirely perfect, could not have inferred from the fluidity and transparency of water that it would suffocate him, or from the light and warmth of fire that it would consume him. No object ever discovers, by the qualities which appear to the senses, either the causes which produced it, or the effects which will arise from it; nor can our reason, unassisted by experience, ever draw any inference concerning real existence and matter of fact.

24. This proposition, "that causes and effects are discoverable, not by reason but by experience", will readily be admitted with regard to such objects, as we remember to have once been altogether unknown to us; since we must be conscious of the utter inability, which we then lay under, of foretelling what would arise from them. Present two smooth pieces of marble to a man who has no tincture of natural philosophy; he will never discover that they will adhere together in such a manner as to require great force to separate them in a direct line, while they make so small a resistance to a lateral pressure. Such events, as bear little analogy to the common course of nature, are also readily confessed to be known only by experience; nor does any man imagine that the explosion of gunpowder, or the attraction of a loadstone, could ever be discovered by arguments "a priori". In like manner, when an effect is supposed to depend upon an intricate machinery or secret structure of parts, we make no difficulty in attributing all our knowledge of it to experience. Who will assert that he can give the ultimate reason, why milk or bread is proper nourishment for a man, not for a lion or a tiger?

But the same truth may not appear, at first sight, to have the same evidence with regard to events, which have become familiar to us from our first appearance in the world, which bear a close analogy to the whole course of nature, and which are supposed to depend on the simple qualities of objects, without any secret structure of parts. We are apt to imagine that we could discover these effects by the mere operation of our reason, without experience. We fancy, that were we brought on a sudden into this world, we could at first have inferred that one Billiard-ball would communicate motion to another upon impulse; and that we needed not to have waited for the event, in order to pronounce with certainty concerning it. Such is the influence of custom, that, where it is strongest, it not only covers our natural ignorance, but even conceals itself, and seems not to take place, merely because it is found in the highest degree.

25. But to convince us that all the laws of nature, and all the operations of bodies without exception, are known only by experience, the following reflections may, perhaps, suffice. Were any object presented to us, and were we required to pronounce concerning the effect, which will result from it, without consulting past observation; after what manner, I beseech you, must the mind proceed in this operation? It must invent or imagine some event, which it ascribes to the object as its effect; and it is plain that this invention must be entirely arbitrary. The mind can never possibly find the effect in the supposed cause, by the most accurate scrutiny and examination. For the effect is totally different from the cause, and consequently can never be discovered in it. Motion in the second Billiard-ball is a quite distinct event from motion in the first; nor is there anything in the one to suggest the smallest hint of the other. A stone or piece of metal raised into the air,

and left without any support, immediately falls: but to consider the matter "a priori", is there anything we discover in this situation which can beget the idea of a downward, rather than an upward, or any other motion, in the stone or metal? And as the first imagination or invention of a particular effect, in all natural operations, is arbitrary, where we consult not experience; so must we also esteem the supposed tie or connection between the cause and effect, which binds them together, and renders it impossible that any other effect could result from the operation of that cause. When I see, for instance, a Billiard-ball moving in a straight line towards another; even suppose motion in the second ball should by accident be suggested to me, as the result of their contact or impulse; may I not conceive, that a hundred different events might as well follow from that cause? May not both these balls remain at absolute rest? May not the first ball return in a straight line, or leap off from the second in any line or direction? All these suppositions are consistent and conceivable. Why then should we give the preference to one, which is no more consistent or conceivable than the rest? All our reasoning "a priori" will never be able to show us any foundation for this preference.

In a word, then, every effect is a distinct event from its cause. It could not, therefore, be discovered in the cause, and the first invention or conception of it, "a priori", must be entirely arbitrary. And even after it is suggested, the conjunction of it with the cause must appear equally arbitrary; since there are always many other effects, which, to reason, must seem fully as consistent and natural. In vain, therefore, should we pretend to determine any single event, or infer any cause or effect, without the assistance of observation and experience.

26. Hence we may discover the reason why no philosopher, who is rational and modest, has ever pretended to assign the ultimate cause of any natural operation, or to show distinctly the action of that power, which produces any single effect in the universe. It is confessed, that the utmost effort of human reason is to reduce the principles, productive of natural phenomena, to a greater simplicity, and to resolve the many particular effects into a few general causes, by means of reasoning from analogy, experience, and observation. But as to the causes of these general causes, we should in vain attempt their discovery; nor shall we ever be able to satisfy ourselves, by any particular explication of them. These ultimate springs and principles are totally shut up from human curiosity and enquiry. Elasticity, gravity, cohesion of parts, communication of motion by impulse; these are probably the ultimate causes and principles which we shall ever discover in nature; and we may esteem ourselves sufficiently happy, if, by accurate enquiry and reasoning, we can trace up the particular phenomena to, or near to, these general principles. The most perfect philosophy of the natural kind only staves off our ignorance a little longer: as perhaps the most

perfect philosophy of the moral or metaphysical kind serves only to discover larger portions of it. Thus the observation of human blindness and weakness is the result of all philosophy, and meets us at every turn, in spite of our endeavors to elude or avoid it.

27. Nor is geometry, when taken into the assistance of natural philosophy, ever able to remedy this defect, or lead us into the knowledge of ultimate causes, by all that accuracy of reasoning for which it is so justly celebrated. Every part of mixed mathematics proceeds upon the supposition that certain laws are established by nature in her operations; and abstract reasoning are employed, either to assist experience in the discovery of these laws, or to determine their influence in particular instances, where it depends upon any precise degree of distance and quantity. Thus, it is a law of motion, discovered by experience, that the moment or force of anybody in motion is in the compound ratio or proportion of its solid contents and its velocity; and consequently, that a small force may remove the greatest obstacle or raise the greatest weight, if, by any contrivance or machinery, we can increase the velocity of that force, so as to make it an overmatch for its antagonist. Geometry assists us in the application of this law, by giving us the just dimensions of all the parts and figures which can enter into any species of machine; but still the discovery of the law itself is owing merely to experience, and all the abstract reasoning in the world could never lead us one step towards the knowledge of it. When we reason "a priori", and consider merely any object or cause, as it appears to the mind, independent of all observation, it never could suggest to us the notion of any distinct object, such as its effect; much less, show us the inseparable and inviolable connection between them. A man must be very sagacious who could discover by reasoning that crystal is the effect of heat, and ice of cold, without being previously acquainted with the operation of these qualities.

PART II

28. But we have not yet attained any tolerable satisfaction with regard to the question first proposed. Each solution still gives rise to a new question as difficult as the foregoing, and leads us on to farther enquiries. When it is asked, "What is the nature of all our reasoning concerning matter of fact?" the proper answer seems to be, that they are founded on the relation of cause and effect. When again it is asked, "What is the foundation of all our reasoning and conclusions concerning that relation?" it may be replied in one word, Experience. But if we still carry on our sifting humor, and ask, "What is the foundation of all conclusions from experience?" this implies a new question, which maybe of more difficult solution and explication. Philosophers that give themselves airs of superior wisdom and sufficiency,

have a hard task when they encounter persons of inquisitive dispositions, who push them from every corner to which they retreat, and who are sure at last to bring them to some dangerous dilemma. The best expedient to prevent this confusion, is to be modest in our pretensions; and even to discover the difficulty ourselves before it is objected to us. By this means, we may make a kind of merit of our very ignorance.

I shall content myself, in this section, with an easy task, and shall pretend only to give a negative answer to the question here proposed. I say then, that, even after we have experience of the operations of cause and effect, our conclusions from that experience are "not" founded on reasoning, or any process of the understanding. This answer we must endeavor both to explain and to defend.

29. It must certainly be allowed, that nature has kept us at a great distance from all her secrets, and has afforded us only the knowledge of a few superficial qualities of objects; while she conceals from us those powers and principles on which the influence of those objects entirely depends. Our senses inform us of the color, weight, and consistence of bread; but neither sense nor reason can ever inform us of those qualities which fit it for the nourishment and support of a human body. Sight or feeling conveys an idea of the actual motion of bodies; but as to that wonderful force or power, which would carry on a moving body for ever in a continued change of place, and which bodies never lose but by communicating it to others; of this we cannot form the most distant conception. But notwithstanding this ignorance of natural powers and principles, we always presume, when we see like sensible qualities, that they have like secret powers, and expect that effects, similar to those which we have experienced, will follow from them. If a body of like color and consistence with that bread, which we have formerly eat, be presented to us, we make no scruple of repeating the experiment, and foresee, with certainty, like nourishment and support. Now this is a process of the mind or thought, of which I would willingly know the foundation. It is allowed on all hands that there is no known connection between the sensible qualities and the secret powers; and consequently, that the mind is not led to form such a conclusion concerning their constant and regular conjunction, by anything which it knows of their nature. As to past "Experience", it can be allowed to give "direct" and "certain" information of those precise objects only, and that precise period of time, which fell under its cognizance: but why this experience should be extended to future times, and to other objects, which for aught we know, may be only in appearance similar; this is the main question on which I would insist. The bread, which I formerly eat, nourished me; that is, a body of such sensible qualities was, at that time, endued with such secret powers: but does it follow, that other read must also nourish me at another time, and that like sensible qualities must always be attended with like secret powers?

The consequence seems nowise necessary. At least, it must be acknowledged that there is here a consequence drawn by the mind; that there is a certain step taken; a process of thought, and an inference, which wants to be explained. These two propositions are far from being the same, "I have found that such an object has always been attended with such an Effect", and "I foresee, that other objects, which are, in appearance, similar, will be attended with similar effects". I shall allow, if you please, that the one proposition may justly be inferred from the other: I know, in fact, that it always is inferred. But if you insist that the inference is made by a chain of reasoning, I desire you to produce that reasoning. The connection between these propositions is not intuitive. There is required a medium, which may enable the mind to draw such an inference, if indeed it be drawn by reasoning and argument. What that medium is, I must confess, passes my comprehension; and it is incumbent on those to produce it, who asserts that it really exists, and is the origin of all our conclusions concerning matter of fact.

30. This negative argument must certainly, in process of time, become altogether convincing, if many penetrating and able philosophers shall turn their enquiries this way and no one be ever able to discover any connecting proposition or intermediate step, which supports the understanding in this conclusion. But as the question is yet new, every reader may not trust so far to his own penetration, as to conclude, because an argument escapes his enquiry, that therefore it does not really exist. For this reason it may be requisite to venture upon a more difficult task; and enumerating all the branches of human knowledge, endeavor to show that none of them can afford such an argument.

All reasoning may be divided into two kinds, namely, demonstrative reasoning, or that concerning relations of ideas, and moral reasoning, or that concerning matter of fact and existence. That there are no demonstrative arguments in the case seems evident; since it implies no contradiction that the course of nature may change, and that an object, seemingly like those which we have experienced, may be attended with different or contrary effects. May I not clearly and distinctly conceive that a body, falling from the clouds, and which, in all other respects, resembles snow, has yet the taste of salt or feeling of fire? Is there any more intelligible proposition than to affirm, that all the trees will flourish in December and January, and decay in May and June? Now whatever is intelligible, and can be distinctly conceived, implies no contradiction, and can never be proved false by any demonstrative argument or abstract reasoning "à priori".

If we be, therefore, engaged by arguments to put trust in past experience, and make it the standard of our future judgment, these arguments must be probable only, or such as regard matter of fact and real existence, according to the division above mentioned. But that there is no argument of this kind, must appear, if our explication of that species of reasoning be admitted as solid and satisfactory. We have said that all arguments concerning existence are founded on the relation of cause and effect; that our knowledge of that relation is derived entirely from experience; and that all our experimental conclusions proceed upon the supposition that the future will be conformable to the past. To endeavor, therefore, the proof of this last supposition by probable arguments, or arguments regarding existence, must be evidently going in a circle, and taking that for granted, which is the very point in question.

31. In reality, all arguments from experience are founded on the similarity which we discover among natural objects, and by which we are induced to expect effects similar to those which we have found to follow from such objects. And though none but a fool or madman will ever pretend to dispute the authority of experience, or to reject that great guide of human life, it may surely be allowed a philosopher to have so much curiosity at least as to examine the principle of human nature, which gives this mighty authority to experience, and makes us draw advantage from that similarity which nature has placed among different objects. From causes which appear "similar" we expect similar effects.

This is the sum of all our experimental conclusions. Now it seems evident that, if this conclusion were formed by reason, it would be as perfect at first, and upon one instance, as after ever so long a course of experience. But the case is far otherwise. Nothing so like as eggs; yet no one, on account of this appearing similarity, expects the same taste and relish in all of them. It is only after a long course of uniform experiments in any kind, that we attain a firm reliance and security with regard to a particular event. Now where is that process of reasoning which, from one instance, draws a conclusion, so different from that which it infers from a hundred instances that are no ways different from that single one? This question I propose as much for the sake of information, as with an intention of raising difficulties. I cannot find, I cannot imagine any such reasoning. But I keep my mind still open to instruction, if any one will vouchsafe to bestow it on me.

32. Should it be said that, from a number of uniform experiments, we "infer" a connection between the sensible qualities and the secret powers; this, I must confess, seems the same difficulty, couched in different terms. The question still recurs, on what process of argument this "inference" is founded? Where is the medium, the interposing ideas, which join propositions so very wide of each other? It is confessed that the color, consistence, and other sensible qualities of bread appear not, of themselves, to have any connection with the secret powers of nourishment and support. For otherwise we could infer these secret powers from the first appearance of these sensible qualities, without the aid of experience; contrary to the sentiment

of all philosophers, and contrary to plain matter of fact. Here, then, is our natural state of ignorance with regard to the powers and influence of all objects. How is this remedied by experience? It only shows us a number of uniform effects, resulting from certain objects, and teaches us that those particular objects, at that particular time, were endowed with such powers and forces. When a new object, endowed with similar sensible qualities, is produced, we expect similar powers and forces, and look for a like effect. From a body of like color and consistence with bread we expect like nourishment and support. But this surely is a step or progress of the mind, which wants to be explained. When a man says, "I have found, in all past instances, such sensible qualities conjoined with such secret powers" And when he says, "Similar sensible qualities will always be conjoined with similar secret powers", he is not guilty of a tautology, nor are these propositions in any respect the same. You say that the one proposition is an inference from the other. But you must confess that the inference is not intuitive; neither is it demonstrative: Of what nature is it, then? To say it is experimental, is begging the question. For all inferences from experience suppose, as their foundation, that the future will resemble the past, and that similar powers will be conjoined with similar sensible qualities. If there be any suspicion that the course of nature may change, and that the past may be no rule for the future, all experience becomes useless, and can give rise to no inference or conclusion. It is impossible, therefore, that any arguments from experience can prove this resemblance of the past to the future; since all these arguments are founded on the supposition of that resemblance. Let the course of things be allowed hitherto ever so regular; that alone, without some new argument or inference, proves not that, for the future, it will continue so. In vain do you pretend to have learned the nature of bodies from your past experience. Their secret nature, and consequently all their effects and influence, may change, without any change in their sensible qualities.

This happens sometimes, and with regard to some objects: Why may it not happen always, and with regard to all objects? What logic, what process of argument secures you against this supposition? My practice, you say, refutes my doubts. But you mistake the purport of my question. As an agent, I am quite satisfied in the point; but as a philosopher, who has some share of curiosity, I will not say skepticism, I want to learn the foundation of this inference. No reading, no enquiry has yet been able to remove my difficulty, or give me satisfaction in a matter of such importance. Can I do better than propose the difficulty to the public, even though, perhaps, I have small hopes of obtaining a solution? We shall at least, by this means, be sensible of our ignorance, if we do not augment our knowledge.

33. I must confess that a man is guilty of unpardonable arrogance who concludes, because an argument has escaped his own investigation, that

therefore it does not really exist. I must also confess that, though all the learned, for several ages, should have employed themselves in fruitless search upon any subject, it may still, perhaps, be rash to conclude positively that the subject must, therefore, pass all human comprehension. Even though we examine all the sources of our knowledge, and conclude them unfit for such a subject, there may still remain a suspicion, that the enumeration is not complete, or the examination not accurate. But with regard to the present subject, there are some considerations which seem to remove all this accusation of arrogance or suspicion of mistake.

It is certain that the most ignorant and stupid peasants—nay infants, nay even brute beasts—improve by experience, and learn the qualities of natural objects, by observing the effects which result from them. When a child has felt the sensation of pain from touching the flame of a candle, he will be careful not to put his hand near any candle; but will expect a similar effect from a cause which is similar in its sensible qualities and appearance. If you assert, therefore, that the understanding of the child is led into this conclusion by any process of argument or ratiocination, I may, rightly, require you to produce that argument; nor have you any pretence to refuse so equitable a demand. You cannot say that the argument is abstruse, and may possibly escape your enquiry; since you confess that it is obvious to the capacity of a mere infant. If you hesitate, therefore, a moment, or if, after reflection, you produce any intricate or profound argument, you, in a manner, give up the question, and confess that it is not reasoning which engages us to suppose the past resembling the future, and to expect similar effects from causes which are, to appearance, similar. This is the proposition which I intended to enforce in the present section. If I be right, I pretend not to have made any mighty discovery. And if I be wrong, I must acknowledge myself to be indeed a very backward scholar; since I cannot now discover an argument which, it seems, was perfectly familiar to me long before I was out of my cradle.

KEY TERMS

A posteriori knowledge is knowledge that is acquired after some experience.

A priori knowledge is knowledge that is arrived at without experience and is necessary and certain (must be true).

Coherentism is a epistemic theory that denies the notion that there are basic foundational belief and instead argue that many of our beliefs are justified by other believes.

Correspondence theory of truth states that a belief is true if and only if it corresponds with something that exists in the world.

Empiricism is a method of acquiring knowledge by means of observation, inquiry, and experience.

Epistemology is the study of theories of knowledge. Epistemic theories attempt to explain the various ways we can arrive at knowledge.

Foundationalism is an epistemic theory that argues our knowledge claims must be based on basic true beliefs and that these basic believes provide a foundation for all knowledge.

JTB theory defines knowledge as requiring three necessary conditions: justification, truth, and belief.

Pragmatic theories of truth claim that, in a sense, truth is relative. Truth may be in a sense relative to: the individual, science, or society.

Rationalism is a method of acquiring knowledge by means of logic and reason.

Reliability theory of knowledge (also known as reliabilism) states that knowledge should be acquired by means of a reliable process. According to reliabilism, a belief is justified based on the method by which it was acquired.

QUESTIONS FOR DISCUSSION AND REVIEW

1. Compare and contrast rationalism and empiricism.
2. Explain the difference between A priori and A posteriori knowledge.
3. Compare and contrast Foundationalism and Coherentism
4. Compare and contrast pragmatic theories of truth with the correspondence theory of truth.
5. What are some of the implications of Gödel's Theorem?

SUGGESTED READINGS

Chalmers, D. (2003). *The Matrix as Metaphysics.*

Descartes, R. (1641). *Meditations on First Philosophy.*

Dewey, J. (1938). *The Theory of Inquiry.*

Hume, D. (1777). *An Enquiry Concerning Human Understanding.*

Internet Encyclopedia of Philosophy. A peer-reviewed academic resource. Available from http://www.iep.utm.edu/

Peirce, C. S. (1868). Nominalism versus Realism. *Journal of Speculative Philosophy*, 2, 1.

Popper, K. (1963). Conjectures and Refutations.

Stanford Encyclopedia of Philosophy. Available from http://plato.stanford.edu/

4

Who Am I? My Mind, Other Minds, and the Nature of Reality

Upon completing this chapter, students should be able to meet the following Learning Outcomes:

4.1 Articulate the views of John Searle and René Descartes on dualism.

4.2 Compare and contrast the views of George Berkeley and Thomas Hobbes on the mind.

4.3 Explain David Hume's criticism of the self and how it is mirrored by Milarepa.

4.4 Analyze the problem of other minds and the various ways the concept of mind can be explained.

4.5 Discuss the concept of artificial intelligence.

The Nature of Substance, Reality, and Mind: Idealism, Dualism, and Materialism

There are a number of complex philosophical issues brought about by a discussion of substance. As you may recall from an earlier chapter, the Ancient Greeks were very much concerned about the question of substance. At present, science tells us everything is made up of material atoms, and yet, philosophers still debate this scientific conclusion. It is not to say that atoms do not exist (although no one has actually seen one, which is another question about scientific realism), but rather a question of what is reality made up of, mind, matter, or a combination of both.

These questions lead to other questions regarding the nature of the human mind. Is it just the brain or does it have an immaterial component? What of the soul? All these questions will be considered in the following sections below.

POWERFUL IDEAS BOX: NATURE OF SUBSTANCE

Materialism claims that all real objects are physical.

Dualism claims that all real objects are either physical or nonphysical.

Idealism claims that all real objects are nonphysical.

Berkeley and Idealism

Berkeley contends that the only things that are real are ideas. This view is known as **idealism**. All the objects we encounter in the world (which is an idea as well) are nonmaterial objects. As bizarre as this may at first sound, what you should be aware of is the fact that the only objects that we do have direct access to in our mind (or brain) are ideas.

We assume that our idea of objects in the world is tied to or come from these objects; some underlying physical substance, yet Berkeley is denying that we have any good reason to infer to this material substance. Berkeley employs a radical empiricism. He thought that we can only acquire knowledge from our experiences—from our perceptions. What is the nature of our perceptions? We assume that we perceive objects directly, yet in fact, what we are doing is experience an idea of the object, which has been constructed by our mind. Berkeley goes on to argue that "to exist is to be perceived."

Berkeley contends that the only things that are real are ideas. All the objects we encounter in the world—which is an idea as well—are nonmaterial objects. As bizarre as this may at first sound, what you should be aware of is the fact that the only objects that we do have direct access to are our ideas. We assume that our idea of objects in the world are tied to or come from those objects (we think those ideas correspond to object in reality), some underlying physical substance, yet Berkeley is denying that we have any good reason to infer to is this material substance.

He may have a point. Consider a strawberry, for example. It has a certain color, shape, and weight; it has a particular texture, taste, and smell. These are all perceptions, ideas in your mind. If you take away the taste of the strawberry, take away its smell, its weight, its shape—what do you have left? Nothing. The strawberry is a bundle of those perceptions. Reality is a bundle of perceptions. In fact, Berkeley believed, "to be is to be perceived": *esse est percipi*. To take another example, consider an object, such as a desk in a room. What do you see besides color, shape, and extension? If all we perceive are these things, and these qualities are ideas in the mind, why posit the existence of some other substance, matter that is unperceived? Berkeley goes on to make a distinction between immediate and mediate objects. **Immediate objects** are those we perceive directly, while **mediate objects** are those that we infer from our immediate perceptions.

In his view, matter or substance is something that we infer exists, but, in fact, we do not directly perceive. Yet what would the matter be like. What would the **noumenal** world (of Immanuel Kant (1724–1804, to be discussed later) be like? Is it not something that we can never know, yet we posit or assume that it exists? What Berkeley says is that we don't need material substance to explain our experiences, and it is an unwarranted inference to draw because there is no reason to assume that our ideas that are of the **phenomenal** world correspond to a physical or material reality.

Berkeley goes on to mark a distinction in the type of minds that exist. He states that the world is composed of two things: ideas and minds. To be an idea, it must be perceived. Perceived by what? A mind. A mind is a perceiving thing. Finite minds can only perceive a limited number of ideas, so what happens to this room when no one is here to perceive it? Does it cease to exist? If that were the case, then how come it always reappears when some perceives it? Would it be the same room?

> "If a tree were to fall on an island where there were no human beings would there be any sound?"
>
> —*The Chautauquan Magazine, 1883, in discussion of Berkeley's metaphysics*

Objects continue to endure, according to Berkeley, because there is one, Infinite Mind. His answer is that it the world continues to endure when we do not perceive it because it continues to be perceived by the infinite mind—God. God is an infinite mind that perceives all things. Ultimately, his entire philosophy can be boiled down to this one profound thought: to exist is to be an idea in the mind of God.

Powerful Thinkers: Immanuel Kant

One of the most influential philosophers in history, Immanuel Kant was born on April 22, 1724, in Königsberg, Prussia. He died there in 1804, never having strayed far from home and having lived a relatively quiet life. Yet, this quiet, lifelong bachelor's works transformed philosophy forever.

Kant, in his monumental (and monumentally difficult) *Critique of Pure Reason* (1781) questioned the necessary conditions of experience, and he explored our possibilities of knowledge. He drew a distinction between phenomena, the reality of appearances in our everyday life as we live it, and noumena, realities that exist independent of the human mind's interpretation. Kant analyzed human experience and the way we organize it in terms of how that reality appears to us phenomenologically but also how it really is—a radically precise reassessment of a problem that goes back to Plato and Aristotle. Kant's transcendental idealism explains how humans interpret the world by imposing structures and order on our perceptions of that world.

The human mind organizes experience based on categories we impose on experience. A priori propositions, such as $2 + 2 = 4$, do not depend on experience. A posteriori propositions rely on experience for justification. For example, the proposition "Sally is hungry" relies on experience to show whether or not it is true.

Kant's contributions to ethics, was as least as influential as his metaphysics. He began with his search for one ultimate principle to guide morals in 1785 *Groundwork for the Metaphysics of Morals* and continued as he explained the rational justification for ethical judgments in his 1788 *The Critique of Practical Reason*. In 1790, *The Critique of Judgment* followed. For Kant, reason is the guiding principle of morals. This principle was his categorical imperative, a product of reason that states simply that you should act always as if according to a maxim that you would turn willingly into a universal law and also that you should always treat humanity—in your own person as well as that of others—as an end in itself and never as a means to an end. Kant's ethics is discussed later in this book in the chapter on ethics.

Kant led a quiet life, and he stuck to his daily constitutional walking schedule so consistently that, so the story goes, housewives in Königsberg would set their clocks by him. He began lecturing at the University of Königsberg in 1755, finally got tenure as professor of logic and metaphysics in 1770, and soon afterwards wrote his first *Critique*.

The only controversy that came his way was when he wrote in his first his first *Critique* that "our age is an age of criticism, and to criticism all our beliefs must submit. Religion in all its holiness, and the state in its majesty, cannot exempt themselves from its tribunal without arousing suspicion against themselves." Kant thought that the question of God could not be answered rationally, an insight not welcomed in conservative Prussia. The King of Prussia in 1792 forbade Kant to his lecture or writing on religion. He continued teaching in Königsberg until he retired in 1796, shortly after the publication of his visionary 1795 political work *Perpetual Peace*.

René Descartes and Substance Dualism

René Descartes (1596–1650) holds a view known as **substance dualism** or **simply dualism**. He maintains that reality is composed of two substances: mind and body. Mind is immaterial essence and body is material essence. All our thoughts and feelings are immaterial and exist in our mind, whereas our body exists in material space. He held that these two substances, one material and the other immaterial, interact with each other at some point in the body.

Mark Yuill/Shutterstock.com

POWERFUL IDEAS BOX: MIND OR BODY

René Descartes gives a number of arguments in an effort to try to prove the mind is not the body. Here are two such arguments:

I can doubt my body

1) I can doubt my body

2) I cannot doubt my mind

3) Since the mind and body have different properties, they must be distinct objects

4) Therefore, my mind and body must be distinct things

From the above argument, Descartes concludes that the mind and body must be different objects. The problem with the above argument is that Descartes' doubt is not an actual property of his body or of his mind—it had no bearing on their existence or nonexistence. Perhaps seeing this flaw, he developed the following argument.

My mind and body have different properties

1) Body is physical

2) Mind is not physical

3) Since the mind and body have different properties, they must be distinct objects

4) Therefore, my mind and body must be distinct things

Physicality is an actual property of objects, so this argument avoids the flaws of the one discussed above. Unfortunately, the materialist will deny premise 2, whereas the idealist will deny the truth of premise 1—this leaves us where we started—unfortunately.

Other Views on the Interaction of Mind and Body

There are various other views on the nature and connection between the mind and the body. **Identity thesis** states that the mind and brain are identical. Dualism as noted above claims that the mind is mental and distinct from the brain is physical. **Parallelism,** which is also known as **Epiphenomenalism,** claims that what happens in the mind also happens at the same time in the brain, but there is no connection between the two things. Finally, **Occasionalism**, which is a version of epiphenomenalism, states that although there is no connection between the mind and brain, magically or supernaturally God makes the two interact—so that when I think of something mentally, my body will follow my thoughts or vice versa.

John Searle—Supervenience

John Searle (b.1932) holds a version of dualism known as **supervenience theory**. At times, he claims it is dualism, and at other times, he claims, it is not. Most philosophers, against his objections, agree that his theory is a version of dualism but, let him call it what he wants. "The history of the philosophy of mind over the past hundred years," Searle wrote, "has been in large part an attempt to get rid of the mental by showing that no mental phenomena exist over and above the physical."

Whereas Descartes is willing to admit that the mental and physical are two different substances (and hence this theory is technically known as **substance dualism**), Searle is unwilling to make that claims; though he thinks there is a mental and a physical, they may be two aspects of a single substance (not unlike Baruch Spinoza (1632–1677)) . He claims that consciousness (the mental thing going on in your head) comes from or *supervenes* upon the physical—in this case, the brain. The mental plays a causal role in explaining behavior and in our actions. The mental may not be immaterial, but it still exists.

This view, along with Berkeley's idealism, and Descartes' substance dualism can make sense of the notion that our thoughts, feelings, and intentions exist, but they are not the same as material objects.

Thomas Hobbes and David Armstrong

Georgios Kollidas/Shutterstock.com

According to Thomas Hobbes (1588–1679), the only things that exist are "bodies [objects] in motion." It is his view that thoughts, ideas, and feelings are physical entities explained by motions in the brain. Writing in the 1600s, he had no notion of neurons or any deep understanding of the human brain, yet he was certain all of these so-called mental properties would reduce to something physical taking place in the brain.

David Armstrong (1926–2014) argues for a strong version of materialism just as Thomas Hobbes does. Armstrong's materialism holds that there is only one substance, and it is material. Whatever consciousness is, it is material. The only things that exist are physical objects. As he says in his book, *The Nature of Mind and Other Essays* (1980), the mind "is not something behind the behavior of the body, it [is] simply part of that physical behavior."

Contemporary Theories of Philosophy of Mind

There are a number of contemporary interpretations of what is collectively known as the mind/body problem. Reductionism is the view that the mind will be reduced to the body. It claims that neuroscience will one day reduce the mental to physical objects such as neurons. **Identity theory** claims that the mind is identical with the brain. **Functionalism** claims that the mind is identical with any object that functions like a brain.

Powerful Thinkers: Alan Turing

Guy Erwood/Shutterstock.com

Can a computer think? Does it have a mind? Asking whether a machine could be taught to imitate the behavior of humans is the main question behind artificial intelligence, and the answer to that question is one of the many contributions of Alan Turing **(1912–1954)**, the visionary mathematician and philosopher of science whose discoveries are the foundation of today's artificial intelligence and computer science. If you study the philosophy of mind or the relation of the mind to mathematics; if you just use a smartphone, a mainframe, or a laptop; if you store information on a cloud; or even if you've seen the 2014 film *The Imitation Game*, you've been touched by the thoughts of this genius.

His tale is as extraordinary as it is tragic. Turing studied quantum mechanics, probability theory, and logic at Cambridge and then at Princeton, returning to England in 1939 to offer himself to the war effort. His individual contribution to victory in World War II has been ranked with those of Winston Churchill and Dwight D. Eisenhower—and that is no exaggeration. It was Turing's cryptanalyses at Bletchley Park that led to breaking the Nazi Enigma code, giving the Allies the necessary information to counter U-boat attacks and save the Battle of the Atlantic. Turing's discoveries saved thousands of lives, but the details of his highly classified secret work did not become public until 2012.

The imitation game Turing devised is an original vision of a computer hardware that could store information and change functions according to the task at hand, so that it did not need to be recalibrated for each computation. In other words, he invented hardware that could imitate the way a person thinks, except the Turing machine could do it much, much faster. In his now famous essay *Computing Machinery and Intelligence*, Turing first asked the question "Can machines think?" setting up a challenge to epistemology and philosophy of mind that goes on to this day.

If consciousness is physical, as materialists believe, then there is no reason why it could not be imitated by a computer—which then could be said to be thinking. The problem with human consciousness, however, is that we in fact have no evidence showing that the mind is indeed made of matter, in this case the brain, than we do that it is not. As Tom Stoppard has the neuroscientist Hilary say near the end of his 2015 play *The Hard Problem*, "when you come right down to it, the body is made of things. And things don't think." That is indeed the hard problem, one we may never solve.

After World War II, Turing continued his research on programming, neural nets, and the budding field of artificial intelligence, while working at the National Physical Laboratory in London. He proposed the first mathematical use of a computer and developed a Turing test for machine intelligence. He began groundbreaking research into the mathematical basis of life and developed a theory of nonlinear biological growth.

The war hero was gay, however, at a time when homosexuality was illegal in England. He was arrested, lost his security clearance, fired, jailed, and sentenced to chemical castration in 1952. He committed suicide in 1954.

Alan Turing received a posthumous royal pardon from Her Majesty Queen Elizabeth II in 2013 on Christmas Eve. Following the pardon and the renewed public gratitude to this powerful thinker who helped the Allies win the war, there is presently a movement to pardon the other 50,000 gay men who were convicted under England's antigay laws.

POWERFUL ANALYSIS: GHOST IN THE MACHINE?

Can a computer have a mind or a soul?

Logical Behaviorism

Gilbert Ryle (1900–1976) holds a view of the mind known as **logical behaviorism**. This view claims that behavior can be explained without positing the existence of a mental realm. Under this conception, it is not logically necessary to discuss the mental when speaking about behavior. He uses the example of the ghost in the machine. This example is that someone might think that a ghost is responsible for the workings of a machine, but there is a different explanation, simply the physical construction of the machine—if you were to examine all of the parts together, you discover that the machine has a completely mechanical explanation for its operations. For example, if you showed a television or tablet PC to some primitive tribesmen, he might think it was magic or had a spirit inside of it, but in fact it is just electronics, circuits, and computer chips—no magic is required. The same may be true of the brain. We think the mind is this magical thing, when it is simply the workings of the brain.

Personal Identity and Artificial Intelligence

David Hume (1711–1776) claims that the self is an illusion and that we can never, in any of our experiences, find a perception of the actual self. In his view, the self is constantly changing and you are never the same person one moment to the next. This view is not unlike some Eastern conceptions of the self and of the mind. It is also close to Jean-Paul Sartre's notion that human beings are nothingness, that is, not-a-thing, and as such cannot be defined. There is no ego, there is no self. According to Hume, all knowledge is based on sense impressions and on experiences. If this is the case, we don't even have any evidence of the self, since any conception of identity must be based on impressions. "It must be some impression that gives rise to every real idea," he wrote in his *Treatise on Human Nature*. "The self is not any one impression, but that to which our several impressions are supposed to have a reference." There is no self. Therefore, as far as our idea of the self, Hume believed "there is no such idea."

> "Listen carefully; what characterizes the mind is clinging to the notion of a self. But if one looks carefully into this 'mind', one actually sees no self at all. If you can learn how really to observe this [apparent] 'nothing', then you'll find that "something" will be seen"
>
> —*Jetsun Milarepa, 1052–1135, The 100,000 Songs of Milarepa*

Although Hume argues against the self, other philosophers have argued for the existence of the self. Thomas Reid (1710–1796) argues that the mental ability of memory gives us reason to hold that the self exist. Daniel Dennett (1942) claims that a fundamental principle of evolution is self preservation as such the self must exist. The debate is not new, but recent scientific developments have made it more of a burning issue. If the self, the human mind, is a complex physical instrument—purely material, as most neuroscientists believe—then it is not only possible but probable that we will eventually explain everything there is to know about the self by studying how the brain works. And it is also possible and probable that a computer system will do that as well.

POWERFUL ANALYSIS: KNOW THY SELF?

Can we know the self, or is the self simple like an empty theater as Hume proclaims?

Materialism is the rule in the science, and that position permeates much philosophy as well; it is certainly an easier proposition to say that all there is, is matter—and thinking is just part of a physical process. Although most people are very likely dualists—anyone who believes in God must be, for example, since God is not material—including atheists such as Jean-Paul Sartre who are not materialists and then have a tough time explaining what the mind is. Still, such an explanation is needed if we are to insist that a computer cannot "think" the way humans can.

That possibility is here, stemming from Alan Turing's original work on artificial intelligence and since then taking off at an exponential rate of success. Computers today not only do what only humans used to do, but they do so faster and more accurately. Does that make them intelligent? Does it mean that computers think? Maybe? In 1962, *Time* Magazine named The Computer its "Man of the Year." And that was just the beginning.

On film at least, of course. The vengeful computer HAL in Stanley Kubrick's *2001: A Space Odyssey* (1968) got the ball rolling in frighteningly believable sci-fi movie, followed by an invasion of smart androids in Ridley Scott's *Bladerunner* (1982), an adorable and tragic little boy robot in Steven Spielberg's *A.I.* (2001), or a sexy disembodied voice online who dumps a real guy for a smarter artificial intelligence in Spike Jonze's *Her* (2013), to name a few of the best.

But there's no need to go to sci-fi movies, just grab your phone. The impressively complex technology involved in designing that computational machine would have been unthinkable only a few decades ago. Maybe computers do think. Still, does the chess program on your laptop feel good when it beats you in every game? Does it judge the music you put on the iCloud? Is your computer punishing you when it freezes? Is it sad when it gets a virus? Does it like chicken soup?

Apple's intelligent personal assistant iOS app Siri, the voice that talks to you in your car or phone, certainly seems intelligent. Siri uses a sophisticated system to interface with your own voice, gets to know you in the sense that her answers—part of the design of her software—will adapt to you the more you ask her. You can ask her "Siri, where is nearest beach?" or "Siri, what is neurophysiology?" But the smartest of smartphones, even with the latest iOS Siri app, is likely to answer your question "Siri, how can I be happy?" with something like "Macy's is on 34th Street." You are not talking the same language. Or, what is more likely, you are conscious and self-conscious, and Siri is not.

Some scientists would say that your own happiness and sadness in fact are not that different from the computer's, as long as what you mean by emotions is precisely whatever goes on in your brain and whatever behavior you perform when you feel those emotions. That is a materialist view, and we do know a lot about matter. The presumption on part here is to assume that our knowing everything there is to know about physical reality leads us to know everything there is to know about the mind. It is fact a popular trend in Anglo-American analytic philosophy to assume just that. The self can or will be explained and understood in physical terms. It's all about the nerve cells and what they do in that complex gray matter called your brain. Anything else is in the realm of mysticism, of returning to Plato, or—God forbid—of psychology. That is, as Tom Stoppard puts it, the hard problem.

And the problem is there, still. To doubt the materialist view of the self is not to doubt science: much of science is as verifiable as $2 + 2 = 4$. Evolution is true, for example. The Big Bang Theory is true, as is the Law of Gravity. The Earth is billions of years old. Intelligent design theory of creation is not so intelligent. The idea is not to ask questions that were answered already and bring about confusion and retrogression, but rather to avoid trusting answers for which there is no foundational evidence. A scientific theory of consciousness is easy, but only if you assume that physics, biology, and chemistry are the way to explain the mind. Yet materialism is a premise, not a conclusion.

We have evidence of dualism, hard as it is to prove it. Kurt Gödel upset many philosophers and mathematicians when he proved that there are true facts that cannot be proved but are nevertheless true. The tough part is explaining them.

READINGS

Searching for a truth that is clear and distinct, René Descartes sets off on a journey of radical doubt that leads to one certain fact he cannot doubt: that he is thinking.

Meditations on First Philosophy

Meditation 1

12. I will suppose, then, not that Deity, who is sovereignty good and the fountain of truth, but that **some malignant demon**, who is at once exceedingly potent and deceitful, has employed all his artifice to deceive me; I will suppose that the sky, the air, the earth, colors, figures, sounds, and all external things, are nothing better than the illusions of dreams, by means of which this being has laid snares for my credulity; I will consider my-self as without hands, eyes, flesh, blood, or any of the senses, and as falsely believing that I am possessed of these; I will continue resolutely fixed in this belief, and if indeed by this means it be not in my power to arrive at the knowledge of truth, I shall at least do what is in my power, viz., [suspend my judgment], and guard with settled purpose against giving my assent to what is false, and being imposed upon by this deceiver, whatever be his power and artifice.

Meditation 2

1. The Meditation of yesterday has filled my mind with so many doubts, that it is no longer in my power to forget them. Nor do I see, meanwhile, any principle on which they can be resolved; and, just as if I had fallen all of a sudden into very deep water, I am so greatly disconcerted as to be unable either to plant my feet firmly on the bottom or sustain myself by swimming on the surface. I will, nevertheless, make an effort, and try anew the same path on which I had entered yesterday, that is, proceed by casting aside all that admits of the slightest doubt, not less than if I had discovered it to be absolutely false; and I will continue always in this track until I shall find something that is certain, or at least, if I can do nothing more, until I shall know with certainty that there is nothing certain. Archimedes, that he might transport the entire globe from the place it occupied to another, demanded only a point that was firm and immovable; so, also, I shall be entitled to entertain the highest expectations, if I am fortunate enough to discover only one thing that is certain and indubitable.

2. I suppose, accordingly, that all the things which I see are false (ficti-tious); I believe that none of those objects which my fallacious memory rep-resents ever existed; I suppose that I possess no senses; I believe that body, figure, extension, motion, and place are merely fictions of my mind. What is there, then, that can be esteemed true ? Perhaps this only, that there is abso-lutely nothing certain.

3. But how do I know that there is not something different altogether from the objects I have now enumerated, of which it is impossible to enter-tain the slightest doubt? Is there not a God, or some being, by whatever name I may designate him, who causes these thoughts to arise in my mind ? But why suppose such a being, for it may be I myself am capable of pro-ducing them? Am I, then, at least not something? But I before denied that I possessed senses or a body; I hesitate, however, for what follows from that? Am I so dependent on the body and the senses that without these I cannot exist? But I had the persuasion that there was absolutely nothing in the world, that there was no sky and no earth, neither minds nor bodies; was I not, therefore, at the same time, persuaded that I did not exist? Far from it; I assuredly existed, since I was persuaded. But there is I know not what being, who is possessed at once of the highest power and the deepest cun-ning, who is constantly employing all his ingenuity in deceiving me. *Doubtless, then, I exist, since I am deceived; and, let him deceive me as he may, he can never bring it about that I am nothing, so long as I shall be conscious that I am something.* So that it must, in fine, be maintained, all things being maturely and carefully considered, that this proposition (pro-nunciatum) I am, I exist, is necessarily true each time it is expressed by me, or conceived in my mind.

4. But I do not yet know with sufficient clearness what I am, though assured that I am; and hence, in the next place, I must take care, lest per-chance I inconsiderately substitute some other object in room of what is properly myself, and thus wander from truth, even in that knowledge (cog-nition) which I hold to be of all others the most certain and evident. For this reason, I will now consider anew what I formerly believed myself to be, before I entered on the present train of thought; and of my previous opinion I will retrench all that can in the least be invalidated by the grounds of doubt I have adduced, in order that there may at length remain nothing but what is certain and indubitable.

5. What then did I formerly think I was? Undoubtedly I judged that I was a man. But what is a man? Shall I say a rational animal? Assuredly not; for it would be necessary forthwith to inquire into what is meant by animal, and what by rational, and thus, from a single question, I should insensibly glide into others, and these more difficult than the first; nor do I now possess enough of leisure to warrant me in wasting my time amid subtleties of this

sort. I prefer here to attend to the thoughts that sprung up of themselves in my mind, and were inspired by my own nature alone, when I applied myself to the consideration of what I was. In the first place, then, I thought that I possessed a countenance, hands, arms, and all the fabric of members that appears in a corpse, and which I called by the name of body. It further occurred to me that I was nourished, that I walked, perceived, and thought, and all those actions I referred to the soul; but what the soul itself was I either did not stay to consider, or, if I did, I imagined that it was something extremely rare and subtitle, like wind, or flame, or ether, spread through my grosser parts. As regarded the body, I did not even doubt of its nature, but thought I distinctly knew it, and if I had wished to describe it according to the notions I then entertained, I should have explained myself in this manner: By body I understand all that can be terminated by a certain figure; that can be comprised in a certain place, and so fill a certain space as there from to exclude every other body; that can be perceived either by touch, sight, hearing, taste, or smell; that can be moved in different ways, not indeed of itself, but by something foreign to it by which it is touched and from which it receives the impression]; for the power of self-motion, as likewise that of perceiving and thinking, I held as by no means pertaining to the nature of body; on the contrary, I was somewhat astonished to find such faculties existing in some bodies.

6. But as to myself, what can I now say that I am], since I suppose there exists an extremely powerful, and, if I may so speak, malignant being, whose whole endeavors are directed toward deceiving me? Can I affirm that I possess any one of all those attributes of which I have lately spoken as belonging to the nature of body? After attentively considering them in my own mind, I find none of them that can properly be said to belong to my-self. To recount them were idle and tedious. Let us pass, then, to the attributes of the soul. The first mentioned were the powers of nutrition and walking; but, if it be true that I have no body, it is true likewise that I am capable neither of walking nor of being nourished. Perception is another attribute of the soul; but perception too is impossible without the body; besides, I have frequently, during sleep, believed that I perceived objects which I afterward observed I did not in reality perceive. Thinking is another attribute of the soul; and here I discover what properly belongs to myself. This alone is inseparable from me. I am--I exist: this is certain; but how often? As often as I think; for perhaps it would even happen, if I should wholly cease to think, that I should at the same time altogether cease to be. I now admit nothing that is not necessarily true. I am therefore, precisely speaking, only a thinking thing, that is, a mind (mens sive animus), understanding, or reason, terms whose signification was before unknown to me. *I am, however, a real thing, and really existent; but what thing? The answer was, a thinking thing. . . .*

R. D. Laing, a pioneer in existential psychoanalysis, analyzes the problem of other minds in this excerpt from his book, *The Politics of Experience*. He explores the fact that we are all in the same boat, but it's still hard to get to know each other.

Us and Them

ONLY WHEN something has become problematic do we start to ask questions. Disagreement shakes us out of our slumbers and forces us to see our own point of view through contrast with another person who does not share it. But we resist such confrontations. The history of heresies of all kinds testifies to more than the tendency to break off communication (excommunication) with those who hold different dogmas or opinions; it bears witness to our intolerance of different *fundamental structures of experience*. We seem to need to share a communal meaning to human existence, to give with others a common sense to the world, to maintain a *consensus*.

But it seems that once certain fundamental structures of experience are shared, they come to be experienced as objective entities. These reified projections of our own freedom are then introjected. By the time the sociologists study these projected-introjected reifications, they have taken on the appearance of things. They are not things ontologically. But they are pseudo-things. They take on the force and character of partially autonomous realities, with their own way of life. A social norm may come to impose an oppressive obligation on everyone, although few people feel it as their own.

At this moment in history, we are all caught in the hell of frenetic passivity. We find ourselves threatened by extermination that will be reciprocal, that no one wishes, that everyone fears, that may just happen to us "because" no one knows how to stop it. There is one possibility of doing so if we can understand the structure of this alienation of ourselves from our experience, our experience from our deeds, our deeds from human authorship. Everyone will be carrying out orders. Where do they come from? Always from elsewhere. Is it still possible to reconstitute our destiny out of this hellish and inhuman fatality?

Within this most vicious circle, we obey and defend beings that exist only insofar as we continue to invent and to perpetuate them. What ontological status have these group beings?

This human scene is a scene of mirages, demonic pseudo-realities, because everyone believes everyone else believes them.

How can we find our way back to ourselves again? Let us begin by trying to think about it.

We act not only in terms of our own experience, but of what we think *they* experience, and how we think they think we experience, and so on in a logically vertiginous spiral to infinity.

Our language is only partially adequate to express this state of affairs. On level 1, two people, or two groups, may agree or disagree. As we say, they see eye to eye or otherwise. They share a common point of view. But on level 2 they may or may not think they agree or disagree, and they may or may not be correct in either case. Whereas level 1 is concerned with agreement or disagreement, level 2 is concerned with understanding or misunderstanding. Level 3 is concerned with a third level of awareness: what do I think you think I think? That is, with realization of or failure to realize second-level understanding or misunderstanding on the basis of first-level agreement or disagreement. Theoretically, there is no end to these levels.

… It is possible to think what everyone else thinks and to believe that one is in a minority. It is possible to think what few people think and to suppose that one is in the majority. It is possible to feel that They feel one is like Them when one is not, and They do not. It is possible to say: I believe this, but They believe that, so I'm sorry, there is nothing I can do.

Gossip and scandal are always and everywhere elsewhere. Each person is the other to the others. The members of a scandal network may be unified by ideas to which no one will admit in his own person. Each person is thinking of what he thinks the other thinks. The other, in turn, thinks of what yet another thinks. Each person does not mind a colored lodger, but each person's neighbor does. Each person, however, is a neighbor of his neighbor. What They think is held with conviction. It is indubitable and it is incontestable. The scandal group is a series of others which each serial number repudiates in himself.

It is always the others and always elsewhere, and each person feels unable to make any difference to Them. I have no objection to my daughter marrying a Gentile *really*, but we live in a Jewish neighborhood after all. Such collective power is in proportion to each person's creation of this power and his own impotence.

This is seen very clearly in the following inverted Romeo and Juliet situation.

John and Mary have a love affair, and just as they are ending it Mary finds she is pregnant. Both families are informed. Mary does not want to marry John. John does not want to marry Mary. But John thinks Mary wants him to marry her, and Mary does not want to hurt John's feelings by telling him that she does not want to marry him—as she thinks he wants to marry her, and that he thinks she wants to marry him.

The two families, however, compound the confusion considerably. Mary's mother takes to bed screaming and in tears because of the disgrace—what people are saying about the way she brought her daughter up. She does not mind the situation "in itself," especially as the girl is going to be married, but she takes to heart what everyone will be saying. No one in their own person in either family (". . . if it only affected me . . .") is in the least concerned for their own sake, but everyone is very concerned about the effect of "gossip" and "scandal" on everyone else. The concern focuses itself mainly on the boy's father and the girl's mother, both of whom require to be consoled at great length for the terrible blow. The boy's father is worried about what the girl's mother will think of him. The girl's mother is worried about what "everyone" will think of her. The boy is concerned at what the family thinks he has done to his father, and so on.

The tension spirals up within a few days to the complete engrossment of all members of both families in various forms of tears, wringing of hands, recriminations, apologies.

Typical utterances are:

MOTHER *to* GIRL: Even if he does want to marry you, how can he ever respect you after what people will have been saying about you recently?

GIRL (*some time later*): I had finally got fed up with him just before I found I was pregnant, but I didn't want to hurt his feelings because he was so in love with me.

BOY: If it had not been that I owed it to my father for all he had done for me, I would have arranged that she got rid of it. But then everyone knew by then.

Everyone knew because the son told his father who told his wife who told her eldest son who told his wife . . . etc.

Such processes seem to have a dynamism divorced from the individuals. But in this and every other case the process is a form of alienation, intelligible when, and only when, the steps in the vicissitudes of its alienation from each and every person can be retraced back to what at each and every moment is their only origin: the experience and actions of each and every single person.

Now the peculiar thing about Them is that They are created only by each one of us repudiating his own identity. When we have installed Them in our hearts, we are only a plurality of solitudes in which what each person has in common is his allocation to the other of the necessity for his own actions. Each person, however, as other to the other, is the other's necessity. Each denies any internal bond with the others; each person claims his own inessentiality: "I just carried out my orders. If I had not done so, someone else would have." "Why don't you sign? Everyone else has," etc. Yet although I can make no difference, I cannot act differently. No single other person is any more necessary to me than I claim to be to Them. But just as he is "one of Them" to me, so I am "one of Them" to him. In this collection of reciprocal indifference, of reciprocal inessentiality and solitude, there appears to exist no freedom. There is conformity to a *presence* that is everywhere *elsewhere*.

The being of any group from the point of view of the group members themselves is very curious. If I think of you and him as together with me, and others again as not with me, I have already formed two rudimentary syntheses, namely, *We* and *They*. However, this private act of synthesis is not in itself a group. In order that *We* come into being as a group, it is necessary not only that I regard, let us say, you and him and me as *We*, but that you and he also think of us as *We*. I shall call such an act of experiencing a number of persons as a single collectivity, an act of rudimentary group synthesis. In this case *We*, that is each of Us, me, you and him, have performed acts of rudimentary group synthesis. But at present these are simply three private acts of group synthesis. In order that a group really jell, I must realize that you think of yourself as one of Us, as I do, and that he thinks of himself as one of Us, as you and I do. I must ensure furthermore that both you and he realize that I think of myself with you and him, and you and he must ensure likewise that the other two realize that this We is ubiquitous among us, not simply a private illusion on my, your or his part, shared between two of us but not all three.

In a very condensed form I may put the above paragraph as follows.

I "interiorize" your and his syntheses, you interiorize his and mine, he interiorizes mine and yours; I interiorize your interiorization of mine and his; you interiorize my interiorization of yours and his. Furthermore, he interiorizes my interiorization of his and yours—a logical ingoing spiral of reciprocal perspectives to infinity.

The group, considered first of all from the point of view of the *experience* of its own members, is not a social object out there in space. It is the quite extraordinary being formed by each person's synthesis of the same multiplicity into *We*, and each person's synthesis of the multiplicity of syntheses.

Looked at from the outside, the group comes into view as a social object, lending, by its appearance and by the apparent processes that go inside it, credence to the organismic illusion.

This is a mirage; as one approaches closer there is no organism anywhere.

A group whose unification is achieved through the reciprocal interiorization by each of each other, in which neither a "common object" nor organizational or institutional structures, etc. have a primary function as a kind of group "cement," I shall call a *nexus*.

The unity of the nexus is in the interior of each synthesis. Each such act of synthesis is bound by reciprocal interiority with every other synthesis of the same nexus, insofar as it is also the interiority of every other synthesis. The unity of the nexus is the unification made by each person of the plurality of syntheses.

This social structure of the completely achieved nexus is its *unity as ubiquity*. It is an ubiquity of *heres*, whereas the series of others is always elsewhere, always *there*.

The nexus exists only insofar as each person incarnates the nexus. The nexus is everywhere, in each person, and is nowhere else than in each. The nexus is at the opposite pole from Them in that each person acknowledges affiliation to it, regards the other as coessential to him, and assumes that the other regards him as coessential to the other.

> We are all in the same boat in a stormy sea,
> And we owe each other a terrible loyalty.
>
> *(G. K. CHESTERTON)*

In this group of reciprocal loyalty, of brotherhood unto death, each freedom is reciprocally pledged, one to the other.

In the nexal family the unity of the group is achieved through the experience by each of the group, and the danger to each person (since the person is essential to the nexus, and the nexus is essential to the person) is the dissolution or dispersion of "the family." This can come about only by one person after another dissolving it in themselves. A united "family" exists only as long as each person acts in terms of its existence. Each person may then act on the other person to coerce him (by sympathy, blackmail, indebtedness, guilt, gratitude or naked violence) into maintaining his interiorization of the group unchanged.

The nexal family is then the "entity" which has to be preserved in each person and served by each person, which one lives and dies for, and which in turn offers life for loyalty and death for desertion. Any defection from the nexus (betrayal, treason, heresy, etc.) is deservedly, by nexus ethics, punishable; and the worst punishment devisable by the "group men" is exile or excommunication: group death.

The condition of permanence of such a nexus, whose sole existence is each person's experience of it, is the successful reinvention of whatever gives such experience its *raison d'être*. If there is no external danger, then danger and terror have to be invented and maintained. Each person has to act on the others to maintain the nexus *in them*.

Some families live in perpetual anxiety of what, to them, is an external persecuting world. The members of the family live in a family ghetto, as it were. This is one basis for so-called maternal overprotection. It is not "over"-protection from the mother's point of view, nor, indeed, often from the point of view of other members of the family.

The "protection" that such a family offers its members seems to be based on several preconditions: (i) a fantasy of the external world as extraordinarily dangerous; (ii) the generation of terror inside the nexus at this external danger. The "work" of the nexus is the generation of this terror. This work is *violence*.

The stability of the nexus is the product of terror generated in its members by the work (violence) done by the members of the group on each other. Such family "homeostasis" is the product of reciprocities mediated under the statutes of violence and terror.

The highest ethic of the nexus is reciprocal concern. Each person is concerned about what the other thinks, feels, does. He may come to regard it as his *right* to expect the others to be concerned about him, and to regard himself as under an obligation to feel concern towards them in turn. I make no move without feeling it as my right that you should be happy or sad, proud or ashamed, of what I do. Every action of mine is always the concern of the other members of the group. And I regard you as callous if you do not concern yourself about my concern for you when you do anything.

A family can act as gangsters, offering each other mutual protection against each other's violence. It is a reciprocal terrorism, with the offer of protection-security against the violence that each threatens the other with, and is threatened by, if anyone steps out of line.

My concern, my concern for your concern, your concern, and your concern for my concern, etc. is an infinite spiral, upon which rests my pride or shame in my father, sister, brother, my mother, my son, my daughter.

The essential characteristic of the nexus is that every action of one person is expected to have reference to and to influence everyone else. The nature of this influence is expected to be reciprocal.

Each person is expected to be controlled, and to control the others, by the reciprocal effect that each has on the other. To be affected by the others' actions or feelings is "natural." It is not "natural" if father is neither proud nor ashamed of son, daughter, mother, etc. According to this ethic, action done to please, to make happy, to show one's gratitude to the other, is the highest form of action. This reciprocal transpersonal cause-effect is a self-actualizing presumption. In this "game," it is a foul to use this interdependence to hurt the other, except in the service of the nexus, but the worst crime of all is to refuse to act in terms of this presumption.

. . . The group, whether We or You or Them, is not a new individual or organism or hyperorganism on the social scene; it has no agency of its own, it has no consciousness of its own. Yet we may shed our own blood and the blood of others for this bloodless presence.

The group is a reality of some kind or other. But what sort of reality? The We is a form of unification of a plurality composed by those who share the common experience of its ubiquitous invention among them.

From outside, a group of Them may come into view in another way. It is still a type of unification imposed on a multiplicity, but this time those who invent the unification expressly do not themselves compose it. Here, I am of course not referring to the outsider's perception of a We already constituted from within itself. The Them comes into view as a sort of social mirage. The Reds, the Whites, the Blacks, the Jews. In the human scene, however, such mirages can be self-actualizing. The invention of Them creates Us, and We may need to invent Them to reinvent Ourselves.

One of the most tentative forms of solidarity between us exists when we each want the same thing, but want nothing from each other. We are united, say by a common desire to get the last seat on the train, or to get the best bargain at the sale. We might gladly cut each other's throats; we may nevertheless feel a certain bond between us, a negative unity, so to speak, in that each perceives the other as redundant, and each person's metaperspective shows him that he is redundant for the other. Each as other-for-the-other is one-too-many. In this case, we share a desire to appropriate the same common object or objects: food, land, a social position, real or imagined, but share nothing between ourselves and do not wish to. Two men both love the same woman, two people both want the same house, two applicants both want the same job. This common object can thus both separate and unite at the same time. A key question is whether it can give itself to all, or not. How *scarce* is it?

The object may be animal, vegetable, mineral, human or divine, real or imaginary, single or plural. A human object uniting people, for instance, is the pop singer in relation to his fans. All can possess him, albeit magically. When this magic confronts the other order of reality, one finds the idol in danger of being torn to shreds by the frenzy of fans seeking any bit of him they can tear off.

The object may be plural. Two rival firms engage in intense competitive advertising, each under the impression that they are losing their consumers to the other. Market research sometimes reveals how riven with fantasy is the scene of such social multiplicities. The laws governing the perception, invention and maintenance of such social beings as "the consumers" are undiscovered.

The common bond between Us may be the Other. The Other may not even be as localized as a definable Them that one can point to. In the social cohesion of scandal, gossip, unavowed racial discrimination, the Other is everywhere and nowhere. The Other that governs everyone is everyone in his position, not of self, but as other. Every self, however, disavows being himself that other that he is for the Other. The Other is everyone's experience. Each person can do nothing because of the other. The other is everywhere elsewhere.

Perhaps the most intimate way We can be united is through each of us being in, and having inside ourselves, the same presence. This is nonsense in any external sense, but here we are exploring a mode of experience which does not recognize the distinctions of analytic logic.

We find this demonic group mysticism repeatedly evoked in the prewar speeches at Nazi Nuremberg rallies. Rudolf Hess proclaims: We are the Party, the Party is Germany, Hitler is the Party, Hitler is Germany, and so on.

We are Christians insofar as we are brothers in Christ. We are in Christ and Christ is in each one of us.

No group can be expected to be held together for long on the pure flame of such unified experience. Groups are liable to disappear through attacks from other groups, or through inability to sustain themselves against the ravages of starvation and disease, from splits through internal dissensions, and so on. But the simplest and perennial threat to all groups comes from the simple defection of its members. This is the danger of evaporation, as it were.

Under the form of group loyalty, brotherhood and love, an ethic is introduced whose basis is my right to afford the other protection from my violence if he is loyal to me, and to expect his protection from his violence if I am loyal to him, and my obligation to terrorize him with the threat of my violence if he does not remain loyal.

. . . Let there be no illusions about the brotherhood of man. My brother, as dear to me as I am to myself, my twin, my double, my flesh and blood, may be a fellow lyncher as well as a fellow martyr, and in either case is liable to meet his death at my hand if he chooses to take a different view of the situation.

The brotherhood of man is evoked by particular men according to their circumstances. But it seldom extends to all men. In the name of our freedom and our brotherhood we are prepared to blow up the other half of mankind, and to be blown up in turn.

The matter is of life or death importance in the most urgent possible sense, since it is on the basis of such primitive social fantasies of who and what are I and you, he and she, We and They, that the world is linked or separated, that we die, kill, devour, tear and are torn apart, descend to hell or ascend to heaven, in short, that we conduct our lives. What is the "being" of "The Reds" to you and me? What is the nature of the presence conjured up by the incantation of this magic sound? Are we sympathizers with "the East"? Do we feel we have to threaten, deter, placate "it" or "her" or "him"? "Russia" or "China" have "being" nowhere else than in the fantasy of everyone, including the "Russians" and "Chinese": nowhere and everywhere. A "being" fantasied by "The Russians" as what they are in and which they have to defend, and fantasied by the non-Russians as an alien super-subject-object from whom one has to defend one's "freedom," is such that if we all act in terms of such mass serialized preontological fantasy, we may all be destroyed by a "being" that never was, except insofar as we *all* invented her or it or him.

The specifically human feature of human groupings can be exploited to turn them into the semblance of nonhuman systems.

We do not now suppose that chemical elements combine together *because* they love each other. Atoms do not explode out of hatred. It is men who act out of love and hatred, who combine for defense, attack, or pleasure in each other's company.

All those people who seek to control the behavior of large numbers of other people work on the *experiences* of those other people. Once people can be induced to experience a situation in a similar way, they can be expected to behave in similar ways. Induce people all to want the same thing, hate the same thing, feel the same threat, then their behavior is already captive—you have acquired your consumers or your cannon-fodder. Induce a common perception of Negroes as subhuman, or of whites as vicious and effete, and behavior can be concerted accordingly.

However much experience and action can be transformed into quantitatively interchangeable units, the schema for the intelligibility of group structures and permanence is of quite a different order from the schema we employ when we are explaining relative constancies in physical systems. In the latter case, we do not, in the same way, retrace the constancy of a pattern back to the reciprocal interiorization of the pattern by whatever one regards as the units comprising it. The inertia of human groups, however, which appears as the very negation of praxis, is in fact the product of praxis and nothing else. This group inertia can only be an instrument of mystification if it is taken to be part of the "natural order of things." The ideological abuse of such an idea is obvious. It so clearly serves the interests of those whose interest it is to have people believe that the status quo is of the "natural order," ordained divinely or by "natural" laws. What is less immediately obvious, but no less confusing, is the application of an epistemological schema, derived from natural systems, to human groups. The theoretical stance here only serves to intensify the dissociation of praxis from structure.

The group becomes a machine—and that it is a man-made machine in which the machine is the very men who make it is forgotten. It is quite unlike a machine made by men, which can have an existence of its own. The group is men themselves arranging themselves in patterns, strata, assuming and assigning different powers, functions, roles, rights, obligations and so on.

The group cannot become an entity separate from men, but men can form circles to encircle other men. The patterns in space and time, their relative permanence and rigidity, do not turn at any time into a natural system or a hyperorganism, although the fantasy can develop, and men can start to live by the fantasy that the relative permanence in space-time of patterns and patterns of patterns is what they must live and die for.

It is as though we all preferred to die to preserve our shadows.

For the group can be nothing else than the multiplicity of the points of view and actions of its members, and this remains true even where, through the interiorization of this multiplicity as synthesized by each, this synthesized multiplicity becomes ubiquitous in space and enduring in time.

It is just as well that man is a social animal, since the sheer complexity and contradiction of the social field in which he has to live is so formidable. This is so even with the fantastic simplifications that are imposed on this complexity, some of which we have examined above.

Our society is a plural one in many senses. Any one person is likely to be a participant in a number of groups, which may have not only different memberships, but quite different forms of unification.

Each group requires more or less radical internal transformation of the persons who comprise it. Consider the metamorphoses that one man may go through in one day as he moves from one mode of sociality to another— family man, speck of crowd dust, functionary in the organization, friend. These are not simply different roles: each is a whole past and present and future, offering differing options and constraints, different degrees of change or inertia, different kinds of closeness and distance, different sets of rights and obligations, different pledges and promises.

I know of no theory of the individual that fully recognizes this. There is every temptation to start with a notion of some supposed basic personality, but halo effects are not reducible to one internal system. The tired family man at the office and the tired businessman at home attest to the fact that people carry over, not just one set of internal objects, but *various internalized social modes of being*, often grossly contradictory, from one context to another.

Nor are there such constant emotions or sentiments as love, hate, anger, trust or mistrust. Whatever generalized definitions can be made of each of these at the highest levels of abstraction, specifically and concretely, each emotion is always found in one or another inflection according to the group mode it occurs in. There are no "basic" emotions, instincts or personality, outside of the relationships a person has within one or another social context.

There is a race against time. It is just possible that a further transformation is possible if men can come to experience themselves as "One of Us." If, even on the basis of the crassest self-interest, we can realize that We and They must be transcended in the totality of the human race, if we in destroying them are not to destroy us all.

As war continues, both sides come more and more to resemble each other. The uroborus eats its own tail. The wheel turns full circle. Shall we realize that We and They are shadows of each other? We are They to Them as They are They to Us. When will the veil be lifted? When will the charade turn to carnival? Saints may still be kissing lepers. It is high time that the leper kissed the saint.

In this accessible, clever essay, Thomas Nagel follows up on Descartes' method of doubt and explores how we can be certain that there are other minds out there.

Other Minds

There is one special kind of skepticism which continues to be a problem even if you assume that your mind is not the only thing there is—that the physical world you seem to see and feel around you, including your own body, really exists. That is skepticism about the nature or even existence of minds or experiences other than your own.

How much do you really know about what goes on in anyone else's mind? Clearly you observe only the bodies of other creatures, including people. You watch what they do, listen to what they say and to the other sounds they make, and see how they respond to their environment—what things attract them and what things repel them, what they eat, and so forth. You can also cut open other creatures and look at their physical insides, and perhaps compare their anatomy with yours.

But none of this will give you direct access to their experiences, thoughts, and feelings. The only experiences you can actually have are your own: if you believe anything about the mental lives of others, it is on the basis of observing their physical construction and behavior.

To take a simple example, how do you know, when you and a friend are eating chocolate ice cream, whether it tastes the same to him as it tastes to you? You can try a taste of his ice cream, but if it tastes the same as yours, that only means it tastes the same *to you*: you haven't experienced the way it tastes *to him*. There seems to be no way to compare the two flavor experiences directly.

Well, you might say that since you're both human beings, and you can both distinguish among flavors of ice cream—for example you can both tell the difference between chocolate and vanilla with your eyes closed—it's likely that your flavor experiences are similar. But how do you know *that*? The only connection you've ever observed between a type of ice cream and a flavor is in your own case; so what reason do you have to think that similar correlations hold for other human beings? Why isn't it just as consistent with all the evidence that chocolate tastes to him the way vanilla tastes to you, and vice versa?

The same question could be asked about other kinds of experience. How do you know that red things don't look to your friend the way yellow things look to you? Of course if you ask him how a fire engine looks, he'll say it looks red, like blood, and not yellow, like a dandelion; but that's because he, like you, uses the word "red" for the color that blood and fire engines look to him, *whatever* it is. Maybe it's what you call yellow, or what you call blue, or maybe it's a color experience you've never had, and can't even imagine.

To deny this, you have to appeal to an assumption that flavor and color experiences are uniformly correlated with certain physical stimulations of the sense organs, whoever undergoes them. But the skeptic would say you have no evidence for that assumption, and because of the kind of assumption it is, you *couldn't* have any evidence for it. All you can observe is the correlation in your own case.

Faced with this argument, you might first concede that there is some uncertainty here. The correlation between stimulus and experience may not be exactly the same from one person to another: there may be slight shades of difference between two people's color or flavor experience of the same type of ice cream. In fact, since people are physically different from one another, this wouldn't be surprising. But, you might say, the difference in experience can't be too radical, or else we'd be able to tell. For instance, chocolate ice cream couldn't taste to your friend the way a lemon tastes to you, otherwise his mouth would pucker up when he ate it.

But notice that this claim assumes another correlation from one person to another: a correlation between inner experience and certain kinds of observable reaction. And the same question arises about that. You've observed the connection between puckering of the mouth and the taste you call sour only in your own case: how do you know it exists in other people? Maybe what makes your friend's mouth pucker up is an experience like the one you get from eating oatmeal.

If we go on pressing these kinds of questions relentlessly enough, we will move from a mild and harmless skepticism about whether chocolate ice cream tastes exactly the same to you and to your friend, to a much more radical skepticism about whether there is *any* similarity between your experiences and his. How do you know that when he puts something in his mouth he even has an experience of the kind that you would call a *flavor*? For all you know, it could be something you would call a sound—or maybe it's unlike anything you've ever experienced, or could imagine.

If we continue on this path, it leads finally to the most radical skepticism of all about other minds. How do you even know that your friend is conscious? How do you know that there are *any minds at all* besides your own?

The only example you've ever directly observed of a correlation between mind, behavior, anatomy, and physical circumstances is yourself. Even if other people and animals had no experiences whatever, no mental inner life of any kind, but were just elaborate biological machines, they would look just the same to you. So how do you know that's not what they are? How do you know that the beings around you aren't all mindless robots? You've never seen into their minds—you couldn't—and their physical behavior could all be produced by purely physical causes. Maybe your relatives, your neighbors, your cat and your dog have *no inner experiences whatever*. If they don't, there is no way you could ever find it out.

You can't even appeal to the evidence of their behavior, including what they say—because that assumes that in them outer behavior is connected with inner experience as it is in you; and that's just what you don't know.

To consider the possibility that none of the people around you may be conscious produces an uncanny feeling. On the one hand it seems conceivable, and no evidence you could possibly have can rule it out decisively. On the other hand it is something you can't *really* believe is possible: your conviction that there are minds in those bodies, sight behind those eyes, hearing in those ears, etc., is instinctive. But if its power comes from instinct, is it really knowledge? Once you admit the *possibility* that the belief in other minds is mistaken, don't you need something more reliable to justify holding on to it?

There is another side to this question, which goes completely in the opposite direction.

Ordinarily we believe that other human beings are conscious, and almost everyone believes that other mammals and birds are conscious too. But people differ over whether fish are conscious, or insects, worms, and jellyfish. They are still more doubtful about whether one-celled animals like amoebae and paramecia have conscious experiences, even though such creatures react conspicuously to stimuli of various kinds. Most people believe that plants aren't conscious; and almost no one believes that rocks are conscious, or kleenex, or automobiles, or mountain lakes, or cigarettes. And to take another biological example, most of us would say, if we thought about it, that the individual cells of which our bodies are composed do not have any conscious experiences.

How do we know all these things? How do you know that when you cut a branch off a tree it doesn't hurt the tree—only it can't express its pain because it can't move? (Or maybe it *loves* having its branches pruned.) How do you know that the muscle cells in your heart don't feel pain or excitement when you run up a flight of stairs? How do you know that a kleenex doesn't feel anything when you blow your nose into it?

And what about computers? Suppose computers are developed to the point where they can be used to control robots that look on the outside like dogs, respond in complicated ways to the environment, and behave in many ways just like dogs, though they are just a mass of circuitry and silicon chips on the inside? Would we have any way of knowing whether such machines were conscious?

These cases are different from one another, of course. If a thing is incapable of movement, it can't give any behavioral evidence of feeling or perception. And if it isn't a natural organism, it is radically different from us in internal constitution. But what grounds do we have for thinking that only things that behave like us to some degree and that have an observable physical structure roughly like ours are capable of having experiences of *any* kind? Perhaps trees feel things in a way totally different from us, but we have no way of finding out about it, because we have no way of discovering the correlations between experience and observable manifestations or physical conditions in their case. We could discover such correlations only if we could observe both the experiences and the external manifestations together: but there is no way we can observe the experiences directly, except in our own case. And for the same reason there is no way we could observe the *absence* of any experiences, and consequently the absence of any such correlations, in any other case. You can't tell that a tree has *no* experience, by looking inside it, any more than you can tell that a worm *has* experience, by looking inside it.

So the question is: what can you really know about the conscious life in this world beyond the fact that you yourself have a conscious mind? Is it possible that there might be much less conscious life than you assume (none except yours), or much more (even in things you assume to be unconscious)?

KEY TERMS

Artificial intelligence   is the scientific and philosophical theory that a computer can perform tasks previously associated with humans.

Dualism   claims that reality is composed of two substances: mind and body; one is physical and the other is nonphysical.

Epiphenomenalism   claims that what happens in the mind also happens at the same time in the brain, but there is no connection between the two things.

Functionalism   claims that the mind is identical with any object that functions like a brain.

Idealism   holds the only objects or things that are real are ideas.

Identity thesis   states that the mind and brain are identical.

Immediate objects   are those we perceive directly.

Logical behaviorism   claims that behavior can be explained without positing the existence of a mental realm.

Mediate objects   are those that we infer from our immediate perceptions.

Noumenal   claims the world how it is beneath or beyond our perceptions.

Occasionalism   is a version of epiphenomenalism states that although there is no connection between the mind and brain. Magically or supernaturally, God makes the two interact, so that when I think of something mentally, my body will follow my thoughts or vice versa.

Parallelism   claims that what happens in the mind also happens at the same time in the brain, but there is no connection between the two things.

Phenomenal   claims that the world is as we experience it through our perceptions.

Substance dualism (dualism)   claims that reality is composed of two substances: mind and body; one is physical and the other is nonphysical.

Reductionism   states that the mind will be reduced to the body. It claims that neuroscience will one day reduce the mental to physical objects such as neurons.

Supervenience theory   claims that although there is a mental and a physical, they may be two aspects of a single substance.

QUESTIONS FOR DISCUSSION AND REVIEW

1. Compare and contrast the views of John Searle and René Descartes on dualism.

2. Compare and contrast the views of George Berkeley and Thomas Hobbes on the mind.

3. Does the materialist position imply a determinist position on the possibility of free will? Explain.

4. Explain what David Hume means by saying that we have no evidence of the self. How is Hume's view related to Milarepa's on this subject?

5. If a computer app beats you every time you play chess, is the computer smarter than you? Does your computer think?

SUGGESTED READINGS

Descartes, R. (1911) *Meditations on First Philosophy.* From *The Philosophical Works of Descartes. (Haldane, E.S. transl.).*

Hodges, A. (2014). *Alan Turing: The Enigma.*

Internet Encyclopedia of Philosophy. A peer-reviewed academic resource. Available from http://www.iep.utm.edu/

Laing, R. D. (1967). *"Us and Them".* From *The Politics of Experience.*

Merleau-Ponty, M. (1945). *Phenomenology of Perception.* (Paul, K. transl.)

Nagel, T. (1987). *"Other Minds".* In *What does it all mean?*

Stanford Encyclopedia of Philosophy. Available from http://plato.stanford.edu/

Free will and Determinism

5

Upon completing this chapter, students will be able to meet the following Learning Outcomes:

5.1 Articulate the problem of free will within determinism or indeterminism.

5.2 Compare and contrast the ideas of Spinoza and Hume on determinism.

5.3 Explain how determinism can be said to be statistically true.

5.4 Articulate the dilemma of determinism and its relation to human freedom as proposed by existentialists from Dostoyevsky to Sartre.

Although many of us believe we can do and act how we want, whenever we want to, philosophers have augured that this is not the case. There are various views on the notion of human freedom. **Free will** is the notion that people make choices and have the capacity to do otherwise than they choose. **Determinism** is the idea that all actions and events are determined or happen necessarily and that human actions are no different. Humanity is as free as a weather vane—a weather vane moves with the direction of the wind, and humans do too. Or to put it more precisely, humans move and act in accordance with desires, impulses, and causes that are beyond our control. For the determinist, there is no freedom of the will. **Indeterminism,** on the other hand, claims that not all actions are determined and that humans have some amount of freedom. In other words, people have some amount of free will.

© The Gallery Collection/Corbis

Our perception of reality seems to indicate to each of us that we are free and have free will; upon closer examination, it is not so obvious. Many philosophers argue that there is no way that humans can have such a thing as free will at all. They call this the dilemma of determinism, as the British philosopher, Colin McGinn (b. 1950), states in his *Problems in Philosophy: The Limits of Inquiry* (1993), that "Either determinism is true or it is not. If it is true, then all our chosen actions are uniquely necessitated by prior states of the world, just like every other event. But then it cannot be the case that we could have acted otherwise, since this would require a possibility determinism rules out. Once the initial conditions are set and the laws fixed, causality excludes genuine freedom."

"On the other hand, if indeterminism is true," McGinn continues, "then, though things could have happened otherwise, it is not the case that we could have chosen otherwise, since a merely random event is no kind of free choice. That some events occur causelessly, or are not subject to law, or only to probabilistic law, is not sufficient for those events to be free choices."

"Man's life is a line that nature commands him to describe upon the surface of the earth, without his ever being able to swerve from it, even for an instant. He is born without his own consent; his organization does in no way depend upon himself; his ideas come to him involuntarily; his habits are in the power of those who cause him to contract them; he is unceasingly modified by causes, whether visible or concealed, over which he has no control, which necessarily regulate his mode of existence, give the hue to his way of thinking, and determine his manner of acting. He is good or bad, happy or miserable, wise or foolish, reasonable or irrational, without his will being for anything in these various states"

—*Paul-Henri Thiry, Baron d'Holbach*

POWERFUL ANALYSIS: FREE OR DETERMINED?

Did you choose to get out of bed this morning, or were you "determined" to do so? Could you have done something else entirely with your day?

POWERUL IDEAS BOX : VIEWS ON HUMAN METAPHYSICAL FREEDOM

Free Will—The notion that people make choices and have the capacity to do otherwise than they choose. In other words, not all actions are predetermined.

Determinism—All actions and events are determined or happen necessarily. There is no free will. Freedom of the will is an illusion.

Indeterminism—Not all actions are determined. People have freedom of the will.

Soft Determinism or **Compatibilism**—All actions are determined, and yet humanity has free will. David Hume (1711–1776) argues for this view. Hume seems to redefine what it means to be "free." "Free" for Hume is doing whatever you are determined to do. This does not sound very "free."

Fatalism—The view that if something is fated to happen, it will happen no matter what; it doesn't even need to be a logical sequence of events that makes it happen.

Baruch Spinoza

Baruch Spinoza (1632–1677) argues that all actions unfold according to the necessary laws that govern the universe. If there was no antecedent cause, there could be no effect. He thinks that there is only one substance and that all things are part of it. He holds that this single substance is God, and that all of creation (including people) are part of God as a single unified whole. In regards to determinism, it is his view that all actions and events are unfolding in a necessary and determined way. There is no choice and there is no freedom. He argues that once we realize we are not free, we should "free" ourselves from regret and remorse for past actions or events as all of those actions and events were determined to happen.

POWERUL IDEAS BOX : SPINOZA THE HINDU?

Similarities between Spinoza's philosophy and Eastern philosophy are very interesting. The nineteenth-century German philosopher Theodore Goldstücker was one of the first academics to notice the similarities between Spinoza's religious conceptions and Hindu traditions of India. Goldstücker said ". . . a western system of philosophy which occupies a foremost rank amongst the philosophies of all nations and ages, and which is so exact a representation of the ideas of the Vedanta, that we might have suspected its founder to have borrowed the fundamental principles of his system from the Hindus. . . . We mean the philosophy of Spinoza, a man whose very life is a picture of that moral purity and intellectual indifference to the transitory charms of this world, which is the constant longing of the true Vedanta philosopher . . . comparing the fundamental ideas of both we should have no difficulty in proving that, had Spinoza been a Hindu, his system would in all probability mark a last phase of the Vedanta philosophy."—W. H. Allen, 1879, *Literary Remains of the Late Professor Theodore Goldstucker*

Jean Buridan and His Donkey

Jean Buridan (1300–1358) used a hypothetical example of a donkey to argue that humanity is not free. The example commonly known as "Buridan's ass (donkey)" is a paradox. According to Buridan (with whom Spinoza agrees), an entirely rational donkey, placed between two stacks of hay of equal size and quality, would starve to death since it cannot make any rational decision to start eating one bale of hay rather than the other.

Spinoza says we are just like the donkey; without some internal or external influence upon us, we would be unable to act. We, like a donkey, would starve to death since our free will is not sufficient for us to produce an action. According to Spinoza without an antecedent cause, there could be no effect. There is no free will. Our desire is not sufficient to produce action.

This example is obviously hypothetical and in principle un-testable. It is not testable because (1) there are no rational donkeys and (2) you cannot remove a person, animal, or object from the causal chain of events in order to place them in perfect "equilibrium" as the example requires.

"I shall consider human actions and desires in exactly the same manner, as though I were concerned with lines, planes and solids"

—Spinoza, The Ethics

As we have noted, Spinoza says that once we understand the nature of the world, we can free ourselves from regret or remorse. Everything that happens in life, all of our choices, and the events that unfold as a result of them, happen necessarily. Events could not unfold differently—things could not have been otherwise. As such, feel happy, feel free and be at peace, free from regret and remorse. This, of course, is easy to say and hard to do.

Compatibilism

Soft determinism, which is also known as Compatibilism, is a theory that states all actions are determined, and yet humanity has free will. David Hume (1711–1776) argues for this view. Hume seems to redefine what it means to be "free." "Free" for Hume is doing whatever you are determined to do. Whereas when most people discuss freedom, they have the idea that they are free to have done otherwise. In other words, you could keep reading this fascinating discussion on free will, or put down the book and have a snack. After the fact, in hindsight, whatever choice you made, you feel was not determined but rather you were open to have make a different decision. Hume's notion of being free as so long as we do what we are determined to do does not sound very "free."

"Man can do what he wills but he cannot will what he wills"

—Arthur Schopenhauer, 1788–1860

Indeterminism

Indeterminism maintains that not all actions are determined. The view holds that people have some measure of freedom of the will. How much freedom we have is highly contested. Some argue we may have just enough to lift our pinky finger, while others think that we are free to perform any action within our abilities or capacities. In other words, we are not free to fly, as we cannot physically do so, but we are free to run, jump, or skip as those are things humans can do. William James (1842–1910) argues that consciousness makes humanity different from material objects, which are governed or determined by the laws of nature and physics. He feels that humans are free, and given his notion of truth, we are free to believe in determinism or indeterminism as it suits us.

"Old-fashioned determinism was what we may call hard determinism. It did not shrink from such words as fatality, bondage of the will, necessitation, and the like. Nowadays, we have a soft determinism which abhors harsh words, and, repudiating fatality, necessity, and even predetermination, says that its real name is freedom; for freedom is only necessity understood, and bondage to the highest is identical with true freedom"

—*William James, The Dilemma of Determinism*

Confronting Freedom:
From Dostoyevsky to Sartre

Deep in the heart of *The Brothers Karamazov* by Fyodor Dostoyevsky (1821–1881) is a story that always rings true. It is about faith and doubt, but it is most of all about freedom. Alexei Fyodorovich Karamazov—Alyosha to his family and friends—is 19 years old at the start of the novel and the youngest of the brothers. He is a deeply religious young man studying to be a priest at a Russian Orthodox Christian monastery. As unassuming and quiet as he is sensitive and loving, Alyosha is different from his brothers and radically different from his brother Ivan, an atheist intellectual and budding writer.

Alyosha reads Ivan's essay "The Grand Inquisitor," a literary conceit on Dostoyevsky's part that succeeds is sounding very much like some else's writing, where Ivan Karamazov famously tells of a silent Christ who is followed by all because it is easier to follow than to choose to take action on your own. There is, Ivan notes, much to be said for knowing clearly what is right and what is wrong, what is allowed and what is not. There is comfort in living under a dictatorship, whether that of religion or that of a czar. "Nothing has ever been more frightening for a human being and for a human society," Ivan Karamazov writes in this book-within-a-book, "than freedom." This insight goers a long way to explain the regime's from those of the Christian Church to those of Czar Nicholas, Lenin, Stalin, and Putin—just to stay within Russia for the moment.

Like the Christ in Ivan's story, Alyosha remains silent; but his brother's arguments reverberate in his consciousness. Alyosha continues his religious studies with father Zosima, who sends him out into the world to practice the love and kindness he preaches. Then something happens, not unexpected but nevertheless shocking: the aged Father Zosima dies, as old people tend to do. The whole monastery expects a sign from God, some sort of indication that this was no ordinary mortal but in fact a saint. They expected at least for there to be the sweet smell of roses around Zosima's body at the funeral—not an unusual belief about Christian saints. But this was summer, and the old man's body not only did not give off a floral scent—it rotted fast and it stank, and the burial had to be rushed.

How could God let this happen?

This question has been asked and still is asked by anyone with religious faith. Why is there cancer? Why are there wars? Or why do you have a bad hair day when you also have a hot date tonight? Looking for reasons can throw you into an anguished fit of doubt, and Alyosha's asking how God could let this happen to the saintly Zosima tested the limits of his faith. Within that suffering and doubt, he realized that he was free, free to believe or not to believe, that the decision was entirely his.

In Richard Brooks' Hollywood epic of *The Brothers Karamazov* (1958), this first of several movie adaptations to date of Dostoyevskky's novel, a young William Shatner—in his Captain Kirk Star Trek days—plays Alyosha. Yul Brynnier plays the nasty brother Dmitri, with Richard Basehart as Ivan. Spoiler alert: Lee J. Cobb in fine form plays the nasty father who gets murdered. That murder, too, was a personal choice.

"What is strange, what would really be marvelous, is not that God should really exist," Dostoyevsky writes, "the marvel is that such an idea, the idea of the necessity of God could enter the head of such a savage, vicious beast as man."

Dostoyevsky calls Alyosha a lover of mankind, and the decision to believe in fact does lead the young man to a life of kindness and even of hope. But what is crucial here is that the choice Alyosha made was and could not be a unique event. Choosing to face freedom, rather than blindly accepting rules, is a lifelong project. To be human is to choose, and in this, Dostoyevsky anticipates twentieth-century existentialism and particularly Jean-Paul Sartre's definition of the human being as freedom itself. The physical is determined by physical laws in nature, but human beings are not just physical things, so they are outside determinism. Alyosha Karamazov, like Sartre's For-Itself in *Being and Nothingness*, is not determined by his past, nor is he bound to a single course of action according to his situation. He is free.

"In phenomenology it is the self which analyzes phenomena, i.e., human consciousness which analyzes that which appears in its sphere . . . . No one motive can influence or determine human consciousness for the simple reason that consciousness carries within itself 'nothing,' is determined in no way, and lies completely outside world determinism. Nothing can determine me because there is 'nothing' in me which can be determined. The relation between my past and my present is such, according to Sartre, that what I am is not the foundation of what I shall be"

—Wilfrid Desan, The For-Itself, 1954, *The Tragic Finale*

We are in fact condemned to be free, as Sartre points out. Within brutal physical limits—we are all going to die, for instance; and we do not choose where or when we are born—and within the limits of brute facticity or what Karl Marx called material conditions, we are in fact totally free. That is of course a difficult paradox to face. But it is refreshing to remember that the fact that a question is difficult does not mean that is does not have an answer. It just means that the question is difficult.

A Brief History of the Universe
(and Why Determinism Is, Statistically True)

As contrary to our supposed perception of freedom and choice as determinism is, it is not as outrageous a claim as one might at first think. Most objects in this universe are governed by laws of nature, and the behavior of those objects is "determined."

> "[Determinism] professes that those parts of the universe already laid down absolutely appoint and decree what the other parts shall be. The future has no ambiguous possibilities bidden in its womb; the part we call the present is compatible with only one totality. Any other future complement than the one fixed from eternity is impossible. The whole is in each and every part, and welds it with the rest into an absolute unity, an iron block, in which there can be no equivocation or shadow of turning"

> —William James, *The Dilemma of Determinism*

J. J. C. Smart (1920–2012) states two definitions regarding this issue, one for determinism and other for randomness. He thinks that between the two that they are exhaustive of all possibilities for how events unfold in this reality. He argues that given the available options, we cannot be free. Smart defines the two possibilities as follows:

Dl: I shall state the view that there is "unbroken causal continuity" in the universe as follows. It is in principle possible to make a sufficiently precise determination of the state of a sufficiently wide region of the universe at time to, and sufficient laws of nature are in principle ascertainable to enable a superhuman calculator to be able to predict any event occurring within that region at an already given time t'.

D2: I shall define the view that "pure chance" reigns to some extent within the universe as follows. There are some events that even a superhuman calculator could not predict, however precise his knowledge of however wide a region of the universe at some previous time (J. J. C. Smart, July 1961, "Free-Will, Praise and Blame," *Mind*)

Smart goes on to say that, "For the believer in free will holds that no theory of a deterministic sort or of a pure chance sort will apply to everything in the universe: he must therefore envisage a theory of a type which is neither deterministic nor indeterministic in the senses of these words which I have specified by the two definitions DI and D2; and I shall argue that no such theory is possible."

Let us consider an example and see how humanity is somehow different from the objects considered. When a pen rolls of your desk and falls to the floor, did it "choose" to fall? When I am teaching this topic in class, I have a habit of dropping markers on purpose to demonstrate that markers always "choose" to fall down. I also drop books, keys, or anything I have around that is handy for the demonstration—frustratingly, each and every time (and it has been about 10,000 times at this point) the objects I drop fall down. I secretly hope they will fall up, or maybe even levitate but they never do.

Now we all know objects do not "choose" to fall down. Objects are, in fact, *determined* to fall down as a result of the laws of nature and physics—specifically gravity, which govern their behavior. They have no free will, nor are the events that follow (once I drop an object) free to unfold any differently than the laws of nature dictate.

From the moment the universe popped into existence some 14 billion years ago with an event known as the big bang, events were determined by the laws of nature. For millions of years after that big bang astrophysicists maintain that it was so hot that no physical matter could form, but when the universe cooled, hydrogen atoms began to form (they did not choose to form, they had to form based on the laws of physics). Eventually, gravity made (or determined) the hydrogen coalesce into stars. As those stars ignited (which, again, was determined, by the laws of physics), nuclear fusion began (again determined by the laws of physics and nuclear chemistry) to create helium, and eventually heavier elements. When those stars burned out, most went supernova and created even more heavy elements (any and all of the naturally found elements in our periodic table—of which there are 92).

Eventually, about five billion years ago or so, our solar system formed. The Earth was formed, collided with some other proto-planet, and created the moon, and over billions of years slowly but surely life evolved within its biosphere. The point of this very brief history of the universe is this: each and every event described above had to happen—it was determined to happen, by the initial state of the universe after the big bang and the laws of physics that govern material objects in this realm.

So approximately 100,000 to 200,000 years ago, *Homo sapiens* show up on planet Earth, and we have the audacity to believe that although determinism reigned for approximately 14 billion years, now we are somehow free or beyond the laws of nature that govern reality. This is statistically very improbable (given 14 billion years of determinism) and also very arrogant on the part of mankind.

Clearly, the laws of nature that govern our behavior are more complicated than the laws of gravity. The laws that govern human behavior are some sort of psychological/biological laws, many of which remain unknown to us today, but that does not mean we are free of them. It is hard to accept, and perhaps just as hard to understand; but the preponderance of evidence is on the side of determinism, although many of us, like a good pragmatics, choose to believe otherwise.

READINGS

In this essay and public address, William James argues for human freedom in the face of the material and detemermistic science of his day. He argues that indeterminism—chance—is a feature of the universe that permits "alternative futures" and the possibility of freedom. Free actions are chance happenings that humans have the ability to partake in.

THE DILEMMA OF DETERMINISM
By William James

A common opinion prevails that the juice has ages ago been pressed out of the free-will controversy, and that no new champion can do more than warm up stale arguments which everyone has heard. This is a radical mistake. I know of no subject less worn out, or in which inventive genius has a better chance of breaking open new ground—not, perhaps, of forcing a conclusion or of coercing assent, but of deepening our sense of what the issue between the two parties really is, of what the ideas of fate and of free will imply. At our very side almost, in the past few years, we have seen falling in rapid succession from the press works that present the alternative in entirely novel lights. Not to speak of the English disciples of Hegel, such as Green and Bradley; not to speak of Hinton and Hodgson, nor of Hazard here—we see in the writings of Renouvier, Fouillée, and Delbœuf how completely changed and refreshed is the form of all the old disputes. I cannot pretend to vie in originality with any of the masters I have named, and my ambition limits itself to just one little point. If I can make two of the necessarily implied corollaries of determinism clearer to you than they have been made before, I shall have made it possible for you to decide for or against that doctrine with a better understanding of what you are about. And if you prefer not to decide at all, but to remain doubters, you will at least see more plainly what the subject of your hesitation is. I thus disclaim openly on the threshold all pretension to prove to you that the freedom of the will is true. The most I hope is to induce some of you to follow my own example in assuming it true, and acting as if it were true. If it be true, it seems to me that this is involved in the strict logic of the case. Its truth ought not to be forced willy-nilly down our indifferent throats. It ought to be freely espoused by men who can equally well turn their backs upon it. In other words, our first act of freedom, if we are free, ought in all inward propriety to be to affirm that we are free. This should exclude, it seems to me, from the freewill side of the question all hope of a coercive demonstrations,—a demonstration which I, for one, am perfectly contented to go without.

With thus much understood at the outset, we can advance. But not without one more point understood as well. The arguments I am about to urge all proceed on two suppositions: first, when we make theories about the world and discuss them with one another, we do so in order to attain a conception of things which shall give us subjective satisfaction; and, second, if there be two conceptions, and the one seems to us, on the whole, more rational than the other, we are entitled to suppose that the more rational one is the truer of the two. I hope that you are all willing to make these suppositions with me; for I am afraid that if there be any of you here who are not, they will find little edification in the rest of what I have to say. I cannot stop to argue the point; but I myself believe that all the magnificent achievements of mathematical and physical science—our doctrines of evolution, of uniformity of law, and the rest—proceed from our indomitable desire to cast the world into a more rational shape in our minds than the shape into which it is thrown there by the crude order of our experience. The world has shown itself, to a great extent, plastic to this demand of ours for rationality. How much farther it will show itself plastic no one can say. Our only means of finding out is to try; and I, for one, feel as free to try conceptions of moral as of mechanical or of logical rationality. If a certain formula for expressing the nature of the world violates my moral demand, I shall feel as free to throw it overboard, or at least to doubt it, as if it disappointed my demand for uniformity of sequence, for example; the one demand being, so far as I can see, quite as subjective and emotional as the other is. The principle of causality, for example—what is it but a postulate, an empty name covering simply a demand that the sequence of events shall someday manifest a deeper kind of belonging of one thing with another than the mere arbitrary juxtaposition which now phenomenally appears? It is as much an altar to an unknown god as the one that Saint Paul found at Athens. All our scientific and philosophic ideals are altars to unknown gods. Uniformity is as much so as is free will. If this be admitted, we can debate on even terms. But if anyone pretends that while freedom and variety are, in the first instance, subjective demands, necessity and uniformity are something altogether different, I do not see how we can debate at all.

To begin, then, I must suppose you acquainted with all the usual arguments on the subject. I cannot stop to take up the old proofs from causation, from statistics, from the certainty with which we can foretell one another's conduct, from the fixity of character, and all the rest. But there are two words which usually encumber these classical arguments, and which we must immediately dispose of if we are to make any progress. One is the eulogistic word freedom, and the other is the opprobrious word chance. The word "chance" I wish to keep, but I wish to get rid of the word "freedom." Its eulogistic associations have so far overshadowed all the rest of its meaning that both parties claim the sole right to use it, and determinists today insist that they alone are freedom's champions. Old-fashioned determinism was what we may call hard determinism. It did not shrink from such words as fatality, bondage of the will, necessitation, and the like. Nowadays, we have a soft determinism which abhors harsh words, and, repudiating fatality, necessity, and even predetermination, says that its real name is freedom; for freedom is only necessity understood, and bondage to the highest is identical with true freedom. Even a writer as little used to making capital out of soft words as Mr. Hodgson hesitates not to call himself a "free-will determinist."

Now, all this is a quagmire of evasion under which the real issue of fact has been entirely smothered. Freedom in all these senses presents simply no problem at all. No matter what the soft determinist means by it,—whether he means the acting without external constraint; whether he means the acting rightly, or whether he means the acquiescing in the law of the whole,— who cannot answer him that sometimes we are free and sometimes we are not? But there is a problem, an issue of fact and not of words, an issue of the most momentous importance, which is often decided without discussion in one sentence,--nay, in one clause of a sentence,—by those very writers who spin out whole chapters in their efforts to show what "true" freedom is; and that is the question of determinism, about which we are to talk tonight.

Fortunately, no ambiguities hang about this word or about its opposite, indeterminism. Both designate an outward way in which things may happen, and their cold and mathematical sound has no sentimental associations that can bribe our partiality either way in advance. Now, evidence of an external kind to decide between determinism and indeterminism is, as I intimated a while back, strictly impossible to find. Let us look at the difference between them and see for ourselves. What does determinism profess?

It professes that those parts of the universe already laid down absolutely appoint and decree what the other parts shall be. The future has no ambiguous possibilities bidden in its womb; the part we call the present is compatible with only one totality. Any other future complement than the one fixed from eternity is impossible. The whole is in each and every part, and welds it with the rest into an absolute unity, an iron block, in which there can be no equivocation or shadow of turning. "With earth's first clay they did the last man knead, And there of the last harvest sowed the seed. And the first morning of creation wrote What the last dawn of reckoning shall read. Indeterminism, on the contrary, says that the parts have a certain amount of loose play on one another, so that the laying down of one of them does not necessarily determine what the others shall be. It admits that possibilities may be in excess of actualities, and that things not yet revealed to our knowledge may really in themselves be ambiguous. Of two alternative futures which we conceive, both may now be really possible; and the one becomes impossible only at the very moment when the other excludes it by becoming real itself. Indeterminism thus denies the world to be one unbending unit of fact. It says there is a certain ultimate pluralism in it; and, so saying, it corroborates our ordinary unsophisticated view of things.

To that view, actualities seem to float in a wider sea of possibilities from out of which they are chosen; and, somewhere, indeterminism says, such possibilities exist, and form a part of truth.

Determinism, on the contrary, says they exist nowhere, and that necessity on the one hand and impossibility on the other are the sole categories of the real. Possibilities that fail to get realized are, for determinism, pure illusions: they never were possibilities at all. There is nothing inchoate, it says, about this universe of ours, all that was or is or shall be actual in it having been from eternity virtually there. The cloud of alternatives our minds escort this mass of actuality withal is a cloud of sheer deceptions, to which "impossibilities" is the only name that rightfully belongs.

The issue, it will be seen, is a perfectly sharp one, which no eulogistic terminology can smear over or wipe out. The truth must lie with one side or the other, and its lying with one side makes the other false.

The question relates solely to the existence of possibilities, in the strict sense of the term, as things that may, but need not, be. Both sides admit that a volition, for instance, has occurred. The indeterminists say another volition might have occurred in its place: the determinists swear that nothing could possibly have occurred in its place. Now, can science be called in to tell us which of these two point-blank contradicters of each other is right? Science professes to draw no conclusions but such as are based on matters of fact, things that have actually happened; but how can any amount of assurance that something actually happened give us the least grain of information as to whether another thing might or might not have happened in its place? Only facts can be proved by other facts. With things that are possibilities and not facts, facts have no concern. If we have no other evidence than the evidence of existing facts, the possibility-question must remain a mystery never to be cleared up.

And the truth is that facts practically have hardly anything to do with making us either determinists or indeterminists. Sure enough, we make a flourish of quoting facts this way or that; and if we are determinists, we talk about the infallibility with which we can predict one another's conduct; while if we are indeterminists, we lay great stress on the fact that it is just because we cannot foretell one another's conduct, either in war or statecraft or in any of the great and small intrigues and businesses of men, that life is so intensely anxious and hazardous a game. But who does not see the wretched insufficiency of this so-called objective testimony on both sides? What fills up the gaps in our minds is something not objective, not external. What divides us into possibility men and anti-possibility men is different faiths or postulates,—postulates of rationality. To this man the world seems more rational with possibilities in it,—to that man more rational with possibilities excluded; and talk as we will about having to yield to evidence, what makes us monists or pluralists, determinists or indeterminists, is at bottom always some sentiment like this.

The stronghold of the deterministic sentiment is the antipathy to the idea of chance. As soon as we begin to talk indeterminism to our friends, we find a number of them shaking their heads. This notion of alternative possibilities, they say, this admission that any one of several things may come to pass, is, after all, only a roundabout name for chance; and chance is something the notion of which no sane mind can for an instant tolerate in the world. What is it, they ask, but barefaced crazy unreason, the negation of intelligibility and law? And if the slightest particle of it exists anywhere, what is to prevent the whole fabric from falling together, the stars from going out, and chaos from recommencing her topsy-turvy reign?

Remarks of this sort about chance will put an end to discussion as quickly as anything one can find. I have already told you that "chance" was a word I wished to keep and use. Let us then examine exactly what it means, and see whether it ought to be such a terrible bugbear to us. I fancy that squeezing the thistle boldly will rob it of its sting.

The sting of the word "chance" seems to lie in the assumption that it means something positive, and that if anything happens by chance, it must needs be something of an intrinsically irrational and preposterous sort. Now, chance means nothing of the kind. It is a purely negative and relative term, giving us no information about that of which it is predicated, except that it happens to be disconnected with something else-not controlled, secured, or necessitated by other things in advance of its own actual presence. As this point is the most subtle one of the whole lecture, and at the same time the point on which all the rest hinges, I beg you to pay particular attention to it. What I say is that it tells us nothing about what a thing may be in itself to call it "chance." It may be a bad thing, it may be a good thing. It may be lucidity, transparency, fitness incarnate, matching the whole system of other things, when it has once befallen, in an unimaginably perfect way. All you mean by calling it "chance" is that this is not guaranteed, that it may also fall out otherwise. For the system of other things has no positive hold on the chance-thing. Its origin is in a certain fashion negative: it escapes, and says, Hands off! coming, when it comes, as a free gift, or not at all.

This negativeness, however, and this opacity of the chance-thing when thus considered ab extra, or from the point of view of previous things or distant things, do not preclude its having any amount of positiveness and luminosity from within, and at its own place and moment. All that its chance-character asserts about it is that there is something in it really of its own, something that is not the unconditional property of the whole. If the whole wants this property, the whole must wait till it can get it, if it be a matter of chance. That the universe may actually be a sort of joint-stock society of this sort, in which the sharers have both limited liabilities and limited powers, is of course a simple and conceivable notion.

Nevertheless, many persons talk as if the minutest dose of disconnectedness of one part with another, the smallest modicum of independence, the faintest tremor of ambiguity about the future, for example, would ruin everything, and turn this goodly universe into a sort of insane sand-heap or nulliverse, no universe at all. Since future human volitions are as a matter of fact the only ambiguous things we are tempted to believe in, let us stop for a moment to make ourselves sure whether their independent and accidental character need be fraught with such direful consequences to the universe as these.

What is meant by saying that my choice of which way to walk home after the lecture is ambiguous and matter of chance as far as the present moment is concerned? It means that both Divinity Avenue and Oxford Street are called; but that only one, and that one either one, shall be chosen. Now, I ask you seriously to suppose that this ambiguity of my choice is real; and then to make the impossible hypothesis that the choice is made twice over, and each time falls on a different street. In other words, imagine that I first walk through Divinity Avenue, and then imagine that the powers governing the universe annihilate ten minutes of time with all that it contained, and set me back at the door of this hall just as I was before the choice was made. Imagine then that, everything else being the same, I now make a different choice and traverse Oxford Street. You, as passive spectators, look on and see the two alternative universes,—one of them with me walking through Divinity Avenue in it, the other with the same me walking through Oxford Street. Now, if you are determinists you believe one of these universes to have been from eternity impossible: you believe it to have been impossible because of the intrinsic irrationality or accidentality somewhere involved in it. But looking outwardly at these universes, can you say which is the impossible and accidental one, and which the rational and necessary one? I doubt if the most ironclad determinist among you could have the slightest glimmer of light on this point. In other words, either universe after the fact and once there would, to our means of observation and understanding, appear just as rational as the other. There would be absolutely no criterion by which we might judge one necessary and the other matter of chance. Suppose now we relieve the gods of their hypothetical task and assume my choice, once made, to be made forever. I go through Divinity Avenue for good and all. If, as good determinists, you now begin to affirm, what all good determinists punctually do affirm, that in the nature of things I couldn't have gone through Oxford Street,—had I done so it would have been chance, irrationality, insanity, a horrid gap in nature,—I simply call your attention to this, that your affirmation is what the Germans call a Machtspruch, a mere conception fulminated as a dogma and based on no insight into details. Before my choice, either street seemed as natural to you as to me. Had I happened to take Oxford Street, Divinity Avenue would have figured in your philosophy as the gap in nature; and you would have so proclaimed it with the best deterministic conscience in the world.

But what a hollow outcry, then, is this against a chance which, if it were presented to us, we could by no character whatever distinguish from a rational necessity! I have taken the most trivial of examples, but no possible example could lead to any different result. For what are the alternatives which, in point of fact, offer themselves to human volition? What are those futures that no seem matters of chance? Are they not one and all like the Divinity Avenue and Oxford Street of our example? Are they not all of them kinds of things already here and based in the existing frame of nature? Is anyone ever tempted to produce an absolute accident, something utterly irrelevant to the rest of the world? Do not an the motives that assail us, all the futures that offer themselves to our choice, spring equally from the soil of the past; and would not either one of them, whether realized through chance or through necessity, the moment it was realized, seem to us to fit that past, and in the completest and most continuous manner to interdigitate with the phenomena already there?

The more one thinks of the matter, the more one wonders that so empty and gratuitous a hubbub as this outcry against chance should have found so great an echo in the hearts of men. It is a word which tells us absolutely nothing about what chances, or about the modus operandi of the chancing; and the use of it as a war cry shows only a temper of intellectual absolutism, a demand that the world shall be a solid block, subject to one control,—which temper, which demand, the world may not be found to gratify at all. In every outwardly verifiable and practical respect, a world in which the alternatives that now actually distract your choice were decided by pure chance would be by me absolutely undistinguished from the world in which I now live. I am, therefore, entirely willing to call it, so far as your choices go, a world of chance for me. To yourselves, it is true, those very acts of choice, which to me are so blind, opaque, and external, are the opposites of this, for you are within them and effect them. To you they appear as decisions; and decisions, for him who makes them, are altogether peculiar psychic facts. Self-luminous and self-justifying at the living moment at which they occur, they appeal to no outside moment to put its stamp upon them or make them continuous with the rest of nature. Themselves it is rather who seem to make nature continuous; and in their strange and intense function of granting consent to one possibility and withholding it from another, to transform an equivocal and double future into an unalterable and simple past.

But with the psychology of the matter we have no concern this evening. The quarrel which determinism has with chance fortunately has nothing to do with this or that psychological detail. It is a quarrel altogether metaphysical. Determinism denies the ambiguity of future volitions, because it affirms that nothing future can be ambiguous. But we have said enough to meet the issue. Indeterminate future volitions do mean chance. Let us not fear to shout it from the house-tops if need be; for we now know that the idea of chance is, at bottom, exactly the same thing as the idea of gift,—the one simply being a disparaging, and the other a eulogistic, name for anything on which we have no effective claim. And whether the world be the better or the worse for having either chances or gifts in it will depend altogether on what these uncertain and unclaimable things turn out to be.

And this at last brings us within sight of our subject. We have seen what determinism means: we have seen that indeterminism is rightly described as meaning chance; and we have seen that chance, the very name of which we are urged to shrink from as from a metaphysical pestilence, means only the negative fact that no part of the world, however big, can claim to control absolutely the destinies of the whole. But although, in discussing the word "chance," I may at moments have seemed to be arguing for its real existence, I have not meant to do so yet. We have not yet ascertained whether this be a world of chance or no; at most, we have agreed that it seems so. And I now repeat what I said at the outset, that, from any strict theoretical point of view, the question is insoluble. To deepen our theoretic sense of the difference between a world with chances in it and a deterministic world is the most I can hope to do; and this I may now at last begin upon, after all our tedious clearing of the way.

I wish first of all to show you just what the notion that this is a deterministic world implies. The implications I call your attention to are all bound up with the fact that it is a world in which we constantly have to make what I shall, with your permission, call judgments of regret. Hardly an hour passes in which we do not wish that something might be otherwise; and happy indeed are those of us whose hearts have never echoed the wish of Omar Khayam-

> That we might clasp, ere closed, the book of fate,
> And make the writer on a fairer leaf
> Inscribe our names, or quite obliterate.
> Ah! Love, could you and I with fate conspire
> To mend this sorry scheme of things entire,
> Would we not shatter it to bits, and then
> Remold it nearer to the heart's desire?

Now, it is undeniable that most of these regrets are foolish, and quite on a par in point of philosophic value with the criticisms on the universe of that friend of our infancy, the hero of the fable "The Atheist and the Acorn,"— Fool! had that bough a pumpkin bore, Thy whimsies would have worked no more, etc. Even from the point of view of our own ends, we should probably make a botch of remodeling the universe. How much more then from the point of view of ends we cannot see! Wise men therefore regret as little as they can. But still some regrets are pretty obstinate and hard to stifle,—regrets for acts of wanton cruelty or treachery, for example, whether performed by others or by ourselves.

The refuge from the quandary lies, as I said, not far off. The necessary acts we erroneously regret may be good, and yet our error in so regretting them may be also good, on one simple condition; and that condition is this: The world must not be regarded as a machine whose final purpose is the making real of any outward good, but rather as a contrivance for deepening the theoretic consciousness of what goodness and evil in their intrinsic natures are. Not the doing either of good or evil is what nature cares for, but the knowing of them. Life is one long eating of the fruit of the tree of knowledge. I am in the habit, in thinking to myself, of calling this point of view the gnostical point of view. According to it, the world is neither an optimism nor a pessimism, but a Gnosticism.

Epictetus (55–135) was a Greek Stoic philosopher. He practiced Stoicism, about 400 years after the stoic system was introduced in Athens. There were originally eight books in his work, the *Discourses*—the current version we have (after approximately 2000 years) is incomplete. The book addresses a variety of topics, and the selection here deals with human freedom.

EPICTETUS
ON FREEDOM

THAT man is free, who lives as he wishes, who is proof against compulsion and hindrance and violence, whose impulses are untrammelled, who gets what he wills to get and avoids what he wills to avoid.

Who then would live in error?

No one.

Who would live deceived, reckless, unjust, intemperate, querulous, abject?

No one.

No bad man then lives as he would, and so no bad man is free. Who would live in a state of distress, fear, envy, pity, failing in the will to get and in the will to avoid?

No one.

Do we then find any bad man without distress or fear, above circumstance, free from failure?

None. Then we find none free.

If a man who has been twice consul hear this, he will forgive you if you add, 'But you are wise, this does not concern you.' But if you tell him the truth, saying, 'You are just as much a slave yourself as those who have been thrice sold', what can you expect but a flogging?

'How can I be a slave?' he says; 'my father is free, my mother is free, no one has bought me; nay, I am a senator, and a friend of Caesar, I have been consul and have many slaves.'

In the first place, most excellent senator, perhaps your father too was a slave of the same kind as you, yes and your mother and your grandfather and the whole line of your ancestors. And if really they were ever so free, how does that affect you? What does it matter if they had a fine spirit, when you have none, if they were fearless and you are a coward, if they were self-controlled and you are intemperate?

'Nay, what has this to do with being a slave?' he replies.

Does it seem to you slavery to act against your will, under compulsion and with groaning?

'I grant you that,' he says, 'but who can compel me except Caesar, who is lord of all?'

Why, then, your own lips confess that you have one master: you must not comfort yourself with the thought that he is, as you say, the common master of all, but realize that you are a slave in a large household.

However, let us leave Caesar for the moment if you please, but tell me this: Did you never fall in love with any one, with a girl, or a boy, or a slave, or a free man?

'What has that to do with slavery or freedom?'

Were you never commanded by her you loved to do anything you did not wish? Did you never flatter your precious slave-boy? Did you never kiss his feet? Yet if any one compel you to kiss Caesar's, you count it an outrage, the very extravagance of tyranny. What is this if not slavery? Did you never go out at night where you did not wish, and spend more than you wished and utter words of lamentation and groaning? Did you put up with being reviled and shut out? If you are ashamed to confess your own story, see what Thrasonides says and does: he had served in as many campaigns or more perhaps than you and yet, first of all, he has gone out at night, at an hour when Getas does not dare to go, nay, if he were forced by his master to go, he would have made a loud outcry and have gone with lamentations over his cruel slavery, and then, what does he say?

> A worthless girl has made a slave of me,
> Whom never foe subdued.

Menander, Fragment 338

Poor wretch, to be slave to a paltry girl and a worthless one too! Why do you call yourself free then any more? Why do you boast of your campaigns? Then he asks for a sword, and is angry with the friend who refuses it out of goodwill, and sends gifts to the girl who hates him, and falls to praying and weeping, and then again when he has a little luck he is exultant. How can we call him free when he has not learnt to give up desire and fear?

The slave is anxious to be set free at once. Why? Do you think it is because he is anxious to pay the tax on his manumission? No! the reason is he imagines that up till now he is hampered and ill at ease because he has not got his freedom. 'If I am enfranchised,' he says, 'at once all will be well, I heed nobody, I talk to all men as an equal and one of their quality, I go where I will, I come whence I will and where I will.' Then he is emancipated, and having nothing to eat he straightway looks for someone to flatter and to dine with; then he either has to sell his body to lust and endure the worst, and if he gets a manger to eat at, he has plunged into a slavery much severer than the first; or if perchance he grows rich, being a low-bred fellow he dotes on some paltry girl and gets miserable and bewails himself and longs to be a slave again.

'What ailed me in those days? Another gave me clothes and shoes, another fed me and tended me in sickness, and the service I did him was a small matter. Now, how wretched and miserable I am, with many masters instead of one! Still, if I can get rings on my fingers I shall live happily and prosperously enough.'

And so first, to get them, he puts up with what he deserves, and having got them repeats the process. Next he says, 'If I go on a campaign I am quit of all my troubles.' He turns soldier and endures the lot of a criminal, but all the same he begs for a second campaign and a third. Lastly, when he gets the crown to his career and is made a senator, once more he becomes a slave again as he goes to the senate; then he enjoys the noblest and the sleekest slavery of all.

Let him not be foolish, let him learn, as Socrates said, what is the true nature of everything, and not apply primary conceptions at random to particular facts. For this is the cause of all the miseries of men, that they are not able to apply their common primary conceptions to particular cases. One of us fancies this, another that. One fancies he is ill. Not at all; it is only that he does not apply his primary conceptions. Another fancies that he is poor, that his father or mother is cruel, another that Caesar is not gracious. But really it is one thing, and one thing only; they do not know how to adjust their primary conceptions. For who has not a primary notion of evil—that it is harmful, to be shunned, by every means to be got rid of? One primary notion does not conflict with another, the conflict is in the application.

To have a quiet mind, to be happy, to do everything as he will, to be free from hindrance and compulsion. Very well: when he becomes Caesar's friend is he relieved from hindrance and compulsion, is he in peace and happiness? Of whom are we to inquire? Whom can we better trust than the very man who has become Caesar's friend?

Come forward and tell us! when was your sleep more tranquil, now or before you became Caesar's friend?

Tell me, when did you dine more agreeably, now or before?

Hear again what he says about this: if he is not invited, he is distressed, and if he is invited he dines as a slave with his lord, anxious all the while for fear he should say or do something foolish. And what do you think he fears? To be flogged like a slave? How should he come off so well? No, so great a man as he, and Caesar's friend, must fear to lose his neck. When did you bathe with more peace of mind, or exercise yourself more at your ease? In a word, which life would you rather live, today's or the old life? No one, I can swear, is so wanting in sense or feeling, that he does not lament his lot the louder the more he is Caesar's friend.

Inasmuch then as neither those who bear the name of kings nor kings' friends live as they will, what free men are left? Seek, and you shall find, for nature supplies you with means to find the truth. If, with these means and no more to guide you, you cannot find the answer for yourself, then listen to those who have made the search. What do they say?

Does freedom seem to you a good thing?

'Certainly.'

Can then one who possesses so great and precious and noble a thing be of a humble spirit?

'He cannot.'

Therefore when you see a man cringing to another or flattering him against his true opinion, you may say with confidence that he too is not free, and not only if he does it for a paltry dinner, but even if he does it for a province or a consulship. But those who do it for small objects you may call slaves on a small scale, and the others, as they deserve, slaves on a large scale.

'I grant you this too.'

Again, does freedom seem to you 'to be something independent, owning no authority but itself?

'Certainly.'

Then whenever a man can be hindered or compelled by another at will, assert with confidence that he is not free.

What is it then which makes man his own master and free from hindrance? Wealth does not make him so, nor a consulship, nor a province, nor a kingdom; we must find something else. Now what is it which makes him unhindered and unfettered in writing?

'Knowledge of how to write.'

What makes him so in flute-playing?

'Knowledge of flute-playing.'

So too in living, it is knowledge of how to live. You have heard this as a general principle; consider it in detail. Is it possible for one who aims at an object which lies in the power of others to be unhindered? Is it possible for him to be untrammelled?

'No.'

It follows that he cannot be free. Consider then: have we nothing which is in our power alone, or have we everything? Or only some things in our power, and some in that of others?

'How do you mean?'

When you wish your body to be whole, is it in your power or not?

'It is not.'

And when you wish it to be healthy?

'That is not in my power.'

And when you wish it to be beautiful?

'That is not in my power.'

And to live or die?

'That is not mine either.'

The body then is something not our own and must give an account to an one who is stronger than ourselves.

'Granted.'

Is it in your power to have land when you will, and as long as you will, and of the quality you will?

'No.'

And clothes?

'No.'

And your bit of a house?

'None of these things.'

And if you wish your children or your wife or your brother or your friends to live, whatever happens, is that in your power?

'No, that is not either.'

Have you nothing then which owns no other authority, nothing which you alone control, or have you something of that sort?

'I do not know.'

Look at the matter thus and consider it. Can anyone make you assent to what is false?

'No one.'

Well, then, in the region of assent you are unhindered and unfettered.

'Granted.'

Again, can anyone force your impulse towards what you do not wish?

'He can; for when he threatens me with death or bonds, he forces my impulse.'

Well now, if you despise death and bonds, do you heed him any longer?

'No.'

Is it your doing then to despise death, or is it not yours?

'Mine.'

It rests with you then to be impelled to action, does it not?

'I grant it rests with me.'

And impulse not to act, with whom does that rest? It is yours too.

'Supposing that my impulse is to walk, and he hinders me, what then?'

What part of you will he hinder? Your assent?

'No, but my poor body.'

Yes, as a stone is hindered.

'Granted; but I do not walk anymore.'

Who told you that it is your business to walk unhindered? The only thing I told you was unhindered was your impulse; as to the service of the body, and its cooperation, you have heard long ago that it is no affair of yours.

'I grant you this too.'

Can any one compel you to will to get what you do not wish?

'No one.'

Or to purpose or to plan, or in a word to deal with the impressions that you meet with?

'No one can do this either; but if I will to get something a man will hinder me from obtaining it.'

How will he hinder you, if you set your will upon things which are your own and beyond hindrance?

'Not at all.'

But no one tells you that he who wills to get what is not his own is unhindered.

'Am I then not to will to get health?'

Certainly not, nor anything else that is not your own. For nothing is your own, that it does not rest with you to procure or to keep when you will. Keep your hands far away from it; above all, keep your will away, or else you surrender yourself into slavery, you put your neck under the yoke, if you admire what is not your own, and set your heart on anything mortal, whatever it be, or anything that depends upon another.

'Is not my hand my own?'

It is a part of you, but by nature a thing of clay, subject to hindrance and compulsion, slave to everything that is stronger than itself. Nay, why do I name you the hand? You must treat your whole body like a poor ass, with its burden on its back, going with you just so far as it may, and so far as it is given you; but if the king's service calls, and a soldier lays hands on it, let it go, do not resist or murmur; if you do, you will only get a flogging and lose your poor ass all the same.

But when this is your proper attitude to your body, consider what is left for you to do with other things that are procured for the body's sake. As the body is the poor ass, other things become the ass's bridle and pack-saddle, shoes and barley and fodder. Give them up too, let them go quicker and with a lighter heart than the ass itself.

And when you have prepared and trained yourself thus to distinguish what is your own from what is not your own, things subject to hindrance from things unhindered, to regard these latter as your concern, and the former as not, to direct your will to gain the latter and to avoid the former, then have you any one to fear anymore?

'No one.'

Of course. What should you fear for? Shall you fear for what is your own, that is, for what makes good and evil for you? Nay, who has authority over what is yours?

Why, what have you been studying all along but to distinguish what it yours from what is not yours, what is in your power from what is not in your power, things subject to hindrance from things unhindered? Why did you go to the philosophers? Was it that you might be just as unfortunate and miserable as ever? I say that so trained you will be free from fear and perturbation.

What has pain to do with you now, for it is only things that cause fear in expectation which cause pain when they come? What shall you have desire for any longer, for your will is tranquil and harmonious, set on objects within its compass to obtain, objects that are noble and within your reach, and you have no wish to get what is beyond your will, and you give no scope to that jostling element of unreason which breaks all bounds in its impatience?

When once you adopt this attitude towards things, no man can inspire fear in you any longer. For how can man cause fear in man by his aspect or his talk or by his society generally, any more than fear can be roused by horse or dog or bee in another horse or dog or bee? No, it is things which inspire fear in every man; it is the power of winning things for another or of taking them away from him that makes a man feared.

I act as the more cautious travellers do. A man has heard that the road is infested by robbers; he does not dare to venture on it alone, but waits for company—a legate, or a quaestor, or a proconsul—and joining him he passes safely on the road. The prudent man does the same in the world; in the world are many haunts of robbers, tyrants, storms, distresses, chances of losing what is dearest.

This is what you ought to practice from sunrise to sunset, beginning with the meanest things and those most subject to injury—a jug or a cup. From this go on to a tunic, a dog, a horse, a field; and from that to yourself, your body and its members, your children, your wife, your brothers. Look carefully on all sides and fling them away from you. Purify your judgements, and see that nothing that is not your own is attached to you or clings to you, that nothing shall give you pain if it is torn from you. And as you train yourself day by day, as in the lecture-room, say not that you are a philosopher (I grant you that would be arrogant), but that you are providing for your enfranchisement; for this is freedom indeed.

He is free, whom none can hinder, the man who can deal with things as he wishes. But the man who can be hindered or compelled or fettered or driven into anything against his will, is a slave. And who is he whom none can hinder? The man who fixes his aim on nothing that is not his own. And what does 'not his own' mean? All that it does not lie in our power to have or not to have, or to have of a particular quality or under particular conditions. The body then does not belong to us, its parts do not belong to us, our property does not belong to us. If then you set your heart on one of these as though it were your own, you will pay the penalty deserved by him who desires what does not belong to him. The road that leads to freedom, the only release from slavery is this, to be able to say with your whole soul:

> Lead me, O Zeus, and lead me, Destiny,
> Whither ordainèd is by your decree.
>
> *Cleanthes*

But, what say you, my philosopher, suppose the tyrant call on you to say something unworthy of you? Do you assent or refuse? Tell me. 'Let me think it over.'

You will think it over now, will you? And what, pray, did you think over when you were at lecture? Did you not study what things are good and what are evil, and what are neither?

'Yes, I did.'

What conclusion did you approve then?

'That things right and noble were good, things wrong and shameful bad.'

Is death evil?

'No.'

Is prison?

'No.'

If you really imagined shameful acts to be bad, and noble acts good, and all else to be indifferent, you would not have proceeded to raise this question: not at all: you would at once have been able to decide the question by intuition, as an act of sight. For when do you question whether black things are white, or heavy things light, instead of following the obvious conclusions of your senses? Why then do you talk now of considering whether things indifferent are more to be shunned than things evil? These are not your judgements: prison and death do not seem to you indifferent, but the greatest evils, nor do base words and acts seem evil, they seem not to matter for us.

This is the habit to which you have trained yourself from the first. 'Where am I? In the lecture-room. And who are listening to me? I am talking to philosophers. But now I have left the lecture-room. Away with those sayings of pedants and fools!' That is how a philosopher gives witness against a friend, that is how a philosopher turns parasite: that is how he hires himself out at a price, and speaks against his real opinion in the Senate, while in his heart his judgement cries aloud, not a flat and miserable apology for an opinion, hanging to idle discussions as by a hair-thread, but a judgement strong and serviceable, trained by actions, which is the true initiation. Watch yourself and see how you take the news, I do not say that your child is dead (how should that befall you?), but that your oil is spilt, or your wine drunk up: well may one who stands by, as your temper rises high, say just this to you, 'Philosopher, you use different language in the lecture-room: why do you deceive us? Why, worm that you are, do you call yourself a man?' I would fain stand by one of these men when he is indulging his lust, that I might see how eager he is, and what words he utters, and whether he remembers his own name, or the discourses which he hears or delivers or reads.

'Yes, but what has this to do with freedom?'

Make this your study, study these judgements, and these sayings: fix your eyes on these examples, if you wish to be free, if you set your desires on freedom as it deserves. It is no wonder that you pay this great, this heavy price for so vast an object. Men hang themselves, or cast themselves down headlong, nay sometimes whole cities perish for the sake of what the world calls 'freedom', and will you not repay to God what He has given, when He asks it, for the sake of true freedom, the freedom which stands secure against all attack? Shall you not practise, as Plato says, not death only, but torture and exile and flogging, in a word practise giving back all that is not yours? If not, you will be a slave among slaves, even if you are consul ten thousand times, and no less, if you go up into Caesar's Palace; and you will discover that 'what philosophers say may be contrary to opinion', as Cleanthes said, 'but not contrary to reason'. For you will really get to know that what they say is true, and that none of these objects that men admire and set their hearts on is of any use to those who get them, though those who have never chanced to have them get the impression, that if only these things were theirs their cup of blessings would be full, and then, when they get them, the sun scorches them and the sea tosses them no less, and they feel the same boredom and the same desire for what they have not got.

For freedom is secured not by the fulfilling of men's desires, but by the removal of desire. To learn the truth of what I say, you must spend your pains on these new studies instead of your studies in the past: sit up late that you may acquire a judgement that makes you free: pay your attentions not to a rich old man, but to a philosopher, and be seen about his doors: to be so seen will not do you discredit: you will not depart empty or without profit, if you approach in the right spirit. If you doubt my word, do but try: there is no disgrace in trying.

KEY TERMS

Free will is the notion that people make choices and have the capacity to do otherwise than they choose. In other words, not all actions are predetermined.

Determinism claims that all actions and events are determined or happen necessarily. There is no free will. Freedom of the will is an illusion.

Indeterminism is the idea that not all actions are determined. People have freedom of the will.

Soft determinism or compatibalism states that all actions are determined, and yet, humanity has free will. David Hume argues for this view. Hume seems to redefine what it means to be "free." "Free" for Hume is doing whatever you are determined to do. (Which does not sound very "free.")

QUESTIONS FOR DISCUSSION AND REVIEW

1. Is free will possible if there is such a thing as God's plan?
2. Explain the paradox of Buridan's donkey, and what Spinoza makes of this paradox.
3. In what sense does Alyosha Karamazov realize that he is free in Dostoyevsky's *The Brothers Karamazov*.
4. For existentialists from Dostoyevsky to Sartre, in what sense are human beings outside determinism?
5. Summarize, explain, and evaluate the main points of the reading by William James.
6. Summarize, explain, and evaluate the main points of the reading by Epictetus.

SUGGESTED READINGS

Dostoyevsky, F. (1958). *The Brothers Karamazov.* (Komroff, M. transl.)

Dostoyevsky, F. (2002). *The Brothers Karamazov.* (Pevear, R. and Volokhonsky, L. transl.).

Internet Encyclopedia of Philosophy. A peer-reviewed academic resource. Available from http://www.iep.utm.edu/

Kim, J. and Sosa.E. eds. (2002). *A Companion to Metaphysics.*

McGinn, C. (1993). *Problems in Philosophy: The Limits of Inquiry.*

Rocca, M. (1996). *Representation and the Mind-Body Problem in Spinoza.*

Safranski, R. (1991). *Schopenhauer and the Wild Years of Philosophy.*

Sartre, J-P. (1956). *Being and Nothingness.* (Barnes, H. transl.).

Stanford Encyclopedia of Philosophy. Available from http://plato.stanford.edu/

What about God? Philosophy of Religion in the Western Tradition

6

Upon completing this chapter, students should be able to meet the following Learning Outcomes:

6.1 Articulate the views of Anselm and Gaunilo regarding the ontological argument.

6.2 Compare and contrast Freud, Nietzsche, Tolstoy, and Kierkegaard on the rationality of religious belief.

6.3 Explain and evaluate the problem of evil.

Your parents may have told you to never discuss religion or politics—nothing leads to a bigger debate or perhaps the loss of a friendship faster. Unfortunately, in a philosophy class, we discuss both. Existence, life, and death are complex matters. Religions have existed since the beginning of human history and, in many cases, predate any written word. Many older religions have morphed into or been absorbed into existing ones. Some even have secret, unknown histories that are only revealed by heretics.

In this chapter, we will focus on Western conceptions of God and discuss the God of the Jews, Christians, and Muslims (who, ironically, is the same being—which has been interpreted in different ways by various Holy books and religions). The discussion will mainly focus on proofs of God's existence, the rationality of religious belief, and the problem of evil (both logical and evidential).

> **POWERFUL ANALYSIS: DOES THE PRACTICE MATTER OR THE BELIEF IN GOD?**
>
> Does it matter what religion you follow? Do good people go to heaven and the wicked go to hell regardless of their faith?

The Existence and Nature of God

The God of the Jews, Christians, and Muslims is purported to have three main qualities or attributes. These qualities and attributes have not been assigned or gleamed by philosophers, but rather, by theologians (religious scholars), who study ancient Holy books and documents. The qualities that God (also known as the three omni God) have are omniscience, omnipotence, and omnibenevolence. That is to say, God is all-knowing, all-powerful, and all-good.

St. Teresa of Ávila

This extraordinary woman made religious belief a personal, sensual matter. Teresa Sánchez de Cepeda y Ahumada, canonized as **St. Teresa of Jesus** and popularly known as **St. Teresa of Ávila** was both a revolutionary theologian and a pioneer of women's rights. The great Castilian poet and mystic, while remaining cloistered among her Carmelite sisters in Ávila most of her life, managed to outwit the Spanish Inquisition, refined what would become the language of Cervantes in the Golden Age of Spanish literature, and hold her own as a philosopher and theologian.

> "Let nothing disturb you
> Let nothing frighten you
> Everything passes
> But God never does
> Patience brings everything
> With God you lack nothing
> God is enough"
>
> —*St. Teresa of Ávila, 1515–1582*

rook76/Shutterstock.com

St. Teresa of Ávila was a key figure in the Catholic Counter-Reformation that began with the Council of Trent (1545–1563) as the Catholic Church found itself besieged by the newly minted protestant faiths. Sixteenth-century Protestants such as Luther and Calvin brought on what was in effect a return to Augustinian—which is to say, Platonic—approaches to faith. Popular and populist, this revivalist Christian spirit contributed to the spread of Protestantism in Europe and presented the Catholic Church in its Thomistic apex with a formidable challenge. Reason, of the brand that St. Thomas Aquinas preached as he perverted Aristotle into Natural Law, now was seen as part of the problem. Teresa's importance to the Catholic Church lay precisely in not resting on a foundation of reason—and in this she anticipated Kierkegaard and the twentieth-century existentialist Christians including Gabriel Marcel. She made faith an intensely personal affair.

Teresa's mysticism took the theological conversation away from reason and into a very personal realm of quiet prayer and meditation that led to spiritual ecstasy. Gian Lorenzo Bernini's marble statue *The Ecstasy of St. Teresa* in the church of Santa Maria della Vittoria in Rome illustrates a famous episode from Teresa's *Autobiography (Libro de la Vida)*, where an angel came to her:

"I saw a golden spear in his hand, with what looked like fire at the tip. He thrust the spear into my heart, my breast, and he left me on fire with a great love of God. The pain was so great it made me moan. And yet the pain also was so overwhelmingly sweet that I did not want it to end."

The sheer sensuality of Teresa's ecstasy as she describes it was not without controversy. But her desire to make the intangible tangible, to make religious belief physical and personal, even sexual, itself calls for piety. Teresa, along with her fellow Spanish mystic and poet St. John of the Cross (1542–1591), embraced the dangerous sensuality of the religious experience, and she proved that it may well be the essence of Christianity to court that danger. Later readers, in or outside the Catholic faith, found recognition and inspiration in the depth of St. Teresa's vivid description of the practice of quiet, private prayer and meditation. Apart from any considerations of the metaphysics of religion, Teresa got the psychology of religion right.

Particularly in her masterpieces, *The Interior Castle* and *The Road to Perfection*, as well as in her spiritual *Autobiography*, Teresa's work was a call to freedom, a challenge for men and women alike and as equals to reach the greatness of human possibilities. She was canonized in 1622 by Pope Gregory XV, and she was declared a Doctor of the Church by Pope Paul VI in 1970. St. Teresa today is celebrated as the patron saint of Spanish writers.

St. Anselm

Various philosophers and theologians have attempted to provide either inductive or deductive logical proofs for God's existence. From the outset, we may note that none of the proofs seem to work—if they did, they would most like be carved into every church, temple, or mosque across the world. Nevertheless, they are worth considering. St. Anselm (1033–1109) attempts to produce a deductive proof for God's existence. He argues that a perfect being necessary exists. His argument is deductive in nature. It is based upon the meaning of certain terms and does not rely upon empirical evidence.

His argument is sometimes called the **ontological argument** because it is based upon the nature of being. He says that if we imagine two objects, both identical, but one exists and the other does not, then the one that exist is more perfect. Since God is already a perfect being, he cannot be more perfect, therefore he must exist. Gaunilo, a French monk of Anselm's time, provided a counterargument to Anselm. He argues that existence does not make something more perfect. He employs a **reductio ad absurdum** (reduce to an absurd conclusion) argument. A reductio argument employs the same structure but changes one word, thereby making the conclusion absurd. In logic, if the argument works in one case, it should work in all cases, all things being equal.

In this case, Gaunilo claims that if perfection entails existence, the by the same token, a perfect island must exist, because, after all it is perfect. Gaunilo does not doubt God's existence, nor does he believe in the perfect island. His point is that, in his view, Anselm's arguments do not work.

Again, in Gaunilo's view, if Anselm is correct in his assertion regarding God's necessary existence, then the same would be true for a perfect island. Does believing in the perfect island make it real? This is absurd—hence this is a reductio ad absurdum (reduce to an absurd conclusion) argument. According to Gaunilo, it is an absurdity to conclude that God necessary exists simply because we can imagine or conceive of him. Anselm agrees that it is absurd to conclude that the perfect island exists just because you think of it, and yet, he claims that in the case of God it is a different matter all together. He maintains that God's existence is guaranteed by his perfection.

In the end, this twelfth-century debate was left unresolved with both men claiming victory. Ultimately, Anselm became Saint Anselm and Gaunilo was lucky to not be excommunicated for his heretical objection to the argument.

St. Thomas Aquinas

In the *Summa Theologica*, which was written between 1265 and 1274, St. Thomas Aquinas' explained the sacred doctrines of Christianity in the clearest way possible. In the work, Aquinas provides **five proofs (or ways) for God's Existence**.

The first four ways fail for various reasons, but the fifth way has some promise and has found its way into our contemporary thought. The five proofs for Gods existence are Motion, Efficient Cause, Possibility and Necessity, Degrees of Perfection, and Design.

From each of these arguments, he attempts to draw conclusions from things that we see in everyday life (empirical evidence) regarding the nature of reality. He starts with motion: if something is in motion, then it must have been set into motion by something else and there is not an infinite chain of movers; so, the first unmoved mover who sets the world in motion is God. This argument is a version of Aristotle's "unmoved mover" argument. Aristotle took existence and creation very seriously and thought it was logically impossible for the universe to be eternal. His answer was to maintain there was a first thing or force that he termed the unmoved mover that set the universe into motion and created, well creation. The problem with the argument is that one premise states that all things are set into motion by something else, but the conclusion says there is one thing that is not set into motion by itself—it is either one or the other but not both, so the argument commits a logical contradiction. All of the other arguments (Efficient Cause, Possibility and Necessity, Degrees of Perfection) have similar logical flaws.

The only argument that does not suffer from serious logical flaws is the Design argument, although it does not prove a number of things.

ST. THOMAS AQUINAS AND DESIGN

St. Thomas Aquinas and the Argument from Design

1) **Among objects that have goals or a purpose, some have minds and others do not.**

2) An object that has a goal, but does not have a mind, must have been designed by a being that had a mind.

3) So there exists a being with a mind who designed all of the mindless objects that act for ends.

4) Hence this Being is God and he does exist.

In the argument, Aquinas claims all objects have a goal or purpose. A pen, for example, has a purpose but does not have a mind. The fact that it has a purpose means it was created by a being with a mind which assigned that purpose. In his view, if an object has a goal or purpose but no mind, then something with a mind must have designed it. Therefore, there is one, single being that has a mind that designed all the mindless objects that have goals or a purpose—of course that Being is God.

From the outset, you may see an issue, pens are mindless objects, but they were not created by God. Furthermore, any human creation or artifact was not created by a single individual or person. By analogy, we could argue that natural creatures and objects may not have a single creator (or a creator at all). Why should we assume there is a single being that created all natural creatures and objects?

William Paley and a Watch on the Beach

William Paley (1743–1805) asked us to imagine that we are walking on a beach and find a watch. He says we may question, how did it get there? One answer is that it was created randomly—perhaps by the action of the waves and the sand on the beach. Paley, however, thinks this is an absurd idea. He thinks that given the complexity of the watch, it would be reasonable to conclude that the watch had a creator or designer— even if we had never seen a watch in our lives. Of those two hypothesis which seems to be the most likely? Paley thinks, just as you most probably do, that it makes more sense to talk about the watch having a designer. Paley's version of the design argument is an argument from analogy. He wants to draw an analogy between the watch and nature. He wants us to look at the complexity of the watch and compare it to the complexity of nature and natural organisms. He thinks that if we consider how complex natural creatures and the universe as a whole is, we will conclude that they must have a designer as they are much more complicated than a simple watch.

David Hume (1711–1776) argues that this is a poor or weak analogy. It is one thing to talk about watches, it is another to talk about living organisms, and still another to talk about the universe. He claims that the argument does not make it rational to conclude that the universe has a designer. Hume thinks Paley is comparing apples to oranges or better human artifact (watches) to natural creatures and the universe. Watches are manmade, living creatures are not. Watchs are inanimate things, organisms are alive. A Gucci and Rolex watch will not procreate and create a Golex. So in Hume's view, Paley is drawing a bad comparison and making a weak inference. Ultimately, it seems Hume may be mistaken, it is not the living or innate nature that is at issue, it is the complexity. And no matter how complex my watch might be, our little pinky finger has more complexity in it. The question is, was it the result of a random or natural process or the result of design?

POWERFUL IDEAS BOX: PROBLEMS WITH THE DESIGN ARGUMENT

1) It does not prove there is an interactive designer. (God could be an architect who creates the universe and moves on to other realms—this view is known as Deism.)

2) It does not prove there is only one designer. (There could be many god or goddesses.)

3) It does not clearly show who the designer is. (It does not prove one religion over another.)

A Scientific Alternative: Evolution

A few years ago, scientists from Harvard University published an article in the journal, *Nature*, providing the result of a genetic analysis of humans and many other primates. The genetic analysis suggests a messy split between the two lineages that lead to humans and the other great apes lineages. According to the scientist, the evolutionary split between humans and our nearest evolutionary cousins, chimpanzees, may have occurred more recently than we thought, according to a new comparison of the respective genetic sequences. Previous estimates put the split at as much as 7 million years ago. This would mean that Toumaï, a fossil dating from at least 6.5 million years ago in Chad and assigned to the species *Sahelanthropus tchadensis*, which had been thought to be the earliest known member of the line that gave rise to modern humans is in fact an ancestor to both species.

Researchers led by David Reich of Harvard Medical School in Boston, Massachusetts, now calculate that the split may have occurred no more than 6.3 million years ago, and possibly as recently as 5.4 million. That would make Toumaï older than the time of the split. The researchers make their claim after comparing the genetic codes of humans, chimpanzees, gorillas, and other primates in unprecedented detail—more than 20 million DNA "letters" in all. By checking the differences between different species' DNA sequences, they were able to estimate the time since they first diverged. The research involved the study of fossils, mathematical algorithms (to calculate the amount of change in the human and ape DNA as well as the time required to produce those changes), and finally genetic analysis. Ultimately, the research helps to confirm the ideas first put forth by Charles Darwin in 1859 in his book, *The Origin of Species* and supports the view that humans evolved from earlier forms of life on the planet.

> "When we read about Creation in Genesis, we run the risk of imagining God was a magician, with a magic wand able to do everything. But that is not so, He created human beings and let them develop according to the internal laws that he gave to each one so they would reach their fulfillment. Evolution in nature is not opposed to the notion of Creation, because evolution presupposes the creation of beings that evolve"

—*Pope Francis, October 27, 2014 at the Pontifical Academy of Sciences*

There is, however, one great irony in this notion, Charles Darwin, the creator of evolutionary theory was a theist and Christian when he wrote his book to explain his theory. He went so far as to place this quote in the beginning of his book "But with regard to the material world, we can at least go so far as this-we can perceive that events are brought about not by insulated interposition of Divine power, exerted in each particular case, but by the establishment of general laws"—William Whewell, *Bridgewater Treatise* (1833), as found in Darwin's *Origin of Species* (1859)

The above quote is by William Whenwell (1794–1866), a British philosopher, scientist, and theologian. He argues that events in this world are not caused by God acting in each particular case, but rather by the establishment of laws of nature. In other words, when objects fall, we do not think God makes each of them fall in every instance, but we believe that gravity (a law of nature) dictates their fall (and for theist is a law of nature created by God).

Darwin, in the same way, feels he has stumbled upon laws of biology that dictate how events will unfold. We do not worry that dogs will give birth to cats or vice versa, as we now understand that genetics and other laws of biology require dogs to give birth to puppies and cats to give birth to kittens. God does not need to employ his will or divine powers to make such things happen, rather, on this view, God established laws of nature that include laws of biology and genetics, which govern these events.

Finally, there is good news for Catholics. In 2014, Pope Francis declared that evolution does not conflict with Catholicism. As Pope Francis states at the Pontifical Academy of Sciences in 2014 "When we read about Creation in Genesis, we run the risk of imagining God was a magician, with a magic wand able to do everything. But that is not so, He created human beings and let them develop according to the internal laws that he gave to each one so they would reach their fulfillment . . . . Evolution in nature is not opposed to the notion of Creation, because evolution presupposes the creation of beings that evolve."

Although persons on both side of the debate feel they are in the right, creation by a God and evolution are not mutually exclusive. It could be the case that there is no God and that humanity is the result of natural law and processes or it could be the case that God employs those natural laws and processes to create humanity.

POWERFUL IDEAS BOX: HYPOTHESES THAT EXPLAIN LIFE ON EARTH

Of the four likely hypotheses for the creation of the universe and humanity, only two seem possible:

Hypothesis 1: Random   (false)
Hypothesis 2: Designer   (false)
Hypothesis 3: Evolution and No Designer (possible)
Hypothesis 4: Evolution and Designer (possible)

Evolution does not rule out the possibility of "intelligent design" for the universe. The notions of evolution and a creator deity are not mutually exclusive.

POWERFUL ANALYSIS: GOD'S EXISTENCE

Can science resolve the issue of God's existence?

Hopes, Bets, and Beliefs

There are numerous other statements and arguments for and against God's existence. The arguments against will be discussed later in the section on the "The Problem of Evil." Immanuel Kant (1724–1804) claims that we should all hope that God exist. In that way, justice will be served to those who have lived a wicked and unjust life and yet prospered in this world. In Kant's view, if you are a moral agent (which I do hope you believe in ethics), then you must assume the God's existence in order to be rational. Having said this, plenty of philosophers and people are atheist and still hold to ethical truth and values.

"The heart has reasons that reason does not know"

—*Blaise Pascal*

© Georgios Kollidas/Shutterstock.com

Blaise Pascal (1623–1662) thought belief in God served our rational self-interest. He proposed a **prudential argument** for God's Existence. He felt that it was in our self-interest to believe in God, as the benefits of such a belief far outweighed any loss.

POWERFUL IDEAS BOX: PASCAL'S WAGER

Your Belief	God Exists	God Does Not Exist
You believe in God	Infinite bliss (heaven)	+/– some small amount
You don't believe in God	Infinite damnation (hell)	+/– some small amount

Possible outcomes:

1) If you believe in God, and he exist, then you are going to heaven and are going to reap infinite rewards.

2) If you don't believe in God, and he does exist, then you are going to hell and suffer infinite pain.

3) If you believe in God, and he does not exist, you have wasted some small measure of energy.

4) If you don't believe in God, and he does not exist, then you have saved some small measure of energy.

There are, of course, a few flaws with Pascal's prudential argument. To begin, if this were the only reason you believed in God, I doubt you would get passed the pearly gates of Heaven. Second, it is an over simplification of the options. There are thousands of religions and gods? Which one ought you to choose? Even if you were to choose, Christianity, Judaism, or Islam, each of those faiths have specific practices and the orthodox teaching hold all other believers are destine for hell. In other words, Pascal's wager is much more of a long shot than he appears to understand or maintain.

Lefteris Papaulakis/Shutterstock.com

William James (1842–1910) thinks that the existence of God cannot be proved or refuted by science. He feels that is something we can make ourselves believe. He thinks belief in God is "open" for most of us to believe in even though there is not sufficient evidence for it. In fact, he goes so far as to say we can "Will ourselves to believe" in God. James says we may believe any "open" hypothesis. James defines a hypothesis as a proposed belief. Such a hypothesis may be live or dead, forced or avoidable, momentous or trivial.

A "live" hypothesis is something we are open to. If we have already made up our minds on an issue, then such a hypothesis is "dead" and we cannot make ourselves believe it. Another two conditions for James are that a hypothesis must be forced and also momentous. In other words, we must be having some sort of existential crisis or serious problem in our life, which forces us to consider the issue. Also the belief must be momentous and very important. We cannot will ourselves to belief trivial or mundane things. When a hypothesis is live, forced, and momentous, then it is a genuine option for us to choose to believe in it. At which point we would attempt to obtain the belief. As far as religion goes, that would mean engaging in the practices of those that do believe, such as going to temple, reciting mantras, or reciting prayers. James feels that over time a person can eventually believe just as any other believer.

POWERFUL ANALYSIS: COMPELLING ARGUMENT?

Is there any argument that you feel is compelling for the existence of God?

POWERFUL IDEAS BOX: CHRISTIANITY AND THE LINK TO MITHRAISM

The First Council of Nicaea also known as First Ecumenical Council of the Catholic Church was called in 325 AD under the leadership of the Roman Emperor Constantine. At the council, Constantine organized the early church and codified the books of the Bible. There was not a single Christian Holy book at that time and various churches had different gospels or books.

Constantine himself, claimed to have converted to Christianity after he had a vision of the cross and of Jesus before the battle of Milvian Bridge (a battle he won during a Roman civil war). It is interesting to note, however, in 312, when his biographer wrote of the battle with Maxentius at the Milvian Bridge he omits any discussion of Constantine's visions.

In fact, as was the custom at the time, after he won the civil war and became undisputed emperor of the Roman Empire, he built a victory arch in Rome (an arch that stands to this day). Although he later claims to have been inspired to victory by Jesus, he omits any Christian symbolism from the arch. Further, he adds various pagan gods including the God Mithra.

Mithra is a son of the Sun god, Apollo, who was born on December 25 to a virgin mother, crucified, and rose from the dead—although he predates Jesus by hundreds of years. (Not unlike the Egyptian god, Horus, who predate Jesus by a few thousand years). Interestingly, in 325, just prior to the council of Nicaea, Constantine "remembered" his visions and makes his biographer rewrite his biography. Found in many early Roman churches, under the church in catacombs, are alters to Mithra. Although belief in Christianity had swept over the slaves and soldiers of the Roman Empire, the Roman elite continued to practice pagan worship and held belief in various gods, including Mithra.

POWERFUL ANALYSIS: PAGAN EMPEROR

If the Roman Emperor Constantine was a pagan, is it problematic (for a Christian) that he was able to shape and mold the Christian Bible and Christian Church into the image he saw fit?

The Rationality of Religious Belief

Friedrich Nietzsche (1844–1900) famously said, "God is dead!" Although in truth he did not believe God had died, but rather, he had never existed in the first place. It was his view that if you are and intelligent person that is able to reason, then you understand that God is a fable, a fairy tale used by the powerful (like Roman Emperors) to control the weak.

Sigmund Freud (1856–1939) had a similar take upon religious belief. In the book, *The Future of an Illusion* (1927), Freud applies his psychological theory to religious belief. According to Freud, most religious belief is captured by the idea that there is a God, one who cares about us, and that will provide us with a eternal happiness after this life. An archetypal protective father figure. Freud argues that the origin of such a belief, which is lacking almost any empirical evidence, is wish fulfillment. It is the result of the psychological desire for protection from a cold brutal reality. Ultimately, belief in God is simply wishful thinking on our part. As Freud says, "Ignorance is Ignorance; no right to believe anything can be derived from it . . . . Scientific work is the only road which can lead us to knowledge of reality outside of ourselves." And in Freud's view, the logical, scientific answer is that belief in God is not a viable, rational belief.

Boris15/Shutterstock.com

In an opposite vain, Søren Kierkegaard (1813–1855) argues that belief in God and Jesus is not (or perhaps, beyond human rationality). True understanding of God is beyond our comprehension. In his view, God exist in a realm that is beyond time and space and yet Jesus became part of time part of space. Jesus, as the son of God and part of the trinity (in which the father, son, and Holy Spirit are all one) became a contradiction, a paradox. In Kierkegaard's view, truth is subjective and relative. And although belief in God is contradictory and irrational, it is still possible.

Leo Tolstoy (1828–1910) expresses a similar view to that of Kierkegaard in his work, the *Confessions* (1880). In the *Confessions,* he notes that the notion that faith is irrational has long been pervasive in philosophy. The dichotomy between faith and reason dates back to antiquity and was taken for granted by medieval thinkers such as St. Augustine and St. Thomas Aquinas. Tolstoy was searching for the meaning and purpose of life. He says that "I realized that it was impossible to search for an answer to my questions in rational knowledge; rational knowledge had led me to recognize that life is meaningless. My life came to a halt and I wanted to kill myself."

He felt that science and reason could not provide any answer to the question as to why we are here, only the how—if that. He goes on to say, "As I looked around at people, at humanity as a whole, I saw that they lived and affirmed that they knew the meaning of life. I looked at myself—I had lived as long as I knew the meaning of life. For me, as for others, faith provided the meaning of life and the possibility of living." Tolstoy would not disagree with Nietzsche or Freud, he would simply say there is more to life than rational belief.

POWERFUL ANALYSIS: IS RATIONALITY REQUIRED?

Does belief in a higher power have to be rational or quantifiable by science? Can our irrational beliefs still be true?

The Problem of Evil

The problem of evil can be put as follows: Can an all knowing all powerful all good being allow evil to exist? If God is all powerful, all knowing and all good, then why does Evil exists in the world? There are no easy answers to these questions. Theologians have been struggling to provide answers, known as theodicies for ages. J. L. Mackie (1917–1981) argues that if we consider the notion of three Omni being with the attributes mentioned above, then he argues that an omni-benevolent being will attempt to stop all evil; that an all powerful being could stop all evil.

Therefore, if such a being exists, then evil should not. In Mackie's view, the fact that the world is filled with pain, suffering, and evil, three omni God does not exist. This argument is known as the logical problem of evil. It is to be distinguished from the evidential problem of evil, which basically says that there is so much evil in the world (and so little good, that clearly God does not exist). Mackie and many philosophers after him maintain that we don't need to employ induction or abduction to resolve the issue of God's existence; we can simply use deductive logic.

POWERFUL IDEAS BOX: J. L. MACKIE'S LOGICAL PROBLEM OF EVIL

J. L. Mackie's deductive argument can be constructed as follows:

1) If a being is omnibenevolent, he will try to stop all evil.
2) If a being is all powerful, he can do anything (including stopping all evil).
3) If a being is all knowing, then he knows everything (including every instance of evil).
4) So if such a being existed, he would not permit any evil; for such an omnibenevolent being will try to remove all evil from the world and an omnipotent being can do anything.
5) Since evil exists, three omni God does not.

Mackie's conclusion is that if God does exist, he must lack one of the three qualities. Either God is not all-knowing, so He cannot stop all evil, He is not all-powerful, so He cannot stop all evil, or He is not omni-benevolent, in which case He is indifferent to evil.

Theologians respond in different ways. Often, they claim that evil is necessary or that it is the result of human free will. Mackie argues that it should not be necessary, and that humans could still have free will even if God prevented us from committing evils. Does humanity needs evil to know good? But why should this be the case? Must we know and experience evil in order to know good? How many rapes or murders do we need before we all know evil? This line of thinking is a limitation upon God's power. God could (if he were all powerful) allow us to know good and evil without having to experience it. He does not need Sally to die in order to save Jim because he can save both.

"Where were you when I laid the earth's foundation?"

—God, Book of Job, Chapter 38, verse 4

POWERFUL IDEAS BOX: WHERE WERE YOU WHEN I LAID THE FOUR CORNERS OF THE EARTH?

The book of *Job*, which is found in the Hebrew Bible and the Old Testament, is an interesting piece of literature (historical or otherwise). To summarize the story succinctly: Satan visits God in Heaven and the two make a wager on Job's fidelity and loyalty to the Lord. Satan says Job is a good servant because God has "built a hedge around his house" and has rewarded him. To this the Lord says test his faith. The Lord tells Satan, he can do anything to Job, or his family, but he may not kill him. Satan does just that. He destroys all his land and livestock, kills all his children and inflicts great pain upon Job. In the end, Job asks God why? . . . to which God says, "Where were you when I laid the earth's foundation?" And then God goes on to list the various things he has done, which are beyond Job's power and how he has the audacity to question his creator. In the end, Job gets double of everything and all is well.

POWERFUL ANALYSIS: IS IT MORAL TO BET ON A PERSON'S LIFE?

If a powerful person (in a position similar to God) made a similar bet, on a man's life and the lives of his children, would we consider him moral?

Theodicy

St. Augustine (354–430) argues that evil is not really, real—it is a privation. A privation is a lack of something. For example, it is not evil or bad that a person is blind, they simply *lack* sight. He goes on to say that "All evil is either sin or punishment for sin." Which would be plausible if evil only befell the wicked, but it does also happen to children for whom the sins they have committed could never equal the pain and suffering they endure.

St. Irenaeus (130–202 AD) has a more interesting explanation of evil. It severs a purpose (one God could have resolved in other ways). On his view, evil provides the necessary problems through which we take part in what he calls "soul-making." Evil, ultimately, is a means to an end. If it did not exist, there would be no means of spiritual development. He maintains that creation is a two-step process. God first made man in his image, as it is stated in genesis and is now making us into his likeness.

According to this view, God's purpose in creation was not to make a perfectly comfortable dwelling place for fully formed human beings, but to put rational creatures with the potential for growth in an imperfect environment where they could, through their freely chosen responses to difficulties they encounter, attain maturity. In other words, we need to struggle in order to grow spiritually—if we are never tested, we can neither fail nor succeed.

What the world would be like with three omni god around would be nearly unfathomable.

Earthquakes could be stopped before they started. Hurricanes would meander harmlessly over the open ocean. Bullets could stop in midair; infants falling out a high rises would land softly on the ground as those they had wings. God could interact with this reality and bring peace and happiness to all. And yet, it does not seem that such a world does exist. Our existence is not one where we interact with such a powerful deity—or rather where such a powerful deity has any interest in helping us. The three omni God appears not to exist because of the vast amount of evil in the world. God seems to lack omnipotence, omniscient, or omni-benevolence—otherwise, God could stamp out all evil. In the end, this topic is a matter of faith, and faith does not need a rational justification. In order to have faith, all you need to do is believe.

POWERFUL ANALYSIS: IS EVIL A PROBLEM?

Does the problem of evil casts doubt on the existence of a three omni God?

READINGS

William James was born in 1842, in New York City. He was born into high status and intellectual prowess. James began the study of chemistry at Lawrence Scientific School at Harvard University in 1861. He completed his medical degree in 1869, but he eventually decided to follow a career in psychology and philosophy. James's brother, Henry James, was a highly influential novelist.

"The Will to Believe"

In the recently published Life by Leslie Stephen of his brother, Fitz-James, there is an account of a school to which the latter went when he was a boy. The teacher, a certain Mr. Guest, used to converse with his pupils in this wise: "Gurney, what is the difference between justification and sanctification?— Stephen, prove the omnipotence of God!" etc. In the midst of our Harvard freethinking and indifference we are prone to imagine that here at your good old orthodox College conversation continues to be somewhat upon this order; and to show you that we at Harvard have not lost all interest in these vital subjects, I have brought with me to-night something like a sermon on justification by faith to read to you,—I mean an essay in justification of faith, a defense of our right to adopt a believing attitude in religious matters, in spite of the fact that our merely logical intellect may not have been coerced. 'The Will to Believe,' accordingly, is the title of my paper.

I have long defended to my own students the lawfulness of voluntarily adopted faith; but as soon as they have got well imbued with the logical spirit, they have as a rule refused to admit my contention to be lawful philosophically, even though in point of fact they were personally all the time chock-full of some faith or other themselves. I am all the while, however, so profoundly convinced that my own position is correct, that your invitation has seemed to me a good occasion to make my statements more clear. Perhaps your minds will be more open than those with which I have hitherto had to deal. I will be as little technical as I can, though I must begin by setting up some technical distinctions that will help us in the end.

I

Let us give the name of "hypothesis" to anything that may be proposed to our belief; and just as the electricians speak of live and dead wires, let us speak of any hypothesis as either "live" or "dead". A live hypothesis is one which appeals as a real possibility to him to whom it is proposed. If I ask you to believe in the Mahdi, the notion makes no electric connection with your nature,—it refuses to scintillate with any credibility at all. As an hypothesis it is completely dead. To an Arab, however (even if he be not one of the Mahdi's followers), the hypothesis is among the mind's possibilities: it is alive. This shows that deadness and liveness in an hypothesis are not intrinsic properties, but relations to the individual thinker. They are measured by his willingness to act. The maximum of liveness in an hypothesis means willingness to act irrevocably. Practically, that means belief; but there is some believing tendency wherever there is willingness to act at all.

Next, let us call the decision between two hypotheses an "option". Options may be of several kinds. They may be—1, "living" or "dead"; 2, "forced" or "avoidable"; 3, "momentous" or "trivial"; and for our purposes we may call an option a "genuine" option when it is of the forced, living, and momentous kind.

1. A living option is one in which both hypotheses are live ones. If I say to you: "Be a theosophist or be a Mohammedan," it is probably a dead option, because for you neither hypothesis is likely to be alive. But if I say: "Be an agnostic or be a Christian," it is otherwise:

trained as you are, each hypothesis makes some appeal, however small, to your belief.

2. Next, if I say to you: "Choose between going out with your umbrella or without it," I do not offer you a genuine option, for it is not forced. You can easily avoid it by not going out at all. Similarly, if I say, "Either love me or hate me," "Either call my theory true or call it false," your option is avoidable. You may remain indifferent to me, neither loving nor hating, and you may decline to offer any judgment as to my theory. But if I say, "Either accept this truth or go without it," I put on you a forced option, for there is no standing place outside of the alternative. Every dilemma based on a complete logical disjunction, with no possibility of not choosing, is an option of this forced kind.

3. Finally, if I were Dr. Nansen and proposed to you to join my North Pole expedition, your option would be momentous; for this would probably be your only similar opportunity, and your choice now would either exclude you from the North Pole sort of immortality altogether or put at least the chance of it into your hands. He who refuses to embrace a unique opportunity loses the prize as surely as if he tried and failed. "Per contra" (on the contrary) the option is trivial when the opportunity is not unique, when the stake is insignificant, or when the decision is reversible if it later proves unwise. Such trivial options abound in the scientific life. A chemist finds a hypothesis live enough to spend a year in its verification: he believes in it to that extent.

But if his experiments prove inconclusive either way, he is quit for his loss of time, no vital harm being done. It will facilitate our discussion if we keep all these distinctions well in mind.

KEY TERMS

Five proofs (or Ways) for God's Existence put forth by St. Thomas Aquinas are Motion, Efficient Cause, Possibility and Necessity, Degrees of Perfection, and Design.

God (also known as the three omni God) has the qualities of omniscience, omnipotence, and omnibenevolence. In other words, God is all-knowing, all-powerful, and all-good.

Ontological argument presented by St. Anselm is based upon the nature of being. Anselm says that if we imagine two objects, both identical, but one exists and the other does not, then the one that exist is more perfect.

Prudential argument proposed by Pascal that it was in our self-interest to believe in God, as the benefits of such a belief far outweighed any loss.

Reductio ad absurdum literally means in Latin reduce to an absurd conclusion. A reductio argument employs the same structure but changes one word, thereby making the conclusion absurd.

QUESTIONS FOR DISCUSSION AND REVIEW

1. Explain, compare and contrast the views of Anselm and Gaunilo regarding the Ontological argument.
2. Explain and evaluate the views of Freud and Nietzsche, on the rationality of religious belief.
3. Explain and evaluate the views of Tolstoy and Kierkegaard, on the rationality of religious belief.
4. Explain and evaluate Pascal's Wager. Would belief based on such an argument get you into heaven?
5. Does believing in an afterlife affect the meaning of life for you? What about not believing in an afterlife?

SUGGESTED READINGS

Aquinas, T. (1998). *Selected Philosophical Writings*. (McDermott, T. transl.).

Pascal, Blaise. (1670). *Pensées*.

Flew, A. (1961). *Hume's Philosophy of Belief: A Study of His First Inquiry.*

Hitchens, C. (2007). *God Is Not Great.*

Internet Encyclopedia of Philosophy. A peer-reviewed academic resource. Available from http://www.iep.utm.edu/

James, W. (1896). *The Will to Believe.*

Mackie, J.L. (1982). *The Miracle of Theism: Arguments for and Against the Existence of God.*

Plantinga, A. (1965). *The Ontological Argument from St. Anselm to Contemporary Philosophers.*

St. Teresa of Avila. (1980). *The Collected Works of Saint Teresa of Avila*, Vols. 1 and 2. (Kavanaugh, K. and Rodriguez, O. transl.)

Stanford Encyclopedia of Philosophy. Available from http://plato.stanford.edu/

Swinburne, R. (1991). *The Existence of God.*

Enlightenment, Nirvana, Rebirth— Eastern Religion and Thought

7

Upon completing this chapter, students should be able to meet the following Learning Outcomes:

7.1 Articulate the main tenets of Hinduism, Buddhism, and Taoism.

7.2 Compare and contrast the various views of Hinduism, Buddhism, and Taoism.

7.3 Explain the connection between the Tao, Ying, and Yang.

7.4 Articulate how principles of Taoism serve as the foundation of the art of Feng Shui

Unlike the West, where most religious systems embrace the notion of monotheism, with one, all powerful deity in control of reality, the East is filled with a myriad of polytheistic deities systems. Many of these systems embrace similar concepts such as the belief that enlightenment is in our own hands, and that karma and that the place and the form we reincarnate into depend upon our action in this life. **Hinduism**, **Buddhism**, and **Taoism** all share notions of **karma, samsara** (the cycle of birth, death, and rebirth), and **reincarnation**, and the purpose of our existence is to reach **enlightenment (Nirvana)**.

Karma is sometimes known as the Law of Cause and Effect. Karma can also be described as the Law of Moral Causation. According to Eastern philosophy, all of our actions have consequences for us. If we perform bad actions, negative consequences

167

will eventually ensue for us. If we perform positive actions, positives consequences will eventually follow. Unlike the causality discussed in other chapters, the cause and the effect may not immediately appear. For example, when you lie or steal, you may not immediately be caught. In fact, karma we have generated in previous lives may now be bearing fruit.

Samsara is the cycle of birth, death, and rebirth. The notion goes hand in hand with reincarnation as it is believed by most Eastern systems that people live many lives in many lifetimes. Reincarnation is the belief that either our soul, consciousness, or some other aspect of our spiritual being is reborn into a physical body in another lifetime. In other words, the spiritual part of us, what some call a soul, and other call consciousness, transcends our physical body and will endure (and maybe have endured) through many lifetimes.

In the West, evidence of this is controversial, although there are various physiologist and scientists who have studied the "past life phenomena." Dr. Brian Weiss in one such scientist, and he has detailed a number of these cases in various books, including *Many Lives, Many Masters* (1988). By using past life therapy, he has been able to cure a number of patients of psychological aliments. In fact, in many of his regression therapy sessions, patients would go into very precise detail about daily activities that happened hundreds or even thousands of years ago. As noted, although reincarnation is met with skepticism by many Westerners, it is taken as a certainty by most Eastern religions.

POWERFUL ANALYSIS

Do you think people who remember past lives provide evidence for reincarnation?

The notion of enlightenment is certainly one of the most varied of Eastern concepts. Generally, it is believed by the various systems (Hinduism, Buddhism, and Taoism) that a soul (or some aspect of our consciousness) will reincarnate time and again until they reach a state of enlightenment. Enlightenment is a personal journey and cannot simply be granted by a Buddha or god, but rather by one's own study and spiritual practice. For the Buddhist, when one achieves such a state, you will no longer reincarnate and will, in a sense, become one with the universe. Some beings that reach enlightenment choose the option of becoming a Buddha and of returning to this realm to help other beings reach enlightenment as well. For a Taoist, you may leave the earthly realm and join the immortals in a Taoist heaven. The specifics of this idea of achieving enlightenment are as varied as the religions and sects of those religions that believe in the concept.

Hinduism

Hinduism is one of the world's oldest religions. It predates written records and its actual origins are lost to the past. The term Hinduism refers to the collection of faiths that are believed to have originated in India, but other scholars believe that it was brought to India thousands of years ago by nomadic peoples. It is a polytheistic system with various gods and goddesses as well as lesser deities. A complete list of the deities (in their various incarnations) is beyond the scope of this text, but some of the chief deities include Brahma, Shiva, Sakti, and Vishnu.

> "On Earth whatever has been gained perishes. So dies, whatever is acquired for the next world by austerities, and so called good deeds. Those who leave here without knowing the Self, as consciousness, reality, love, will not find freedom in any world"
>
> —Book VIII, Part 1, verse 6 of *The Chandogya Upanishad*

Brahma is considered by many Hindus as the superior god and the creator of this reality. Together with Shiva and Vishnu, he forms a trinity of gods: Brahma is the creator, Shiva is the destroyer, and Vishnu is the preserver. Brahma's job was creation of the world and all creatures. His name should not be confused with **Brahman**, who is the supreme god force present within all things. Many Hindus believe that Shiva's powers of destruction and recreation are used to destroy the illusions and imperfections of this world, paving the way for beneficial change. According to the Hindu belief, this destruction is not arbitrary, but constructive.

Vishnu is a personal god and a protector of this realm. The Buddha was an incarnation of the god Vishnu according to some Hindu sects. Vishnu's purpose is to return to the earth in troubled times and restore the balance of good and evil. It is believed that he has been incarnated nine times (taking on various forms known as avatars). Some Hindus believe that he will be reincarnated one last time close to the end of this world.

POWERFUL IDEAS BOX: NOTABLE AVATARS OF VISHNU

Vishnu has appeared in various incarnations nine times on this earth.

Rama was a greatest warrior. In this form, he kills the demon King Ravana, who abducted his wife Sita.

Krishna was a great thinker and is the hero of the *Mahabharata*, an epic poem. He also delivered his famous message known as the *Baghavad Gita*.

Buddha appeared in the fifth-century BCE and founded the teaching of Buddhism.

Kalki is expected to appear at the end of this present age of decline. He will be a person on earth appearing seated on a white horse.

Buddhism and The Buddha

A philosophical tradition, founded by Gautama Siddhartha Buddha in the fifth-century BCE, that took on various forms as a religion and spread throughout Asia. In a sense, it is related to Hinduism in the same way that Judaism is related to Christianity (in that the Buddhist teachings come out of earlier ideas found in Hinduism in the same way that Christian ideas come out of earlier teachings found in Judaism).

Although many ideas are similar, there are various differences, and Buddhism is a distinct philosophical/religious system. The primary difference is that Buddhist do not worship the large Parthenon of deities found in Hinduism. Some Buddhists make offerings to the various Buddhas, but do not necessarily worship the Buddhas as god. It is important to note that most schools of Buddhism recognize various Buddhas beyond the historical one. Some lived human lives as Gautama Siddhartha did, and other Buddhas exist in other realms and realities. The Tibetans, for example, recognize Padmasambhāva, (also known as Guru Rinpoche), founder of Buddhism in Tibet as a Buddha.

Regardless of the school or precise practices, Buddhism attempts to help the individual conquer the suffering and mutability of human existence through the elimination of desire and ego and attainment of the state of nirvana. This is done by mitigating the past negative karma of past lives. There are various schools and sects of Buddhism. Some schools focus on prayer and ritual, and other schools focus on meditation or study.

POWERFUL ANALYSIS

Do you believe in karma? Why or why not?

The Buddha's Eightfold Noble Path and Four Noble Truths

Buddha's answer to the central problem of life is captured by what is known as the "**Four Noble Truths**." (1) *The Truth of Suffering*, there is suffering; (2) *The Truth of the Cause of Suffering*, suffering has specific and identifiable causes (ignorance, ego, attachment, and desire); (3) *The Truth of the Ending of Suffering*, suffering can be ended by letting go of the causes of suffering; and (4) *The Truth of the Path Leading to the Ending of Suffering*, the way to end suffering is through enlightened living, as expressed in the **Eightfold Path**.

POWERFUL IDEAS BOX: THE EIGHTFOLD PATH

1) Right Understanding

To understand the Law of Cause and Effect and the Four Noble Truths.

2) Right Attitude

Let go of thoughts of greed and anger.

3) Right Speech

Avoid lying, gossip, and harsh speech.

4) Right Action

Not to destroy any life, not to steal or commit adultery.

5) Right Livelihood

Avoid occupations that bring harm to oneself and others.

6) Right Effort

Work hard to do one's best in the right direction.

7) Right Mindfulness

Always being aware and attentive.

8) Right Concentration

Make the mind steady and calm in order to realize the true nature of things.

Meditation and Practice

There is not a uniform system of practice and study. In fact, there is no uniform set of Buddhist writings. There are various mantras and sutras found throughout the Buddhist community. Mantras are mystical symbols or sounds that are written or chanted. Sutras are religious text. Some of these texts are attributed to the Buddha or a close disciple, but others are written by various other Buddhist masters since the time of the Buddha. Many practitioners of Buddhism and other Eastern religions will have a small alter or place to meditate at home. Offerings and prayers are often performed on a daily basis.

Photo courtesy of Matthew Schuh.

Powerful Thnkers: Jetsun Milarepa

Milarepa was originally a practitioner of black magic. He studied the dark practices, in an effort to avenge his suffering at the hands of his aunt and uncle, whom stole his property and inheritance and made him, his mother, and his sister work as slaves in their own home and lands. He sent a powerful storm to his village that killed many people and fled into exile. He eventually studied under the Tibetan Master *Marpa the Translator* and spent many years suffering at his master's hands (so that he could remove the negative karma he had generated by his previous actions). He achieved enlightenment in a single lifetime, by means of decades of solitary meditation and practice. He is honored by the title Jetsun which is a Tibetan title meaning "venerable" or "reverend".

Two books, *The Life of Milarepa* and *The 100,000 songs of Milarepa*, recount various aspects of his life and practice. He was also renowned for the practice of an ancient yoga known as Tummo, or inner fire. He is said to have been able to melt ice and snow and live in the mountains in just rags because of the heat he was able to generate with the yoga. Milarepa's advice to those seeking enlightenment was, "Life is short, and the time of death is uncertain; so apply yourself to meditation. Avoid doing evil, and acquire merit, to the best of your ability, even at the cost of life itself. In short, act so that you will have no cause to be ashamed of yourselves; and hold fast to this rule".

Lao Tzu, Founder of Taoism

Lao Tzu (ca. 570 BCE), the founder of Taoism, regarded that the Tao is ineffable and beyond our ability to alter or change. He emphasized the importance of effortless non-striving and living in accordance with the principles of the universe. These principles are found in the Tao, which is a single force that guides events in the universe. Lao Tzu believed that human life, like everything else in the universe, is constantly influenced by outside forces. He believed "simplicity" to be the key to truth and freedom. Lao Tzu encouraged his followers to observe and seek to understand the laws of nature, to develop intuition and build up personal power, and to use that power to lead life with love and without force.

The Tao, Ying, and Yang

All of us have seen the yin–yang symbol, but few of us realize its relationship to Taoism. The main idea is that the universe is run by a single principle, the Tao, or "Great Ultimate." The Tao itself can be divided into two opposite principles, or two principles that oppose one another in their actions, yin and yang. All the opposites one perceives in the universe can be reduced to one of the opposite forces. The yin and yang represent all the opposite principles one finds in the universe. Under yang are the principles of maleness, the sun, creation, heat, light, heaven, dominance, and so on, and under yin are the principles of femaleness, the moon, completion, cold, darkness, material forms, submission, and so on.

Each of these principles produce the other: Heaven creates the ideas of things under yang, the earth produces their material forms under yin, and vice versa; creation occurs under the principle of yang, the completion of the created thing occurs under yin, and vice versa, and so on.

The yin and yang accomplish changes in the universe through the five material agents, or *wu hsing*, which both produce one another and overcome one another. All change in the universe can be explained by the workings of yin and yang and the progress of the five material agents (wood, fire, metal, water, and earth) as they either produce one another or overcome one another. Yin–yang and the five agents explain all events within the universe.

Feng Shui

The principles of Taoism serve as the foundation of the art of **Feng Shui**. Feng Shui is an art of divination (or predicting the future) and a method of influencing our destiny, which is based on Taoist principles. For the most part, the knowledge of Feng Shui has been a closely guarded secret in the East and completely misunderstood in the West. There are various schools of Feng Shui and books that find their way to Western books stores are usually a jumbled mess. There is much more to the practice such as buying a bamboo plant and placing it in your living room.

For thousands of years, Feng Shui masters and their few handpicked "in house" students tightly guarded ancient classical Feng Shui concepts and formulas.

Its secrets poetically disguised in Chinese verses called the *Classics*. This secrecy made Feng Shui difficult to comprehend. Only masters with lifetimes of training and experience knew how to use these secrets to keep men in power, win battles, and amass wealth. Historically, only noble and high ranking people were allowed to engage in Feng Shui practices. In an effort to discover the secrets of Feng Shui's power, some sought to become scholars of the Classics. Others paid astronomical prices to obtain formulas hidden in various classical texts on the subject.

Powerful Thinkers: Angel de Para

Photo courtesy of Angel De Para, Earthluck International.

Master Angel de Para is a modern Feng Shui practitioner that lives in the United States. He has studied under many of the world's leading Feng Shui masters and routinely travels around the world to continue his studies and to provide Feng Shui readings. He has worked to gain deeper levels of understanding of the art and has studied many of the classical teachings and textbooks. With a background in aeronautic quality control, he has rigorously applied scientific methods and practice to demonstrate the veracity (or truth) of Feng Shui practices. He has worked to test the various theories and formulas by means of extensive, worldwide research, observation, application, and documentation.

Through his rigorous studies and private practice, he further discovered and continues to systematically prove a multitude of his own formulas and theories (based upon the classical teachings that go back thousands of years in the East). He has been trained in various schools, but his practice is most heavily based in a school of Feng

Shui known as Flying Stars. This school incorporates an element of time which changes with each lunar cycle. He is also working to advance Feng Shui practices with twenty-first century applications. His teachings clarify and transform the many misconceptions and ineffective formulas that are confusing and frustrating those who want to learn and practice authentic Feng Shui.

Through his extensive experience as a highly effective practitioner, he found the teachings of his masters to be strong; however, the methodology of applying Feng Shui needed to adapt to the many changes in our universe. Changes in our means of social interaction and communication, the way we conduct business, construct buildings, apply science, create economic strategies, and so on. Currently, Master de Para is the only Feng Shui master who has preserved the essence of the ancient art while scientifically developing it to synchronize with our modern world.

Confucius and the Confucian Tradition

Confucius (ca. 550 BCE) was the founder of one of the most dominant system of thought in China. He wrote with an emphasis toward the perfectibility of people and their ability to affect things for the better. Confucius himself had a simple moral and political teaching: to love others, to live with honor, to act ethical not egoistically, and to practice "reciprocity," that is "don't do to others what you would not want yourself."

Confucius was very critical of the government. He believed that government and rulers should lead by example, not by force. He felt that a government based upon laws and punishments could keep people in line, but governments led by rulers that exemplified virtues and good manners would enable people to act socially and to control themselves. This was seldom the case during his lifetime and China was in a nearly perpetual state of civil war with various factions controlling the country. His critical views regarding the behavior of the government bureaucrats, and of the abuses of civil Chinese authority led to his teachings being banned at various times throughout Chinese history.

Conclusion

There are thousands of religions that exist in the world today. There are hundreds of variations of the four that have been mentioned in this chapter. No single chapter in an introductory textbook can do justice to the topics of Eastern religions. Thousand of books have been written on each of the four religions discussed and on the hundreds of other religions that were omitted. In closing, religion and practice are often integrated into everyday life and culture in the East, so that there is no separation at times between secular and religious life.

READINGS

Theos Bernard entered Columbia University in the fall of 1934 and was awarded the degree of Masters of Arts (AM) in 1936. He authored several books *Heaven Lies Within Us* and *Penthouse of the Gods*, which were both published following his trips to India and Tibet that took place from 1936 to 1937. Upon travelling to Tibet, he was recognized by the Tibetan religious leaders as a reincarnation of a great Buddhist teacher. In his works, at times, he seems to represent himself as a reincarnation of the Buddha Padmasambhāva.

The Tibetans were generally wary of outsiders, but Bernard was able to gain access to the most secret temples, monasteries, and religious practices. He has also given many books by the Tibetan leaders (books that number in the hundreds and may have been otherwise lost as a result of the Chinese occupation of Tibet). All of the books were written in Tibetan, and few have yet to be translated into other languages. In his work, *Hinduism*, he gives a basic introduction to Hindu beliefs and practices.

Hinduism

There is innate in the human heart a metaphysical hunger to know and understand what lies beyond the mysterious and illusive veil of nature. This is true from savage to savant. Each in his own way, according to his own capacity, tries to fathom the eternal mystery of life. From the beginning of time, teachers have endeavoured to bridge the gap between the seen and the unseen and to show cause for the inescapable experiences of sorrow and suffering that engulf mankind. But the questions still remain: What is the nature of Reality? What is the nature of human existence? What is the cause of pleasure and pain? How can Liberation be attained?

The solutions and explanations offered by man range from the simplest superstitions to the most subtle philosophical speculations. In the West, man's perceptual knowledge of the external world has been his measuring rod, his basis for theorizing. The primitive who is unable to see beyond the physical manifestation of forces displayed by nature constructs an animism or a pantheism; the scientist examining the depths of matter with his microscope and sweeping the heavens with his telescope postulates a materialism. Nowhere is there any record. Mystery still remains.

Since the dawn of Western Civilization, there have been few achievements in the realm of philosophy that have been able to out-live the scientific findings of a single century. With the advent of every new discovery, we have to revise our scheme of things. The entire sea of science is strewn with theories that have had to be abandoned because the inventive genius of man has

From *Hindu Philosophy* by Theos Bernard, PH.D, The Philosophical Thoughts Library, Inc., 1947.

been able to bring to light new facts that would not fit into the previous theories. The latest ideas are always called improvements and "evolution."

The West refuses to accept the postulate that the world of mind and matter is but an appearance of a deeper reality which lies beyond the perception of our senses, regardless of how magnified these may be by powerful instruments of precision. One of the reasons for this is due to the preconceived notion that man cannot know metaphysical truths by direct experience; therefore, at best, metaphysical truths can only be speculations, inferences, or ungrounded faith. Even if it were possible, the West maintains that no man has ever attained such supreme knowledge. Another attitude is that all systems of thought must be mutually contradictive, and that, if one of them be true, the rest must be false. There is little place left for various interpretations of a single philosophy to suit different minds.

In the Orient, it has been accepted that man can know metaphysical truths by direct experience. He need not depend upon speculation, inference, or faith. The literature is replete with the writings of men who are said to know the whole truth of Nature and human existence, and the teachings of these men have been set forth in the philosophical systems of ancient India.

Purpose of Hindū Philosophy

All systems of Hindū Philosophy are in complete agreement that the purpose of philosophy is the extinction of sorrow and suffering and that the method is by the acquisition of knowledge of the true nature of things which aims to free man from the bondage of ignorance which all teachers agree is the cause of human suffering.

Hindū Philosophy does not attempt to train one to discern metaphysical truths; it offers a way of thinking which enables one rationally to understand the reality experienced by self-fulfilled personalities, and thereby to lead one to the realization of Truth. In this light, philosophy is seen as an art of life and not a theory about the universe, for it is the means of attaining the highest aspirations of man. It is not for the discovery, but for the understanding of Truth.

There are said to be three stages by which the student can arrive at this realization of the true nature of things. They are: (1) Faith; (2) Understanding; and (3) Realization. The first stage is that of accepting the laws of nature as taught by the great minds of the past. In the next stage, through the process of analysis, the student arrives at a rational and logical conviction; however, reasoning and speculation about transcendental principles can never lead to more than probability, for there can never be certainty in reason as a means of discovering transcendental truths. At best, reasoning is merely a means of understanding the principles of nature and it is the purpose of philosophy to guide and aid the reasoning of the student. The last stage enables the individual actually to become one with the Ultimate Reality.

This is accomplished through the practice of Yoga. The techniques and methods used for the attainment of this end have been treated at length in a previous book[1] by the author.

These stages are not unlike those employed in teaching geometry. First the student is given the proposition that the sum of the angles of a triangle is equal to two right angles. This must be accepted as axiomatic, until it is finally demonstrated through reason to be an actual fact. Still it is only a rational conviction which does not necessarily carry certainty. The truth of this proposition can be verified only by actually cutting out from a piece of paper a triangle and measuring the angles, thereby actually experiencing beyond any measure of doubt that the sum total of the three angles is 180 degrees or the equivalent of two right angles. This last procedure of obtaining direct knowledge or realization of a geometrical truth might be said to correspond to the realization of transcendental truth through Yoga.

Test of Philosophy

Philosophy is one of life's noblest pursuits; although its wisdom is the reward of few, it ought to be the aspiration of all. If a philosophy is going to satisfy the intellectual life of the modern world, its conclusions must be able to withstand the acid test of analysis in the dry light of reason. Nothing can be taken for granted; the necessity of every assumption must be established. It must be capable of explaining all things from the Great Absolute to a blade of grass; it must not contradict the facts of experience, conceptual or perceptual. Its hypothesis must satisfy all the demands of our nature; it must account for all types of experience: waking, dreaming, sleeping, and those moments which are claimed by the religious ascetic during his deep contemplation. It must be realistic as well as idealistic; it must not be a brutal materialism, worshipping facts and figures and ignoring values, idealizing science and denying spirituality. Nor must it be predominantly a philosophy of values which evades and ignores all connection with facts. It must be comprehensive enough to account for every new discovery of science; it must embrace all the concepts of religion and other philosophical systems. All ideas must receive recognition and find their proper place within the border of its synthesis; every fact of the universe, every aspect of life, every content of experience must immediately fall within the scope of its mould. The March of Science must justify it at every step.

It is not enough merely to interpret reality as perceived by the senses; it must explain both sides of reality, the change and the unchangeable, being and becoming, permanent and impermanent, animate and inanimate. The emphasis on one or the other of these two aspects brings about many of the

---

[1] *Hatha Yoga*, New York, Columbia University Press, 1944.

radical differences in philosophy. The need is to unite them in a deep abiding harmony. All these conditions have been satisfied by the philosophical systems of India.

The Darśanas

According to Indian tradition there is only one Ultimate Reality, but there are six fundamental interpretations of that Reality. These are called the Sad Darśanas or "six insights," because they give man sight of the sensible verities and enable him to understand in the light of reason the super-sensible Truth attainable only through the revealed scriptures or through the experience of ṛṣis (sages). The word darśana comes from the root *dṛś* , "to see," and is the Sanskrit term used for philosophy. The six darśanas constitute the classic philosophical systems of India. They are Nyāya, Vaiśeṣika, Sāṁkhya, Yoga, Mīmāṁsä, and Vedānta. They are not the creation of any one mind nor the discovery of any single individual. The real founders are unknown, and there is considerable controversy as to when they were first reduced to writing, but neither of these conditions detracts from the value of their principles. Together they form a graduated interpretation of the Ultimate Reality, so interrelated that the hypothesis and method of each is dependent upon the other. In no way are they contradictory or antagonistic to one another, for they all lead to the same practical end, knowledge of the Absolute and Liberation of the Soul.

They have many characteristics in common. They all grew out of the Upanisads, the philosophical portion of the Veda which is accepted as the supreme authority; they are delivered in the Sūtra style, that is as aphorisms; as such, they are extremely concise, avoiding all unnecessary repetition and employing a rigid economy of words, making it difficult to understand them correctly in their original form without the use of commentaries, for they use many of the same terms, but each system gives its own meaning to the use of the term. They rest their conclusions on several common concepts: all accept the eternal cycle of Nature which is without beginning and end, and which consists of vast periods of creation, maintenance, and dissolution; all accept the principle of regeneration of the soul that maintains that life and death are but two phases of a single cycle to which the soul is bound and to which it clings because of ignorance of the true nature of things; all accept Dharma as the moral law of the universe that accounts for these eternal cycles of Nature, as well as the destiny of the human soul; all agree that knowledge is the path to freedom and that Yoga is the method to attain final liberation.

Sogyal Rinpoche has been a teacher of the Dalai Lama and founded a number of monstaries and religious centers in America and Europe. In his work, *The Tibetan Book of Living and Dying (1994),* he explains many of the main elements of Tibetan Buddhism in a manner accessible and easy to comprehend for Westerners. This short excerpt details the ideas.

The Tibetan Book of Living and Dying

Death In The Modern World

When I first came to the West, I was shocked by the contrast between the attitudes to death I had been brought up with and those I now found. For all its technological achievements, modern Western society has no real understanding of death or what happens in death or after death.

I learned that people today are taught to deny death, and taught that it means nothing but annihilation and loss. That means that most of the world lives either in denial of death or in terror of it. Even talking about death is considered morbid, and many people believe that simply mentioning death is to risk wishing it upon ourselves.

Others look on death with a naive, thoughtless cheerfulness, thinking that for some unknown reason death will work out all right for them, and that it is nothing to worry about. When I think of them, I am reminded of what one Tibetan master says: "People often make the mistake of being frivolous about death and think, 'Oh well, death happens to everybody. It's not a big deal, it's natural. I'll be fine.' That's a nice theory until one is dying."[3]

Of these two attitudes toward death, one views death as something to scurry away from and the other as something that will just take care of itself. How far they both are from understanding death's true significance!

All the greatest spiritual traditions of the world, including of course Christianity, have told us clearly that death is not the end. They have all handed down a vision of some sort of life to come, which infuses this life that we are leading now with sacred meaning. But despite their teachings, modern society is largely a spiritual desert where the majority imagine that *this life* is all that there is. Without any real or authentic faith in an afterlife, most people live lives deprived of any ultimate meaning.

I have come to realize that the disastrous effects of the denial of death go far beyond the individual: They affect the whole planet. Believing fundamentally that this life is the only one, modern people have developed no long-term vision. So there is nothing to restrain them from plundering the planet for their own immediate ends and from living in a selfish way that

Rinpoche, Sogyal. Excerpts from pp. 7-13 [2689 words] from *The Tibetan Book Living and Dying* by Sogyal Rinpoche and edited by Patrick Gaffney & Andrew Harvey. Copyright © 1993 by Rigpa Fellowship. Reprinted by permission of HarperCollins Publishers.

could prove fatal for the future. How many more warnings do we need, like this one from the former Brazilian Minister for the Environment, responsible for the Amazon rain forest?

> *Modern industrial society is a fanatical religion. We are demolishing, poisoning, destroying all life-systems on the planet. We are signing IOUs our children will not be able to pay ... We are acting as if we were the last generation on the planet. Without a radical change in heart, in mind, in vision, the earth will end up like Venus, charred and dead.*[4]

Fear of death and ignorance of the afterlife are fueling that destruction of our environment that is threatening all of our lives. So isn't it all the more disturbing that people are not taught what death is, or how to die? Or given any hope in what lies after death, and so what really lies behind life? Could it be more ironic that young people are so highly educated in every subject except the one that holds the key to the entire meaning of life, and perhaps to our very survival?

It has often intrigued me how some Buddhist masters I know ask one simple question of people who approach them for teaching: Do you believe in a life after this one? They are not being asked whether they believe in it as a philosophical proposition, but whether they feel it deeply in their heart. The master knows that if people believe in a life after this one, their whole outlook on life will be different, and they will have a distinct sense of personal responsibility and morality. What the masters must suspect is that there is a danger that people who have no strong belief in a life after this one will create a society fixated on short-term results, without much thought for the consequences of their actions. Could this be the major reason why we have created a brutal world like the one in which we are now living, a world with little real compassion?

Sometimes I think that the most affluent and powerful countries of the developed world are like the realm of the gods described in the Buddhist teachings. The gods are said to live lives of fabulous luxury, reveling in every conceivable pleasure, without a thought for the spiritual dimension of life. All seems to go well until death draws near and unexpected signs of decay appear. Then the gods' wives and lovers no longer dare approach them, but throw flowers to them from a distance, with casual prayers that they be reborn again as gods. None of their memories of happiness or comfort can shelter them now from the suffering they face; they only make it more savage. So the dying gods are left to die alone in misery.

The fate of the gods reminds me of the way the elderly, the sick, and the dying are treated today. Our society is obsessed with youth, sex, and power, and we shun old age and decay. Isn't it terrifying that we discard old people when their working life is finished and they are no longer useful? Isn't it disturbing that we cast them into old people's homes, where they die lonely and abandoned?

Isn't it time also that we took another look at how we sometimes treat those suffering with terminal illnesses like cancer and AIDS? I know a number of people who have died from AIDS, and I have seen how often they were treated as outcasts, even by their friends, and how the stigma attached to the disease reduced them to despair, and made them feel their life was disgusting and had in the eyes of the world already ended.

Even when a person we know or love is dying, so often people find they are given almost no idea of how to help them; and when they are dead, we are not encouraged to give any thought to the future of the dead person, how he or she will continue, or how we could go on helping him or her. In fact, any attempt to think along these lines risks being dismissed as nonsensical and ridiculous.

What all of this is showing us, with painful clarity, is that now more than ever before we need a fundamental change in our attitude toward death and dying. Happily, attitudes are beginning to change. The hospice movement, for example, is doing marvelous work in giving practical and emotional care. Yet practical and emotional care are not enough; people who are dying need love and care, but they also need something even more profound. They need to discover a real meaning to death, and to life. Without that, how can we give them ultimate comfort? Helping the dying, then, must include the possibility of spiritual care, because it is only with spiritual knowledge that we can truly face, and understand, death.

I have been heartened by the way in which in recent years the whole subject of death and dying has been opened up in the West by pioneers such as Elisabeth Kübler-Ross and Raymond Moody. Looking deeply into the way that we care for the dying, Elisabeth Kübler-Ross has shown that with unconditional love, and a more enlightened attitude, dying can be a peaceful, even transformative experience. The scientific studies of the many different aspects of the near-death experience that followed the brave work of Raymond Moody have held out to humanity a vivid and strong hope that life does not end with death, and there is indeed a "life after life."

Some, unfortunately, did not really understand the full meaning of these revelations about death and dying. They went to the extreme of glamorizing death, and I have heard of tragic cases of young people who committed suicide because they believed death was beautiful and an escape from the depression of their lives. But whether we fear death and refuse to face it, or whether we romanticize it, death is trivialized. Both despair and euphoria about death are an evasion. Death is neither depressing nor exciting; it is simply a fact of life.

How sad it is that most of us only begin to appreciate our life when we are on the point of dying. I often think of the words of the great Buddhist master Padmasambhava: "Those who believe they have plenty of time get ready only at the time of death. Then they are ravaged by regret. But isn't it far too late?" What more chilling commentary on the modern world could there be than that most people die unprepared for death, as they have lived, unprepared for life?

The Journey through Life and Death

According to the wisdom of Buddha, we *can* actually use our lives to prepare for death. We do not have to wait for the painful death of someone close to us or the shock of terminal illness to force us into looking at our lives. Nor are we condemned to go out empty-handed at death to meet the unknown. We can begin, here and now, to find meaning in our lives. We can make of every moment an opportunity to change and to prepare—wholeheartedly, precisely, and with peace of mind—for death and eternity.

In the Buddhist approach, life and death are seen as one whole, where death is the beginning of another chapter of life. Death is a mirror in which the entire meaning of life is reflected.

This view is central to the teachings of the most ancient school of Tibetan Buddhism. Many of you will have heard of the *Tibetan Book of the Dead*. What I am seeking to do in this book is to explain and expand the *Tibetan Book of the Dead*, to cover not only death but life as well, and to fill out in detail the whole teaching of which the *Tibetan Book of the Dead* is only a part. In this wonderful teaching, we find the whole of life and death presented together as a series of constantly changing transitional realities known as *bardos*. The word "bardo" is commonly used to denote the intermediate state between death and rebirth, but in reality bardos *are occurring continuously throughout both life and death*, and are junctures when the possibility of liberation, or enlightenment, is heightened.

The bardos are particularly powerful opportunities for liberation because there are, the teachings show us, certain moments that are much more powerful than others and much more charged with potential, when whatever you do has a crucial and far-reaching effect. I think of a bardo as being like a moment when you step toward the edge of a precipice; such a moment, for example, is when a master introduces a disciple to the essential, original, and innermost nature of his or her mind. The greatest and most charged of these moments, however, is the moment of death.

So from the Tibetan Buddhist point of view, we can divide our entire existence into four continuously interlinked realities: (1) life, (2) dying and death, (3) after death, and (4) rebirth. These are known as the four bardos: (1) the natural bardo of this life, (2) the painful bardo of dying, (3) the luminous bardo of *dharmata*, and (4) the karmic bardo of becoming....

... Our exploration necessarily begins with a direct reflection on what death means and the many facets of the truth of impermanence—the kind of reflection that can enable us to make rich use of this life while we still have time, and ensure that when we die it will be without remorse or self-recrimination at having wasted our lives. As Tibet's famous poet saint, Milarepa, said: "My religion is to live—and die—without regret."

Contemplating deeply on the secret message of impermanence—what lies in fact beyond impermanence and death—leads directly to the heart of the ancient and powerful Tibetan teachings: the introduction to the essential "nature of mind." Realization of the nature of mind, which you could call our innermost essence, that truth we all search for, is the key to understanding life and death. For what happens at the moment of death is that the ordinary mind and its delusions die, and in that gap the boundless sky-like nature of our mind is uncovered. This essential nature of mind is the background to the whole of life and death, like the sky, which folds the whole universe in its embrace.

The teachings make it clear that if all we know of mind is the aspect of mind that dissolves when we die, we will be left with no idea of what continues, no knowledge of the new dimension of the deeper reality of the nature of mind. So it is vital for us all to familiarize ourselves with the nature of mind while we are still alive. Only then will we be prepared when it reveals itself spontaneously and powerfully at the moment of death; be able to recognize it "as naturally," the teachings say, "as a child running into its mother's lap"; and by remaining in that state, finally be liberated.

A description of the nature of mind leads naturally into a complete instruction on meditation, for meditation is the only way we can repeatedly uncover and gradually realize and stabilize that nature of mind. An explanation will then be given of the nature of human evolution, rebirth, and *karma*, so as to provide you with the fullest possible meaning and context of our path through life and death. . . .

. . . My students often ask me: How do we know what these bardos are, and from where does the astonishing precision of the bardo teachings and their uncannily clear knowledge of each stage of dying, death, and rebirth come? The answer may seem initially difficult to understand for many readers, because the notion of mind the West now has is an extremely narrow one. Despite the major breakthroughs of recent years, especially in mind/body science and transpersonal psychology, the great majority of scientists continue to reduce the mind to no more than physical processes in the brain, which goes against the testimony of thousands of years of experience of mystics and meditators of all religions.

From what source or authority, then, can a book like this be written? The "inner science" of Buddhism is based, as one American scholar puts it, "on a thorough and comprehensive knowledge of reality, on an already assessed, depth understanding of self and environment; that is to say, on the complete enlightenment of the Buddha."[5] The source of the bardo teachings is the enlightened mind, the completely awake buddha mind, as experienced, explained, and transmitted by a long line of masters that stretches back to the Primordial Buddha. Their careful, meticulous—you could almost say scientific—explorations and formulations of their discoveries of mind over many centuries have given us the most complete picture possible of both life and death. It is this complete picture that, inspired by Jamyang Khyentse and all my other great masters, I am humbly attempting to transmit for the very first time to the West.

Eva Wong is a Taoist and Feng Shui master. She has written many books on the technical aspects of feng shui, such as *A Master Course in Feng-Shui* (2001), and on Taoist folklore. This section from Seven Taoist Masters details some of the key teachings of Taoist practice as explained by the main character of the story.

Seven Taoist Masters

On the appointed day, Ma Yü and Sun Yüan-chen approached Wang Ch'ung-yang and formally became his disciples. Wang Ch'ung-yang told them, "The Taoist path is a path of awakening and knowing. Those who walk it will return to the truth. Entrance to the path should be gradual. Your training should follow a sequence, starting from the easy and graduating to the difficult. Those who aspire to cultivate the Tao must first find their original nature. Original nature is the original state of things, or "Earlier Heaven." You must cultivate your original nature until it is smooth and bright. If original nature is not cultivated, feelings will be wild. Untamed feelings are like tigers and dragons. If you cannot tame these animals in you, how can you become one with the void? The Tao is without form. You must dissolve your ego, for the ego is the source of form and attachment. You must learn how to subdue the tiger and the dragon and tame the monkey and the wild horse. A wild intelligence is like a monkey. It plays tricks on you and makes you mistake the impermanent for the real. Egotistic intentions are like wild horses. They drag you away from the purity and stillness of original nature. If you do not tame the wild horse and the mischievous monkey, then you will not understand the mysteries of heaven and earth, the balance of *yin* and *yang*, and the power of silence in moving the universe. The clockwise path is mortality; the counterclockwise path is immortality. To empty the heart of desire and thoughts, to be in the void, is to emerge with the Tao. The Tao cannot be grasped by thoughts. It must be experienced directly with the heart....

. . . When Ch'ung=yang said, "I shall explain original nature to you with a picture. However, understand that original nature cannot be conceptualized or described. My drawing is therefore only an approximation." Taking a brush, he dipped it into some ink and drew a circle on a piece of paper. Inside the circle he drew a dot. Then he said to Ma Tan-yang and Sun Puerh, "Do you know what this represents?" They replied, "Sir, we do not know. Instruct us." Wang Ch'ung-yang said, "The circle represents the undifferentiated whole, a state of existence before heaven and earth emerged. This state is called *Wu-chi*. From *Wu-chi*, *T'ai-chi* is born. This is the dot in the circle. From *T'ai-chi*, everything in the universe is born. The life-giving breath of *T'ai-chi* is the one breath of Earlier Heaven. From the one breath of Earlier Heaven emerges original nature. Original nature was there before we were born. It will be there after we die. Original nature is also called the knowing spirit. It is not born, and it never dies. Everyone has original nature. We do not see it because it is often clouded by craving, desire, and evil thoughts. If we do not sweep away that which hides our original nature, we will lose our connection with Earlier Heaven and be doomed to countless lifetimes of suffering. How does one reconnect with Earlier Heaven? Earlier Heaven must be experienced with the heart of the Tao. If one tries to understand Earlier Heaven with the ego, one will never find it. Earlier Heaven and original nature are in front of us. We cannot see it because the ego has constructed a barrier. If we are able to dissolve the ego, then original nature, or the heart of the Tao, will emerge. When the heart of the Tao emerges, Earlier Heaven will appear. How does one cultivate the heart of the Tao and dissolve the egotistic heart? When a person is ill, simply getting rid of the symptom will not ensure that the illness will never return. The cause of the illness must be eradicated. Similarly, we must find the root of the barriers which separate us from Earlier Heaven. The ancient sages and immortals have understood these causes and have set down guidelines for eradicating them. I shall transmit their teachings to you.

"If you want to get rid of the sickness of spirit and body, you must get to its cause. If you know the cause, then you will know the cure. The primary cause of ill health is none other than craving. Craving creates the obstacles to health. These obstacles are desire for liquor, sexual desire, greed for riches, and bad temper. Those who wish to cultivate health and longevity must first remove these obstacles. Sever all attachment to external things and dissolve desires. Then the internal illness will disappear and the root of ill health will be eradicated. Once health is regained, the cultivation of the Tao and the attainment of immortality are possible.

"First, let us discuss the obstacle of liquor. Many people know that liquor can disrupt reason and therefore want to abstain from it. Others abstain because they are persuaded to do so by friends and relatives. Yet others abstain because the law forbids it. However, when they see liquor or when they see others drink, they desire it. Even if no liquor has touched their lips, the very craving shows that they have not overcome the obstacle. Craving originates in thoughts. Even before the thought becomes action, craving already exists and the damage has been done. Getting rid of the obstacle of liquor requires the absence of craving in thought as well as in action.

"Now, take sexual desire. Many people know that sexual desire drains the generative energy and want to abstain from it. However, when they see an attractive person they fantasize about having sex or secretly desire sexual company. When these thoughts arise, even if one is not engaged in sex physically, one is already prey to the obstacle. You now understand that the cause of craving after liquor and sex lies in the mind. If you want to remove these obstacles, you must start with eradicating the thoughts of desire from your mind. Tame the heart [mind], and the intentions will not run wild. When the heart is emptied of desire, the cause of ill health will disappear. Cut the attachments externally, and the internal injuries will be healed. Your heart should be clear and calm like a still lake reflecting the light of the moon. If ripples appear on the water, then the image of the moon will be distorted and the Tao will never be realized in you.

"How does one go about eradicating the desire for liquor and sex? The ancient sages offer this advice: If it is not proprietous, do not look at it. If it is not proprietous, do not do it. If it is in front of you, behave as if you saw nothing. If it is spoken to you, behave as if you heard nothing. The Buddhists teach: "Forget the other, forget oneself, forget everyone." The Taoists teach: "Look but do not see it; hear but do not listen." [That is, if you are not attached to the liquor or the sexual attraction, those things will lose their attractiveness. Attraction is not in the object itself but in the attitude that we carry around with us.] If you can do this, then you will have eradicated the desire for liquor and sex.

"As for riches, this is a difficult obstacle to overcome. There are those who are poor and need to work hard to earn a living for themselves and their family. Therefore, they do not have much choice but to focus their attention on acquiring money. People in this condition must live with their karma and wait for another lifetime to relinquish their ties with money. Then there are those who crave riches so that they may display their wealth and earn the respect and admiration of others. Yet further there are those who crave riches for a life of luxury and waste. And then there are those who accumulate riches because they wish to exploit misfortune and see others suffer. It is these latter kinds of craving for riches that prevent one from discovery of the Tao.

"Temper is the result of emotions running wild. There are positive and negative feelings. Positive feelings like compassion, empathy, and humility are to be cultivated, but negative feelings such as anger, bad temper, and cruelty should be dissolved. Bad temper is the result of self-importance. Bad temper is harmful to health because it creates bad *ch'i* in our bodies. Verbal arguments, competitiveness, aggressiveness, impatience, frustration, annoyance are all manifestations of bad temper. How can people with these dispositions attain the Tao?

"If you wish to eradicate the bad temper and the desire for riches, listen to the sages. They give good advice. The Confucianists say, 'Riches that do not rightfully belong to me I see as empty as the floating clouds. Take control of your reason, and you will not lose your temper.' The Buddhists say, 'Do not crave rewards. Virtue comes from the ability to resist provocation.' The Taoists say, 'Know the illusion of material goods. Cultivate compassion, and your temper will be calmed.' Take these words of advice and you will be able to eradicate bad temper and desire for riches.

"To eradicate the four obstacles to health—liquor, sexual desire, riches, and bad temper—one must cultivate the heart. Once the heart is tamed, the cause of ill health will disappear. The Confucianists tell us to 'awaken.' The Buddhists tell us to 'understand.' The Taoists tell us to 'act intuitively.' First, we need to *awaken* to the fact that we have fallen prey to the obstacles. Second, we need to *understand* what the obstacles are and their causes. Lastly, we need to *act intuitively*, that is, to act spontaneously from a heart that is tamed of desire and craving. If you can do these things, then you will have no problem attaining the Tao."

Ma Tan-yang and Sun Pu-erh asked about meditation. Wang Ch'ung-yang said, "In meditation all thoughts must cease. When the ego is dead, the spirit emerges. When you sit, sit on a cushion. Loosen your clothing. At the hour of *tzu* (11:00 P.M.), cross your legs gently and sit facing east. Clasp your hands together and place them in front of your body. Your back should be straight. Strike your teeth together and swallow your saliva. Place the tongue against the palate of your mouth. You should be alert in listening, but do not be attached to sounds. Let your eyes drop, but do not close them. Focus on the light that you see in front of you and concentrate on the Lower *t'an-t'ien*. In meditation it is very important to stop thinking. If thoughts arise, the spirit will not be pure, and your efforts of cultivation will come to nothing. In addition, you should drop all feelings. Once feelings arise, the heart will not be still, and the attainment of the Tao is impossible."

Wang Ch'ung-yang continued, "Sit on a cushion and you will be able to sit long and not feel tired. Loosen your clothing so the movement of internal energy will not be constricted. The hour of *tzu* is when the first ray of *yang* appears. Face east because the breath of life flows in from the east at the hour of first *yang*. Clasp your hands in the *t'ai-chi* symbol, because it symbolizes emptiness of form. Sit with your back straight, because only with a vertical spine can the energy rise to the head. Close your mouth and place the tongue against the palate so that the internal energy cannot dissipate. The ear is associated with generative energy. Being attached to sound will dissipate this energy. Do not close your eyes, for they let the light in to shine on your spirit. If you close your eyes, the spirit will be dimmed. If you open them too wide, the spirit will escape. Therefore you should lower the lids but not close them. Concentrate on the Lower *t'an-t'ien* as if to reflect the light of your eyes on it because here is the mystery of all things. Minimize speech, as this conserves vital energy. Rest your ears, as this conserves generative energy. Dissolve thoughts to conserve spiritual energy. When all these energies are not dissipated, then you will attain immortality."

Ma Tan-yang and Sun Pu-erh thanked Wang Ch'ung-yang for his instructions. Wang Ch'ung-yang added, "Staying on the path of the Tao requires discipline. You should take this knowledge seriously and practice it all the time. Otherwise, even though you know what to do, you will accomplish nothing." Ma Tan-yang and Sun Pu-erh bowed and left. They returned to their rooms and began to meditate according to Wang Ch'ung-yang's instructions. A few months passed in this way, and they began to experience changes in their bodies. Thinking that they had now grasped all the teachings of the Tao, they stopped visiting Wang Ch'ung-yang for further instruction.

One day Ma Tan-yang was meditating in his room and saw Wang Ch'ung-yang enter. Ma Tan-yang stood up to welcome his teacher. Wang Ch'ung-yang said, "The Tao is limitless. It can be used continuously and yet never dry up. It is flexible and can cloak itself in countless shapes. Do not hold on to one of its many manifestations. Be sincere and humble in your learning. Only then will your body benefit from your training."

Wang Ch'ung-yang continued to teach Ma Tan-yang. "If your heart is not true, you cannot cultivate the Tao. Every action and every thought must come from a true heart. If your heart is sick, then it must be healed. Tame the selfish heart with a selfless heart. Tame the desirous heart with a heart of reason. Tame the heart of extreme tendencies with moderation. Tame the proud heart with a humble heart. Find where the problems are and counter each of them. If you are able to do this, then the problems will never arise. Your heart will be like the spring wind. Your mind will be bright as the moon in a clear sky. Your heart will be open like the wide plains, and your being will be as still and rooted as the mountains. The internal energy will circulate through your body. Without realizing it, you will have attained the Tao."

KEY TERMS

Brahman is the supreme God force present within all things according to the Hindu beliefs.

Buddhism is a philosophical tradition, founded by Gautama Siddhartha Buddha in the fifth-century BCE, which took on various forms as a religion and spread throughout Asia.

Eightfold path is the path the Buddha says we must follow to reach enlightenment.

Feng Shui an art of divination, which is based on Taoist principles.

Four noble truths are the philosophy of Buddha on suffering and happiness.

Hinduism refers to the collection of faiths that are believed to have originated in India, but other scholars believe that it was brought to India thousands of years ago by nomadic peoples. It is a polytheistic system with various gods and goddesses as well as lesser deities.

Karma, sometimes known as the Law of Cause and Effect, refers to the notion that all of our actions bring about positive or negative consequences for ourselves now or in the future.

Reincarnation is the belief that either our soul, consciousness, or some other aspect of our spiritual being is reborn into a physical body.

Samsara is the cycle of birth, death, and rebirth that all being undergo until they achieve enlightenment.

Taoism was founded by Lao Tzu (ca. 570 BCE), founder of Taoism, held that the Tao is ineffable and beyond our ability to alter or change. It is believed that human life, like everything else in the universe, is constantly influenced by outside forces that act in accordance with the Tao.

QUESTIONS FOR DISCUSSION AND REVIEW

1. Compare and contrast various views of Hinduism, Buddhism, and Taoism.
2. Explain the connection between the Tao, Ying, and Yang.
3. Articulate how principles of Taoism serve as the foundation of the art of Feng Shui.
4. Summarize, explain, and evaluate the main points of the reading by Theos Bernard.
5. Summarize, explain, and evaluate the main points of the reading by Sogyal Rinpoche.

SUGGESTED READINGS

Alexander, E. (2012). *Proof of Heaven: A Neurosurgeon's Journey into the Afterlife.*

Bernard, T. (1939). *Heaven Lies Within Us.*

Bernard, T. (1945). *Philosophical Foundations of India.*

Bhaskarananda, S. (2002). *The Essentials of Hinduism: A Comprehensive Overview of the World's Oldest Religion.*

Burpo, T. (2010). *Heaven is for Real.*

Hill, N. (1937). *Think and Grow Rich.*

Internet Encyclopedia of Philosophy. A peer-reviewed academic resource. Available from http://www.iep.utm.edu/

Milarepa, J. (1999). *The Hundred Thousand Songs of Milarepa.* (Chang, G.C.C. transl.).

Padmasambhāva. (2008). *Natural Liberation: Padmasambhāva's Teaching on the Six Bardos.* (Wallace, B.A. transl.)

Ray, R. (2002) *Secrets of the Varja World: The Tantric Buddhism of Tibet.*

Rinpoche, D.K. (1999). *Guru Yoga.* (Ricard, M. transl.)

Rinpoche, D.K. (1992). *The Heart Treasure of the Enlightened Ones.* (Ricard, M. transl.)

Rinpoche, K. K. (1993). *Luminous Mind: The Way of the Buddha.*

Rinpoche, K.P.S. and Rinpoche, K.T.D. (2008). *The Dark Red Amulet: Oral Instructions on the Practice of Vajrakilaya. (Samye Translation group transl.).*

Rinpoche, S. (1994) *The Tibetan Book of Living and Dying.*

Stanford Encyclopedia of Philosophy. Available from http://plato.stanford.edu/

Veenhof, D. (2011). *White Lama: The Life of Tantric Yogi Theos Bernard, Tibet's Emissary to the New World.*

Weiss, B. (1988). *Many Lives, Many Masters.*

Wong, E. *(2001). A Master Course in Feng Shui.*

Wong, E. (2004). *Seven Taoist Masters.*

Wong, E. (2011). *Taoism: An Essential Guide.*

Twentieth-Century American Philosophy— "What Is, 'Is'?"

8

Upon completing this chapter, students should be able to meet the following Learning Outcomes:

8.1 Explain the idea of analytic philosophy in contrast with other schools of philosophy.

8.2 Compare and contrast the logical positivist to the natural language theorist.

8.3 Explain the role of the "Vienna Circle" in the history of analytic philosophy.

Analytic philosophy was created as a distinct school of philosophical thought by many of the great minds in the first half of the twentieth century. There were various founders: Bertrand Russell is one of the founders of analytic philosophy along with his predecessor Gottlob Frege, as well as his colleague G. E. Moore, and their student Ludwig Wittgenstein.

"Modern analytical empiricism . . . differs from that of Locke, Berkeley, and Hume by its incorporation of mathematics and its development of a powerful logical technique. It is thus able, in regard to certain problems, to achieve definite answers, which have the quality of science rather than of philosophy. It has the advantage, in comparison with the philosophies of the system-builders, of being able to tackle its problems one at a time, instead of having to invent at one stroke a block theory of the whole universe. Its methods, in this respect, resemble those of science. I have no doubt that, in so far as philosophical knowledge is possible, it is by such methods that it must be sought; I have also no doubt that, by these methods, many ancient problems are completely soluble"

—*Bertrand Russell, 1945, A History of Western Philosophy*

What differentiates analytic philosophy from other school of philosophical thought is unclear. In his book, *The Dialogue of Reason* (1986), L. Jonathan Cohen (1923–2006) argues that there are three ways by which analytic philosophy may be separated from other philosophical schools of thought. The first possibility is that analytic philosophy holds different foundational doctrines or tenets than other areas of philosophy. This was the view adopted by the **logical positivist (or empirical positivist)** at the beginning of the last century. In the view of the logical positivist, only statements verifiable either logically or empirically are cognitively meaningful—anything else (primarily metaphysics) is meaningless or nonsense.

The second possibility as to what differentiates analytic philosophy as a distinct school of philosophy is that it employs doctrines distinct from other branches of philosophy. This notion was employed by the **natural language theorists** in the middle of the last century. Finally, the third possibility is that analytic philosophy is concerned with different problems than other branches of philosophy. Jonathan Cohen argues for the third possibility in his book and claims that what separate analytic philosophy from other schools of philosophy is that it is primarily focused on "normative problems about reasons and reasoning."

Powerful Thinkers: L. Jonathan Cohen

L. Jonathan Cohen was a fellow of the Queen's College, Oxford (1957–1990) and of the British Academy. He contributed to the various areas of philosophy including epistemology, logic, the philosophy of law, language, psychology, and philosophy of science. He was awarded a scholarship to Balliol College, Oxford, where he read literature and began his interest in philosophy. His studies, however, were interrupted by the World War II. Cohen trained as a codebreaker, and after learning Japanese, he served in British naval intelligence in the Far East from 1942 to 1945.

Upon completing his studies, he began his career at Queen's College, Oxford. In his second book, *The Diversity of Meaning* (1962), he examined the nature of meaning from the different perspectives of linguistics, sociology, the history of ideas, as well as analytic philosophy. The book was one expression of his dissent from the prevailing philosophical fashions in Britain.

In his work, *The Probable and the Provable* (1977), he developed a "Baconian" analysis of probability, which is opposed to the more standard a "Pascalian" analysis of probability. The analysis provided unique solutions to a number of open problems and paradoxes, including a proof of when the testimony of two witnesses corroborates one another. He applied his inductive logic to questions of metaphor, explanation and skepticism.

"I found myself filled with semi-mystical feelings about beauty . . . and with a desire almost as profound as that of the Buddha to find some philosophy which should make human life endurable"

—*Bertrand Russell, 1872–1970, The Autobiography of Bertrand Russell, 1956.*

Powerful Thinkers: Michael Dummett

Michael Dummett (1925–2011) supports many of Cohen's claims regarding the nature and foundation of analytic philosophy in his book, *Truth and Other Enigmas* (1978). He says that, "The goal of [analytic] philosophy is the analysis of the structure of thought; secondly, that the study of thought is to be sharply distinguished from the psychological process of thinking; and finally, the only proper method for analyzing thought consist in the analysis of language . . . the acceptance of these three tenets is common to the entire analytical school."

POWERFUL ANALYSIS: ONLY THE ANALYSTS?

Is the analytic school the only one in the history of philosophy to deal with "normative problems about reasons and reasoning"? Or is that what every philosopher since Socrates has done?

Logical Positivism

Logical positivism is a twentieth-century school of philosophy, which argues that all meaningful propositions (or statements/utterances) are either: analytic, verifiable, or confirmable by means of observation and experiment. The proponents of this view argue that metaphysical theories are therefore strictly meaningless (as such the mind or soul do not exist, or at least cannot be confirmed, since they cannot be observed). This view is also sometimes known as logical empiricism.

One of its chief proponents and founders was Rudolph Carnap. The notion of analytic can be stated as "true by virtue of the meaning of the words or concepts used to express it," so that its denial would be a self-contradiction. An alternative definition, one that is proposed by natural language theorist, is that "analytic statements tend to not alter the form of its words and to use word order rather than inflection or agglutination to express grammatical structure."

Powerful Thinkers: Vienna Cirlce and A. J. Ayer

The "Vienna Circle" has been described as a group of philosophical thugs or as the patron saints of twentieth-century philosophy—the truth, no doubt, is somewhere in the middle. The members of the "Vienna Circle" founded a school of thought known as empirical or logical positivism, which is, in fact, a recognized school of philosophy. As such, the group has as much right to be a "school" of philosophy as any other "school" developed in the twentieth century.

As noted above, some have called this group, which is traditionally known as the "the Vienna Circle," "a gang of philosophers" (which is certainly the most boring "gang" ever assembled). The group included various philosophers including Rudolph Carnap and Kurt Godel, they were the founders of the group, which started meeting in Vienna in the twentieth century—hence the name.

The so-called "Vienna Circle" dedicated themselves to the reconciling philosophy with the new sciences and so determined to take it upon themselves to evaluate the truth solely in terms of the empirical verifiability or logic of language—which lead philosophy down an interesting path, from which it is still recovering. This was termed either of "Logical Positivism" or "Empirical Positivism."

A. J. Ayers's *Language, Truth and Logic* (1936) represent a modified version of logical Positivism, which he called "logical empiricism." The book questioned all aspects of philosophy that did not deal with what he consecrated empirical or verifiable issues. He called into question the entire enterprise of metaphysics by saying it was "nonsense" and that questions of value were nonexistent . . . which leads to various other issues (like why get out of bed since nothing have axiological significance), which they missed.

It is interesting to note that Ayer himself realized the shortcomings of *Language, Truth and Logic*, and he recanted and/or clarified many of his views in the introduction to the 1946 edition of the book.

"True philosophic contemplation, finds its satisfaction in every enlargement of the not-Self, in everything that magnifies the objects contemplated, and thereby the subject contemplating. Everything, in contemplation, that is personal or private, everything that depends upon habit, self-interest, or desire, distorts the object, and hence impairs the union which the intellect seeks"

—*Bertrand Russell, 1912, The Value of Philosophy*

Natural Language Philosophy

Natural Language Philosophy (also known as Linguistic Philosophy or Ordinary Language Philosophy) approaches traditional philosophical problems as being rooted in misunderstandings in a language. The proponents of the view claim that many of the philosophical problems undertaken as a result of a misuse or misunderstanding of language.

Some philosophers argue that it is a separate school of philosophy and is a reaction against the analytic philosophy, while others argue it as just an extension of the analytic tradition Ludwig Josef Johann Wittgenstein (1889–1951), Gilbert Ryle (1900–1976), J. L. Austin (1911–1960), Peter Strawson (1919–2006), and John Wisdom (1904–1993) were all proponents of this school of thought. Of the group, Wittgenstein was ultimately the most accomplished (as well as misunderstood of the group).

Wittgenstein's early and late works (if they do not contradict one another) certainly provide very different philosophical views regarding the nature of language and of philosophy itself. His philosophy is often divided into an early period, exemplified by the *Tractatus*, and a later period, articulated in the *Philosophical Investigations*. The early Wittgenstein was concerned with the logical relationship between propositions and the world and believed that by providing an account of the logic underlying this relationship, he had solved all philosophical problems. The later Wittgenstein rejected many of the assumptions of the *Tractatus*, arguing that the meaning of words is best understood as their use within a given language game.

Some members of this school of thought were willing to accept metaphysical statements (or at least entertain them) such as Wittgenstein. As he said, "What we do is bring words back from their metaphysical to their everyday usage."

"Philosophy is a battle against the bewitchment of our intelligence by means of language"

—*Ludwig Wittgenstein*

READINGS

Alan Montefiore (b. 1926) and Bernard Williams (1929–2003) collaborated on a collection of essays on analytic philosophy published in 1966. Both were leaders in the field. They both had a great influence on philosophical thought in the latter half of the twentieth century.

The Analytic Tradition

WHAT constitutes a philosophical movement? The movements or schools of the past had their unity—or were given it by the historian of philosophy—most often in one of two ways. Either there was some great philosopher to whom the movement owed its leading ideas and its name, as when a group of philosophers were styled in antiquity 'Epicureans', or, more recently, 'Kantians' or 'Hegelians'; or, alternatively, it was more directly the terms of some broad agreement of philosophical doctrine and conclusion that provided the unity, as with the 'Stoicism' of antiquity or the 'Logical Positivism' of the twenties and thirties of this century. In this sort of sense, it is not easy to identify 'schools' of philosophy in contemporary Western thought. Leaving on one side the extremely special case of Marxism, even those movements in Europe that have a self-conscious title, notably the 'existentialist' and 'phenomenological' movements, do not display straightforwardly the unity either of allegiance or of doctrine that is to be found at earlier times in the history of philosophy. While the figure of Husserl stands behind phenomenology, it is certainly not as 'Husserlians' that phenomenologists go forth; again, to recognize some philosophical writings as 'existentialist' is to recognize rather a style and a type of concern rather than a readily isolable body of doctrine.

If this is true of movements such as these, it is still more evidently true of the kind of philosophy represented by the essays in this book. In some part, no doubt, this difference between the philosophy of the present day and some philosophy of the past is due merely to its being *the present day*: the comforting unities in past schools appear only as the falsifying effect of distance and the inevitable over-simplifications of history. But even when allowance has been made for this, a contrast remains, a contrast that has its roots in the historical development of philosophy in the last hundred years and, more particularly, in this century. This is most conspicuously true of the sort of philosophy presented here, but it also has some application to the Continental movements. The kind of unity that rested on a group of philosophers sharing the same doctrines and conclusions presupposes, of course, that there are characteristic philosophical conclusions to be shared; while the allegiance to a great philosophical figure—at least that sort of allegiance that gives his name to a school, unlike, for instance, the allegiance to Socrates—characteristically demands that the followers suppose their master to have discovered, at least in outline, the final truth. The notion of 'final truths' in philosophy is one that the modern temper tends to treat with scepticism; and indeed, more radically than this, even the idea of there being doctrines or conclusions at all in philosophy (whether final or not) is open to question. Such doctrines have usually offered themselves in the past as contributions to theoretical knowledge, while yet being characteristically different from the theoretical knowledge embodied in the natural and mathematical sciences; and the overwhelming practical and intellectual achievements of those sciences in the present time have inevitably reinforced in a powerful way a certain doubt that has been lurking in philosophy at least from the time of Kant, and indeed earlier: the doubt that all genuine theoretical knowledge is scientific, and that it cannot be as a contribution to such knowledge that philosophy has its peculiar, non-scientific, role to play.

Whatever the justice of such a doubt, it certainly appears as no accident that the characteristic agreements and disagreements between philosophers of the same and different schools at this time should not express themselves so much in doctrine, as in method. It is in certain styles and methods of thought, certain types of questions and certain sets of terms and ideas for discussing them, that the unity of existentialist thought, for example, most obviously appears; and similarly with the essays collected in this book. They are all examples of methods of philosophical discussion that have been most influential and important in Great Britain and elsewhere in the English-speaking world since the war, and which (it is fair to say) remain so. The range of styles and subject matter to be found even in this collection, limited as it necessarily is, illustrate the fact that a certain definite unity in this philosophical style is compatible with considerable variety in both philosophical interests, and in general belief. It is perhaps worth remarking in particular, as something more readily taken for granted in this style of philosophy than in many European styles, that the authors (who represent, incidentally, the younger age-group among English-speaking philosophers, being mostly in their thirties or early forties) include both Christians and non-Christians. This variety is further witnessed in the movement's not having any agreed name: 'linguistic philosophy', 'linguistic analysis', even 'Oxford philosophy' (with reference to the university where these methods have been, not so much originated, as most influentially practised), are all titles which have been applied to these ways of philosophical discussion. It is notable that these titles have been more enthusiastically employed by critics or expositors of these ideas than by the philosophers in question themselves, who prefer in general to describe their activity merely as 'doing philosophy'. To some people, this description might seem to embody the claim that these were the only ways of doing philosophy. To some extent, the rejection of labels is more connected with a dislike of 'taking sides in philosophy' (to use a phrase of Professor Gilbert Ryle's), a wholesale rejection of programmatic aspirations and zealotry, than it is with an exclusive claim to have *the* programme of philosophy; however, it is also true that many of these philosophers would claim that their way of approaching philosophical problems was better—more illuminating, more realistic, and more rational—than others. Such a claim is a proper consequence of their believing in what they are doing. Though the 'English-speaking' style of philosophy is an academic style—a point that we shall come back to—it does not suffer from that particularly barren form of academicism which blankly accords equal respect to any activity that calls itself 'philosophy'.

...There is a well-known textbook contrast between the traditions of British and of Continental philosophy; that British philosophy is empirical, down-to-earth, and sober in expression, while that of the Continent tends to be speculative, metaphysical, and either obscure in utterance or, if not, to have the special sort of clarity that goes with an ambitious rationalism. This contrast is, of course, an absurd caricature. It does, like many caricatures, make a gesture towards something true; in particular, so far as the present situation is concerned, there is a genuine divergence between a rather matter-of-fact tone in the British style, and the darker and more intense note that is struck by much writing on the Continent. The cause is neither banal superficiality on the part of the British philosopher, nor pretentious obscurity on the part of the Continental one—though the divergence is itself marked by the fact that when they succumb to their characteristic vices, these are the vices that each succumbs to. The divergence is rather connected with a genuine disagreement about what constitutes seriousness in philosophy; this, again, is a point that we shall come back to later in this Introduction.

In other respects, the caricature that we have just referred to is extremely misleading. It particularly misleads in suggesting that British philosophy is empirical, if what this means is that it is the *philosophy of empiricism*, directly in the tradition of Locke, Berkeley and Hume. Such a philosophy certainly has had in recent times distinguished exponents: notably Bertrand Russell, and—in a rather different manner—A. J. Ayer, though Ayer has modified his position considerably from the extreme empiricism of *Language, Truth and Logic* (1936) and *The Foundations of Empirical Knowledge* (1940). It is also true that British philosophy retains certain empiricist interests (see, for instance, Mr Quinton's contribution to this book), and even certain empiricist (though not necessarily exclusively empiricist) principles and attitudes, notably a scepticism about large-scale metaphysical conclusions supposedly founded on the deliverances of reason or intuition. But more generally it is certainly not in any allegiance to traditional empiricism that this philosophy is distinguished from the philosophies of the Continent. Indeed, in so far as British philosophy is sceptical of large-scale metaphysical conclusions, it will be as suspicious of the metaphysics of empiricism—the attempt to establish the basic constituents of the universe as experiences—as of any other.

There is a further point. Traditionally, empiricism has been expressed in psychological terms; it was as a theory of the human mind that it typically appeared, and its vocabulary was that of ideas, impressions and the powers of association. The appearance of being a kind of *a priori* psychology is not, however, essential to empiricism; it has been characteristic of many sorts of philosophy in the twentieth century to try to shake off the idiom of psychologism; this it has done under such diverse influences as those of Frege, Husserl and G. E. Moore, in some part because of the new birth in the last hundred years of logic as a non-psychological science, and also in some part because of the growth of psychology itself as a natural science independent of philosophy. Empiricism was able to respond to this change, and what was essentially the empiricism of Hume, though with many refinements, was presented, particularly by the logical positivists of the Vienna Circle, not in a psychological, but in a logical and linguistic form: as a doctrine not about the powers and nature of the mind, but as a theory of language and the limits of meaning. But while this was a possible expression of empiricism, its linguistic emphasis has proved more powerfully influential than its empiricist content. The concern with meaning, with what can be sensibly and pointfully said in what circumstances, and more generally with the conditions of meaningful discourse, has in a sense turned against empiricism itself, particularly against its characteristic doctrine of the primacy of the 'data' of immediate sense-experience.

This has led—by what some philosophers (but perhaps not these philosophers) might regard as a typically dialectic movement—to the development of a certain underlying tension in contemporary British philosophy. On the one hand, the mood and intent are still predominantly empiricist; on the other hand, the implications of many of the methods used and of the insights attained are not. This tension, too, is to be felt in the collection of essays of this book; in some cases, perhaps, within the individual essays themselves, but certainly within the collection taken as a whole. How this tension is to be resolved may be seen as one of the most general of the questions facing British philosophy at the present time.

All this may suggest that the present gap between British and Continental philosophy may lie in a rather different place than the emphasis on empiricism would indicate. It does, however, at the same time suggest a new and real kind of difficulty in bridging the gap. For it may be wondered whether there are not certain objections *in principle* to this linguistic philosophy ever moving outside the English-speaking world by the medium of translation. The concern with language in this philosophy is not merely abstract and general as it is in the general science of linguistics and in communication theory and such studies. It is rather that particular features of the use of language, particularly in the most ordinary concerns of everyday life, are thought both to give rise to some philosophical problems, and to provide at least clues to their solution. The language whose uses are studied by these philosophers is, not surprisingly, their own—English. It may well be suggested that this sort of concern with the everyday workings of a natural language must inevitably defy satisfactory translation: if English-speaking philosophy is linguistic, then it must inevitably remain the philosophy of English speakers.

If we did not think that this objection could be answered, we should clearly not have asked our contributors to write essays to be translated—we should not have embarked on assembling this book at all. In fact, we believe that there is a number of answers to this objection relating to different aspects of so-called 'linguistic' philosophy. First, for a good deal of the work which recognizably belongs to this type of philosophy, it is not true that its arguments make any direct appeal to features of the English, or any other, language. It is 'linguistic' only in being constantly aware of the presence of language, not merely in the negative sense of being sensitive to the dangers of being misled by words and trapped into empty verbal argument if we do not ask 'what is the point of using language in this way?', but also in the more positive sense of an awareness that in discussing, as philosophy always has, the relations between concepts and the nature of various ideas, one always comes back to the expression of such things in the human activity of thinking and talking about the world.

There has been some discussion and disagreement in the past years about the question of to what extent formalized languages can fruitfully be applied to philosophical problems. All would agree that there were certain subjects, most obviously the philosophy of mathematics, to which the application of formalized languages was valuable, perhaps essential; their wider application, however, is more favoured by some philosophers (notably in the United States, such as Quine) than by others (notably certain Oxford philosophers, such as Strawson). One essay in this book offers to some extent such a formal treatment of its problems, Mr Harré's on the philosophy of science.

Thus a good deal of so-called 'linguistic' philosophy is not so linguistic as all that, in the sense at least of its arguments referring to particular features of some natural language such as English. Some of it, however, does undoubtedly proceed by making explicit references to distinctions embodied in the English language. Nevertheless, even in these cases, translation is not necessarily a hopeless task. For in very many cases, the distinctions that are being made are of a general and important kind which it is highly probable will also be reflected in very similar distinctions made in other natural languages. In these respects, the problem of translating English 'linguistic' philosophy will be no more radical than that of translating, for instance, Aristotle or other philosophers who have claimed to discover important distinctions which they have explained by reference to structures in their own languages. The linguistic interest in such cases is not peculiar to the philosopher's own language, although it is in that language, and by reference to it, that his points are made. A striking example of this type of philosophy in the recent tradition is the work of Professor Gilbert Ryle. His *Concept of Mind* (1950) is a work that uses very many examples drawn from English forms of speech; his points, however, are of a sufficiently general kind for the book to have been successfully translated into Italian by F. Rossi-Landi (under the title *Lo Spirito come Comportamento*). In so far as essays in the present book do use explicitly linguistic arguments, we can only ask the reader to judge for himself whether they have been successfully translated by seeing whether they make their point.

It must be admitted, however, that there is one sort of work in recent British philosophy which presents a problem to a translator of a kind more radical than, for instance, Ryle's work presents, or the essays in this book. This is work of a type practised and advocated by the late Professor J. L. Austin (whose work is described by Mr Pears in this book, and in one respect criticized by Mr Seatle). Austin's concern was with extremely fine distinctions in the meaning and use of certain English expressions, and it differed from Ryle's interests, for example, in not being concerned only with distinctions of a rather broad and general kind such as we have argued are very probably to be found also in other languages. Ryle's concentration on some fairly broad distinctions at the expense of others is connected with his willingness to accept from the philosophical tradition some large-scale distinctions of category, such as that between an event, a process, a disposition, etc., in terms of which he handles his philosophical problems. Austin's approach was in a sense more radical; he, like others before him, sought 'new beginnings' in philosophy, and was unwilling to accept traditional categorial structures, or even traditional philosophical problems. Accordingly, he felt that no distinction embodied in everyday speech could safely be overlooked, and was prepared to consider nuances of meaning which other philosophers would probably dismiss as trivial or of no philosophical significance. Some of his writings in this manner and those of his followers might well prove, as they stand, untranslatable, since the shades of meaning for which Austin had a peculiarly fine ear, often lie at a level at which one is certainly concerned with idiosyncracies of the English language.

While this is so, it does not follow that Austin's *philosophy* could not be practised by non-English speakers. This would be to assume that only English had fruitfully distinguishable nuances. It is rather that some of his work, instead of being translated from English, would need to be carried on as a fresh enterprise in terms of another language.

... On the one hand, he sometimes spoke as though the aim of his activity was to get away from philosophy as traditionally understood, and rather lay the foundations for a systematic and empirical study of language; and some of the concepts that he developed for the description of language, such as that of a 'speech-act', may well come to play an important part in the developing science of linguistics. On the other hand, Austin clearly thought that many of the distinctions to which he drew attention were highly relevant to the issues which (in his view) philosophers had in the past wildly over-simplified in their discussions; and his discussions of the language of perception, or again of the ways in which we describe human actions, were certainly intended to undercut much of what has in the past gone on in the philosophical treatment of those issues. In this connection, Austin's concern with nice distinctions of English usage appears at once as more philosophical and, in a sense, less essential. For the use of the distinctions there was essentially to *recall one to the facts*; the immensely complex facts of perception and action which the philosophers have traditionally treated in such a cavalier fashion. The aim was essentially to make one realize in a concrete way the complex variety of situations to which the language of perception and action applies, and in this respect there are analogies between Austin and the later work of Wittgenstein (some of which Mr Pears explores in the paper already referred to). Both wished to recall philosophy to the world, and in this attempt the concern with our ordinary speech, the ways in which we unreflectively describe the world in our ordinary concerns, has a double role. First, it was the *means* of recall: reflection on ordinary language could realize for one the distinctions in the world; this was so for Austin more than for Wittgenstein, and it is a significant fact that Wittgenstein's works were written not in English, but in German, being published in each case together with an English translation. Secondly, the language was itself part of the world, of the human world which philosophy had to understand instead of embarking on the vast and over-simplified theories which have always been its bane—not merely, it should be said, in the form of the ambitious speculative metaphysics which has often been mistrusted, but even in the form of less ambitious empiricist theories which were not to be trusted any the more because they were not obviously high-flown.

This concern with the return to the facts was something that in their different ways Austin and Wittgenstein seem to have had in common. By this phrase one is, of course, immediately reminded of Husserl: and indeed Austin was prepared to call his studies by the name of 'linguistic phenomenology'. But the resemblance does not go all that deep. For the facts to which both Austin and Wittgenstein wished to recall philosophy were very commonplace and everyday facts of ordinary life, not construed as data of consciousness; nor themselves products of any particular supposed insight into phenomena: just facts of the common world, shared with the least philosophical human observer. In this respect Austin and Wittgenstein resembled each other. But their ways were very different; their temperament and approach almost diametrically opposed. For Wittgenstein, a man of strongly metaphysical temper, philosophy was an agonizing activity, which aimed at depth of insight. Austin's outlook was more that of a scholarly man who had also a great respect for the world of affairs; he felt that what philosophy needed was principally a lot more unvarnished *truth*, to be secured by hard work, patience and accuracy. Those were characteristics and aims which to a considerable extent were shared by a powerfully influential figure in the British philosophy of this century, G. E. Moore.

These differences of temperament between these philosophers are of more than biographical interest. For they are connected with certain features of British philosophy which certainly contribute strongly to the existing lack of *rapport* between it and most contemporary philosophy on the continent of Europe; features which range from a fairly superficial difference of tone to a more fundamental difference in their basic concern. These are the sorts of difference which can make a less familiar way of philosophizing seem unsympathetic at the outset, and discourage one from ever coming to grips with what it has to offer; accordingly, we should like to end this Introduction with some general remarks on these kinds of difference.

If Wittgenstein had been as powerful an influence on the *spirit* of British philosophy as he has been on its content, European philosophers would have been readier perhaps than they have been to grant the seriousness of that philosophy. Wittgenstein's deep personal commitment to philosophy, the powerfully individual and pungent quality of his writing, which some have compared to Nietzsche, and the peculiar affinity which, despite all the obvious oppositions, some aspects of his thought bear to some nineteenth-century German philosophy, notably that of Schopenhauer: all these features carry a kind of conviction which, one would have thought, would be instantly recognizable in the European tradition. If, as has perhaps been the case, even the writings of Wittgenstein himself have not received the attention elsewhere that they have in the English-speaking world, this can only be for a reason that we shall return to below—the fact that in most of his later work his concern is with philosophy itself, in particular, with the philosophy of logic and language, and does not express itself in any explicit way on moral or political topics.

But, in any case, the truth is that in spirit and tone, it is not so much the Wittgensteinian mode that prevails in contemporary British writing, as that which earlier we identified with Austin and Moore: it is a certain academic dryness, a deliberate rejection of the literary and dramatic, that is for the most part the style of this philosophy. Critics who are oppressed by these characteristics tend to ascribe them to some sort of intellectual cowardice, a failure of nerve in face of the more challenging aspects of experience. But this is certainly a superficial criticism, and there is more than one reason why the prevailing British style should be as it is. First, there are undoubtedly factors of straightforward historical tradition, which can almost, if not totally— be summed up in the fact that British philosophy responded to Kant in ways quite different from those in which Continental philosophy did: in particular it has never fundamentally been influenced by Hegel, and therefore not by the manifold post-Hegelian developments and reactions which constitute the mainstream of the German, and indeed other Continental, subsequent tradition. To state this fact, is not, of course, to explain anything; the fact itself invites explanation. Nevertheless, it is to the point that it is not a unique feature of *contemporary* British philosophy that a divergence should exist from the Continental style—it dates back to the end of the eighteenth century.

To come to more particular points: it is an important feature of British philosophy that it is self-consciously academic, in the sense that its exponents are aware of being engaged jointly with others in a subject which is taught to undergraduates and is a subject of research in universities. It is not, of course, alone in this—all this is equally true of philosophy on the continent of Europe. What is perhaps peculiar, however, is certain consequences that are felt to follow from the philosopher's academic standing, about both the responsibilities and the limitations of his position; connected, perhaps, with certain differences in the structure of academic life. The adoption of a relatively sober and undramatic style and an objective form of argument responds to the demands, not just (as some critics urge) of academic respectability, but of a professional conscience. This point raises, in fact, the whole question of how philosophy can honestly be taught at all—*philosophy*, that is to say, as opposed to the mere history of philosophy on the one hand, or a sterile dogmatic system on the other; and this is a puzzling enough question. The nature of the 'British style' in philosophy is certainly connected with one view on this question: a view that emphasizes the availability of the subject in objective instruction and rational discussion. It is a view whose emphasis is on *the colleague* rather than on *the master*.

However, these are perhaps not points of the first importance. The rejection of the dramatic style goes deeper than this; and we would suggest that there is a genuine difference between much British and much Continental philosophy in this respect, which causes genuine misunderstanding. It comes out in the different role or treatment of examples in the two cases. It is a characteristic of much Continental writing that if a concept or idea is under discussion, the examples that are given to make it come to life, to illustrate its application, are either themselves of a striking or intense kind, or, if not, are described in a striking and intense manner. A literary perception is brought to bear on the example which seeks to elicit the force of the example in terms which have an emotional impact. A very striking example of this is, of course, Sartre: a typical case would be the well-known passage in *L'Etre et le Néant* in which, seeking the fundamental basis of negation, he gives a powerfully realized description of a man's consciousness of a café *not* containing someone whom he expected to see there. This is not the only sort of negative judgement he admits, of course; but the significant point is that it is such examples that he regards as centrally important, as not being 'merely abstract', and as having 'a real foundation'. Sartre is, perhaps, an untypical example, being as distinguished a creative writer as philosopher; the point, however, applies more generally—Merleau-Ponty's *Phénoménologie de la Perception*, for instance, contains many phenomenological descriptions whose aim is clearly to heighten the intensity of our awareness of what we see and feel in certain situations by description of what is in fact an intense awareness of such things. Common to both, and to many other writers, one might say, is this: that reflection on our ordinary consciousness takes the path of the description of a reflective consciousness, where a reflective consciousness is precisely marked by a certain emotional intensity and single-mindedness.

A British philosopher will tend to say, on the other hand: if you want to understand the notion of negation, you must see it in its most humdrum applications; not those in which the recognition that someone is not there is intensified by a personal sense of disappointment, but just the case where, for instance, one finds that one's shoes are not under the bed, and so forth. And of those occasions, one must give descriptions that match precisely the unexciting everyday character of such incidents. The aim is indeed to reflect on everyday consciousness, but it will be a falsification of that to represent it, in reflective description, as intense: for everyday consciousness is not intense. The *essence* of ordinary experience emerges in its ordinariness, and ordinary experience—it is a simple tautology to say—is where most of our concepts most typically do their work.

This deliberate rejection of the idea that situations of heightened consciousness are those that reveal the most important features of our thought is very fundamental to British philosophy, and is one of the particular influences of Wittgenstein—the dramatic intensity of whose approach to *the subject* revealed this idea with an impact lacking in Moore, who in a quiet transfixed sort of way took it for granted. We suggested earlier that there was a genuine disagreement between the British school and many Continental ones about what constituted seriousness in philosophy; and this disagreement comes to a focus at this point. Seriousness and intensity are for the British outlook certainly different: for while a serious study may itself have to be an intense study, a serious representation of the world is not the representation of a world of intensity. On the contrary, it is a representation of the world which takes seriously the way that the world presents itself to ordinary, practical concerns of common life.

For many of the concepts and features of human thought studied by philosophy, this general attitude of the British philosopher must surely be correct. Yet it obviously has its dangers. For there are other aspects of human experience in which intensity of consciousness is itself, one might say, part of the issue, and where it will be a contrary falsification to suppose that the most everyday styles of thought were the most revealing. Such may well be the case with moral and aesthetic experience, and to some extent with politics. Politics is necessarily a special case, since the intensity of political experience in a society is so evidently a function of history; and the lack of political philosophy in the recent British tradition (commented on by Professor Wollheim in his essay in this book), and most obviously, of course, the lack of a Marxist tradition (discussed by Mr Taylor) are clearly connected with the freedom from disruptive change in British history, the sort of change that demands fundamental political reflection on questions that *have* to be answered. It is interesting that in recent years there has been a strong indication of dissatisfaction with these aspects of British philosophy among younger students in particular, which comes very probably from a sense of fundamental political issues which now face the British in common with everyone else. There are some signs of a growing recognition of such issues, and a corresponding revival in significant political philosophy.

Moral issues present a more complex problem, since the role of intensity of consciousness can itself be, in a sense, a moral issue. To illustrate this very crudely: it is possible for a moral philosopher to see a rather settled structure of rights, duties and human aims (something which is often—and, he may even think, *rightly*—taken for granted), as constituting the basic fabric of moral thought, and to concentrate on trying to systematize and explain this; while another sees this only as a background to creative acts of moral imagination, born of intense moral reflection, which he regards as the most important element to be considered in reflecting on moral thought and action. The difference between these two is scarcely just a theoretical difference. It is a familiar enough picture that regards the first as dead and the second alive; or the first unfree, and the second free; or the first in bad faith, and the second an honest man; but these, in their turn, are scarcely theoretical descriptions. Thus, there is no simple or uncommitted position from which to evaluate, in these sorts of respects, the contributions of a style of moral philosophy. The contributions of recent British philosophy to moral issues have primarily been to the study of morality as, one might say, an anthropological concept: how moral principles are to be distinguished from other rules or institutions in society, and similar questions. In part, this emphasis has been conditioned by a certain theoretical belief about philosophical morality, the so-called distinction between fact and value; but—as Mr Montefiore's discussion of this in his essay tries to show—this is not a pure theoretical belief itself, and the peculiar role it has played in structuring a style of moral philosophy which, while often illuminating, has undoubtedly been rather formal, demure and unadventurous, itself requires explanation, perhaps of a sociological kind, which we shall not attempt here. This, again, is an aspect of British philosophical thought that shows signs of awakening to a more vital kind of life than it has often achieved recently.

Bertrand Russell (1872–1970) was a British philosopher, logician, mathematician, historian, writer, social commentator, and activist. He was also considered by some at various points in his career as a liberal, a socialist, and a pacifist—although he denied any serious allegiance to any of these views. He did his best to apply philosophy to life and that is what you find in this short selection from his book.

The Value Of Philosophy

from Bertrand Russell's *The Problems of Philosophy*

... it will be well to consider, in conclusion, what is the value of philosophy and why it ought to be studied. It is the more necessary to consider this question, in view of the fact that many men, under the influence of science or of practical affairs, are inclined to doubt whether philosophy is anything better than innocent but useless trifling, hair-splitting distinctions, and controversies on matters concerning which knowledge is impossible.

This view of philosophy appears to result, partly from a wrong conception of the ends of life, partly from a wrong conception of the kind of goods which philosophy strives to achieve. Physical science, through the medium of inventions, is useful to innumerable people who are wholly ignorant of it; thus the study of physical science is to be recommended, not only, or primarily, because of the effect on the student, but rather because of the effect on mankind in general. This utility does not belong to philosophy. If the study of philosophy has any value at all for others than students of philosophy, it must be only indirectly, through its effects upon the lives of those who study it. It is in these effects, therefore, if anywhere, that the value of philosophy must be primarily sought.

But further, if we are not to fail in our endeavour to determine the value of philosophy, we must first free our minds from the prejudices of what are wrongly called 'practical' men. The 'practical' man, as this word is often used, is one who recognizes only material needs, who realizes that men must have food for the body, but is oblivious of the necessity of providing food for the mind. If all men were well off, if poverty and disease had been reduced to their lowest possible point, there would still remain much to be done to produce a valuable society; and even in the existing world the goods of the mind are at least as important as the goods of the body. It is exclusively among the goods of the mind that the value of philosophy is to be found; and only those who are not indifferent to these goods can be persuaded that the study of philosophy is not a waste of time.

Philosophy, like all other studies, aims primarily at knowledge. The knowledge it aims at is the kind of knowledge which gives unity and system to the body of the sciences, and the kind which results from a critical examination of the grounds of our convictions, prejudices, and beliefs. But it cannot be maintained that philosophy has had any very great measure of success in its attempts to provide definite answers to its questions. If you ask a mathematician, a mineralogist, a historian, or any other man of learning, what definite body of truths has been ascertained by his science, his answer will last as long as you are willing to listen. But if you put the same question to a philosopher, he will, if he is candid, have to confess that his study has not achieved positive results such as have been achieved by other sciences. It is true that this is partly accounted for by the fact that, as soon as definite knowledge concerning any subject becomes possible, this subject ceases to be called philosophy, and becomes a separate science. The whole study of the heavens, which now belongs to astronomy, was once included in philosophy; Newton's great work was called 'the mathematical principles of natural philosophy'. Similarly, the study of the human mind, which was a part of philosophy, has now been separated from philosophy and has become the science of psychology. Thus, to a great extent, the uncertainty of philosophy is more apparent than real: those questions which are already capable of definite answers are placed in the sciences, while those only to which, at present, no definite answer can be given, remain to form the residue which is called philosophy.

This is, however, only a part of the truth concerning the uncertainty of philosophy. There are many questions—and among them those that are of the profoundest interest to our spiritual life—which, so far as we can see, must remain insoluble to the human intellect unless its powers become of quite a different order from what they are now. Has the universe any unity of plan or purpose, or is it a fortuitous concourse of atoms? Is consciousness a permanent part of the universe, giving hope of indefinite growth in wisdom, or is it a transitory accident on a small planet on which life must ultimately become impossible? Are good and evil of importance to the universe or only to man? Such questions are asked by philosophy, and variously answered by various philosophers. But it would seem that, whether answers be otherwise discoverable or not, the answers suggested by philosophy are none of them demonstrably true. Yet, however slight may be the hope of discovering an answer, it is part of the business of philosophy to continue the consideration of such questions, to make us aware of their importance, to examine all the approaches to them, and to keep alive that speculative interest in the universe which is apt to be killed by confining ourselves to definitely ascertainable knowledge.

Many philosophers, it is true, have held that philosophy could establish the truth of certain answers to such fundamental questions. They have supposed that what is of most importance in religious beliefs could be proved by strict demonstration to be true. In order to judge of such attempts, it is necessary to take a survey of human knowledge, and to form an opinion as to its methods and its limitations. On such a subject it would be unwise to pronounce dogmatically; but if the investigations of our previous chapters have not led us astray, we shall be compelled to renounce the hope of finding philosophical proofs of religious beliefs. We cannot, therefore, include as part of the value of philosophy any definite set of answers to such questions. Hence, once more, the value of philosophy must not depend upon any supposed body of definitely ascertainable knowledge to be acquired by those who study it.

The value of philosophy is, in fact, to be sought largely in its very uncertainty. The man who has no tincture of philosophy goes through life imprisoned in the prejudices derived from common sense, from the habitual beliefs of his age or his nation, and from convictions which have grown up in his mind without the co-operation or consent of his deliberate reason. To such a man the world tends to become definite, finite, obvious; common objects rouse no questions, and unfamiliar possibilities are contemptuously rejected. As soon as we begin to philosophize, on the contrary, we find, as we saw in our opening chapters, that even the most everyday things lead to problems to which only very incomplete answers can be given. Philosophy, though unable to tell us with certainty what is the true answer to the doubts which it raises, is able to suggest many possibilities which enlarge our thoughts and free them from the tyranny of custom. Thus, while diminishing our feeling of certainty as to what things are, it greatly increases our knowledge as to what they may be; it removes the somewhat arrogant dogmatism of those who have never travelled into the region of liberating doubt, and it keeps alive our sense of wonder by showing familiar things in an unfamiliar aspect.

Apart from its utility in showing unsuspected possibilities, philosophy has a value—perhaps its chief value—through the greatness of the objects which it contemplates, and the freedom from narrow and personal aims resulting from this contemplation. The life of the instinctive man is shut up within the circle of his private interests: family and friends may be included, but the outer world is not regarded except as it may help or hinder what comes within the circle of instinctive wishes. In such a life there is something feverish and confined, in comparison with which the philosophic life is calm and free. The private world of instinctive interests is a small one, set in the midst of a great and powerful world which must, sooner or later, lay our private world in ruins. Unless we can so enlarge our interests as to include the whole outer world, we remain like a garrison in a beleaguered fortress, knowing that the enemy prevents escape and that ultimate surrender is inevitable. In such a life there is no peace, but a constant strife between the insistence of desire and the powerlessness of will. In one way or another, if our life is to be great and free, we must escape this prison and this strife.

One way of escape is by philosophic contemplation. Philosophic contemplation does not, in its widest survey, divide the universe into two hostile camps—friends and foes, helpful and hostile, good and bad—it views the whole impartially. Philosophic contemplation, when it is unalloyed, does not aim at proving that the rest of the universe is akin to man. All acquisition of knowledge is an enlargement of the Self, but this enlargement is best attained when it is not directly sought. It is obtained when the desire for knowledge is alone operative, by a study which does not wish in advance that its objects should have this or that character, but adapts the Self to the characters which it finds in its objects. This enlargement of Self is not obtained when, taking the Self as it is, we try to show that the world is so similar to this Self that knowledge of it is possible without any admission of what seems alien. The desire to prove this is a form of self-assertion and, like all self-assertion, it is an obstacle to the growth of Self which it desires, and of which the Self knows that it is capable. Self-assertion, in philosophic speculation as elsewhere, views the world as a means to its own ends; thus it makes the world of less account than Self, and the Self sets bounds to the greatness of its goods. In contemplation, on the contrary, we start from the not-Self, and through its greatness the boundaries of Self are enlarged; through the infinity of the universe the mind which contemplates it achieves some share in infinity.

For this reason greatness of soul is not fostered by those philosophies which assimilate the universe to Man. Knowledge is a form of union of Self and not-Self; like all union, it is impaired by dominion, and therefore by any attempt to force the universe into conformity with what we find in ourselves. There is a widespread philosophical tendency towards the view which tells us that Man is the measure of all things, that truth is man-made, that space and time and the world of universals are properties of the mind, and that, if there be anything not created by the mind, it is unknowable and of no account for us. This view, if our previous discussions were correct, is untrue; but in addition to being untrue, it has the effect of robbing philosophic contemplation of all that gives it value, since it fetters contemplation to Self. What it calls knowledge is not a union with the not-Self, but a set of prejudices, habits, and desires, making an impenetrable veil between us and the world beyond. The man who finds pleasure in such a theory of knowledge is like the man who never leaves the domestic circle for fear his word might not be law.

The true philosophic contemplation, on the contrary, finds its satisfaction in every enlargement of the not-Self, in everything that magnifies the objects contemplated, and thereby the subject contemplating. Everything, in contemplation, that is personal or private, everything that depends upon habit, self-interest, or desire, distorts the object, and hence impairs the union which the intellect seeks. By thus making a barrier between subject and object, such personal and private things become a prison to the intellect. The free intellect will see as God might see, without a here and now, without hopes and fears, without the trammels of customary beliefs and traditional prejudices, calmly, dispassionately, in the sole and exclusive desire of knowledge—knowledge as impersonal, as purely contemplative, as it is possible for man to attain. Hence also the free intellect will value more the abstract and universal knowledge into which the accidents of private history do not enter, than the knowledge brought by the senses, and dependent, as such knowledge must be, upon an exclusive and personal point of view and a body whose sense-organs distort as much as they reveal.

The mind which has become accustomed to the freedom and impartiality of philosophic contemplation will preserve something of the same freedom and impartiality in the world of action and emotion. It will view its purposes and desires as parts of the whole, with the absence of insistence that results from seeing them as infinitesimal fragments in a world of which all the rest is unaffected by any one man's deeds. The impartiality which, in contemplation, is the unalloyed desire for truth, is the very same quality of mind which, in action, is justice, and in emotion is that universal love which can be given to all, and not only to those who are judged useful or admirable. Thus contemplation enlarges not only the objects of our thoughts, but also the objects of our actions and our affections: it makes us citizens of the universe, not only of one walled city at war with all the rest. In this citizenship of the universe consists man's true freedom, and his liberation from the thraldom of narrow hopes and fears.

Thus, to sum up our discussion of the value of philosophy; Philosophy is to be studied, not for the sake of any definite answers to its questions since no definite answers can, as a rule, be known to be true, but rather for the sake of the questions themselves; because these questions enlarge our conception of what is possible, enrich our intellectual imagination and diminish the dogmatic assurance which closes the mind against speculation; but above all because, through the greatness of the universe which philosophy contemplates, the mind also is rendered great, and becomes capable of that union with the universe which constitutes its highest good.

KEY TERMS

Logical positivist (or empirical positivist) is an approach that sought to legitimize philosophical discourse on a basis shared with the best examples of empirical sciences. Only statements verifiable either logically or empirically are cognitively meaningful.

Natural language theorists claim that analytic statements tend to not alter the form of its words and to use word order rather than inflection or agglutination to express grammatical structure.

QUESTIONS FOR DISCUSSION AND REVIEW

1. Explain the idea of analytic philosophy in contrast with other schools of philosophy.
2. Compare and contrast the logical positivist to the natural language theorist.
3. Explain the role of the "Vienna circle" in the history of analytic philosophy.
4. Summarize, explain, and evaluate the main points of the reading by Bernard Williams and Alan Montefiore.
5. Summarize, explain, and evaluate the main points of the reading by Bertrand Russell.

SUGGESTED READINGS

Carnap, R. (1947). *Meaning and Necessity*.

Internet Encyclopedia of Philosophy. A peer-reviewed academic resource. Available from http://www.iep.utm.edu/

Russell, B. (1912). *The Problems of Philosophy*.

Russell, B. (1912). *The Value of Philosophy*.

Russell, B. (1927). *An Outline of Philosophy*.

Ryle, G. (1949). *The Concept of Mind*.

Stanford Encyclopedia of Philosophy. Available from http://plato.stanford.edu/

Wittgenstein, L. (1922). *Tractatus Logico-Philosophicus*. (Ogden,C.K. transl.).

Wittgenstein, L. (1953). *Philosophical Investigations*.

Wittgenstein, L. (1958). *The Blue and Brown Books*: Notes Dictated in English to Cambridge Students from 1933–1935.

Quine, W. V. O. (1951). Two Dogmas of Empiricism. *The Philosophical Review*, 60, 20–43.

Quine, W. V. O. (1969). *Ontological Relativity and Other Essay*.

Existentialism and Humanism

9

Upon completing this chapter, students should be able to meet the following Learning Outcomes:

9.1 Articulate the main themes found in existentialism.

9.2 Explain why Kierkegaard and Dostoyevsky are considered predecessors of existentialism.

9.3 Critically analyze Husserl's phenomenology and how it informed existentialism.

9.4 Explain the meaning of being and nothingness according to Sartre.

9.5 Discuss the concept of absurdity in Albert Camus' philosophy.

Reason Is Not Enough—Existentialism before Existentialism

The word existentialism came into use in the twenty-first century, but its themes go back a bit farther. Philosophers, theologians, and artists of the past such as Søren Kierkegaard (1813–1855) and Fyodor Dostoyevsky(1821–1881) already shared existentialist concerns such as the fact that we are bound to be here and now, that in more than one sense, existence precedes essence—or at least whatever meaning we find it is a meaning we bring. We all find ourselves first existing in the world—without or rhyme or reason, without essence before us—then it is up to us to decide what to make of our existence. There also has been the existentialist concern with the human search for identity and meaning, a deep form of humanism independent on whether or not one believed in God. Above all, existentialists then and now share a sense of interconnectedness with others, a way of taking stock of human freedom that links it to responsibility for ourselves and for others. It leads to an ethics of personal responsibility, if only in the realization that whatever we do and whatever we are, we are the ones choosing that. And reason is not nearly enough to justify that choice. It is personal. It is an always personal revolt against reason.

> "Since the beginning of the century many great books have expressed the revolt of life's immediacy against reason. Each in its own way has said that the rational arrangement of a system of morals or politics, or even of art, is valueless in the face of the fervor of the moment, the explosive brilliance of an individual life, the premeditation of the unknown. It would seem that the communion of man and his power to choose cannot long be endured. . . . As soon as we desire something or call others to witness, as soon as we live, we imply that the world is, in principle, in harmony with itself and others with ourselves. We are born into reason as into language. But the reason at which we arrive must not be the same reason we abandoned with such a flourish. The experience of reason cannot simply be forgotten: we must form a new idea of reason"
>
> —*Maurice Merleau-Ponty, Sense and Non-Sense*
> *(H. L. Dreyfus and P. A. Dreyfus, trans.),*
> *Northwestern University Press)*

Dostoyevsky masterfully portrayed the anguish that comes with doubt and the necessity of choosing to confront that doubt personally in his novels such as *The Brothers Karamazov* and *Crime and Punishment*. His own choice to believe in God was personal, a way to escape the anguish of facing everyday existence in this world.

Kierkegaard emphasized personal choice over reason, and he saw that the realization of just how lonely that choice can be leads to, in his words, a sickness-unto-death. As a Protestant Christian, Kierkegaard thought that all the previous proofs of the existence of God were meaningless. In his particular case, the philosopher found that the way to avoid the otherwise inescapable dread of living in doubt was to choose to believe. To take a leap of faith.

One reason Kierkegaard is often considered an existentialist is not that he found a way to believe in God without needing a proof through reason—most existentialists are atheists, in fact. But arguably what makes Kierkegaard an existentialist is that what matters to him is the realization that believing or not was his choice. Moral codes, including those of the church but also those of philosophers up to this time, were simply a crutch. We have to take responsibility for our choices, and it is the act of choosing that matters. It is what makes us human.

POWERFUL IDEAS BOX: LEAP OF FAITH?

Have you ever met anyone who believes in God because he or she saw a good proof of his existence? Maybe Kierkegaard is right, and faith is a matter of taking a leap of faith. There is no reason to believe, one just chooses to do so, or not. And that choice is as personal as it is constant. That is, choosing is never a one-time event, but rather a constant state of affairs. To be human is to choose.

POWERFUL ANALYSIS: A LEAP OF FAITH?

Should we be willing to believe ideas without any evidence and take a leap of faith as Kierkegaard argues?

From Hegel to Existentialism

The rules of the game changed with **Georg Wilhelm Friedrich Hegel** (1770–1831), an idealist of a different stripe from Plato or Berkeley. Hegel opened the door to doubt. The strikingly original and difficult philosophy he developed in *The Phenomenology of Mind* (1807), and later in his *Logic* (1816) and *Philosophy of Right* (1821), showed that everything depends on our apprehending the truth not only as substance but also as subject. Hegel believed the world, our world, was an unfolding of an idea, and that this idea—also called mind or spirit—was constantly unfolding in a dialectic of a thesis that contained within itself its own destruction, of the antithesis that contained that destruction, and of a synthesis that absorbed both. That synthesis then became a thesis, and the Hegelian dialectic would go on. The thesis needs the antithesis, just as subjectivity (that which thinks) and objectivity (that which is thought of) are dialectical opposites that form a synthesis that is constantly unfolding. Idea and nature, too, are dialectical opposites, perennially unfolding forward in a vision of human consciousness as the unfolding of reason.

GEORG WILHELM HEGEL 1770-1831

DEUTSCHE BUNDESPOST

20

© Boris15 / Shutterstock.com

This unfolding move forward provided the means to understand human consciousness and thought. It has its own unique reason. There is reason in history, for example, but it is nearly impossible, if possible at all, for us to understand that because we ourselves are the actors in that history.

> "All the great philosophical ideas of the past century—the philosophies of Marx and Nietzsche, phenomenology, German existentialism, and psychoanalysis—has their beginning in Hegel. It was he who started the attempt to explore the irrational and integrate it into an expanded reason that remains the task of our century. He is the inventor of that reason, broader than the understanding, which can respect the variety and singularity of individual consciousnesses, civilizations, ways of thinking, and historical contingency but which nevertheless does not give up the attempt to master them in order to guide them to their own truth"
>
> —*Maurice Merleau-Ponty*

This is a radical departure from traditional logic, and to this day some philosophers have difficulty reading Hegel much less understanding his phenomenological-dialectical logic. Since each era has its own internal logic, it is through critically examining human experience in all its facets that may approach understanding its meaning. That meaning, as Hegel points out in *The Phenomenology of Mind*, is the process consciousness understanding itself, free of any *a priori* concepts or categories of the mind. In a radical departure from Kant's metaphysics, Hegel's phenomenology starts with humanity's efforts to comprehend its fundamental situation, assuming no such thing as a noumenal level of reality Kant's noumena—as opposed to phenomena—are unknowable, therefore unthinkable. If it is unthinkable, then it does not exist. Only the phenomenon exists, or at the very least, it is only to the phenomena that we have access. It is humanity's responsibility to re-appropriate itself by understanding the phenomenon of its own existence as well as that of history. In this sense, Hegel is the ancestor of Edmund Husserl and modern phenomenology, of the existential philosophy, and of the twentieth and twenty-first centuries humanist interpretations of Marxism.

© Bettmann/CORBIS

Husserl: Phenomenology and Existential Philosophy

The father of phenomenology, Edmund Husserl was born on April 8, 1859 in Moravia, what is now the Czech Republic. He was active in Germany and died in Freiburg on April 27, 1938. Husserl's revolutionary philosophy is aimed at a scientific analysis of experience as it is lived. Consciousness, he thought, has intentionality—it is always consciousness of something. In this sense, intentional thoughts and intentional acts are defined through consciousness. In a process of phenomenological reduction, the existence of the world beyond our experience of it can be neither confirmed nor denied. Through transcendental reduction, phenomenology allows us to return to the self, that is, to the self that is required to know a complete empirical self-consciousness.

© adoc-photos/Corbis

That consciousness itself cannot be separated from the object of consciousness is the crux of Husserl's phenomenology, solving the problem of the gap between the knower and the known. The intentionality of the mind—a concept that influenced the existentialism of Jean-Paul Sartre, Simone de Beauvoir, and Albert Camus considerably—means that in an ontological sense, the two must exist together as two aspects of a single phenomenon. The self is not the act but rather it observes the act, it is present to it. Since his 1913 highly original work *Ideas*, through his 1931 *Cartesian Meditations,* and the valedictory 1936 *The Crisis of European Sciences and Transcendental Phenomenology: An Introduction to Phenomenological Philosophy*, Husserl reworked his transcendental reduction, reaching what he called a sphere of own-ness. The transcendental ego is dialectically connected to the lived body of another ego. Husserl called this interconnectedness of two consciousnesses as transcendental inter-subjectivity.

After Husserl: Existentialism

The phenomenological approach that suggested examining life experiences as a way to understand the subject of that experience in the world led to new and revolutionary ways of doing philosophy. Although Husserl's initial project was to return to the things in themselves as experienced in everyday life as it is lived, the philosophers that followed first in Germany and immediately afterwards in France concentrated on the self and its encounter with others and with the world.

Powerful Thinkers: Martin Heidegger

Martin Heidegger (1889–1976) was Husserl's student assistant at the University of Freiburg in 1919, eventually took over as department chairperson and continued the exploration of the self in the world. In his 1927 *Being and Time*, Heidegger analyzed the nature of Being in human terms, referring to us all as *Dasein*, or "Being there." We ask ourselves what we ourselves are, and we apprehend immediately that we are always "there," that is, we are thrown into a world not of our choosing: free as we might be there, there is where we are. We should be seen as "Being-in-the-world," a situation filled with things that are not us. The identity of *Dasein* is determined by its relation to others as well as to the world.

© adoc-photos/Corbis

After the 1933 election of Adolf Hitler and the Nazi racial laws that soon followed, Husserl was suspended from the University of

Freiburg for being a Jew. Martin Heidegger, Husserl's former star pupil who had dedicated his own *Being and Time* to Husserl, joined the Nazi Party, became Rector of the University of Freiburg, and refused his old teacher library privileges. Husserl died in 1938, sparing himself the gas chamber that awaited millions of Jews.

Jean-Paul Sartre

Also following Husserl, but transforming the ontology resulting from his method, Sartre believed that consciousness in fact can negate what the empiricists called reality. The role of the imagination, of intentionality at its most basic, emerges outside the order of causality. That was the beginning of French existentialism.

The leading figure of French existentialism, and one of the most influential writers of our time, Jean-Paul Charles Aymard Sartre (1904–1980) studied philosophy at the École Normale Supèrieur in his native Paris. He was profoundly influenced by the phenomenology of Edmund Husserl (1858–1938), with whom Sartre's friend Maurice Merleau-Ponty had just finished studying in Germany before World War II broke out. It was Husserl's revolutionary insight that human consciousness cannot be separated from its presence to the world, that is, from the object of consciousness. Consciousness is always consciousness of something, and the two together make up a phenomenon. Philosophy then must concert itself with that relationship: our intentionality, that is, our presence as witnesses to the world creates the meaning of that world that we are not. Philosophy became the study of life as it is actually lived.

© Michel Ginfray/Apis/Sygma/Corbis

To say that Sartre was inspired by Husserl's phenomenology when he first heard about it from Merleau-Ponty over drinks in at Les Deux Magots café in Paris' Left Bank would be a spectacular understatement—he took Husserl's idea and created a new philosophy from it himself. It was then that history intervened. In quick succession, Husserl died, the Germans invaded France, and Sartre joined the army and fought against the Nazis. Shortly thereafter he became a German prisoner of war, escaped, and worked in the Resistance movement against the German occupation.

During the German occupation, Sartre wrote both *Being and Nothingness* (1943), the seminal text of existentialism, and *No Exit* (1944), the first play staged in Paris after the liberation and arguably the clearest dramatization of existentialist philosophy. He also found time for ghost-writing anti-Nazi articles for the resistance underground paper *Combat* with his friend Albert Camus (1913–1969), and with his lifelong partner Simone de Beauvoir (1913–1960).

© Manuel Litran/Corbis

In *Being and Nothingness*, Sartre introduces a new concept: We are Nothingness, that is, we are not things. The world is a thing, it is solid, knowable—it's just there. Human beings, on the other hand, are defined by not-being, that is, by Nothingness. You can know this book you're reading, you can know your shoe, you can know your house. You can know everything there is to know about these things precisely because they are things. Your presence to them defines them. But you can never say that about the student sitting next to you: Whatever you think you know about another person, there's more there. There is always more.

Sartre refers to these two categories of reality as Being-in-itself (the world, *Être-en-soi*) and being-for-itself (us, *Êtrepour-soi*). We are defined by freedom. We are condemned to be free. Our existence precedes essence precisely because it is our existence, our presence to Being that gives Being its meaning. We are witnesses to our lives, in other words, and we are constantly creating its meaning. We are always projecting ourselves into a future. "I am the Self that I will be," Sartre remarked. This can be and often is difficult, even intolerable. So an easy way out of this is to pretend to be a thing, or to pretend that others are things. That is what Sartre calls bad faith, and he points out that we know better.

"Dostoyevsky once wrote 'if God did not exist, everything would be permitted,' and that, for existentialism, is the starting point. Everything is indeed permitted if God does not exist, and man is in consequence forlorn, for he cannot find anything to depend upon either within or outside himself. For if indeed existence precedes essence, one will never be able to explain one's actions by reference to a given and specific human nature. In other words, there is no determinism, man *is* freedom. We are left alone, without excuse"

—*Jean-Paul Sartre*

A novelist, screenwriter, and playwright as well as a philosopher and political activist, Sartre was awarded the Nobel Prize for Literature in 1964, with the Nobel Academy praising "his work which, rich in ideas and filled with the spirit of freedom and the quest for truth, has exerted a far-reaching influence on our age." True to form, and not wanting to become an institution, Sartre respectfully refused the award.

Sartre, Beauvoir, and Camus all practiced what they preached, not only in their heroic work for the French resistance against the Nazis, but also in committing themselves to the fights against colonialism, against racism, for women's equality, for a woman's reproductive rights, for gay rights, against tyranny anywhere. He was the conscience of a generation, a witness to his century. Jean-Paul Sartre died in Paris on April 15, 1980. A crowd of 60,000 Parisians marched in his funeral. He is buried alongside Simone de Beauvoir in the Montparnasse Cemetery, not far from where they lived their whole lives. Fittingly, the city of Paris in 2000 renamed its Place de St. Germain, in the heart of the Left Bank, the Place Sartre-Beauvoir.

Existentialism and The Arts

Especially following the spectacular critical and popular success of Sartre, Beauvoir, and Camus, existentialism became a sensibility that permeated the arts. The stereotype of the goateed intellectual in a black turtle neck sweater spouting deep thoughts and sipping coffee in the Left Bank made its way to Stanley Donen's 1957 musical *Funny Face*, starring Audrey Hepburn and Fred Astaire, with the beautiful Hepburn as a "sympaticalist." French existentialism made it to the cover of *Time* and *Life* magazines. It was news.

The themes were there before, of course: the individual confronts the world alone, asking the world for reasons is simply absurd since the world does not offer any, anxiety and doubt are inescapable or escapable only by lying to oneself, everything that matters does so in an intensely personal way, confronting the need to choose can be as painful as it is necessary—all these ideas emerged previously not just in philosophy but also in literature and the arts.

Fyodor Dostoyevsky's novels *The Brothers Karamazov* and *Crime and Punishment*, Miguel de Unamuno's novel *La Tía Tula* and his essay *The Tragic Sense of Life*—just as later the novels of Franz Kafka, the plays of the Nobel Prize laureates Samuel

Beckett and Harold Pinter, and the early short stories of Guillermo Cabrera Infante all were drenched in existentialist themes that nevertheless were and are best illustrated in the novels and plays of Sartre, Beauvoir, and Camus.

But it is on film, which Sartre called "the art of the twentieth century," that existentialism best found a home outside the academy. The Jean-Luc Godard (b. 1930) portrayed alienation and the sheer absurdity of life as it is actually lived beginning with his revolutionary *À bout de souffle (Breathless)* (1960) and especially the intensely personal *Vivre sa vie (My Life To Live)* (1962). Alain Resnais (1922–2014), followed his controversial 1959 *Hiroshima Mon Amour* with the 1961 cinematic masterpiece *Last Year at Marienbad*, bursting asunder the doors of existentialism in film with an exquisite explosion of disorientation, elegantly and heartbreakingly portraying the utter loneliness of life and questioning the meaning of memory.

Michelangelo Antonioni (1912–2007), the Italian master of existentialist film, created a body of work that remains one of the best and most accessible ways to understand the existentialist worldview and the absurdity of the human situation, particularly in his pioneering black-and-white trilogy of in *L'avventura* (1960), *La notte* (1961), and *L'Eclisse* (1962). There, as well as in his first color films *Il deserto rosso (The Red Desert*, 1964) and *Blowup* (1966), Antonioni created existential puzzles without solutions, much as in life itself. The alienation inherent in human relations, and the impossible attempts to find meaning in them, have seldom if ever been portrayed with such cruel clarity as in *L'Eclisse*, starring Alain Delon and Antonioni's muse Monica Vitti. Alienation is inevitable, drenched in immensities of sadness, and any hope to be found is a hope to be created by us. Life is on us. Antonioni's pictures illuminate existentialism in visual terms, dazzlingly, starkly.

Near the end of the twentieth century, Krzysztof Kieślowski (1941–1996) added bitter irony to the existentialist themes of alienation and absurdity with his *Trois Couleurs (Three Colors: Red, White, and Blue)* trilogy in 1993–1994.

Albert Camus: Existentialism, Absurdity, and Life

The outlier of existential philosophy, Albert Camus (1913–1960) was born in Algeria, worked in France, and remained ambiguous about his identity in every sense. Like Sartre and Beauvoir, he worked in the French resistance during World War II; like them, too, he enjoyed immense success in literature, theater, and philosophy. In social issues, he was on-and-off friend or enemy of his Left Bank colleagues—he was very much of the Left but never a communist, existentialist in his metaphysics but humanistic in his politics. He celebrated resistance and rebellion, but he denounced terrorism from the Left or the Right, decrying the use of violence in the name of an idea—any idea. Progressive to the core, Camus nevertheless refused to become a fellow traveler in any way. "All the dead," he wrote in a newspaper article about both sides of the Algerian conflict, "belong to the same tragic family."

Sergey Goryachev/Shutterstock.com

Existentialists believe that an intellectual must be engaged in the actual life of his or her world that philosophy in particular must focus on the confrontation of the individual with a world that reason simply cannot explain. Camus' philosophical position, everywhere from his novels and plays to his essays, was in this sense the definition of French existentialism. Camus made the concept of absurdity a key concern of his oeuvre, from the novels *The Stranger* (1942) and *The Plague* (1947) right through *The Fall* (1956) and the posthumously published *A Happy Death* (1971) and *The First Man* (1995); absurdity is also a central theme in his plays *Caligula* (1945), and *State of Siege* (1948) as well as in philosophical essays including *The Myth of Sisyphus* (1942), *The Rebel*, (1951), and *Resistance, Rebellion, and Death* (1961). In *The Myth of Sisyphus*, the eponymous hero was punished by the gods likely because he had stolen some of their secrets. The punishment was cruel and simple: Sisyphus was condemned to roll a heavy rock uphill, and when at last he got to the mountaintop, the rock rolled back downhill. Sisyphus had to roll it back up, up he kept on pushing, and down the rock went again, and again . . . Forever. This hopeless labor was his punishment, this hopeless situation his condition. What interested Camus here was Sisyphus as he headed back down, smiling: he is an absurd hero in this tale, a witness to his own absurdity. The situation is as absurd as it is real. At the end of the story, Camus exhorts us to imagine Sisyphus happy.

POWERFUL ANALYSIS: IS THE CHECK IN THE MAIL?

Should we work to better our lot in this life, or simply hope for the after-life? Is the check in the mail (after our deaths)? In other words should we hope that God will reward us in the next life as opposed to in this life? Or is it really better to bet on this life than on the next, as Camus wrote?

The world is not absurd for Camus, but life is. The world is a thing, neither absurd nor rational. Life is absurd because we keep asking the world for reasons, and the world remains and always will remain silent. We are alone. Yet we have a choice: suicide or just be happy. He chose to be happy, by all accounts having a rich and joyful life, by any standards enjoying great literary success. He was given the Nobel Prize in Literature in 1957, at the age of 44, with the Nobel Academy citing him "for his important literary production, which with clear-sighted earnestness illuminates the problems of the human conscience in our times." Three years later, he was found dead in a car accident in the South of France, leaving behind, bloodied in the wrecked remains of his new sports car, the manuscript of an unfinished masterpiece, *The First Man*. The absurdity of the situation was as tragic as it was obvious.

"It is better to bet on this life than on the next," wrote Camus in *A Happy Death*. Finding joy—choosing joy—while you can is a difficult but necessary project for all of us. The choice is ours and ours alone.

READINGS

The founder of phenomenolgy Edmund Husserl describes his new philosophy of analyzing the phenomenon of life as it is lived, in this article originally written for the 1927 edition of The *Encyclopedia Britannica*.

Phenomenology

INTRODUCTION

THE TERM 'PHENOMENOLOGY' designates two things: a new kind of descriptive method which made a breakthrough in philosophy at the turn of the century, and an *a priori* science derived from it; a science which is intended to supply the basic instrument for a rigorously scientific philosophy and, in its consequent application, to make possible a methodical reform of all the sciences.

... The first thing that is necessary is a clarification of what is peculiar to experience, and especially to the pure experience of the psychical—and specifically the purely psychical that experience reveals, which is to become the theme of a pure psychology. It is natural and appropriate that precedence will be accorded to the most immediate types of experience, which in each case reveal to us our own psychic being.

Focusing our experiencing gaze on our own psychic life necessarily takes place as reflection, as a turning about of a glance which had previously been directed elsewhere. Every experience can be subject to such reflection, as can indeed every manner in which we occupy ourselves with any real or ideal objects—for instance, thinking, or in the modes of feeling and will, valuing and striving. So when we are fully engaged in conscious activity, we focus exclusively on the specific thing, thoughts, values, goals, or means involved, but not on the psychical experience as such, in which these things are known *as* such. Only reflection reveals this to us. Through reflection, instead of grasping simply the matter straightout—the values, goals, and instrumentalities—we grasp the corresponding subjective experiences in which we become 'conscious' of them, in which (in the broadest sense) they 'appear'. For this reason, they are called 'phenomena', and their most general essential character is to exist as the 'consciousness-of' or 'appearance-of' the specific things, thoughts (judged states of affairs, grounds, conclusions), plans, decisions, hopes, and so forth. This relatedness [of the appearing to the object of appearance] resides in the meaning of all expressions in the vernacular languages which relate to psychic experience—for instance, perception *of* something, recalling *of* something, thinking *of* something, hoping *for* something, fearing something, striving *for* something, deciding on something, and so on. If this realm of what we call 'phenomena' proves to be the possible field for a pure psychological discipline related exclusively to phenomena, we can understand the designation of it as *phenomenological psychology*. The terminological expression, deriving from Scholasticism, for designating the basic character of being as consciousness, as consciousness of something, is *intentionality*. The phenomenological reversal of our gaze shows that this 'being directed' [*Gerichtetsein*] is really an immanent essential feature of the respective experiences involved; they are 'intentional' experiences.

An extremely large and variegated number of kinds of special cases fall within the general scope of this concept. Consciousness of something is not an empty holding of something; every phenomenon has its own total form of intention, but at the same time it has a structure, which in intentional analysis leads always again to components which are themselves also intentional. So for example in starting from a perception of something (for example, a die), phenomenological reflection leads to a multiple and yet synthetically unified intentionality. There are continually varying differences in the modes of appearing of objects, which are caused by the changing of 'orientation'—of right and left, nearness and farness, with the consequent differences in perspective involved. There are further differences in appearance between the 'actually seen front' and the 'unseeable' ['*unanschaulichen*'] and relatively 'undetermined' reverse side, which is nevertheless 'meant along with it'. Observing the flux of modes of appearing and the manner of their 'synthesis', one finds that every phase and portion [of the flux] is already in itself 'consciousness-of'—but in such a manner that there is formed within the constant emerging of new phases the synthetically unified awareness that this is one and the same object. The intentional structure of any process of perception has its fixed essential type [*seine feste Wesenstypik*], which must necessarily be realized in all its extraordinary complexity just in order for a physical body simply to be perceived as such. If this same thing is intuited in other modes—for example, in the modes of recollection, fantasy or pictorial representation—to some extent the whole intentional content of the perception comes back, but all aspects peculiarly transformed to correspond to that mode. This applies similarly for every other category of psychic process: the judging, valuing, striving consciousness is not an empty having knowledge of the specific judgments, values, goals, and means. Rather, these constitute themselves, with fixed essential forms corresponding to each process, in a flowing intentionality. For psychology, the universal task presents itself: to investigate systematically the elementary intentionalities, and from out of these [unfold] the typical forms of intentional processes, their possible variants, their syntheses to new forms, their structural composition, and from this advance towards a descriptive knowledge of the totality of mental process, towards a comprehensive type of a life of the psyche [*Gesamttypus eines Lebens der Seele*]. Clearly, the consistent carrying out of this task will produce knowledge which will have validity far beyond the psychologist's own particular psychic existence.

Psychic life *is* accessible to us not only through self-experience but also through experience of others. This novel source of experience offers us not only what matches our self-experience but also what is new, inasmuch as, in terms of consciousness and indeed as experience, it establishes the differences between own and other, as well as the properties peculiar to the life of a community. At just this point there arises the task of also making phenomenologically understandable the mental life of the community, with all the intentionalities that pertain to it.

The idea of a phenomenological psychology encompasses the whole range of tasks arising out of the experience of self and the experience of the other founded on it. But it is not yet clear whether phenomenological experience, followed through in exclusiveness and consistency, really provides us with a kind of closed-off field of being, out of which a science can grow which is exclusively focused on it and completely free of everything psychophysical. Here [in fact] difficulties do exist, which have hidden from psychologists the possibility of such a purely phenomenological psychology even after Brentano's discovery of intentionality. They are relevant already to the construction of a really pure self-experience, and therewith of a really pure psychic datum. A particular method of access is required for the pure phenomenological field: the method of 'phenomenological reduction'. This *method of 'phenomenological reduction'* is thus the foundational method of pure psychology and the presupposition of all its specifically theoretical methods. Exactly this same thing is true of every kind of awareness directed at something out there in the world. A consistent *epoche* of the phenomenologist is required, if he wishes to break through to his own consciousness as pure phenomenon or as the totality of his purely mental processes. That is to say, in the accomplishment of phenomenological reflection he must inhibit every co-accomplishment of objective positing produced in unreflective consciousness, and therewith [inhibit] every judgmental drawing-in of the world as it 'exists' for him straightforwardly. The specific experience of this house, this body, of a world as such, is and remains, however, according to its own essential content and thus inseparably, experience '*of* this house', this body, this world; this is so for every mode of consciousness which is directed towards an object. It is, after all, quite impossible to describe an intentional experience—even if illusionary, an invalid judgment, or the like—without at the same time describing the object of that consciousness *as* such. The universal *epoche* of the world as it becomes known in consciousness (the 'putting it in brackets') shuts out from the

phenomenological field the world as it exists for the subject in simple absoluteness; its place, however, is taken by the world as given in *consciousness*
(perceived, remembered, judged, thought, valued, etc.) —the world *as
such*, the 'world in brackets', or in other words, the world, or rather individual
things in the world as absolute, are replaced by the respective meaning of
each in *consciousness* [*Bewusstseinssinn*] in its various modes (perceptual
meaning, recollected meaning, and so on).

With this, we have clarified and supplemented our initial determination of
the phenomenological experience and its sphere of being. In going back
from the unities posited in the natural attitude to the manifold of modes of
consciousness in which they appear, the unities, as inseparable from these
multiplicities—but as 'bracketed'—are also to be reckoned among what is
purely psychical, and always specifically in the appearance-character in
which they present themselves. The method of phenomenological reduction (to the pure 'phenomenon', the purely psychical) accordingly consists (1)
in the methodical and rigorously consistent *epoche* of every objective positing in the psychic sphere, both of the individual phenomenon and of the
whole psychic field in general; and (2) in the methodically practiced seizing
and describing of the multiple 'appearances' as appearances of their objective units and these units as units of component meanings accruing to them
each time in their appearances. With this is shown a twofold direction—the
noetic and *noematic* of phenomenological description. Phenomenological
experience in the methodical form of the phenomenological reduction is
the only genuine 'inner experience' in the sense meant by any well-grounded
science of psychology. In its own nature lies manifest the possibility of being
carried out continuously *in infinitum* with methodical preservation of purity.
The reductive method is transferred from self-experience to the experience
of others insofar as there can be applied to the envisaged mental life of the
Other the corresponding bracketing and description according to the subjective 'How' of its appearance and what is appearing ('*noesis*' and '*noema*').
As a further consequence, the community that is experienced in community
experience is reduced not only to the mentally particularized intentional
fields but also to the unity of the community life that connects them all
together, the community mental life in its phenomenological purity (inter-
subjective reduction). Thus results the perfect expansion of the genuine
psychological concept of 'inner experience'.

To every mind there belongs not only the unity of its multiple *intentional
life-process* with all its inseparable unities of sense directed towards the
'object'. There is also, inseparable from this life-process, the experiencing
I-subject as the identical *I-pole* giving a centre for all specific intentionalities,
and as the carrier of all habitualities growing out of this life-process. . . .

If we consider the how of this inclusion, we find that what is meant is that
every *a priori* is ultimately prescribed in its validity of being precisely *as a*

transcendental achievement; i.e., it is together with the essential structures of its constitution, with the kinds and levels of its givenness and confirmation of itself, and with the appertaining habitualities. This implies that in and through the establishment of the *a priori* the subjective *method* of this establishing is itself made transparent, and that for the *a priori* disciplines which are founded within phenomenology (for example, as mathematical sciences) there can be no 'paradoxes' and no 'crises of the foundations'. The consequence that arises [from all this] with reference to the *a priori* sciences that have come into being historically and in transcendental naïveté is that only a radical, phenomenological grounding can transform them into true, methodical, fully self-justifying sciences.

In phenomenology all rational problems have their place, and thus also those that traditionally are in some special sense or other philosophically significant. For out of the absolute sources of transcendental experience, or eidetic intuiting, they first [are able to] obtain their genuine formulation and feasible means for their solution. In its universal relatedness-back-to-itself, phenomenology recognizes its particular function within a possible life of mankind at the transcendental level. It recognizes the absolute norms which are to be picked out intuitively from it [life of mankind], and also its primordial teleo-logical-tendential structure in a directedness towards disclosure of these norms and their conscious practical operation. It recognizes itself as a function of the all-embracing reflective meditation of (transcendental) humanity, [a self-examination] in the service of an all-inclusive praxis of reason; that is, in the service of striving towards the universal ideal of absolute perfection which lies in infinity, [a striving] which becomes free through [the process of] disclosure. Or, in different words it is a striving in the direction of the idea (lying in infinity) of a humanness which in action and thought would live and move [be, exist] in truth and genuineness. It recognizes its self-reflective function [of self-examination] for the relative realization of the correlative practical idea of a genuine human life in the second sense (whose structural forms of being and whose practical norms it is to investigate), namely as one [that is] consciously and purposively directed towards this absolute idea. In short, the metaphysically teleological, the ethical, and the problems of philosophy of history, no less than, obviously, the problems of judging reason, lie within its boundary, no differently from all significant problems whatever, and all [of them] in their inmost synthetic unity and order as [being] of transcendental spirituality.

The Phenomenological Resolution of All Philosophical Antitheses

In the systematic work of phenomenology, which progresses from intuitively given [concrete] data to heights of abstraction, the old traditional ambiguous antitheses of the philosophical standpoint are resolved—by themselves and without the arts of an argumentative dialectic, and without weak efforts and compromises: oppositions such as between rationalism (Platonism) and empiricism, relativism and absolutism, subjectivism and objectivism, ontologism and transcendentalism, psychologism and anti-psychologism, positivism and metaphysics, or the teleological versus the causal interpretation of the world. Throughout all of these, [one finds] justified motives, but throughout also half-truths or impermissible absolutizing of only relatively and abstractively legitimate one-sidednesses.

Subjectivism can only be overcome by the most all-embracing and consistent subjectivism (the transcendental). In this [latter] form it is at the same time objectivism [of a deeper sort], in that it represents the claims of whatever objectivity is to be demonstrated through concordant experience, but admittedly [this is an objectivism which] also brings out its full and genuine sense, against which [sense] the supposedly realistic objectivism sins by its failure to understand transcendental constitution. *Relativism* can only be overcome through the most all-embracing relativism, that of transcendental phenomenology, which makes intelligible the relativity of all 'objective' being [or existence] as transcendentally constituted; but at one with this [it makes intelligible] the most radical relativity, the relatedness of the transcendental subjectivity to itself. But just this [relatedness, subjectivity] proves its identity to be the only possible sense of [the term] 'absolute' being—over against all 'objective.' being that is relative to it—namely, as the 'for-itself'—being of transcendental subjectivity. Likewise: *Empiricism* can only be overcome by the most universal and consistent empiricism, which puts in place of the restricted [term] 'experience' of the empiricists the necessarily broadened concept of experience [inclusive] of intuition which offers original data, an intuition which in all its forms (intuition of *eidos*, apodictic self-evidence, phenomenological intuition of essence, etc.) shows the manner and form of its legitimation through phenomenological clarification. Phenomenology as eidetic is, on the other hand, rationalistic: it overcomes restrictive and dogmatic rationalism, however, through the most universal rationalism of inquiry into essences, which is related uniformly to transcendental subjectivity, to the I, consciousness, and conscious objectivity. And it is the same in reference to the other antitheses bound up with them. The tracing back of all being to the transcendental subjectivity and its constitutive intentional functions leaves open, to mention one more thing, no other way of contemplating the world than the *teleological*. And yet phenomenology also acknowledges a kernel of truth in naturalism (or rather sensationism). That is, by revealing associations as intentional phenomena, indeed as a whole basic typology of forms of passive intentional synthesis with transcendental and purely passive genesis based on essential laws, phenomenology shows Humean fictionalism to contain anticipatory discoveries; particularly in his doctrine of the origin of such fictions as thing, persisting existence, causality—anticipatory discoveries all shrouded in absurd theories.

Phenomenological philosophy regards itself in its whole method as a pure outcome of methodical intentions which already animated Greek philosophy from its beginnings; above all, however, [it continues] the still vital intentions which reach, in the two lines of rationalism and empiricism, from Descartes through Kant and German idealism into our confused present day. A pure outcome of methodical intentions means real method which allows the problems to be taken in hand and completed. In the way of true science this path 'is endless. Accordingly, phenomenology demands that the phenomenologist foreswear the ideal of a philosophic system and yet as a humble worker in community with others, live for a perennial philosophy.

In this short excerpt from his magisterial introduction to Sartre's philosophy, *The Tragic Finale*, Wilfrid Desan (1908–2001) lays out the concept of freedom as the very definition of human consciousness unbound by determinism.

Husserl began his career as a mathematician, and like other mathematicians before and after him he soon found himself concerned with the foundations of mathematics. Obviously, some such inquiry was necessary if he was to convince himself, as he was more than ready to do, that the mathematician could give all the answers to the riddle of the universe. What he discovered, however, was that the mathematician had to come to the philosopher for the understanding of knowledge itself and of several of the most elementary notions, such as space, time, and number. In short, his investigation into the foundations of mathematical knowledge led him into a new and, as it may have seemed, alien field. And here he was to make the same mistake, and to experience the same disillusion, that he had known before; for he assumed that philosophy would have the answers ready-made for him, and that his problems would be settled once and forever. Instead, he found a field bristling with thorns, scarred with rock formations, soggy with the quagmires of two thousand years of philosophical perplexities. Philosophy offered him no clear-cut answer. With the optimism of comparative youth, Husserl set himself the task of bringing order into this philosophical wilderness. We see him now, in retrospect, as another Descartes, with the same faith in reason, the same trust in the mathematical approach. His purpose was to build up philosophy so that eventually it would exhibit the rigorous thinking that characterized science, and the same meticulous precision. He wanted a return "zu den Sachen selbst," from which, in his belief, philosophy had unknowingly divorced itself. In order to acquire this strict objectivity, the philosopher, he said, must turn his whole attention to the exact and careful description of *that which appears to our consciousness*; i.e., the so-called phenomenon. To know is not to act, or to produce, but only to see.[1]

The "phenomenon" being that which manifests itself in *whatever way* it manifests itself, will not be restricted to the sensible appearance alone.[2] Feelings, desires, aversions, political institutions, philosophical doctrines "appear" and "manifest themselves" as "really" as a color does, but in a different way. My inner feelings, for instance, "manifest" themselves to me. In

---

[1] Husserl, *Ideën* (Halle: Niemeyer, 1913), pp. 1off.

[2] This aspect of the Husserlian phenomenology is clearly illustrated by Heidegger in *Sein und Zeit* (Halle: Niemeyer, 1929), p. 28.

fact, they are—even more than public phenomena—something which appears.

When we add to the term "phenomenon" the term "legein" (to examine, to describe), we shall be able to understand that "phenomenology" is a method which wants to describe all that manifests itself *as* it manifests itself.[3]

This precise description of what appears is a phenomenological description. It must be entirely free of all apriority and prejudice.[4] Consequently, no postulate of practical or theoretical reason, no criterion of revelation or tradition, may be admitted. Phenomenology rejects all deductive method, whether Hegelian or Scholastic. In phenomenology it is the Self which analyzes "phenomena"; i.e., human consciousness which analyzes that which appears in its sphere.

. . . To be "outside" being, to be isolated from being, to escape being, to stay out of the causal order of the world, means to be *free*. Human reality, then, is free. Human reality *is* Freedom. Freedom is so essential to the notion of human reality that it makes the formulation of all human essence in a static definition impossible. Freedom, claims Sartre, breaks up all definition: human reality makes itself and invents itself continually. So it appears that "existence precedes essence." *Essence* (what we are) is a result of what we make ourselves to be.

Sartre's freedom is absolute, as I shall explain in detail later. No one motive can influence or determine human consciousness for the simple reason that consciousness carries within itself "nothing," is determined in no way, and lies completely outside world determinism. "It is a generating of the past by means of nothing," concludes Sartre in one of his paradoxical formulas, which often sound more complicated than they are. An example will make this clear: I decide to go to the movies. Why? There is no determinative motive for me to go. Nothing can determine me, because there is "nothing" in me which can be determined. The relation between my past and my present is such, according to Sartre, that *what I was is not the foundation of what I am*, any more than what I *am* is the foundation of what I *shall* be. Once more he concludes with a paradox: I am the one whom I shall be in a way of not being it. This simply means: I am the one whom I *shall be*, without in any way being the *foundation* of what I shall be.

How does freedom manifest itself? How are we conscious of it? We are conscious of our freedom through *anguish*. Anguish is nothing but the fear

---

[3]"Das was sich zeigt, so wie es sich vom ihm selbst her zeigt, von ihm selbst her sehen lassen"— *Sein und Zeit*, p. 34.

[4]"Wir lassen uns durch keine Autorität das Recht verkümmern, alle Anschauungsarten als gleichswertige Rechtsquellen der Erkenntnis anzuerkennen—auch nicht durch die Autorität der 'Modernen Naturwissenschaft'"— *Ideën*, p. 38. (Consequently, the phenomenologists claim to be the real positivists—"die echte Positivisten.")

of ourselves or the painful hesitation before the possibles, my possibles, which only I can determine.

One could perhaps object that although anguish is an essential characteristic of freedom, its manifestations are not frequent. The answer is that most people do not reflect, they simply "act." "The consciousness of an acting man is non-reflective."[5] Real anguish, what could be called ethical anguish, appears only when we have put ourselves in front of our responsibility. In ordinary life, however, in the life of *immediate* consciousness (i.e., the life where we do not reflect), the values appear under the form of a thousand little taboos which are ready-made and to which we are obedient: we must be at the office at nine o'clock, we must keep to the right side of the road, we must not kiss the file clerk. We *reflect*, we face our freedom and are overwhelmed by anguish. Our usual attitude before anguish, however, is *flight*. Even philosophical determinism is an escape from anguish, for if it can be proven that we are no longer responsible for our actions, there is no more reason to be anguished.[6]

. . . In considering ourselves in this way as a "thing," we try to escape anguish.[7] For a "thing" is no longer free, and has no reason to be "anguished."

In summary, then, we may say that negation and non-being under their different forms (interrogation, negative judgment, and destruction) suppose a form of nothingness in the heart of consciousness itself. It is in the absolute and pure subjectivity of human consciousness that we discover the origin of the non-being which we ascribe to things. The act by which the For-itself (or human consciousness) continually generates non-being into the world is called nihilation, or negation: all judgment is in one way or another a negation or nihilation. And since one can only give what one has, human consciousness *is* its own non-being, its own "nihilation." Furthermore, to be "outside" being means also to be *free*. The For-itself is Freedom.

---

[5] *EN*, p. 69.
[6] *EN*, p. 71.
[7] *EN*, p. 81. Cf. Bergson, *La Pensée et le Mouvant*, pp. 143 ff, p. 190.

KEY TERMS

Being-in-itself (**Être-en-soi**) is Sartre's term for matter, the world that is not conscious, that is, an essence.

Being-for-itself (**Être-pour-soi**) is Sartre's term for human consciousness, which is not a thing; the "nothingness" whose existence precedes essence.

Dasein is literally "being there" in German, Heidegger's useful concept that definition of a person always as being there (*Dasein*), thrown into a world that is not of his or her choosing.

Existentialism is a philosophy that concentrates on everyday life as it is lived, noting that existence precedes essence.

Hegelian dialectic is variously interpreted as either a new logic or a new way to use traditional logic, where a thesis not only proves at some point insufficient but also contains within itself its own destruction, an antithesis; the two elements are not opposed in the traditional way but rather are absorbed into a third element: synthesis. The synthesis is itself a new thesis, so the forward progress of the idea moves forward dialectically.

Phenomenology is Husserl's philosophy describing how consciousness is always consciousness of something, and how the two together—the knower and the known—make up a phenomenon.

QUESTIONS FOR DISCUSSION AND REVIEW

1. Articulate the main themes found in existentialism.
2. Explain why Kierkegaard and Dostoyevsky are considered predecessors of existentialism.
3. Critically analyze Husserl's phenomenology and how it informed existentialism
4. Explain the meaning of being and nothingness according to Sartre.
5. Summarize, explain, and evaluate the main points of the reading by Husserl.
6. Summarize, explain, and evaluate the main points of the reading by Wilfrid Desan.

BIBLIOGRAPHY AND SUGGESTED READINGS

Camus, A. (1991). *The Myth of Sisyphus*. (O'Brien, J. transl.).

Desan, W. (1965). *The Marxism of Jean-Paul Sartre*.

Dostoyevsky, F. (2002). *The Brothers Karamazov*. (Pevear, R. and Volokhonsky, L. transl.).

Hegel, G. W. F. (1977). *Phenomenology of Spirit*. (Miller, A.V. transl.).

Husserl, E. (1927). *Phenomenology*. In R. Kearney and M. Rainwater (Eds.), *The Continental Philosophy Reader*.

Internet Encyclopedia of Philosophy. A peer-reviewed academic resource. Available from http://www.iep.utm.edu/

Merleau-Ponty, M. (1964). *Hegel's Existentialism*. In *Sense and Non-sense*. (.Dreyfus, H.L. and Dreyfus, P.A. transl.).

Sartre, J-P. (1948). *Existentialism and Humanism,* (Mairet, P.; transl.)

Sartre, J-P. (1956). *Being and Nothingness*. (Barnes, H. transl.).

Sartre, J-P. (2006). *Critique of Dialectical Reason*, vols. 1 and 2, (Sheridan-Smith, A. and Hoare, Q. transl.).

Stanford Encyclopedia of Philosophy. Available from http://plato.stanford.edu/

Aesthetics— Judging Beauty

10

Upon completing this chapter, students should be able to meet the following Learning Outcomes:

10.1 articulate the connections between pleasure, contemplation, and judgment in aesthetic appreciation.

10.2 explain the how aesthetics, art, and criticism are interrelated.

10.3 evaluate David Hume's view regarding art criticism.

10.4 articulate the notion of 'truth' in art criticism.

10.5 explain if it is possible to have agreement about aesthetic judgments and if that is a problem.

Pleasure, Contemplation, and Judgment

The field of aesthetics casts a very wide net. The arts are many, and they happen in different places all over the world. They always have. Our enjoyment, appreciation, and judgment of art—together with the question of what defines art to begin with—are the key elements to consider in aesthetics. The word itself is derived from the Greek Αισθητική, *aisthetikos*, meaning "coming from the senses."

More than any other branch of axiology, that is, of the philosophy of making value judgments, aesthetics has sensuality built into it as much as it has seductive, ineffable quality in its critical analysis. Still, though some philosophers disagree, it is not just a matter of taste.

Aesthetics, Art, and Criticism

You might ask, what is it critics do, exactly? Serious arts critics have to travel, usually a lot. They contemplate paintings in museums all over the world, listen to different orchestras in different concert halls, witness ballet and opera wherever they may come to life. Critics also often serve on juries, observe the impact of social and political forces on the art of their time, reflect on the art of the past and the art of the future and do so by experiencing that art in person. A literary critic can of course just sit and read a book, and that book will be the same artistic object that everyone elsewhere is reading. But the other arts, especially the performing arts, are different. To analyze painting and sculpture, or theater, music, dance, and opera, the critic has to travel wherever these artistic works may be.

Yes, critics travel. And the toughest journey a critic takes is the vast one from the statement "I like this'" to "This is good." The shortest distance between those two points is seldom a straight line.

> "Today it goes without saying that nothing concerning art goes without saying. Everything about art has become problematic: its inner life, its relation to society, even its right to exist."
>
> —*Theodor Adorno*

One easy way of dividing the arts is between what we like, which must be good, and everything else. On some level, this remains the case even in the most complex aesthetics systems. Blaise Pascal's clever littler dictum that "the heart has its reasons that reason does not know" is as unsettling as it is true. Say something strikes you as absolutely right in the concert hall, something in the theater has a powerful effect on you. You begin to articulate what you will choose to call the reasons for the work's success. But maybe your heart still has other reasons; these reasons do not begin to touch. It is in this sense that criticism defines not so much what the work of art is as what happens when we witness it. The act of witnessing is what transforms a work of art standing alone into the object of our aesthetic experience. This is the moment of attention, the vehicle for the journey from the report of a private experience—"I like this"—to the public utterance and judgment "This is good."

"I like 'x'" or "I don't like 'x'" are always true, and they also are not interesting unless you're talking to your best friend or to your mother: these statement are simply reports on one's own feelings. On the other hand, "'x' is good" or "'x' is bad'" are judgments and require arguments with clearly defined reasons for each judgment.

POWERFUL ANALYSIS: DO THE KARDASHIANS MAKE GREAT TV?

Critically analyze the difference between these two statements:

- I like the TV show *Keeping Up with the Kardashians*.
- *Keeping Up with the Kardashians* is great TV show.

How can you defend the truth of either statement?

Two things are going on here. First, the critic's point of view is not that of the artist. It is, rather, that of the spectator, the witness. We are all witnesses, and art is intrinsically democratic in that sense. Second, there is an implied acknowledgment of the work of art's unique sensuousness. There are real feelings at work, and these feelings not only color but actually may define the aesthetic experience.

And these feelings guide the critic's journey. When we in the audience jointly conspire in what the English poet Samuel Taylor Coleridge (1772–1884) first noted amounts to a "willing suspension of disbelief" while watching a performance, we also agree that there is much more to the object of our attention than its physical ingredients.

POWERFUL IDEAS BOX: CRITICS

"Critics of words use words. Critics of music use words. Those thirteen syllables . . . are as pertinent as any I can make on the matter. If the final comment on a work of art is another work of art, might some critical prose, as art, equal the art it describes? Yes, but that very prose is independent of the art it describes. The best critical writing is superfluous to its subject, and musical criticism is the most superfluous of all."

—*Ned Rorem*

© Christopher Felver/CORBIS

The Phenomenology of Artistic Experience

This is the stuff of objective reporting, elements that are not a matter of opinion: the articulation of a cellist's phrasing, the steps of a dance, the rhythmic texture of an aria, the words of a play, and the notes of a symphony. But the critic, along with the rest of the audience, responds to more than these objective components of a work of art. The object of our attention transcends its material character: suddenly, miraculously, steps are more than steps, words become theater, a string of notes can break your heart. That is why it is fair to call the aesthetic experience sensual.

Of course, it takes two to have any sensual experience. It takes not just the performance and performer, but also the witness who perceives them in a particular way. Our presence at a performance, our perception of a performance, and our feelings about a performance are the happy bundle of elements that create meaning in the arts. This is the phenomenological process, and it is particularly useful in talking about the performing arts. Examining the phenomenon of what happens onstage reveals not just the basic truth of a particular work but also its universality, its inescapable humanity.

Context and dialectic are everything in aesthetics. There is no essential artistic meaning out there waiting to be discovered, and neither is there just a series of language relations waiting to be analyzed. In our time, even with today's dreary deconstructionists or politicized critics, the role of the witness and the dialectic of witnessing remain ever more useful in talking about the arts.

A score unperformed, an aria unsung, a play unread, or a dance merely intended is never the point. Theories of textual truth, political relevance, or social benefit also are never the point. The experience of an actual performance is what matters in criticism. That said, it is also true that the critic cannot claim to be just another witness among many. A critic is not what Virginia Woolf had in mind when she famously described the common reader. There is such a thing as judgment, even if the term has become decidedly unfashionable both in philosophy and in mainstream popular arts criticism.

POWERFUL IDEAS BOX: ART

"The word 'art' first signified a manner of doing and nothing more. This unlimited sense has disappeared from use . . . . . Art, considered as contemporary activity, has had to submit to the conditions of the generalized social life of our time. It has taken its place in the general economy"

—*Paul Valéry*

What Makes a Critic's Opinion Authoritative?

David Hume (1711–1776) believed that emotions are significant in both aesthetics and ethics, as we will discuss in the next chapter. In other words, he thought that a judgment consisted simply of approving or not, a matter of feeling. His theory has more adherents in aesthetics than in ethics today, particularly because aesthetics involves both contemplation and judgment. The problem remains, however, that "I don't like that movie" is no better argument in aesthetics than "I don't like those people" in ethics, although both statements are passed for arguments with alarming frequency.

Still, Hume has a point about the cultivation of taste, and a critic must certainly have good taste and good judgment. A critic's opinion, an aesthetic judgment, depends on knowledge, experience, and passion. Knowledge not just of the arts but also of the mechanics of criticism: aesthetics, logic, and rhetoric. Experience that must come from a thirst for knowledge and a wealth of opportunity. This last may seem cruel, but it remains true; all the theoretical knowledge of music in the world will not help in judging an orchestral performance if all you have heard is one orchestra in one hall, just as acquaintance with only a handful of museums or ballet companies is simply not enough in judging painting or dance with any perspective.

Context also is vital, and often it can help shape an aesthetic judgment. The Abstract Expressionists such as **Willem De Kooning** (1904–1997) and **Robert Motherwell** (1915–1991), who put American art on the map in the twentieth century, were often quite good at explaining their intentions. They were often as helpful and always at least as sensitive as philosophers and poets variously judged and praised their work. Words can help, no matter what the composer Ned Rorem may think.

© Albright-Knox Art Gallery/CORBIS

Truth in Criticism

A critic's passion must be a given. Criticism must be willing to make a case for the art that matters, not just for ways to pass the time. A creeping fear of authority is one of the most disturbing dangers of popular criticism: the suggestion that reviews are mere statements of preference, not judgments.

This is a lie. For example, if a critic believes that Edward Albee's *Three Tall Women*' is a sublime climax to a lifetime of genius, that Tom Morton-Smith's *Oppenheimer* is the most challenging and disturbing dramatic treatment to date of the ethics of the atomic bomb, or that cello concerto Philip Glass composed for the movie *Naqoyqatsi* is one of the most exciting and moving scores of the last 100 years, then that critic must argue vigorously to win over anyone who will listen. If a critic believes that something like *So You Think You Can Dance?* or *The Voice* are trash as dance, music, or television, it would be unimaginable defend it as anything else. The rest is misplaced politeness, timidity, and an abdication of critical responsibility.

© Leemage/Corbis

Socrates roundly condemned the unexamined life as not worth living, but is the unexamined music worth hearing? Is the unexamined dance worth watching? Is it worth dancing? On one level, there must be such a thing as simple, unambitious, and even mindless entertainment. What can be the harm? And yet, what is it that makes a stupid piece irritating? Hope springs eternal each time, the curtain goes up; the joy of discovery is great, but disappointment can be bitter. If art is to matter—and a critic must believe that it does—judgments must be made with almost cruel clarity. Then, the expressions of utter joy at witnessing greatness onstage will ring true.

Powerful Thinkers: Richard Wagner

Radical, transgressive, and revolutionary Richard Wagner (1813–1883) sets out to reinvent theater at the decadent heights of the Romantic Revolution. His opera tetralogy *Der Ring des Nibelungen* (The *Ring of the Nibelung*) premiered in 1876, in a theater built expressly for the then extraordinary staging demands the opera called for the Bayreuther Festspielhaus, where a festival of Wagner operas continues to this day.

Sara Krulwich/The New York Times/Redux

Wagner's vision was to recapture the impact of ancient Greek drama, while synthesizing all the arts in a feast of music, dance, theater, and art—a total work of art, or *Gesamtkunstwerk*.

His influence was and is enormous. He explained Wagnerian aesthetics in a series of essays between 1849 and 1852; but it was in his operas, on stage, that his argument is proved. Particularly between *Tristan and Isolde* (1865)—an ode to impossible love beyond death—and his final masterpiece, the sacred mystery play *Parsifal* (1882), Wagner asks crucial questions about the possibility of ethics in a godless world and the importance of freedom to the fabric of humanity. His operas are about love and death, those constant elements in the dialectic of the human condition.

In Wagner's *Gesamtkunstwerk,* the composer wanted most of all to recapture what he imagined to be the depths, simplicity, and truth of Greek tragedy. He succeeded in theater better than anyone since Shakespeare. He also succeeded in creating plays so rich in meaning that there has been room for wildly different interpretations. *Der Ring des Nibelungen* in particular has been at the mercy of—or has received the richest interpretations by—the greatest stage directors since its creation.

The mystical ring and the magical sword, enchanted water nymphs and flying warrior maidens, and even the building and destruction of the gods in Valhalla and perhaps the end of the divine and the birth of humanity—these have been fodder for interpretation and reinterpretation in our time. There have been Marxist *Rings*—with the fall of the gods seen as the inevitable result of class struggle, just as once there were Nazi *Rings* in which the Norse hero Siegfried was distorted into standing for the Aryan ideal. There have been Freudian and Jungian *Rings,* deconstructionist *Rings*, and postmodern *Rings*. The English National Opera set it in outer space, and the Paris Opera in a fashionable department store. Patrice Chereau's controversial landmark 1976 Bayreuth Festival production was the first to be filmed complete and is perhaps still the best acted, though it's sweet New Left flavor dates it as a nostalgic pre-glasnost affair. Goetz Friedrich set his 1976 *Ring* in a time tunnel with designs inspired by the Washington, DC metro stations—a gift for the American Bicentennial that had a successful run at the Kennedy Center in Washington. Otto Schenck's 1989 *Ring* for the Metropolitan Opera was a rarity by being free of anachronisms, innocent of ideological cant. The Met dropped that production in 2013, in favor of Robert LePage's dementedly expensive, riotously unsuccessful version.

Wagner's *Parsifal* tells the tale of God's own Holy Fool whose role is to save humanity. He is the Wagnerian hero closest to the ideal of Greek tragedy. The opera, Wagner's last, carries an invitation to abstraction that—paradoxically—has made this character easy to recognize as Wagner's creation even in the strangest productions. François Girard's 2012 Met production, with Jonas Kaufmann as Parsifal in a musical and dramatic characterization that set a high standard for years to come, was set in what looked like a vast pool of blood.

Maybe each age has its own Wagner. The theater and opera director Goetz Friedrich once said that "It doesn't really matter what directors do—the score will always be there, the music will always be there, Wagner will always be there."

A critic's work can be a lonely journey, a case of judging and writing against the grain. A critic should aim to rescue the details worth noting from what the great French novelist Nathalie Sarraute (1900–1999) called the magma of everyday banality. Concepts as rich in meaning as "good" or "beautiful" are falling out of favor as popular criticism grows ever more innocent of moral authority.

Elitism and the Arts

In an age when being judgmental has become a bad thing, condemned by those who would destroy the canon and dumb down the arts as far as they will go, criticism may surrender its role out of a sense of survival: television arts critics remain on the air by summarizing movie plots, book reviews become book reports, rap and hip-hop are treated as if on the same level as Beethoven, the concept of elitism has become anathema to those who fund the arts, and even the rules of grammar are seen as quaint suggestions.

Maybe Elitism Is a Good Thing

An elitism of vision, excellence, imagination, and genius. An elitism of talent, taste and bravery are something to treasure. It is not for everyone, but it can represent the best in all of us and it certainly ought to be there for all of us to admire. These are strange times indeed, when the concept of elitism has become an insult, a way to smear the arts. Elitism, often in the eye of the beholder, has become doublespeak for exclusion, for everything that is not politically correct. To be placed in a position of defending, elitism is decidedly awkward.

Enemies of culture cry that the arts should be democratic, ergo the arts have failed. They presume that since not everyone can reach excellence, then excellence, too, is somehow undemocratic. They make use of perverse educational trends that, when arts education takes place at all, preach that everyone can be an artist while showing no one how to be part of an educated audience. Advisory committees, boards of directors, and tribes of ideological guardians today ensure the multicultural, pangeographic, and heterogeneous quality of funded artistic projects, as if great art ever had been created by committee rather than by an individual's unique and passionate vision.

When artistic canons are devalued, and every opinion, no matter how base and uninformed, is worth the same as every other, mediocrity is rewarded and individual genius languishes unrecognized. Shunning the elite, we prop up the bland, the safe, hoping that if we call it great often enough we might believe in its greatness.

> "Not every opinion is worth considering, just as not every work of art is worth our time. There are such things as stupid remarks, ignorant judgments, misplaced affections and, of course, there is such a thing as bad art"
>
> —*Octavio Roca*

Yet consider, for example, that no one would choose a brain surgeon by neighborhood committee vote. If your country were invaded, you would want elite troops for your defense. Only the best will do for things we care about. Yet too often we let artistic discourse be shaped by those who care the least about the arts.

Why not aim for the best in the arts, humanity's highest achievement, as we clearly do in other endeavors? Why allow ourselves to be embarrassed by our culture's greatness? Why tear down what is most sublime in our culture and vulgarize it to the lowest possible level just so everyone, no matter how crass or bigoted, will not be offended by it?

Elitism Is Not the Problem. Elitism Is the Answer

We may be in danger of forgetting how to have a meaningful argument about the arts, a true reckoning of aesthetics. The collectivization and internationalization of popular entertainment, and their worship in much of the popular press, are fast heading toward the hegemony of the banal.

Yet, contrary to popular cant, not every opinion is worth considering, just as not every work of art is worth our time. A flat note in opera is not a matter of opinion, and neither is flawed turnout or lazy *épaulement* in ballet. But we respond to more than these objective components of a work of art. The object of our attention transcends its material character. There are such things as stupid remarks, ignorant judgments, misplaced affections and, of course, there is such a thing as bad art.

Multiculturalism, Art, and Politics

Multiculturalism is at once a reality and a noble goal. But accepting its many advantages should not dampen our courage to call something civilized and something else barbaric, something advanced and something else retrograde, and something good and something else bad. Multiculturalism at its most vulgar amounts to this, in ordinary language: anything goes, so nothing is worth it. That is relativism at its worst.

There is an appalling lack of moral outrage in criticism these days, when few things offend some readers more than a critic's taking offense at anything. With indulgences all but guaranteed for any art, no matter how low, having high standards is considered suspect. **Bishop George Berkely** (1685–1783) remarked that "we ought to think with the learned and speak with the vulgar." The Irish philosopher was not being cynical, just practical. Critics often are tempted to place their faith in small matters, not so much in acceptance of lowered expectations as in resigned enjoyment of modest details. Then just wait to be surprised.

POWERFUL IDEAS BOX: LOOKING AT DANCE, JUDGING DANCE

The easiest way to look at a ballet is just that: look at it. Few things anywhere compare with ballet in being easy to love. There are beautiful people, usually moving to ravishing music, using their bodies in ways that are at once athletic and sublime, telling tales in motion that reveal truths and suggest mysteries we might otherwise be too shy or afraid to see.

Details are everything, and they mean different things to different people. There is a small moment in the first ballet I ever saw that still breaks my heart every time.

In *"Giselle,"* an emotionally shattering ballet and one of the glories of romantic theater, a poor peasant girl suddenly faces a rich, elegant woman who is wearing what must seem like impossibly beautiful clothes: Giselle's simple gesture as she reaches and almost touches the hem of Bathilde's dress embodies innocent hope against all odds, longing for so much happiness that Giselle will never know, and ineffable sadness.

How each ballerina plays that moment can be as telling as how a Violetta in Act One of Verdi's opera *La Traviata* notices the ravages of a fast life staring back in the mirror in the simple line *"O, qual pallor."* "How pale I look." Or it can be as devastating as how the dying Åse in Ibsen's epic *Peer Gynt* can suggest irony, fervor, and terror all at once as she listens to her fantastical liar of a son describe the gates of heaven she will soon enter.

Dancers turn and run, lift and caress each other, stand very still. These are things all of us do in our everyday lives, but it would be wrong to say that dance is like everyday life. It isn't. Every one of those moves is as different from the way ordinary mortals move as Beethoven's Pastoral Symphony is different from the actual sounds of a summer morning.

Gjon Mili / Getty

Ballet, theater, music—each is as unnatural as it is beautiful.

Then again, the power of suggestion may be the most staggering trick in an artist's bag: almost everything listed just now, from balances to good looks, can matter not at all when a great dancer chooses to make us believe in his or her performance. Just as Maria Callas in her last tour had the power to make the audience believe that it had heard notes she clearly had not sung, so could the great Alicia Alonso (b. 1920) in her 50s be the most youthful Giselle we are ever likely to see.

Do we fall in love with the dancer or the dance? The story or the movement? The athletic prowess, poetic interpretation, or sexy good looks? With the emotions brought out by a series of steps or gestures, or with the dazzling geometry of these same phrases? Do we fall in love with the fact that this is the best we have ever seen, or just the first we have ever seen? All of these, as it happens, are good reasons. So is loving *The Nutcracker'* because your little niece Consuelo is making her debut as a dancing lollipop. Whatever makes you return to the theater is a good reason, if only because chances are you will like it even better the next time. You might even begin to judge it.

Keep in mind that a critic most likely works from a theoretical framework as well as from a knowledge of history. But it is worth remembering, however, that what makes the difference in the success of a concerto, a play, or a dance is not its adherence to any theory at all. Bad criticism takes us away from the experience of the arts and into the realm of theory.

That is one problem with Marxist aesthetics, for example, or with other utilitarian views of the arts that can turn critics into propagandists or censors. Talk of whether or not a concerto, a play or a dance is socially relevant or politically useful is all very nice, but the real question is whether it is good or bad. Does Pablo Picasso's immortal *Guernica* (1937) require knowledge of the Spanish Civil War in order to be emotionally devastated by it? Is it part of our aesthetic appreciation or judgment of Dmitri Shostakovich's symphonies or string quartets that they were composed by one of most tragic composer of our time whose life was made nearly impossible by Stalinism? Or can we just listen to it and still judge it to be great music, apart from its historical context?

Artgo/Shutterstock.com

The ballet *Giselle* (1841), the apotheosis and climax of the Romantic Era, is not a communist dance if it is performed by the Ballet Nacional de Cuba in Havana any more than it is a fascist or kleptocratic dance as performed by today's Bolshoi Ballet in Moscow, or a Republican or Democrat dance when brought to life by the American Ballet Theatre in New York. It is just *Giselle*.

Is political criticism of art a form of *ad hominem* argument, or is all art political? Being able to tell the difference, performance by actual performance, moment by living moment, is a critic's responsibility. And that means separating competence from incompetence, acting from acting out, professional polish from mere good intentions, and art from dross or worse.

The phenomenal thing about the arts—in every sense of that very useful term—is that it takes two to give meaning to the phenomenon. There is no unmediated, essential truth in literature, painting, music, theater, or dance. The truth of those art forms arises not in a vacuum but in public, in real life, in the magical moment when the audience witnesses the performers in action.

How You Can Judge

Forget program notes, forget for now how wonderful the arts are for the community. Forget the artists' heartwarming backgrounds or political associations. For heaven's sake, forget Sigmund Freud and V. I. Lenin, whose aesthetic theories are at last achieving the neglect they so richly deserve. A critic first and foremost must concentrate on what is happening on the page or onstage.

In the end, it is still the journey from "I like this" to "this is good," from "I like Marcel Proust" to "Proust is sublime, beautiful, good" that matters.

Is this personal? Sure. Should anyone really want criticism to be impersonal, pretending to be objective, scientific? No. The truth is that, in the arts as in life, you fall in love all of a sudden. Then, if you are lucky, you spend a lifetime working out the details.

READINGS

A leading light of American Abstract Expressionism and one of the great painters of the twentieth century, Willem de Kooning (1904–1997) here disarmingly confesses the meaning of his art and discusses the possibilities of abstraction.

What Abstract Art Means to Me

THE first man who began to speak, whoever he was, must have intended it. For surely it is talking that has put "Art" into painting. Nothing is positive about art except that it is a word. Right from there to here all art became literary. We are not yet living in a world where everything is self-evident. It is very interesting to notice that a lot of people who want to take the talking out of painting, for instance, do nothing else but talk about it. That is no contradiction, however. The art in it is the forever mute part you can talk about forever.

For me, only one point comes into my field of vision. This narrow, biased point gets very clear sometimes. I didn't invent it. It was already here. Everything that passes me I can see only a little of, but I am always looking. And I see an awful lot sometimes.

The word "abstract" comes from the light-tower of the philosophers, and it seems to be one of their spotlights that they have particularly focussed [sic] on "Art." So the artist is always lighted up by it. As soon as it—I mean the "abstract"— comes into painting, it ceases to be what it is as it is written. It changes into a feeling which could be explained by some other words, probably. But one day, some painter used "Abstraction" as a title for one of his paintings. It was a still life. And it was a very tricky title. And it wasn't really a very good one. From then on the idea of abstraction became something extra. Immediately it gave some people the idea that they could free art from itself. Until then, Art meant everything that was in it—not what you could take out of it. There was only one thing you could take out of it sometime when you were in the right mood—that abstract and indefinable sensation, the esthetic part—and still leave it where it was. For the painter to come to the "abstract" or the "nothing," he needed many things. Those things were always things in life—a horse, a flower, a milkmaid, the light in a room through a window made of diamond shapes maybe, tables, chairs, and so forth. The painter, it is true, was not always completely free. The things were

---

Willem de Kooning, "What Abstract Art Means to Me," talk delivered at the "What is Abstract Art?" symposium, The Museum of Modern Art, New York, February 5, 1951. First published in "What Abstract Art Means to Me: Statements by Six American Artists," *The Museum of Modern Art Bulletin* XVIII, no. 3 (Spring 1951): 4-8.

All quotations by Willem de Kooning © Estate of Lisa de Kooning.

not always of his own choice, but because of that he often got some new ideas. Some painters liked to paint things already chosen by others, and after being abstract about them, were called Classicists. Others wanted to select the things themselves and, after being abstract about them, were called Romanticists. Of course, they got mixed up with one another a lot too. Anyhow, at that time, they were not abstract about something which was already abstract. They freed the shapes, the light, the color, the space, by putting them into concrete things in a given situation. They *did* think about the possibility that the things—the horse, the chair, the man—were abstractions, but they let that go, because if they kept thinking about it, they would have been led to give up painting altogether, and would probably have ended up in the philosopher's tower. When they got those strange, deep ideas, they got rid of them by painting a particular smile on one of the faces in the picture they were working on.

The esthetics of painting were always in a state of development parallel to the development of painting itself. They influenced each other and vice versa. But all of a sudden, in that famous turn of the century, a few people thought they could take the bull by the horns and invent an esthetic beforehand. After immediately disagreeing with each other, they began to form all kinds of groups, each with the idea of freeing art, and each demanding that you should obey them. Most of these theories have finally dwindled away into politics or strange forms of spiritualism. The question, as they saw it, was not so much what you *could* paint but rather what you could *not* paint. You could *not* paint a house or a tree or a mountain. It was then that subject matter came into existence as something you ought *not* to have.

In the old days, when artists were very much wanted, if they got to thinking about their usefulness in the world, it could only lead them to believe that painting was too worldly an occupation and some of them went to church instead or stood in front of it and begged. So what was considered too worldly from a spiritual point of view then, became later—for those who were inventing the new esthetics—a spiritual smoke-screen and not worldly enough. These latter-day artists were bothered by their apparent uselessness. Nobody really seemed to pay any attention to them. And they did not trust that freedom of indifference. They knew that they were relatively freer than ever before *because* of that indifference, but in spite of all their talking about freeing art, they really didn't mean it that way. Freedom to them meant to be useful in society. And that is really a wonderful idea. To achieve that, they didn't need *things* like tables and chairs or a horse. They needed ideas instead, social ideas, to make their objects with, their constructions—the "pure plastic phenomena"— which were used to illustrate their convictions. Their point was that until they came along with their theories, Man's own form in space—his body—was a private prison; and that it was because of this imprisoning misery—because he was hungry and overworked and went to a horrid place called home late at night in the rain, and his bones ached and his head was heavy—because of this very consciousness of his own body, this sense of pathos, they suggest, he was overcome by the drama of a crucifixion in a painting or the lyricism of a group of people sitting quietly around a table drinking wine. In other words, these estheticians proposed that people had up to now understood painting in terms of their own private misery. Their own sentiment of form instead was one of comfort. The beauty of comfort. The great curve of a bridge was beautiful because people could go across the river in comfort. To compose with curves like that, and angles, and make works of art with them could only make people happy, they maintained, for the only association was one of comfort. That millions of people have died in war since then, because of that idea of comfort, is something else.

This pure form of comfort became the comfort of "pure form." The "nothing" part in a painting until then—the part that was not painted but that was there because of the things in the picture which were painted—had a lot of descriptive labels attached to it like "beauty," "lyric," "form," "profound," "space," "expression," "classic," "feeling," "epic," "romantic," "pure," "balance," etc. Anyhow that "nothing" which was always recognized as a particular something—and as something particular—they generalized, with their book-keeping minds, into circles and squares. They had the innocent idea that the "something" existed "in spite of" and not "because of" and that this something was the only thing that truly mattered. They had hold of it, they thought, once and for all. But this idea made them go backward in spite of the fact that they wanted to go forward. That "something" which was not measurable, they lost by trying to make it measurable; and thus all the old words which, according to their ideas, ought to be done away with got into art again: pure, supreme, balance, sensitivity, etc.

Kandinsky understood "Form" as *a* form, like an object in the real world; and an object, he said, was a narrative—and so, of course, he disapproved of it. He wanted his "music without words." He wanted to be "simple as a child." He intended, with his "inner-self," to rid himself of "philosophical barricades" (he sat down and wrote something about all this). But in turn his own writing has become a philosophical barricade, even if it is a barricade full of holes. It offers a kind of Middle-European idea of Buddhism or, anyhow, something too theosophic for me.

The sentiment of the Futurists was simpler. No space. Everything ought to keep on going! That's probably the reason they went themselves. Either a man was a machine or else a sacrifice to make machines with.

The moral attitude of Neo-Plasticism is very much like that of Constructivism, except that the Constructivists wanted to bring things out in the open and the Neo-Plasticists didn't want anything left over.

I have learned a lot from all of them and they have confused me plenty too. One thing is certain, they didn't give me my natural aptitude for drawing. I am completely weary of their ideas now.

The only way I still think of these ideas is in terms of the individual artists who came from them or invented them. I still think that Boccioni was a great artist and a passionate man. I like Lissitzky, Rodchenko, Tatlin and Gabo; and I admire some of Kandinsky's painting very much. But Mondrian, that great merciless artist, is the only one who had nothing left over.

The point they all had in common was to be both inside and outside at the same time. A new kind of likeness! The likeness of the group instinct. All that it has produced is more glass and an hysteria for new materials which you can look through. A symptom of love-sickness, I guess. For me, to be inside and outside is to be in an unheated studio with broken windows in the winter, or taking a nap on somebody's porch in the summer.

Spiritually I am wherever my spirit allows me to be, and that is not necessarily in the future. I have no nostalgia, however. If I am confronted with one of those small Mesopotamian figures, I have no nostalgia for it but, instead, I may get into a state of anxiety. Art never seems to make me peaceful or pure. I always seem to be wrapped in the melodrama of vulgarity. I do not think of inside or outside—or of art in general—as a situation of comfort. I know there is a terrific idea there somewhere, but whenever I want to get into it, I get a feeling of apathy and want to lie down and go to sleep. Some painters, including myself, do not care what chair they are sitting on. It does not even have to be a comfortable one. They are too nervous to find out where they ought to sit. They do not want to "sit in style." Rather, they have found that painting—any kind of painting, any style of painting—to be painting at all, in fact—is a way of living today, a style of living, so to speak. That is where the form of it lies. It is exactly in its uselessness that it is free. Those artists do not want to conform. They only want to be inspired.

The group instinct could be a good idea, but there is always some little dictator who wants to make his instinct the group instinct. There *is* no style of painting now. There are as many naturalists among the abstract painters as there are abstract painters in the so-called subject-matter school.

The argument often used that science is really abstract, and that painting could be like music and, for this reason, that you cannot paint a man leaning against a lamp-post, is utterly ridiculous. That space of science—the space of the physicists—I am truly bored with by now. Their lenses are so thick that seen through them, the space gets more and more melancholy. There seems to be no end to the misery of the scientists' space. All that it contains is billions and billions of hunks of matter, hot or cold, floating around in darkness according to a great design of aimlessness. The stars I think about, if I could fly, I could reach in a few old-fashioned days. But physicists' stars I use as buttons, buttoning up curtains of emptiness. If I stretch my arms next to the rest of myself and wonder where my fingers are—that is all the space I need as a painter.

Today, some people think that the light of the atom bomb will change the concept of painting once and for all. The eyes that actually saw the light melted out of sheer ecstasy. For one instant, everybody was the same color. It made angels out of everybody. A truly Christian light, painful but forgiving.

Personally, I do not need a movement. What was given to me, I take for granted. Of all movements, I like Cubism most. It had that wonderful unsure atmosphere of reflection—a poetic frame where something could be possible, where an artist could practise [sic] his intuition. It didn't want to get rid of what went before. Instead it added something to it. The parts that I can appreciate in other movements came out of Cubism. Cubism *became* a movement, it didn't set out to be one. It has force in it, but it was no "force-movement." And then there is that one-man movement, Marcel Duchamp—for me a truly modern movement because it implies that each artist can do what he thinks he ought to—a movement for each person and open for everybody.

If I *do* paint abstract art, that's what abstract art means to me. I frankly do not understand the question. About twenty-four years ago, I knew a man in Hoboken, a German who used to visit us in the Dutch Seamen's Home. As far as he could remember, he was always hungry in Europe. He found a place in Hoboken where bread was sold a few days old—all kinds of bread: French bread, German bread, Italian bread, Dutch bread, Greek bread, American bread and particularly Russian black bread. He bought big stacks of it for very little money, and let it get good and hard and then he crumpled it and spread it on the floor in his flat and walked on it as on a soft carpet. I lost sight of him, but found out many years later that one of the other fellows met him again around 86th street. He had become some kind of a Jugend Bund leader and took boys and girls to Bear Mountain on Sundays. He is still alive but quite old and is now a Communist. I could never figure him out, but now when I think of him, all that I can remember is that he had a very abstract look on his face.

As exquisite a writer as he is a composer, Ned Rorem (b. 1923) here explains what is wrong with music critics.

Thirteen Ways of Looking at a Critic

Critics of words use words. Critics of music use words.

Those thirteen syllables, penned a decade ago, are as pertinent as any I can make on the matter.

If the final comment on a work of art is another work of art, might some critical prose equal, as art, the art it describes? Yes, but that very prose is independent of the art it describes.

The best critical writing is superfluous to its subject, and musical criticism is the most superfluous of all.

3. Some of my best friends are critics; but the basic rapport with, for example, Virgil Thomson or the late William Flanagan, has always been compositional. Flanagan-as-critic was a purveyor of free tickets; Thomson-as-critic was the best in the world and hence free of rules. But that was in another time.

... Whether composers make the best music critics is debatable; but composers, even bad ones, know better than anyone how music is made—providing they have heard their works in good performances.

... A critic must be able to tell—and then to tell you—the first-rate from the second-rate. In every field except music this question has been settled so far as the past is concerned, and concentration centers on the moment. Music critics' chief business should be the discouragement of standard master-pieces. At this point his function is moral: to warn against being beguiled by trends.

Most new music is bad, and it is the critic's duty to say so. But let him say so with sorrow, not with relish. The glee with which some of our head critics declare "I told you so" as yet another première bites the dust is no less contemptible than Casals belittling Stravinsky in order to sit on the Russian's throne. The great unwashed in heeding these spokesmen become exonerated from what should be a normal need for today's music.

The most honest description of the creative process is: making it up as you go along. The most honest description of the critical process is: judgment according to kinetic reaction. Neither process is casual. Do we even know what we believe? If so, how to react to the belief? The not knowing has itself become in America a kind of belief. We like to talk about it more than to listen to it; it is made in order to be reviewed; it does not exist if it is not discussed.

Rorem, Ned. Excerpts from "Thirteen Ways of Looking at a Critic" from *Setting the Tone* by Ned Rorem. Reprinted by permission of Open Road Integrated Media.

Gide's quip, "Don't be too quick to understand me," obtains to us all, since we don't even understand ourselves. A composer doesn't want to be understood, he wants not to be misunderstood. Of course, Gide could also have said, "Don't be too quick to misunderstand me."

If critics are tastemakers, why has none blown the whistle on the concept of greatness—whatever that may be—as absolute and irreversible? Perhaps Beethoven's Ninth is trash. Perhaps even Babbitt and Sessions are antiseptic bores who, if they appeal to executants, appeal through challenge and not pleasure. (And I do allow the role of ugliness-as-pleasure in art: Mozart and Ravel, at their highest, contain ugliness. But when all is ugly, nothing is ugly.)

If critics applaud the emperor's new clothes along with the Philistines, some recognize the real thing when they hear it. But what critic will put his finger on the *absence* of the real thing?

Does public criticism otherwise affect me? And what do I stand to lose by voicing these opinions before critics?

Bad reviews make me feel worse than good reviews make me feel good, but no reviews are saddest. Although I've never read anything about myself that I've agreed with, or even understood, bad or good, I still prefer good to bad, since friends and foes might read it. But mainly I am ignored by the press. If the punishment for complaining is to be further ignored, I have nothing to lose.

In *Thirteen Ways of Looking at a Blackbird* Wallace Stevens wonders

> ... which to prefer,
> The beauty of inflections
> Or the beauty of innuendoes,
> The blackbird whistling
> Or just after.

In music there is no "just after." A critic will never recapture the sound. The writings of even a Proust, a Shaw, a Tovey may be music—evocative, penetrating, ambiguous yet inevitable—but they are not *the* music. We can recall being in love but we cannot revive lovemaking except while making love. Sometimes when we finally hear the piece a critic has so wonderfully extolled we find no link. Stevens has it both ways but only within his poem, and our memory of his poem *is* the poem. Similarly, the memory and therefore the criticism of music lie only within the music.

Nantucket, July 1982

One of the youngest members of the postwar New York School, the American painter Robert Motherwell (1915–1991) boasts an inimitable style of simple shapes and bold strokes that somehow always seem to challenge the engage the heart as well as the intellect in a dialectic of beauty, history, and revolution.

ROBERT MOTHERWELL

Robert Motherwell (1915–1991) never achieved the inviolable fame that came to older artists, such as Pollock, de Kooning, and Rothko, with whom he was associated in the 1950s. But his series of *Elegies to the Spanish Republic*, their ascetic black-and-white orchestrations keyed to the calamitous history of the Spanish Civil War, have long been admired as an essential mid-century achievement, filtering the social and political turmoil of the 1930s through the more personal rhetorical voice of the postwar period. Motherwell, who came from a wealthy West Coast family, had studied at Harvard and Columbia, and he had a knowledge of French language and literature that made him a natural companion for the Surrealists who were in exile in the United States in the 1940s. For many years he was admired as much for his intellectual as for his painterly gifts, and when compared with most writings by American artists, Motherwell's are certainly thick with literary references. He coedited *Possibilities* with Harold Rosenberg, publishing essential statements by Pollock and Rothko, and his 1951 anthology, *The Dada Painters and Poets*, was immensely influential, setting in motion a postwar revaluation of Dada's anarchic spirit. Included here are a statement, "Black or White," written for a 1950 group show at the Kootz Gallery dedicated to the New York School's fascination with the limited palette, and Motherwell's statement for the 1951 panel at the Museum of Modern Art for which Calder and de Kooning also prepared remarks.

What Abstract Art Means to Me

THE emergence of abstract art is one sign that there are still men able to assert feeling in the world. Men who know how to respect and follow their inner feelings, no matter how irrational or absurd they may first appear. From their perspective, it is the social world that tends to appear irrational and absurd. It is sometimes forgotten how much wit there is in certain works of abstract art. There is a certain point in undergoing anguish where one encounters the comic—I think of Miró, of the late Paul Klee, of Charlie Chaplin, of what healthy and human values their wit displays ...

Motherwell, Robert. From *Collected Writings of Robert Motherwell* edited by Stephanie Terenzio (1984): c.880 words from "What Abstract Art Means to Me" (pp. 180-184) © 1994 by Robert Motherwell. By Permission of Oxford University Press.

I find it sympathetic that Parisian painters have taken over the word "poetry," in speaking of what they value in painting. But in the English-speaking world there is an implication of "literary content," if one speaks of a painting as having "real poetry." Yet the alternative word, "aesthetic," does not satisfy me. It calls up in my mind those dull classrooms and books when I was a student of philosophy and the nature of the aesthetic was a course given in the philosophy department of every university. I think now that there is no such thing as *the* "aesthetic," no more than there is any such thing as "art," that each period and place has its own art and its aesthetic—which are specific applications of a more general set of human values, with emphases and rejections corresponding to the basic needs and desires of a particular place and time. I think that abstract art is uniquely modern—not in the sense that word is sometimes used, to mean that our art has "progressed" over the art of the past—though abstract art may indeed represent an emergent level of evolution—but in the sense that abstract art represents the particular acceptances and rejections of men living under the conditions of modern times. If I were asked to generalize about this condition as it has been manifest in poets, painters, and composers during the last century and a half, I should say that it is a fundamentally romantic response to modern life—rebellious, individualistic, unconventional, sensitive, irritable. I should say that this attitude arose from a feeling of being ill at ease in the universe, so to speak—the collapse of religion, of the old close-knit community and family may have something to do with the origins of the feeling. I do not know.

But whatever the source of this sense of being unwedded to the universe, I think that one's art is just one's effort to wed oneself to the universe, to unify oneself through union. Sometimes I have an imaginary picture in mind of the poet Mallarmé in his study late at night—changing, blotting, transferring, transforming each word and its relations with such care—and I think that the sustained energy for that travail must have come from the secret knowledge that each word was a link in the chain that he was forging to bind himself to the universe; and so with other poets, composers, and painters... If this suggestion is true, then modern art has a different face from the art of the past because it has a somewhat different function for the artist in our time.

One of the most striking aspects of abstract art's appearance is her nakedness, an art stripped bare. How many rejections on the part of her artists! Whole worlds—the world of objects, the world of power and propaganda, the world of anecdotes, the world of fetishes and ancestor worship. One might almost legitimately receive the impression that abstract artists don't like anything but the act of painting...

What new kind of *mystique* is this, one might ask. For make no mistake, abstract art is a form of mysticism.

Still, this is not to describe the situation very subtly. To leave out consideration of what is being put into the painting, I mean. One might truthfully say that abstract art is stripped bare of other things in order to intensify it, its rhythms, spatial intervals, and color structure. Abstraction is a process of emphasis, and emphasis vivifies life, as A. N. Whitehead said.

Nothing as drastic an innovation as abstract art could have come into existence, save as the consequence of a most profound, relentless, unquenchable need.

The need is for felt experience—intense, immediate, direct, subtle, unified, warm, vivid, rhythmic.

Everything that might dilute the experience is stripped away. The origin of abstraction in art is that of any mode of thought. Abstract art is a true mysticism—I dislike the word—or rather a series of mysticisms that grew up in the historical circumstance that all mysticisms do, from a primary sense of gulf, an abyss, a void between one's lonely self and the world. Abstract art is an effort to close the void that modern men feel. Its abstraction is its emphasis.

Perhaps I have tried to be clear about things that are not so very clear, and have not been clear about what is clear, namely, that I love painting the way one loves the body of woman, that if painting must have an intellectual and social background, it is only to enhance and make more rich an essentially warm, simple, radiant act, for which everyone has a need . . .

In this excerpt from his book *Cuban Ballet*, Roca makes a case for judging ballet phenomenologically in the context of its own time and place, in the context of history.

Giselle: Ballet is Not Politics, But It Is History

[adapted from Octavio Roca: "Giselle," in *Cuban Ballet*, Gibbs Smith, 2010, ISBN 978-1-4236-0758-8, pp. 200–219; notes omitted]

In the Diaspora, the theft of a Cuban identity, indeed of a Cuban homeland, has led many dancers to a bold refusal to accept that brutal change in their own material conditions. When an artist's—or anyone's—praxis is stolen, the resulting alienation is as clear as it is cruel. It becomes impossible to ignore the material conditions in which art is created. It becomes impossible, too, not to want more than sheer resignation to these conditions. Paradoxically, to accept one's lot is also to refuse. When Alicia Alonso had her dancer's praxis stolen by blindness, she both accepted that brutal physical condition and refused to be determined by it. The rest is history. When Cuban exile dancers in the Diaspora had their praxis stolen by the loss of their country, their refusal led and continues to lead to a dialectical acceptance of their condition that is at once a refusal to accept these limits. Jean-Paul Sartre was right in noting that freedom is what you do with has been done to you.

These Cuban dancers, often far from their homeland and more distinctly Cuban for it, say with every step that, "No, you will not take Cuba away from me." Even more than in the case of Cuba's musical or literary traditions, exile has meant a regeneration and revitalization of Cuban ballet and its rich tradition. Nowhere is that tradition more ravishingly embodied, and nowhere is the example of Alicia Alonso more telling, than in the Cuban *Giselle*.

Most of Alonso's changes to the original 1841 version of *Giselle* are of course not accidental, but rather conscious aesthetic choices. Turning the interpolated Act One peasant pas de dix for the villagers—an impressive tour de force for the male dancers who must display superhuman *ballon* in strings of *jetés*—manages to preserve a beloved scene in the *Giselle* tradition going back to the original Paris production, while at the same time avoiding the dramatic awkwardness of introducing an extra principal couple without a story of their own. Alonso's solution solves that problem. Earlier in Act One, when the entire corps of villagers turns and stares over their shoulders at Hilarion, who is unmistakably identified as outside the community identity embodied in the ensemble, the clarity of dramatic detail also subtly appropriates and elevates what is elsewhere a dispensable connective musical passage. The intense and frantic fugue in Act Two, reinstated by Alonso in 1972 and omitted in virtually all modern productions except Alonso's, preserves the integrity of Adam's score but also vindicates the music by making the scene a revelation of the character of the vengeful Wilis—and a stark contrast to Giselle's gentle, determined spirit as revived by a surprised Myrtha in Act Two. These and other musical matters, incidentally, could by no means be taken for granted before Alonso restored the *Giselle* score to its full splendor in 1972, when her productions both for the Paris Opera and the Ballet Nacional de Cuba boasted the first note-complete versions of Adam's score since the original 1843 revival in Paris. Alonso was simply curious about what the complete original musical score might yield.

What is it about ballet, and what is it about the Cuban *Giselle*, that is so personal? Details are everything, and they mean different personal things to different people. There is a small, emotionally shattering moment in *Giselle* when the poor peasant girl suddenly faces a rich elegant woman who is wearing what must seem like impossibly beautiful clothes: Giselle's simple pantomime—no more than a few bars of music—as she reaches and almost touches the hem of Bathilde's dress embodies innocent hope against all odds, longing for so much happiness that Giselle will never know, and ineffable sadness. The gesture was in the original Paris production, 7 years before the Revolution of 1848 and well before Marxist theories of class differences. Yet there it is, in a different context today, in all its simplicity and timeless universality. How each ballerina plays that moment can be as telling as how a Violetta in Verdi's *La Traviata* notices the ravages of a fast life staring back in the mirror in the simple line, "*O, qual pallor.*" Or it can be as devastating as how the dying Åse in Ibsen's *Peer Gynt* can suggest irony, fervor, and terror all at once as she listens to her fantastical liar of a son describe the gates of heaven she will soon enter. Ballet encompasses dance, music, and drama; it takes place in lived history; it is an ephemeral phenomenon.

A product of the artist's unique labor within specific material conditions, ballet is as unnatural as it is beautiful. Dancers, if one looks closely, also give away an almost immodest, disarmingly personal treasure of details; the sum of choices they have made throughout their lives as dancers, their unique body language and, some might say, their souls. No other artist is as naked before you as a dancer—no singer, no actor. A dancer's body is the instrument of dance, a dancer's emotions its texture. What you see really is what you get. Cuban dancers dance, of course. They also stand, fierce and exposed, in the thickets of living Cuban history.

To a critic with a hammer, everything looks like a nail. Political criticism of Cuban ballet is facile. Talk of whether or not a dance is socially relevant or politically useful is all even interesting, but the real question ought to be whether a dance is good or bad. It is not by any means, at least not necessarily, a political question. Alicia Alonso is not a key figure in the theory and praxis of ballet because of or despite her politics. The truth is that her *Giselle* was not bourgeois art in the 1940s and 1950s, no more than it was communist art after 1959. That would be impossible—it is the same *Giselle*. Antony Tudor was right when he told me that she is only a ballerina, and that is all she is. That is a lot. The material conditions that have shaped her life, as well as the life project through which she shaped those conditions, are dialectically inseparable. It would be as much a mistake to judge the Ballet Nacional de Cuba and its founder solely by its political situation as it would be to judge it hermeneutically as pure movement. There is no such thing.

There is no unmediated, essential truth in ballet. The truth of a ballet arises not in a vacuum but in public, in real life, in the magical moment when the audience witnesses the dancers in motion. Should ballet tell a story at all? Or is ballet at its purest simply a matter of bodies in motion with no meaning other than the movement itself? Alonso's *Giselle* raises questions about what ballet is and what it ought to be. Of course, it raises questions about the role of the artist in a communist society, but here it is the ballet itself and not the society that must be the object of judgment. Situating Alonso and the Cuban School of Ballet means situating the artists and their art in this context, not mainly or even necessarily in the context of the politics of their time.

> "To a critic with a hammer, everything looks like a nail. Political criticism of Cuban ballet is facile. Talk of whether or not a dance is socially relevant or politically useful is all even interesting, but the real question ought to be whether a dance is good or bad"

Audiences everywhere seem to love story ballets, even if most American ballet critics betray an inordinate fondness for ballets devoid of dramatic content. Are such classics of the canon as *Giselle*, *Swan Lake,* and *The Sleeping Beauty*, the highest achievements of an art form or simply guilty pleasures in which an audience must be indulged? Are modern narrative dances such as Paul Taylor's *Company B* or Anjelin Preljocaj's *Le Parc* somehow not as important or successful as the less obviously dramatic new works of Christopher Wheeldon or Alexei Ratmansky? For that matter, is something like Balanchine's *Who Cares?* or Azari Plisetsky's *Canto Vital*, really abstract? Audience preference aside, narrative ballets have not had an easy time around the American dance intelligentsia since the 1940s. They also have been the most highly valued in Cuban critical circles, before and after the revolution.

With the best of intentions, a fanatical embrace of abstraction has led to an often condescending attitude toward the ballets that audiences love most. It is a curious phenomenon. Story ballets such as *The Nutcracker* pay the bills in most companies in capitalist countries, and they historically have attracted some of the great revolutionaries of choreography from August Bournonville and Marius Petipa right through Tudor, Roland Petit, Preljocaj, and William Forsythe. Still, the American critical establishment invariably places abstract ballet on a higher plane than any venture claiming to marry ballet and theater. That is a pity. Abstract ballet is many things in theory, but in reality, it is phenomenologically impossible. A fetish of modern critics, the promotion of abstraction in dance is an impressive feat of sophistry. It is an ersatz opposite of the narrative tradition.

For Alonso, psychological insights would become the way to marry meaning and technique. In the late 1940s and 1950s, as the Ballet Alicia Alonso grew into the Ballet Nacional de Cuba, this dramatic method was simply taken for granted and was in fact the rule in Cuban theatrical circles. The first drama lessons in the Stanislavsky method in Havana were taught by Adolfo de Luis, a Cuban disciple of Stanislavky and Piscator, in Alonso's own Academia de Baile Alicia Alonso in Havana. Method acting, in dance as in the nonmusical stage, was the rule in Cuba as influential new theater companies sprung up in Havana before the revolution, including Las Máscaras, Sala Talía, and El Sótano. This atmosphere mirrored the situation of the theatrical avant-garde in both New York and Moscow. Coincidence or *Zeitgeist*, it was very much part of the material artistic conditions of Alonso's *Giselle* initially in her two companies, the American Ballet Theatre and Ballet Nacional de Cuba. And, in her particular case, it was certainly not the politics of Cuba before or after the revolution that were telling. The key to her art is not political, no matter what political uses may be found for that art. A major element of the Alonso characterization and approach to *Giselle* and all her other roles from the 1940s onwards is the uniquely happy result of George Balanchine's astringent technical demands and Antony Tudor's psychological intensity.

Should abstraction be abandoned as an ideal? Ballet is unique among the arts in holding on to a quaint modernist aesthetic. That same 1950s and 1960s modernism, long abandoned in music, theater, and painting, still entrances American ballet critics and impresarios. Companies such as the Royal Ballet, Covent Garden, the Bolshoi, and the Kirov all become apologetic in the United States when they continue to use ballet to tell a story— and often they are viewed as somehow retrograde, not as advanced as whatever ossified neoclassical model passes for tradition in Manhattan. True, that the opposite has been the case in Russia and in Cuba is in part the result of fetishizing an aesthetic of socialist realism. But it is also true that, well before socialist realism was proclaimed as an artistic ideal of Marxism–Leninism, narrative ballet was the status quo; ballet told stories, period. And in Cuba, also well before the revolution, narrative ballet was the rule at Pro-Arte Musical, at Ballet Alicia Alonso, and at the Ballet Nacional de Cuba. A coincidence of aims does not by any means constitute a relation of cause and effect.

In situating the Cuban *Giselle*, what matters is the *Giselle* tradition in all its lived transformations together with the actual performance practice in and out of Cuba. The material conditions that are the groundwork of Alonso's work are undeniable, and they are undeniably tied to Cuban political realities. But those conditions, over the arc of a lifetime, have had a wide range. Consider then this: Alicia Alonso received honors such as the Orden de Carlos Manuel de Céspedes and was named a Dama de la República when Cuba actually was a republic before 1959; and she also has been named a Hero of Labor and was vice president of the Cuban–Soviet Friendship Association after 1959. Should we posit an "Alonso I" and "Alonso II"? Can these in any meaningful way be claimed as ways to judge her? Or her *Giselle*?

An alternative explanation is more difficult, but it also is necessary to ponder. Alicia Alonso chose to remain in Cuba after 1959. She could have had a career outside her country, as so many dancers everywhere do; she chose not to. Her choices have earned her praise, and they have earned her scorn and vilification. Reflecting on exile, soon after the fateful 1980 Mariel exodus that changed the political tenor of both her audience and her working conditions in Cuba, Alicia Alonso told me that "to emigrate, not just for political reasons but for economic reasons or even for art. . . to emigrate always means that so much is taken away from you. You live for the permanent question; What if?" "So much is robbed from an exile, most of all the admiration of one's possibilities."

She was not about to be robbed of her own possibilities. That this involved a certain willful blindness, quite apart from her physical condition, is clear. The Alonsos kept their company insulated from much of the everyday terror of living in Castro's Cuba, but their influence of course was limited to the company. Elsewhere, Castro's "Words to the Intellectuals" sent a chill through the arts in Cuba soon after the revolution. The Heberto Padilla affair, which soured Jean-Paul Sartre, Simone de Beauvoir, and so many other European left-wing intellectuals on Castro's socialist paradise, not only sidelined that great poet simply because of his poetry but also turned him into an informant. This would become the rule, and writers suffered the worst but were by no means the only artists affected. Arturo Sandoval, a protégé of Dizzy Gillespie and one of the founders of the fusion jazz band Irakere, was monitored carefully and was told by the Minister of Culture Armando Hart Dávalos to take care that his music not sounds "so American." The gay German composer Hans Werner Henze was evicted from Havana, and Alonso had to abandon plans to commission a ballet set to his Cuban oratorio *El Cimarrón*, which was based on Miguel Barnet's Cuban novel. Barnet himself was subsequently reduced to writing sociology rather than fiction. Padilla in his confession to the National Union of Writers and Artists (UNEAC), a grotesque bit of Stalinist theater, accused José Lezama Lima of antisocial tendencies, and the old gay man found all his works withdrawn and never published again in his lifetime; he died in fear in Havana in 1976. Gay men and dissidents were officially classified as antisocial criminals by the National Congress on Education and Culture. Virgilio Piñera was under virtual house arrest; Guillermo Cabrera Infante was exiled; Reinaldo Arenas was jailed, tortured, and eventually put on a fishing boat to Miami during the Mariel exodus. Even as Castro himself singled out the Ballet Nacional de Cuba as heroes of labor in his speech to the First Congress of the Cuban Communist Party in 1975, there was no question that even Alicia Alonso had to be careful—she still does in 2015. It would be facile at this juncture to render a severe judgment of what one might see as Alonso's cowardice in the face of these injustices. It also would be pointless; if she was to remain in Cuba, what else could she do?

"Cuba is such a small country," Alicia told me in 1980 the first time I interviewed her for *The Washington Post*, "and it has suffered so much." The scope of that suffering within Alonso's grasp was and is limited; what she could do artistically and practically to keep her company well and dancing was and is something else. It is worth noting that these are not small details.

Wilhelm Furtwaengler, in wartime Berlin, could do little to alleviate the madness and terror of Hitler's holocaust, but what he could do was keep German culture alive for the future by making music in the present. For decades, Dmitri Shostakovich endured the uncertainty and horror of Stalin's grip, by managing to create beauty the way he could. These are considerable achievements, and it would be foolish and thankless to point out that both artists might have done better by leaving their country. For decades, Alicia Alonso has not left hers. And the ballet company she has nurtured reflects—and has thrived within—the brutal reality of those material conditions. She may be accused of becoming a silent partner in the oppression of the Cuban people, but she must be held at least as responsible for keeping her people's culture alive. Yes, narrative ballet with a message was the way to proceed under a socialist–realist agenda. Yet Alonso did so within the classical canon, not by commissioning agitprop works. This turned her Ballet Nacional de Cuba into one of the world's most aesthetically conservative companies. Cuba is not the place to discover new choreography or new music; there are dancers in that company, in 2010, who have never met a choreographer of new works and who never saw Alonso dance. Yet, within those limits, what a breathtaking achievement it is that the repertory on which her company concentrates has been extraordinarily well served. Cuba is the place to find valid, fresh dancing of the canonical nineteenth-century repertory. Cuba is the home of the truest and most moving *Giselle* staging anywhere in the world.

Not just her work, but Alonso herself long has been a source of political controversy—her name has the power to call up a complex maelstrom of meaning that can only be realized in its totality. This, despite the fact that the passage to political activism was much more difficult for her than for her husbands—Fernando Alonso (a member of the Communist Party since the 1930s) and even Pedro Simón (a philosopher and critic well connected to the Cuban intelligentsia and adept at survival in that environment). The shift from individual artistic discovery and personal excellence to political commitment has been at best shallow in Alicia Alonso; a case of *"cubrir la forma,"* doing enough to survive and to maintain her ability to make dances. She can be accused of never coming to grips with the tragic consequences of the political philosophy she often claims to espouse in the right interviews, just as she can be praised in practical terms for improving the artistic conditions of her dancers in Cuba as well as for more than once springing some of them out of communist jails. "She is a whore," Reinaldo Arenas once told me, far from home, in New York. "But she did get people out of jail, I can tell you that."

"Alicia kept a lot of them from being thrown into the UMAP camps," Arenas continued, referring to the concentration camps of the Unidades Militares de Ayuda a la Producción (UMAP) begun by Raúl Castro in 1965 that interned gays as well as Jehova's Witnesses and other nonconformists to the socialist ideal. The camps continued until 1971, when the United Nations Commission on Human Rights pressured the Cuban government into closing them as such.

Political criticism of Alonso's *Giselle*, of Alonso herself, is pointless. Ballet is not a political tool, but one reason it is in fact so important in Cuban culture is that its nuances carry political meanings that can be very subtle and never oppressive. Her life project has been impeccable, and the results of her labor beautiful. She has remained an elitist in her art, surrounded by fetishized populism. Under any political conditions, and perhaps especially in a climate of oppression, beauty and goodness have to count.

"I helped my country take the first strong, certain steps towards a future of dance," Alonso told me in 1980. "I am very proud of our company. Most of all I believe in the human being, and I believe that art makes us human. I have learned to trust that, over so, so many years."

Her *Giselle*, over all those years and above all her other achievements, has been a profession of that faith. Capturing an era and transcending it in triumph are what makes *Giselle* rank with *Hamlet* and *Le Cid*, with *Parsifal*, and with *Peer Gynt*. Ballet has no richer masterpiece than this deceptively simple, endlessly fascinating dance about a love that overpowers death. Hegel famously observed that the owl of Minerva takes wing at dusk; that wisdom and deepest understanding arrive at the close of an epoch, at the birth of a new day. That is true of *Giselle*, at once the apotheosis of romantic ballet and the glittering model for all classical ballets to come. It is true also of Alonso's staging of this and other masterworks of the classical canon. The text and the context of that canon have been enriched and transformed by her labors.

The twentieth century's greatest interpreter of the most beautiful of all ballets continues to revitalize and redefine this nineteenth-century masterpiece for the twenty-first century. Alicia Alonso truly was born so that *Giselle* would live. Her unique *Giselle* remains a dialectical synthesis of boundless romantic passion and elegant classical rigor, of impeccably schooled respect for our cultural past and indomitable faith in our future. Alonso, born in 1920, first danced *Giselle* in 1943, and owned the role for the next 50 years. In the truest existential sense, she is what she does, and what she does above all else is this. Alicia Alonso is Giselle, in history, and forever in my memory.

The integrity of the Cuban *Giselle* matters. So does technical virtuosity, an element of performance practice that has grown considerably since 1841. The endless secure balances of the ballerinas, the insolent extension and stratospheric jump of the men, all these and others by now necessary details make *Giselle* as instantly accessible as it is thrilling. Alonso's ghostly Wilis, not coincidentally, are the most dramatically charged as anywhere. These are not the abstract dancing patterns seen today in productions from San Francisco to St. Petersburg. These Wilis are avenging spirits, and their vengeance resounds in their moves. In some of the finest American and European classical troupes, when the corps de ballet is not nurtured dramatically as well as technically, it shows. The sensible Marxist directive to make art clearly accessible to the people—to all of all the people—has no quarrel here with Alonso's artistic integrity. The changes she has organically integrated into her reconstruction of this nineteenth-century jewel only make it shine that much brighter for audiences, any audiences, in the twenty-first century. These are valid changes because they remain true to the text of the original ballet and they also reflect and transform the context of that ballet today. The material conditions of the *Giselle* text are given, the transformation of those conditions within the phenomenon of performance is dialectical, and the performance in practice again and again revitalizes the artistic context itself. Here in Alonso's *Giselle* is praxis dictating theory, theory reflecting truth on stage.

In performance, the beauty of Alonso's dancers at home and abroad is that one can take so much for granted: balances are solid and assured, the line is exquisitely uniform and historically informed, épaulement and port de bras are exquisite and subtle, the technique is superhuman but the acting is always humane. From corps dancers, coryphées, and soloists up through the splendid principals, Cuban dancers tend to dance as if their lives depend on it.

Conscious of the dialectical, transforming role she has played in the project that has defined her life, Alonso is proud of the success of her Cuban *Giselle*. She is proud that, "after Paris I also later staged it for the Teatro San Carlo in Naples, the cradle of Italian ballet and, consequently, of world ballet. You can see, then, how it is possible for us to return a gift we received from Europe, revitalized and enriched, quite apart from the infinite possibilities of our own, original Latin American arts across all genres, whether the original artistic expression be from Scandinavia or from China. We, of course, are Cubans, but art is universal."

Alonso's deeply humanistic interpretation of *Giselle* ranks as the finest in the late twentieth century as well as now. Her choreography improbably emerges as the epitome of the romantic ballet tradition. "Real tradition," Alonso has said, "living, valid, and positive tradition must be open. It must be received from all around. One has to search out tradition, study it, acquire it, and then feel free to live it freely; this way, a dance becomes a dialectical assimilation, not an imposed anachronism. This way everything depends on the creative talent that must be the starting point of any artistic endeavor."

"Romantic ballet can be conceived not only as a style from a past era, but also as a state of mind, a sensibility, an emotional necessity that can emerge—and in fact has emerged—in every era, in every place," wrote Alonso in 1981. "Even as its expressions vary into infinity, the romantic era, examined historically, brought dance a series of timeless values that are inseparable from the most treasured in the culture of humanity."

In 1983, after taking the ballet on a whirlwind international tour from Santo Domingo, Colombia, and Venezuela to Turkey and Syria, she returned to Havana to celebrate the fortieth anniversary of her debut in the role. On December 24, 1980, at the Sala Garcia Lorca of the Gran Teatro de La Habana, she danced *Giselle* complete for the last time in Cuba. She had danced *Giselle* for half a century. Again in her hometown, on December 29, 1991, for celebrations of the one hundred and fiftieth anniversary of the 1841 world premiere of *Giselle*—and this truly must be considered miraculous even by her own standards—Alonso at age 70 danced the Mad Scene, as well as the two Act Two pas de deux. She was unforgettable. Recent years have brought much change, and doubtless even more changes are in store as Alonso, no longer dancing the role and in fact leading her company blind from a wheelchair, keeps alive this Cuban corner of the world's *Giselle* tradition. Her Cuban dancers, her living legacy both in Havana and in the growing Cuban Diaspora, today take this most beautiful element of the Cuban School of Ballet to every corner of the world. This is a sign of hope. Just as Russia's Bolshoi Ballet preceded and has outlived Soviet communism, so the Ballet Nacional de Cuba is managing to survive and even thrive through the darkest decades in Cuban history—and will likely go on dancing gloriously into the millennium after Cuba is finally free.

KEY TERMS

Abstract expressionism, an American school of art that flourished from the end of World War II to the 1960s and the emergence of Pop Art; also referred to as the **New York School.**

Aesthetics, a branch of philosophy dealing with the pleasure, contemplation, and above all judgment of art.

Gesamkunstwerk, Wagner's aim in what he called his music dramas; a total work of art that synthesizes and makes use of all the arts.

QUESTIONS FOR DISCUSSION AND REVIEW

1. Explain the connections between Pleasure, Contemplation, and Judgment in aesthetic appreciation.

2. Explain how Aesthetics, Art, and Criticism are interrelated.

3. Evaluate David Hume's view regarding art criticism.

4. Articulate the notion of 'truth' in art criticism.

5. Explain if it is possible to have agreement about aesthetic judgments and if that is a problem.

6. Name at least two examples of great art—from any art form including painting and sculpture, literature, theater, film, television, music, or dance—and explain what you think makes them great. Do your examples have any critical standards in common?

7. Ned Rorem notes that "Critics of words use words. Critics of music use words." Is it unfair or misguided to use words in judging, say, music, dance, or painting? What else can you suggest?

8. In what sense is liking something different from saying it is good? Give examples.

9. Discuss some of what might be the objective, verifiable facts one might take into account in judging a piece of art. In other words, what things are clearly not a matter of opinion?

10. In what sense are emotions aesthetically significant, that is, what if anything do your feelings have to do with judging art?

11. Paul Valéry believes that art "has taken its place in the general economy. Should the fact that art is an economic commodity affect our aesthetic judgement?

12. Opera and ballet, to name just two great forms of art, don't make a profit in today's economy. Should art be supported with public funds, as it is in many countries, in the same manner that public schools and hospitals are?

13. Given what the American painters Willem De Kooning and Robert Motherwell write in this chapter, do you think art can ever be abstract? Explain.

BIBLIOGRAPHY AND SUGGESTED READINGS

Adorno, T. W. (1970). *Aesthetic Theory*.

Aristotle. (1895). *Poetics*. (Butcher, S.H. transl.).

De Kooning, W. (2014). What Abstract Art Means to Me. In Perl, J. (Ed.), *Art in America 1945–1970*.

Hume, D. (1918). *Of the Standard of Taste and Other Essays*.

Internet Encyclopedia of Philosophy. A peer-reviewed academic resource. Available from http://www.iep.utm.edu/

Marcuse, H. (1978). *The Aesthetic Dimension: Toward a Critique of Marxist Aesthetics*.

Motherwell, R. (1992). What Abstract Art Means to Me. In *Collected Writings of Robert Motherwell*.

Motherwell, R. *Elegy to the Spanish Republic*. Available from http://www.moma.org/collection_images/resized/938/w500h420/CRI_203938.jpg

Roca, O. (2010). *Giselle*, in *Cuban Ballet*, with forewords by A. Alonso and M. Baryshnikov.

Roca, O. (1990) interviewed with Alicia Alonso, in Pedro Simón's Giselle.

Roca, O. (1989).Interview with Friedrich Hegel, in Beitraege zum Musiktheater.

Spice, N. *Is Wagner Bad for Us?* In London review of books. April 11, 2013.

Stanford Encyclopedia of Philosophy. Available from http://plato.stanford.edu/

Ethics and the Good Life

11

Upon completing this chapter, students should be able
to meet the following Learning Outcomes:

11.1 Discuss the elements of any moral dilemma: the act, the
consequences of the act, and the moral agent.

11.2 Critically analyze the false starts in moral philosophy
including relativism and Divine Command.

11.3 Discuss the practical and logical problems with Aquinas'
Natural Law moral theory.

11.4 Explain how ethics can be said to be always personal
and often political.

The Meaning of Ethics

Ethics is, in a very real sense, philosophy in an emergency. Most philosophical questions—everything from the possible existence of a god and our place in the universe to the nature of beauty and the pleasures of identifying it—invite leisurely discussion over long periods of time. Someone facing an ethical problem, on the other hand, more often than not has to make a personal decision about that dilemma with little chance of waiting around. Decisions concerning academic integrity, professional behavior, and sexual ethics, for example, often fall in this category. A woman who has just found out that she is pregnant and happens to be pondering the morality of abortion had better decide that moral point herself soon or the decision will be made for her.

POWERFUL IDEAS BOX: BETTER TO BE SILENT

"Whereof one cannot speak, thereof one must be silent"

—*Ludwig Wittgenstein, Tractatus Logico-Philosophicus*

Anglo-American analytic philosophers in particular tend to agree with Wittgenstein that, basically, if you can't be clear about something, just be quiet.

This tenet, nourished by an increasing trust in science as well as a trust that science has good foundational arguments for certainty, have led in the twentieth and twenty-first centuries to a quasi-scientific view of moral philosophy and to such academic balkanizations as met-ethics (asking "where did that moral question come from and what does it mean?"), normative ethics (asking "How do you define a moral standard?"), and applied ethics (at last asking "Now what should I do?"). Continental philosophers for the most part have stayed with this last question, often asserting that all ethics is applied and most often it is also political.

These philosophers, too, aim for clarity. But they also understand that clarity is not always possible and that action is always necessary. Civil rights, women's rights, reproductive rights, marriage equality, abortion, assisted suicide and euthanasia, , legalization of drugs, capital punishment—all of these burning issues need solid moral arguments and ethically justified action. The action is the aim of all moral theories discussed in this chapter. Questions about right and wrong and questions about the right way to live are the subject of ethics. In that sense, and, this is crucial, ethical theory is never abstract: it concerns real human problems. The discussion in this chapter is an introduction to moral philosophy. Moral philosophy will be considered through critical analyses of the most common types of theories as well as of some examples that help illustrate these different ways to look at life. These include the theories underlying **Aristotelian**, **Kantian**, and **Utilitarian** arguments as they pertain to everyday life we live. Moral dead-ends such as relativism and divine command theories are also considered, along with the lasting influence of the Middle Ages' Natural Law ethics. The goal of this chapter is to apply critical thinking to help develop reasoned justifications for judgments on diverse moral issues, an exercise of reason that can point the way to better understanding of the role ethics plays in our daily lives.

Moral Dead-Ends

There are various moral dead-ends including all the people who think they are experts in ethics (without any formal study of the subject). Cultural relativism and the divine command theory of morals are in fact discredited in the field of philosophy, but both remain powerful in their cultural impact. Natural Law, which aimed higher than either of these but ultimately failed, is also examined later.

Cultural Relativism

The educator and critic Allan Bloom has noted with dismay that most of today's students arrive at college as relativists. Remarks such as "Who's to say who is right?" or "Who am I to judge" and "Maybe it's right for them, just not for me" reflect common and well-intentioned attitudes that nevertheless can destroy the possibility of responsible ethical judgment. While it is true that different cultures have different moral codes, must it follow that therefore there is no objective truth in morality? There are major drawbacks in accepting this form of cultural relativism, both from within a given culture and for outsiders to that culture.

If you are within the culture in question, relativism leaves no room for dissent or progress, since the culture is right by definition. If you are outside that culture in question, relativism leaves the outsider with no moral standing. The massacres committed by the religious extremists of ISIS, the treatment of women in the Middle East, the lunching of Blacks in the American South, or the Holocaust murder of millions of Jews by the Nazis all would be beyond your judgment if you don't happen to be part of these cultures. The beheading of gays or the stoning to death of adulterous women, as our allies in Saudi Arabia do, is something we have every right to condemn even if you are not a citizen of that country. Relativism would force you to respect that culture to the point of standing by and not passing judgment at all.

Ethics, at the very least, should enable us to say that something is right or wrong, no matter where and no matter who is involved. Relativism precludes that judgment.

Divine Command

If relativism claims that the way we have always done things must be right for us, Divine Command claims that without doubt the right thing to do is whatever our god or gods command. Like relativism, this is one of the most primitive ethical theories. Some common problems range from the difficulty of identifying and verifying god's commands to the undeniable challenge that several competing gods present in a multicultural world. Whose god are we talking about? Whose scriptures, or whose interpretation of those scriptures? What about trusting the messenger? When several presidential candidates state that Jesus commanded them to run for president, and clearly only one of them might win an election, does that mean the Jesus was just messing with the others?

The biggest problem with Divine Command theory, however, is put most clearly, most unsettlingly, by Socrates in Plato's *Euthyphro*: is something right because the gods command it, or do the gods command it because it is right? Why is this a problem?

POWERFUL ANALYSIS BOX: THE EUTHYPHRO PROBLEM

Is something right because god said so, or did god say so because it is right?

Is It Right Because God Says It Is Right . . .

If something is right because god commands it, then given his omnipotence, god could command anything. Murder is wrong, but perhaps it will be right tomorrow afternoon at 3. This is not a frivolous crazy example—god commanded Abraham to slaughter his own child, and that act would be right as long as god said so. That merciless god is not the one most people worship. It also makes ethics impossible in that you would have no way of deciding what to do since the concepts of right or wrong could change on a whim.

On the other hand, if your god wouldn't do that and god commands something because it is right—an omniscient god would not steer you wrong and, after all, he know everything—the you have diminished his authority and turned him into a good source of information. When you mother teaches you not to cross the street without looking both ways, she does so because she know better; once you learn that bit of truth, you don't need your mother to tell you again. This second option turns god into a divine Google.

One way you take away your god's power, the other way you take away his mercy. In fact, the omniscience and omnipotence of any god are a major dilemma for theologians to this day.

Either way, divine command theory destroys your idea of god. Theologians agree. And in fact St. Thomas Aquinas came up with a clever, but fatally flawed, way of avoiding the Euthyphro Problem.

Natural Law

St. Thomas Aquinas used Aristotle's metaphysics to build a moral philosophy. The result was his Natural Law, a theory that is no longer taken seriously among most philosophers but one which nevertheless has remained influential in the public imagination. If reason reveals to us how nature works—as Aristotle believes—and if we also know that God made nature, then it follows that reason reveals to us that this is the way it has to work, since God made it that way. So it is the case that the right thing to do ends up being what God commands, but not because God commands it but rather because "in the light of reason" you yourself find that moral truth revealed to you. Unnatural equals bad, natural equals good. That is Natural Law according to St. Thomas Aquinas.

rook76/Shutterstock.com

Never mind that, for example, the most natural thing in life would be to die of cancer, slowly and in pain. It is a good bet few people today would call chemotherapy, radiation therapy, and pain killers wrong—though they are all certainly unnatural. If you have ever taken an aspirin, you have committed an unnatural act. The idea that "unnatural" means "bad," or that "letting nature take its course" is always a good thing are just two examples of the influence of Aquinas' Natural Law—as is the Catholic church's continuing endorsement of all of Aquinas' teachings. This is not merely an academic topic: such current issues as the morality of condom use, abortion, and homosexuality are still discussed in some quarters in terms of Natural Law. Is there a natural way to do things? Do you think everything in the universe has a proper function? Does reason reveal this to you?

"An 'is' is not an 'ought'"

—*David Hume*

David Hume, a brilliant Scottish philosopher, proposed some devastating critiques of Natural Law, namely that one can't get an "ought" out of an "is." How is a law of nature different from a law of morals? Even if Aquinas had been right about every description of nature that his reason apparently revealed to him—and clearly he was not: the Earth is not flat, though many people were burned at the stake for saying that it wasn't—merely describing something is not the same thing as prescribing or judging it. Science is descriptive, ethics is prescriptive, normative.

One needs reasons, clear and impartial reasons, to begin making ethical arguments. One cannot obtain a prescriptive or normative statement—that is, a moral judgment—from a descriptive statement. As Hume pointed out in one of the most devastating, pithy claims in all of moral philosophy, an "is" is not an "ought." Natural Law rests on a mistake.

POWERFUL IDEAS BOX: HOW DO YOU JUDGE?

There are three elements to consider in making a moral judgment: the act in question, the consequences of that act, and the moral agent, that is, the person performing that act. Which do you think matters the most?

John Stuart Mill and the Utilitarians

Everett Historical/Shutterstock.com

Mill's no-nonsense philosophy is behind most of today's civil rights, privacy rights, marriage equality, and reproductive rights arguments. In his groundbreaking essay *On Liberty*, he points out that over one's own body and mind, one is sovereign, and no government or individual has a right to interfere. Classical utilitarianism, based on the ideas of Mill and others, is also called consequentialism and encompasses three propositions. First, in judging an action right or wrong, consider only the consequences; nothing else matters. Second, is assessing those consequences, consider only the amount of happiness or unhappiness they bring; nothing else matters. Third, and this remains perhaps the most controversial, the happiness of each and every person affected by the action counts the same.

POWERFUL ANALYSIS: DO CONSEQUENCES MATTER?

Are the consequences of an act what matter the most in making a moral decision? Would you call yourself a utilitarian? Why, or why not?

Immanuel Kant and the Categorical Imperative

Are some things simply always right and some others wrong no matter what? Kant's philosophy is also called deontological, from the Greek word for duty. There are actions that reason shows us it is our duty to take, and actions that are always wrong no matter what. Kant's **Categorical Imperative** revolutionized ethics and remain perhaps the most influential uses of reason applied to moral matters: "Act only according to that maxim by which you can at the same time will that it should become a universal law," and "Act so that you treat humanity, whether in your own person or in that of another, always as an end and never only as a means." In other words, don't do something you wouldn't want everyone else to do. And don't treat people as things, because you know better.

This theory has wide implications. For example, it is wrong to kill innocent people and you would not want anyone to do that—that would go against the categorical imperative that your own reason shows you. So you can't do it, even if the innocent person is a terminal cancer patient experiencing excruciating pain, even if it is you. The main argument against suicide today is Kantian. The main argument favoring assisted suicide is utilitarian: the consequences of the act are the end of suffering for the person who is suffering, that is a good consequence that it the patient's choice, and no one else's happiness or unhappiness is affected directly in the same way.

Aristotle and The Ethics of Virtue

The oldest moral philosophy we have is in many ways still the freshest. Socrates, in Plato's *Republic*, tells us that ethics is about "no small matter, but how we ought to live." Three generations after Socrates, around 325 BC, Aristotle in his *Nichomachean Ethics*—the first full, comprehensive treatment of the subject in the history of humanity—put this crucial question not in terms of the right thing to do, but rather of the right way to be: for Aristotle, ethics is a question of character. The most desirable character is that of a virtuous person because, according to Aristotle, that person simply will fare better in life. That is, a virtuous person in the long run is likelier to be happy.

Lefteris Papaulakis/Shutterstock.com

So What Is Virtue?

Aristotle defines it as a midpoint between two extremes, those of excess and deficiency. For example, a generous person is neither cheap nor extravagant. A courageous soldier is neither reckless nor coward—to which Aristotle adds that "courage in an unworthy cause is no courage at all." These and other virtues are cultivated by habit: no one is born friendly, industrious, dependable, tactful, thoughtful, or tolerant.

Just as it is only by practicing and competing that one becomes a great Olympic athlete, Aristotle mentions in one of his examples, it is only by doing the things a virtuous person does that one becomes virtuous. Loyalty, fairness, honesty, consideration, discretion, and even love all are things we learn only by doing and by doing them well.

They are also qualities that are likelier to lead to a happy life.

The ethics of virtue has become a powerful force in current moral debates. Particularly in an increasingly secular world, the ethics of virtue provides common ground for dialog among believers and nonbelievers alike, as among Jews, Christians, and Muslims—all of whom, incidentally, have been greatly influenced by Aristotle in matters of theology as well as in ethics. Regardless of the source of one's beliefs, it seems eminently sensible to ask both what makes people happy and what traits of character make for a good person. In other words, it makes more sense to ask "What kind of person would do this?" or "Would a good person do such a thing? than to ask "Is this right? or "Is this wrong?"

Elizabeth Anscombe, a British philosopher known not only for her neo-Kantian views but also for having gravitated toward Aristotle near the end of her life, perhaps put it best in her 1958 *Modern Moral Philosophy* when she claimed that "The concepts of obligation—*moral* obligation and *moral* duty, that is to say—and of what is morally right and morally wrong, and of the moral sense of 'ought,' ought to be jettisoned . . . .. It would be a great improvement if, instead of 'morally wrong,' one always named a genus such as 'untruthful,' 'unchaste,' 'unjust.'". These, Aristotle and his followers believe, all are things everyone needs. That is, despite all our differences, we all want to be happy, and we all can approach happiness by leading virtuous lives.

Ethics Is Always Personal

Aristotelian ethics plays well with others, and it has not only gained ground among Kantians but also closed parallels in existentialist ethics of ambiguity. This ambiguity is always personal, and it is part of human existence.

POWERFUL IDEAS BOX: LIFE HERE AND NOW

"From the moment he is born, from the instant he is conceived, man begins to die ... Man knows it. For him, this life that makes itself by unmaking itself is not just a natural process; it itself thinks itself. He affirms himself as pure interiority against which no exterior power could take hold, and he also submits himself as a thing crushed by the obscure weight of other things" (S. de Beauvoir, *Introduction to an Ethics of Ambiguity*)

The consoling metaphysics Beauvoir mentions in passing is actually a couple of thousand years' worth of moral philosophy, from Aristotle to Kant and Mill, to this day. There is no such thing as ethics in a vacuum, as Aristotle noticed in his magisterial *Nicomachean Ethics*. Fond of using examples from sports and the arts—there were good games in nearby Olympia, after all, and Athens by all accounts had a fine theater scene—Aristotle points of what virtues are needed to help lead athletes and artists alike reach excellence in their chose fields.

Natursports/Shutterstock.com

According to Aristotle, we learn how to do something by doing it well, and by doing it that way often enough that it becomes a habit. Excellence in, say, playing the lyre requires many virtues including talent, education, persistence, practice and more practice and then actually showing up to play and play well. Excellence in sports wants many of the same virtues, talent, education, persistence, practice and more practice and then actually showing up to play and play well. Lionel Messi, arguably the world's greatest football player, reached that goal of excellence through years of training, persistence, practice, and by making use of his talent by belonging to a great training program and a great team. He also showed up, and he keeps showing up, getting better and better—no one stays the same, and that direction up or down is always personal as well as in relation to material conditions. It is not what you mean to do or what you able to do that counts for Aristotle. It is what you actually do and do well.

In both sports and music, you also need equipment: the lyre player needs a lyre; the football player needs a ball and a team. Someone has to pay for these, and there the ethical question becomes political: a good piano, for example, costs about $30,000, and the most musically talented child may never reach his or her potential as a great pianist if that piano is not available. Who will pay for that? Who has the right to opportunity—the young musician with the talent or the one with the money? This particular element of the discussion is political and is at the heart of the chapter that follows.

In ethics, Aristotle was among the first to notice the obvious but often overlooked requirement talent, education, practice us to happiness, and how excellence in any of the virtues is likelier than its opposite to help anyone reach that happiness.

We are not alone here, we are with other people who themselves are facing the same moral decisions.

". . . This means that in establishing a certain conduct as a possibility and precisely because it is *my* possibility, I am aware that *nothing* can compel me to adopt that conduct. Yet I am already there in the future, and in this sense there is a relation between my future being and my present being. But a nothingness has slipped into the heart of this relation. What I am now is not the foundation of what I will be. I am the self which I will be in the sense of not being it"

—Jean-Paul Sartre, *Being and Nothingness.*

These hard questions don't go away. Beauvoir and Sartre are right in their phenomenological description of what goes on when we make any moral decision. Moral pitfalls remain, too, and this is itself a good reason to strive for as much clarity as possible in making moral judgments. Different, sound moral theories from Aristotle to this day alarmingly can lead to different and often opposing ethical positions on specific ethical problems in everyday life. There is in fact a lot to be said for helping ourselves to these theories that have emerged over millennia of moral philosophy. But the moral decision is still yours to make, and the action is yours to take. Ethics is personal, and it is definitely on you.

READINGS

Aristotle (384–322 BCE) analyzes the meaning of virtue and its role in the good life in this excerpt from his Nicomachean Ethics, the first full treatment of moral philosophy we have.

Aristotle: The Virtues

Now if the function of man is an activity of soul which follows or implies a rational principle, and if we say 'so-and-so-and 'a good so-and-so' have a function which is the same in kind, e.g. a lyre, and a good lyre-player, and so without qualification in all cases, eminence in respect of goodness being added to the name of the function (for the function of a lyre-player is to play the lyre, and that of a good lyre-player is to do so well): if this is the case, and we state the function of man to be a certain kind of life, and this to be an activity or actions of the soul implying a rational principle, and the function of a good man to be the good and noble performance of these, and if any action is well performed when it is performed in accordance with the appropriate excellence: if this is the case, human good turns out to be activity of soul in accordance with virtue, and if there are more than one virtue, in accordance with the best and most complete. But we must add "over a lifetime," for one swallow does not a summer make, nor does one day; and so too one day, or a short moment of pleasure and joy, does not make anyone blessed and truly happy.

If happiness is activity in accordance with virtue, it is reasonable that it should be in accordance with the highest virtue; and this will be that of the best thing in us. Whether it be reason or something else that is this element which is thought to be our natural ruler and guide and to take thought of things noble and divine, whether it be itself also divine or only the most divine element in us, the activity of this in accordance with its proper virtue will be perfect happiness. That this activity is contemplative we have already said.

Now such a thing happiness, above all else, is held to be; for this we choose always for self and never for the sake of something else, but honor, pleasure, reason, and every virtue we choose indeed for themselves (for if nothing resulted from them we should still choose each of them), but we choose them also for the sake of happiness, judging that by means of them we shall be happy. Happiness, on the other hand, no one chooses for the sake of these.

Virtue too is distinguished into kinds in accordance with this difference; for we say that some of the virtues are intellectual and others moral, philosophic wisdom and understanding and practical wisdom being intellectual, liberality and temperance moral. For in speaking about a man's character we do not say that he is wise or has understanding but that he is good-tempered or temperate; yet we praise the wise man also with respect to his state of mind; and of states of mind we call those which merit praise virtues.

It is also plain that none of the moral virtues arises in us by nature; for nothing that exists by nature can form a habit contrary to its nature. For instance the stone which by nature moves downwards cannot be habituated to move upwards, not even if one tries to train it by throwing it up ten thousand times; nor can fire be habituated to move downwards, nor can anything else that by nature behaves in one way be trained to behave in another. Neither by nature, then, nor contrary to nature do the virtues arise in us; rather we are adapted by nature to receive them, and are made perfect by habit. For the things we have to learn before we can do them, we learn by doing them, e.g. men become builders by building and lyre players by playing the lyre; so too we become just by doing just acts, temperate by doing temperate acts, brave by doing brave acts. Again, it is from the same causes and by the same means that every virtue is both produced and destroyed, and similarly every art; for it is from playing the lyre that both good and bad lyre-players are produced. And the corresponding statement is true of builders and of all the rest; men will be good or bad builders as a result of building well or badly. For if this were not so, there would have been no need of a teacher, but all men would have been born good or bad at their craft. This, then, is the case with the virtues also; by doing the acts that we do in our transactions with other men we become just or unjust, and by doing the acts that we do in the presence of danger, and being habituated to feel fear or confidence, we become brave or cowardly. The same is true of appetites and feelings of anger; some men become temperate and good-tempered, others self-indulgent and irascible, by behaving in one way or the other in the appropriate circumstances. Thus, in one word, states of character arise out of like activities. This is why the activities we exhibit must be of a certain kind; it is because the states of character correspond to the differences between these. It makes no small difference, then, whether we form habits of one kind or of another from our very youth; it makes a very great difference, or rather all the difference.

For people are good in but one way, but bad in many. Virtue, then, is a state of character concerned with choice, lying in a mean, that is, the mean relative to us, this being determined by a rational principle, and by that principle by which the man of practical wisdom would determine it. Now it is a mean between two vices, that which depends on excess and that which depends on defect; and again it is a mean because the vices respectively fall short of or exceed what is right in both passions and actions, while virtue both finds and chooses that which is intermediate. Hence in respect of its substance and the definition which states its essence virtue is a mean, with regard to what is best and right an extreme.

But not every action nor every passion admits of a mean; for some have names that already imply badness, e.g. spite, shamelessness, envy, and in the case of actions adultery, theft, murder; for all of these and suchlike things imply by their names that they are themselves bad, and not the excesses or deficiencies of them. It is not possible, then, ever to be right with regard to them; one must always be wrong. Nor does goodness or badness with regard to such things depend on committing adultery with the right woman, at the right time, and in the right way, but simply to do any of them is to go wrong. It would be equally absurd, then, to expect that in unjust, cowardly, and voluptuous action there should be a mean, an excess, and a deficiency; for at that rate there would be a mean of excess and of deficiency, an excess of excess, and a deficiency of deficiency. But as there is no excess and deficiency of temperance and courage because what is intermediate is in a sense an extreme, so too of the actions we have mentioned there is no mean nor any excess and deficiency, but however they are done they are wrong; for in general there is neither a mean of excess and deficiency, nor excess and deficiency of a mean.

And what we said before' will apply now; that which is proper to each thing is by nature best and most pleasant for each thing; for man, therefore, the life according to reason is best and pleasantest, since reason more than anything else is man. This life therefore is also the happiest.

Only the act in question counts in making moral judgments according to Immanuel Kant (1724–1804), and he explains how his categorical imperative lets us judge an act, in this selection from his *Groundwork for the Metaphysics of Morals.*

Immanuel Kant: The Categorical Imperative

The conception of the will of every rational being as one which must consider itself as giving in all the maxims of its will universal laws, so as to judge itself and its actions from this point of view- this conception leads to another which depends on it and is very fruitful, namely that of a kingdom of ends. By a kingdom I understand the union of different rational beings in a system by common laws. Now since it is by laws that ends are determined as regards their universal validity, hence, if we abstract from the personal differences of rational beings and likewise from all the content of their private ends, we shall be able to conceive all ends combined in a systematic whole (including both rational beings as ends in themselves, and also the special ends which each may propose to himself), that is to say, we can conceive a kingdom of ends, which on the preceding principles is possible. For all rational beings come under the law that each of them must treat itself and all others never merely as means, but in every case at the same time as ends in themselves. Hence results a systematic union of rational being by common objective laws, i. e., a kingdom which may be called a kingdom of ends, since what these laws have in view is just the relation of these beings to one another as ends and means. It is certainly only an ideal.

A rational being belongs as a member to the kingdom of ends when, although giving universal laws in it, he is also himself subject to these laws. He belongs to it as sovereign when, while giving laws, he is not subject to the will of any other. A rational being must always regard himself as giving laws either as member or as sovereign in a kingdom of ends which is rendered possible by the freedom of will. He cannot, however, maintain the latter position merely by the maxims of his will, but only in case he is a completely independent being without wants and with

Morality consists then in the reference of all action to the legislation which alone can render a kingdom of ends possible. This legislation must be capable of existing in every rational being and of emanating from his will, so that the principle of this will is never to act on any maxim which could not without contradiction be also a universal law and, accordingly, always so to act that the will could at the same time regard itself as giving in its maxims universal laws. If now the maxims of rational beings are not by their own nature coincident with this objective principle, then the necessity of acting on it is called practical necessitation, i. e., duty. Duty does not apply to the sovereign in the kingdom of ends, but it does to every member of it and to all in the same degree.

We can now end where we started at the beginning, namely, with the conception of a will unconditionally good. That will is absolutely good which cannot be evil- in other words, whose maxim, if made a universal law, could never contradict itself. This principle, then, is its supreme law: *"Act only as if according to a maxim which can at the same time be willed to be a universal law."* This is the sole condition under which a will can never contradict itself; and such an imperative is categorical. Since the validity of the will as a universal law for possible actions is analogous to the universal connection of the existence of things by general laws, which is the formal notion of nature in general, the categorical imperative can also be expressed thus: *"So act as if your maxim were to serve likewise as the universal law for all rational beings".* A kingdom of ends is thus only possible on the analogy of a kingdom of nature, the former however only by maxims, which is self-imposed rules, the latter only by the laws of efficient causes acting under necessitation from without. Nevertheless, although the system of nature is looked upon as a machine, yet so far as it has reference to rational beings as its ends, it is given on this account the name of a kingdom of nature. Now such a kingdom of ends would be actually realized by means of maxims conforming to the canon which the categorical imperative prescribes to all rational beings, if they were universally followed.

But although a rational being, even if he punctually follows this maxim himself, cannot reckon upon all others being therefore true to the same, nor expect that the kingdom of nature and its orderly arrangements shall be in harmony with him as a fitting member, so as to form a kingdom of ends to which he himself contributes, that is to say, that it shall favor his expectation of happiness, still that law: *"Act only as if according to a maxim of a member of a merely possible kingdom of ends legislating in it universally,"* remains in its full force, inasmuch as it commands categorically. And it is just in this that the paradox lies; that the mere dignity of man as a rational creature, without any other end or advantage to be attained thereby, in other words, respect for a mere idea, should yet serve as an inflexible precept of the will, and that it is precisely in this independence of the maxim on all such springs of action that its sublimity consists; and it is this that makes every rational subject worthy to be a legislative member in the kingdom of ends: for otherwise he would have to be conceived only as subject to the physical law of his wants.

The objective necessity of actions from obligation is called duty. From what has just been said, it is easy to see how it happens that, although the conception of duty implies subjection to the law, we yet ascribe a certain dignity and sublimity to the person who fulfils all his duties. There is not, indeed, any sublimity in him, so far as he is subject to the moral law; but inasmuch as in regard to that very law he is likewise a legislator, and on that account alone subject to it, he has sublimity. We have also shown above that neither fear nor inclination, but simply respect for the law, is the spring which can give actions a moral worth.

John Stuart Mill (1806–1873) proposes that actions are right in proportion to their creation of happiness, wrong if they produce its opposite. In refining Bentham's Utilitarianism by analyzing how not every happiness is the same, Mill set the blueprint for every argument for individual human rights to this day.

John Stuart Mill: Utilitarianism

From the dawn of philosophy, the question concerning the summum bonum, or, what is the same thing, concerning the foundation of morality, has been accounted the main problem in speculative thought, has occupied the most gifted intellects, and divided them into sects and schools, carrying on a vigorous warfare against one another. And after more than two thousand years the same discussions continue, philosophers are still ranged under the same contending banners, and neither thinkers nor mankind at large seem nearer to being unanimous on the subject, than when the youth Socrates listened to the old Protagoras, and asserted (if Plato's dialogue be grounded on a real conversation) the theory of utilitarianism against the popular morality of the so-called sophist.

It is true that similar confusion and uncertainty, and in some cases similar discordance, exist respecting the first principles of all the sciences, not excepting that which is deemed the most certain of them, mathematics; without much impairing, generally indeed without impairing at all, the trustworthiness of the conclusions of those sciences. An apparent anomaly, the explanation of which is, that the detailed doctrines of a science are not usually deduced from, nor depend for their evidence upon, what are called its first principles. Were it not so, there would be no science more precarious, or whose conclusions were more insufficiently made out, than algebra; which derives none of its certainty from what are commonly taught to learners as its elements, since these, as laid down by some of its most eminent teachers, are as full of fictions as English law, and of mysteries as theology. The truths which are ultimately accepted as the first principles of a science, are really the last results of metaphysical analysis, practiced on the elementary notions with which the science is conversant; and their relation to the science is not that of foundations to an edifice, but of roots to a tree, which may perform their office equally well though they be never dug down to and exposed to light. But though in science the particular truths precede the general theory, the contrary might be expected to be the case with a practical art, such as morals or legislation. All action is for the sake of some end, and rules of action, it seems natural to suppose, must take their whole character and color from the end to which they are subservient. When we engage in a pursuit, a clear and precise conception of what we are pursuing would seem to be the first thing we need, instead of the last we are to look forward to. A test of right and wrong must be the means, one would think, of ascertaining what is right or wrong, and not a consequence of having already ascertained it.

Although the non-existence of an acknowledged first principle has made ethics not so much a guide as a consecration of men's actual sentiments, still, as men's sentiments, both of favor and of aversion, are greatly influenced by what they suppose to be the effects of things upon their happiness, the principle of utility, or as Bentham latterly called it, the greatest happiness principle, has had a large share in forming the moral doctrines even of those who most scornfully reject its authority. I might go much further, and say that to all those a priori moralists who deem it necessary to argue at all, utilitarian arguments are indispensable. It is not my present purpose to criticize these thinkers; but I cannot help referring, for illustration, to a systematic treatise by one of the most illustrious of them, the Metaphysics of Ethics, by Kant. This remarkable man, whose system of thought will long remain one of the landmarks in the history of philosophical speculation, does, in the treatise in question, lay down a universal first principle as the origin and ground of moral obligation; it is this: "So act asif according to a maxi that you would willingly admit admit of being adopted as a law by all rational beings." But when he begins to deduce from this precept any of the actual duties of morality, he fails, almost grotesquely, to show that there would be any contradiction, any logical (not to say physical) impossibility, in the adoption by all rational beings of the most outrageously immoral rules of conduct. All he shows is that the consequences of their universal adoption would be such as no one would choose to incur.

On the present occasion, I shall attempt to contribute something towards the understanding and appreciation of the Utilitarian or Happiness theory, and towards such proof as it is susceptible of. It is evident that this cannot be proof in the ordinary and popular meaning of the term. Questions of ultimate ends are not amenable to direct proof. Whatever can be proved to be good must be so by being shown to be a means to something admitted to be good without proof. The medical art is proved to be good by its conducing to health; but how is it possible to prove that health is good? The art of music is good, for the reason, among others, that it produces pleasure; but what proof is it possible to give that pleasure is good? If, then, it is asserted that there is a comprehensive formula, including all things which are in themselves good, and that whatever else is good, is not so as an end, but as a mean, the formula may be accepted or rejected, but is not a subject of what is commonly understood by proof. We are not, however, to infer that its acceptance or rejection must depend on blind impulse, or arbitrary choice. The subject is within the cognizance of the rational faculty; and neither does that faculty deal with it solely in the way of intuition. Considerations may be presented capable of determining the intellect either to give or withhold its assent to the doctrine; and this is equivalent to proof.

The creed which accepts as the foundation of morals, Utility, or the Greatest Happiness Principle, holds that actions are right in proportion as they tend to promote happiness, wrong as they tend to produce the reverse of happiness. By happiness is intended pleasure, and the absence of pain; by unhappiness, pain, and the privation of pleasure. To give a clear view of the moral standard set up by the theory, much more requires to be said; in particular, what things it includes in the ideas of pain and pleasure; and to what extent this is left an open question. But these supplementary explanations do not affect the theory of life on which this theory of morality is grounded- namely, that pleasure, and freedom from pain, are the only things desirable as ends; and that all desirable things (which are as numerous in the utilitarian as in any other scheme) are desirable either for the pleasure inherent in themselves, or as means to the promotion of pleasure and the prevention of pain.

Now, such a theory of life excites in many minds and among them in some of the most estimable in feeling and purpose, inveterate dislike. To suppose that life has (as they express it) no higher end than pleasure- no better and nobler object of desire and pursuit- they designate as utterly mean and groveling; as a doctrine worthy only of swine, to whom the followers of Epicurus were, at a very early period, contemptuously likened; and modern holders of the doctrine are occasionally made the subject of equally polite comparisons by its German, French, and English assailants.

When thus attacked, the Epicureans have always answered, that it is not they, but their accusers, who represent human nature in a degrading light; since the accusation supposes human beings to be capable of no pleasures except those of which swine are capable. If this supposition were true, the charge could not be gainsaid, but would then be no longer an imputation; for if the sources of pleasure were precisely the same to human beings and to swine, the rule of life which is good enough for the one would be good enough for the other. The comparison of the Epicurean life to that of beasts is felt as degrading, precisely because a beast's pleasures do not satisfy a human being's conceptions of happiness.

Human beings have faculties more elevated than the animal appetites, and when once made conscious of them, do not regard anything as happiness which does not include their gratification. I do not, indeed, consider the Epicureans to have been by any means faultless in drawing out their scheme of consequences from the utilitarian principle. To do this in any sufficient manner, many Stoic, as well as Christian elements require to be included. But there is no known Epicurean theory of life which does not assign to the pleasures of the intellect, of the feelings and imagination, and of the moral sentiments, a much higher value as pleasures than to those of mere sensation. It must be admitted, however, that utilitarian writers in general have placed the superiority of mental over bodily pleasures chiefly in the greater permanency, safety, least costly, etc., of the former- that is, in their circumstantial advantages rather than in their intrinsic nature. And on all these points utilitarians have fully proved their case; but they might have taken the other, and, as it may be called, higher ground, with entire consistency. It is quite compatible with the principle of utility to recognize the fact, that some kinds of pleasure are more desirable and more valuable than others. It would be absurd that while, in estimating all other things, quality is considered as well as quantity, the estimation of pleasures should be supposed to depend on quantity alone.

If I am asked, what I mean by difference of quality in pleasures, or what makes one pleasure more valuable than another, merely as a pleasure, except its being greater in amount, there is but one possible answer. Of two pleasures, if there be one to which all or almost all who have experience of both give a decided preference, irrespective of any feeling of moral obligation to prefer it, that is the more desirable pleasure. If one of the two is, by those who are competently acquainted with both, placed so far above the other that they prefer it, even though knowing it to be attended with a greater amount of discontent, and would not resign it for any quantity of the other pleasure which their nature is capable of, we are justified in ascribing to the preferred enjoyment a superiority in quality.

The principle of utility either has, or there is no reason why it might not have, all the sanctions which belong to any other system of morals. Those sanctions are either external or internal. Of the external sanctions it is not necessary to speak at any length. They are the hope of pleasure and the fear of displeasure. There is evidently no reason why all these motives for observance should not attach themselves to the utilitarian morality, as completely and as powerfully as to any other. Indeed, those of them which refer to our fellow creatures are sure to do so, in proportion to the amount of general intelligence; for whether there be any other ground of moral obligation than the general happiness or not, men do desire happiness; and however imperfect may be their own practice, they desire and commend all conduct in others towards themselves, by which they think their happiness is promoted. With regard to the religious motive, if men believe, as most profess to do, in the goodness of God, those who think that conduciveness to the general happiness is the essence, or even only the criterion of good, must necessarily believe that it is also that which God approves.

The internal sanction of duty, whatever our standard of duty may be, is one and the same- a feeling in our own mind; a pain, more or less intense, attendant on violation of duty, which in properly cultivated moral natures rises, in the more serious cases, into shrinking from it as an impossibility. This feeling, when disinterested, and connecting itself with the pure idea of duty, and not with some particular form of it, or with any of the merely accessory circumstances, is the essence of Conscience; though in that complex phenomenon as it actually exists, the simple fact is in general all encrusted over with collateral associations, derived from sympathy, from love, and still more from fear; from all the forms of religious feeling; from the recollections of childhood and of all our past life; from self-esteem, desire of the esteem of others, and occasionally even self-abasement. This extreme complication is, I apprehend, the origin of the sort of mystical character which, by a tendency of the human mind of which there are many other examples, is apt to be attributed to the idea of moral obligation, and which leads people to believe that the idea cannot possibly attach itself to any other objects than those which, by a supposed mysterious law, are found in our present experience to excite it. Its binding force, however, consists in the existence of a mass of feeling which must be broken through in order to do what violates our standard of right, and which, if we do nevertheless violate that standard, will probably have to be encountered afterwards in the form of remorse. Whatever theory we have of the nature or origin of conscience, this is what essentially constitutes it.

The ultimate sanction, therefore, of all morality (external motives apart) being a subjective feeling in our own minds, I see nothing embarrassing to those whose standard is utility, in the question, what is the sanction of that particular standard? We may answer the same as of all other moral standards- the conscientious feelings of mankind. Undoubtedly this sanction has no binding efficacy on those who do not possess the feelings it appeals to; but neither will these persons be more obedient to any other moral principle than to the utilitarian one

To be incapable of proof by reasoning is common to all first principles; to the first premises of our knowledge, as well as to those of our conduct. But the former, being matters of fact, may be the subject of a direct appeal to the faculties which judge of fact- namely, our senses, and our internal consciousness. Can an appeal be made to the same faculties on questions of practical ends? Or by what other faculty is cognizance taken of them?

Questions about ends are, in other words, questions what things are desirable. The utilitarian doctrine is that happiness is desirable, and the only thing desirable, as an end; all other things being only desirable as means to that end. What ought to be required of this doctrine- what conditions is it requisite that the doctrine should fulfill- to make good its claim to be believed?

The only proof capable of being given that an object is visible is that people actually see it. The only proof that a sound is audible is that people hear it: and so of the other sources of our experience. In like manner, I apprehend, the sole evidence it is possible to produce that anything is desirable, is that people do actually desire it. If the end which the utilitarian doctrine proposes to itself were not, in theory and in practice, acknowledged to be an end, nothing could ever convince any person that it was so. No reason can be given why the general happiness is desirable, except that each person, so far as he believes it to be attainable, desires his own happiness. This, however, being a fact, we have not only all the proof which the case admits of, but all which it is possible to require, that happiness is a good: that each person's happiness is a good to that person, and the general happiness, therefore, a good to the aggregate of all persons. Happiness has made out its title as one of the ends of conduct, and consequently one of the criteria of morality.

On the Connection between Justice and Utility.

To recapitulate: the idea of justice supposes two things; a rule of conduct, and a sentiment which sanctions the rule. The first must be supposed common to all mankind, and intended for their good. The other (the sentiment) is a desire that punishment may be suffered by those who infringe the rule. There is involved, in addition, the conception of some definite person who suffers by the infringement; whose rights (to use the expression appropriated to the case) are violated by it. And the sentiment of justice appears to me to be, the animal desire to repel or retaliate a hurt or damage to oneself, or to those with whom one sympathizes, widened so as to include all persons, by the human capacity of enlarged sympathy, and the human conception of intelligent self-interest. From the latter elements, the feeling derives its morality; from the former, its peculiar impressiveness, and energy of self-assertion.

I have, throughout, treated the idea of a right residing in the injured person, and violated by the injury, not as a separate element in the composition of the idea and sentiment, but as one of the forms in which the other two elements clothe themselves. These elements are a hurt to some assignable person or persons on the one hand, and a demand for punishment on the other. An examination of our own minds, I think, will show that these two things include all that we mean when we speak of violation of a right. When we call anything a person's right, we mean that he has a valid claim on society to protect him in the possession of it, either by the force of law, or by that of education and opinion. If he has what we consider a sufficient claim, on whatever account, to have something guaranteed to him by society, we say that he has a right to it. If we desire to prove that anything does not belong to him by right, we think this done as soon as it is admitted that society ought not to take measures for securing it to him, but should leave him to chance, or to his own exertions.

To have a right, then, is, I conceive, to have something which society ought to defend me in the possession of. If the objector goes on to ask, why it ought? I can give him no other reason than general utility. If that expression does not seem to convey a sufficient feeling of the strength of the obligation, nor to account for the peculiar energy of the feeling, it is because there goes to the composition of the sentiment, not a rational only, but also an animal element, the thirst for retaliation; and this thirst derives its intensity, as well as its moral justification, from the extraordinarily important and impressive kind of utility which is concerned. The interest involved is that of security, to every one's feelings the most vital of all interests. All other earthly benefits are needed by one person, not needed by another; and many of them can, if necessary, be cheerfully foregone, or replaced by something else; but security no human being can possibly do without on it we depend for all our immunity from evil, and for the whole value of all and every good, beyond the passing moment; since nothing but the gratification of the instant could be of any worth to us, if we could be deprived of anything the next instant by whoever was momentarily stronger than ourselves.

Our notion, therefore, of the claim we have on our fellow-creatures to join in making safe for us the very groundwork of our existence, gathers feelings around it so much more intense than those concerned in any of the more common cases of utility, that the difference in degree (as is often the case in psychology) becomes a real difference in kind. The claim assumes that character of absoluteness, that apparent infinity, and incommensurability with all other considerations, which constitute the distinction between the feeling of right and wrong and that of ordinary expediency and inexpediency. The feelings concerned are so powerful, and we count so positively on finding a responsive feeling in others (all being alike interested), that "ought" and "should" grow into "must," and recognized indispensability becomes a moral necessity.

KEY TERMS

Categorical imperative   the key point in Kant's moral philosophy, a basic rule for telling right from wrong based on the universalizability of your act.

Deontology   from the Greek word for duty, a term for Kantian and neo-Kantian ethics.

Consequentialism   see Utilitarianism.

Natural law   Aquinas' ethical theory.

Relativism   a primitive ethical theory that defines right and wrong according to the mores of a particular time and place.

Divine command   a primitive moral theory that defines right as whatever god commands and wrong as whatever god forbids.

Utilitarianism   also called **consequentialism,** the moral theory that bases judgment of right and wrong on the consequences of an act.

Virtue ethics   another name for Aristotle's ethics, in which it is a person's character that matters in making a moral judgment, rather than an act that person performs or the consequences of that act.

QUESTIONS FOR DISCUSSION AND REVIEW

1. Explain the elements of any moral dilemma: the act, the consequences of the act, and the moral agent.
2. Critically analyze the false starts in moral philosophy including relativism and Divine Command.
3. Discuss the practical and logical problems with Aquinas' Natural Law moral theory.
4. Explain how ethics can be said to be always personal and often political.
5. Summarize, explain, and evaluate the main points of the reading by Aristotle.
6. Summarize, explain, and evaluate the main points of the reading by Immanuel Kant.
7. Summarize, explain, and evaluate the main points of the reading by John Stuart Mill.

BIBLIOGRAPHY, SUGGESTED READINGS, AND USEFUL LINKS

Anscombe, G. E. M. (1958). *"The Ethics of Virtue Today"*. [From *Modern Moral Philosophy*, by G. E. M. Anscombe; originally published in *Philosophy 33*, No. 124

Aristotle (1902). The Nicomachaean Ethics, Vols. 1 and 2. (Ross. W.D. transl.).

Aquinas, T. (1998). *Selected Philosophical Writings*. (McDermott, T. transl.).

Bentham, J. (1861). *An Introduction to the Principles of Morals and Legislation*.

de Beauvoir, S. (2004). *Introduction to an Ethics of Ambiguity*. (Timmermann, M. transl.).

Internet Encyclopedia of Philosophy a peer-reviewed academic resource. Available from http://www.iep.utm.edu/

MacIntyre, A. (1981). *After Virtue: A Study in Moral Theory*.

Mill, J. S. (1861). *Utilitarianism*.

Plato. (1892). *Euthyphro*. In Authors (Ed.), *The Dialogues of Plato*. (Jowett, B. transl.).

Sartre, J-P. (1956). *Being and nothingness*, (Barnes, H. transl.).

Sartre, J-P. (2006). *Critique of dialectical reason*, Vols. 1 and 2. (Sheridan-Smith, A. and Hoare, Q. transl.).

Sartre, J-P. (1992). *Notebooks for an Ethics*. (Pellauer, D. transl.).

Stanford Encyclopedia of Philosophy. Available from http://plato.stanford.edu/

We are not Alone Here—Political Philosophy

12

Upon completing this chapter, students should be able to meet the following Learning Outcomes:

12.1 Articulate the salient points of the state of nature for Locke and Hobbes.

12.2 Compare and contrast the various views of Hobbes and Locke on the state of nature and natural rights.

12.3 Explain the difference between Locke's labor theory of property and Marx's theory of surplus value.

12.4 Discuss Karl Marx's analysis of class struggle as presented in his *Communist Manifesto*.

12.5 Explain the views of Nozick and Hospers regarding legitimate laws and the role of government.

12.6 Compare and contrast Rawls and Nozick on justice.

There are various questions raised by rise of civilized society and the formation of government. Governments are arranged in various ways. Some governments have a single leader, elected by no one while other governments are lead by leaders elected by the citizens. The economic distribution and redistribution also vary in a number of ways. In this chapter, we examine some classic views on government as well as some contemporary views on the notion of justice.

POWERFUL IDEA BOX: SYSTEMS OF GOVERNMENT

Democracy—rule by the people, after Ancient Athens always through elected officials.

Socialism—rule by the people, with its elected government guaranteeing their welfare.

Monarchy—rule by a king.

Oligarchy—rule by a group.

Theocracy—rule by religious leaders.

Despotism or Dictatorship—rule by someone who has seized the government by force.

POWERFUL ANALYSIS: FREEDOM OR CONTROL?

What should the balance be between individual freedom, our individual autonomy, and social control?

Natural Right's Theorists: Thomas Hobbes, John Locke, and Jean-Jacques Rousseau

Thomas Hobbes and John Locke both discuss their views on political philosophy within a school of thought known as natural rights theory. **Natural rights** are rights we have without a government. They are rights that we have in virtue of our humanity. Natural rights are akin to what we now call human rights although there are important philosophical differences. One key difference is that natural rights are argued to exist even in the absence of government or civil society. Many of the "human rights" argued for by groups like Amnesty International or the United Nations are the rights that could only be held within a civil society.

Often, when you hear people discussing human rights abuses, they mean abuses of certain basic rights. Unlike the notion of human rights (which can be rather muddled as various organizations and groups define such rights in different ways), natural rights have a long detailed history in philosophy. Rights such as the right to life or the right to liberty are often argued to be natural rights.

Natural rights are rights that people have without any legislation or action by the government; some (such as Hobbes and Locke) argue that they would exist even if there were no government. These rights should be distinguished from **positive rights,** which are created by an act of legislation by the government. The government makes a law, and a right is created. Dogs have positive rights. Even trees can have positive rights so long as the government passes a law granting them certain protections. For example, at present, people living in the state of Colorado have a right to smoke marijuana, whereas no such right exists in the state of Florida. In Colorado, the voters (by means of political process) have obtained the right—a right which is not a natural right. Positive rights vary from state to state and country to country.

There is no clear philosophical foundation for natural rights. Writers such as Hobbes and Locke argued that natural rights were granted by God. However, this view carries little philosophical weight. It may simply be that there existence is simply a basic supposition of political theory.

POWERFUL ANALYSIS: WHERE DO RIGHTS COME FROM?

We assume we have many rights, but where do our rights originate? Do all of our rights come from the government?

Hobbes and Locke also argue for natural rights in the context of the **state of nature**. The state of nature is a hypothetical situation where mankind is living without any government. Rousseau discusses the state of nature as well, but mainly to criticize the conception of it presented by Hobbes and Locke.

Thomas Hobbes

Thomas Hobbes was born in Wiltshire, on April 5, 1588. His father was the vicar of a parish. He studied at Magdalen Hall in Oxford entering the college with a firm grasp of both Greek and Latin. He left Oxford in 1608 and became the private tutor for the eldest son of Lord Cavendish of Hardwick (later known as the Earl of Devonshire). He traveled with the Cavendish family across Europe tutoring their young son. Given his connections to the noble family, he had the opportunity to meet many of his contemporary thinkers including Francis Bacon, Herbert of Cherbury, and Ben Johnson.

In 1651, Hobbes published his most influential book, *Leviathan*. Hobbes argues that the government can be seen as a great creature (The leviathan, a mythical serpent) composed of the citizens with the king as its head. Hobbes argued that the government's main purpose was the protection of people from their own selfishness. A ruler with absolute authority was the only one who could maintain peace.

Hobbes argues for this analysis of government by discussing the state of nature. According to him, mankind was born into the state of nature. As noted above, the state of nature is a hypothetical situation where mankind is living with no government. In such a situation, there is no one in charge to make political or legal decisions. On Hobbes' view, life in the state of nature is "short nasty and brutish." There are no arts or letters, only a "war of all against all." In this state, all people have an equal right to everything. Right, in Hobbes' view, is equal to freedom, "the freedom, to do what he would, and against whom he thought fit, and to possess, use and enjoy all that he would or could get."

Although we have a bare right to all, we also have two natural rights. As Hobbes says, "The right of nature, which writers commonly call jus natural, is the liberty each man hath to use his own power as he will himself for the preservation of his own nature; that is to say, his own life, and consequently, of doing anything which, in his own judgment and reason, he shall conceive to be the most apt means thereunto." In other words, we are at liberty to do anything we must for the preservation of our life.

On his view, the life of war ultimately becomes tiresome, for even the strongest must sleep, and even then the weakest could kill them. The constant fear of death and loss leads mankind out of the state of nature. In order to leave the state of nature, we must employ our natural reason, which he believes allows us to be aware of two laws of nature. The laws of nature are to "seek peace and follow it" and two, "be willing, were others are willing to do so too, as far as needed for peace, and defense of himself as he shall think it necessary, to lay down his right to all things; and be contented with so much liberty against other men, as he would allow against himself." From these two laws of natural reason, Hobbes concludes that all men should lay down their bare right to everything and alienate all of their rights to one individual, the sovereign.

Hobbes goes on to argue that once we form a social contract and leave the state of nature, we are bound by the contract for eternity. In other words, we may not revolt against the government since we have promised to obey the sovereign. The reality, of course, is that none of us where there when the original social contract was formed, so it is unclear if we are bound by the hypothetical/historical oath.

Contemporary political philosophy may argue that although many citizens may have never given express consent to be governed, we give our tacit consent by remaining in the country. Express consent is when a person actually states an oath of allegiance or a promise to obey the government. Persons that become naturalized citizens do this when they take an oath, as do men whom are 18 years of age and fill out a draft card for military service. Tacit consent is consent that is "unexpressed, unspoken, unsaid, and implicit." The fact that we remain present in the country is taken are our tacit consent to obey its laws and constitution.

John Locke

John Locke was born on August 29, 1632, in Warrington, a village in Somerset, England. In 1668, he was elected as a fellow of the Royal Society; in 1674, he graduated as a bachelor of medicine; and in 1675, he was appointed to a medical studentship at the college. Although he was formally trained in medicine, he worked in a number of advisory positions to high-level government leaders such as the Earl of Shaftesbury who became Lord Chancellor in 1672.

Locke wrote his major political work, *Two Treatises of Civil Government* in the 1680s, but in a time of political turmoil and upheaval in England, the ideas and the works expressed were thought to be revolutionary and contrary to royal authority. Locke had to flee into exile in Holland during this period in his life. The work was finally published in 1690. In the works he puts forth his theory of natural law and natural rights in which he makes a distinction between legitimate and illegitimate civil governments. He also argues that there can be times when revolution is justified. He argues that the reason the government is established is to protect the life, liberty, and property of a people. If these goals are not fulfilled by the government, then rebellion is legitimate.

POWERFUL IDEAS BOX: JOHN LOCKE AND THE AMERICAN REVOLUTION

John Locke had a powerful influence upon the American Revolution. His ideas served as the basis for various documents including the Declaration of Independence. Thomas Jefferson, the author of the Declaration of Independence readily admitted that he based it upon John Locke's political philosophy. The most obvious example found in the Declaration is the phrase, "life, liberty and pursuit of happiness," which mirrors Locke' notion of the natural rights to "life, liberty and property." Locke's philosophy provided a philosophical legitimacy for the American Revolution and revolutions against tyrannical governments everyone.

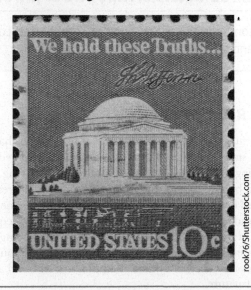

rook76/Shutterstock.com

John Locke argues from the state of nature to the foundations of political society. Locke's conception of the state of nature differs from Hobbes. He says that it is not a state of war but rather, "Men living together according to reason, without a common superior on Earth with authority to judge between them is, properly, the state of nature." Locke argues that we have certain fundamental natural rights. We are endowed with these rights even in absence of any government or political association.

> "The labor of his body, and the work of his hands, we may say, are properly his. Whatsoever then he removes out of the state that nature hath provided, and left it in, he hath mixed his labor with, and joined to it something that is his own, and thereby makes it his property"

> —*John Locke, 1690, Two Treatises of Civil Government*

Locke argues that mankind has three natural rights: life, liberty, and property. He says that in the state of nature, we can acquire property rights. He employs a notion known as the **labor theory of property**. The labor theory of property, succinctly put, states that if you work for something, and it is not already owned by someone, then you acquire ownership of it. This is to be distinguished from the theory of surplus value analyzed by Karl Marx, which is discussed below.

Locke argues that because we can have property rights in the state of nature, but we cannot adequately protect it, we ought to enter into a civil government. On Locke's view, we do not give up all of our rights to the government rather the government has a duty to protect us and our rights. Governments that fail to protect our basic rights are illegitimate and we may revolt against them.

POWERFUL ANALYSIS: THE STATE OF NATURE

Compare and contrast the various views of Hobbes and Locke on the state of nature and natural rights.

Jean-Jacques Rousseau

Jean-Jacques Rousseau claims that both Hobbes and Locke mischaracterize the state of nature. In a true state of nature, man is not motivated by greed, envy, or acquisition of material things. On Rousseau's view, natural man (living in a true state of nature) is motivated by love of self and only cares about self-preservation. Natural man is not motivated by greed or love of material goods. One does not see wild animals wearing gold and jewels. Even the higher primates do not acquire property—so in Rousseau's mind, a true state of nature would be mankind living together in peace and harmony. He seems to assume there would be enough resources for people to survive without war or conflict, but in his view, that is a true and accurate representation of the state of nature.

"The first man who, having enclosed a piece of ground, bethought himself of saying This is mine, and found people simple enough to believe him, was the real founder of civil society. From how many crimes, wars, and murders, from how many horrors and misfortunes might not any one have saved mankind, by pulling up the stakes, or filling up the ditch, and crying to his fellows: Beware of listening to this imposter; you are undone if you once forget that the fruits of the earth belong to us all, and the earth itself to nobody"

—*Jean-Jacques Rousseau, 1754, Discourse on Inequality.*

Lefteris Papaulakis/Shutterstock.com

The state of nature presented by Hobbes and Locke is what Rousseau calls pre-political man. Pre-political man has yet to form a government but has been corrupted from the natural state by the goals of acquisition of property and wealth. Ultimately, mankind completely leaves its natural state and enters into civil society once we move from the goal of self-preservation toward the goal of acquiring property and wealth. At this point, mankind becomes motivated by greed and corrupted by envy.

"Man is born free, and everywhere he is in chains. One man thinks himself the master of others, but remains more of a slave than they are"

—*Jean-Jacques Rousseau, 1762, The Social Contract*

Rousseau is highly critical of civil society. He is so critical in fact that he began his literary career by entering (and winning) an essay contest in which writers were supposed to applaud and praise civilization by writing an essay expressing the exact opposite views. He argued that morals had become corrupted by science and technology and that mankind had placed too much emphasis on logic at the expense of our natural senses and feelings.

In regards to his political views, he argues that all of mankind is in chains. He thinks we all are prisoners and slaves of the government. We are controlled by laws, rules, and regulations we did not impose on ourselves but rather that were imposed on us from outside political forces and politicians. He thinks that we can only be truly free when we are part of a **direct democracy**. Direct democracy is the notion that each citizen has an active role in the government and has an equal say and role in the creation of laws. Given the fact that most countries have millions or hundreds of millions of citizens, it seems to be a very impractical (if not impossible) approach to governance.

Most democratic countries rely upon **representative democracy**. Under such a system, the citizens vote for representatives that represent their political interest.

Although Rousseau's approach seems rather improbable, he does argue that it would lead mankind toward freedom in that we all would be executives and citizens at once. Each person would be the government, and at the same time, subject to laws of their own creation.

Rousseau continues his romantic idealism by maintaining that under such a system, the people must be guided by the **general will**. The general will is the opinion people will reach, if they consider a matter objectively and determine what is best for society as a whole (and are not swayed by their personal interest). Rousseau believes that if given the unbiased facts, everyone in a society could unanimously agree about what is the correct course of action that will benefit the common good of society.

In contrast to the general will, Rousseau discusses the dangers of the **will of all**. The will of all is simply the will of the majority, considering only their self-interest—not what is best for society. At present, it would seem most political elections end in results which are motive by the will of all, not the general will. The will of all is the will of the majority, it is what the majority of people desire, it may not have the common good of all society as its goal. This notion of rule by majority is a serious problem for Rousseau, and in his view this leads to an immoral government.

Social Justice, Equality, and Liberty

John Stuart Mill was a social reformer and proponent of liberty and freedom. He worked to reform and revised Jeremy Bentham's statement of the ethical theory of utilitarianism and was a precursor to libertarian ideals. In his essay *On Liberty*, he argues that the limiting principle against positive legislations of government is *harm*. The government must not extent into the private affairs of its citizens except to stop harm to others. So, the only legitimate laws according to Mill are laws that protect you from others, but not from yourself.

In *On Liberty*, John Stuart Mill puts forth a famous liberty limiting principle that is known as "**the Harm Principle**." This principle is probably the most permissive of the liberty limiting principles. It says, in extended form, " The sole end for which mankind are warranted, individually or collectively, in interfering with the liberty of action of any of their number, is self-protection. The only purpose for which power can be rightfully exercised over any member of a civilized community, against his will, is to prevent harm to others. His own good, either physical or moral, is not a sufficient warrant. He cannot rightfully be compelled to do or forbear because it will be better for him to do so, because it will make him happier, because, in the opinion of others, to do so would be wise, or even right . . . The only part of the conduct of anyone, for which he is amenable to society, is that which concerns others. In the part which merely concerns himself, his independence is, of right, absolute. Over himself, over his own body and mind, the individual is sovereign."

Libertarianism

John Hospers is a contemporary philosopher who argues for libertarian views. **Libertarians** argue for a limited government, one that has as its sole purpose, protection. Hospers states that of the three types of laws that government enacts: 1) laws protecting you from yourself, 2) laws protecting you from others, and 3) laws making you help others, only the second class of laws are legitimate. The other two are the result of government superseding its bounds.

In his 1974 book, *Anarchy, State and Utopia*, Robert Nozick argues for a modern libertarian view, similar to that of John Hospers. Nozick argues for a minimalist state, one limited whose sole purpose is to provide to protection to its citizens. He maintains that citizens need protection from: force, fraud, and breach of contract. In his view, a government, which acts like more than a night-watchman, is infringing upon the rights and liberty of its citizens. Nozick also defends a view known as the entitlement notion of justice. Under this view, a person is entitled to what they have rightly acquired, and justice consists in each person's retaining control over their acquisitions.

Justice as Fairness

John Rawls defined justice as fairness. He argues that everyone ought to have the same basic liberties, and any social or economic inequality ought to benefit the poor instead of the rich. Inequality, say in taxes, ought to be at the expense of the rich in order to benefit the poor. He argues that we would arrive at these principles if we were in the **original position**. The original position is a hypothetical situation where there is no government.

He argues that these two principles are the guiding force behind his conception:

1) Each person has an equal right to the most extensive scheme of equal basic liberties compatible with a similar scheme of liberties for all.

2) Social and economic inequalities are to meet two conditions: they must be (a) to the greatest expected benefit to the least advantaged; (b) attached to offices and positions open to all under conditions of fair equality of opportunity (*A Theory of Justice*, 1971).

PhotoStockImage/Shutterstock.com

In the original position, each participant represents various social groups that are present in society. In the original position, each participant is under the **veil of ignorance**. The veil of ignorance is a hypothetical thought experiment where one is to imagine oneself as a representative of the populous as a whole. Under the veil, you will be looking for guiding principles of justice and begin to stipulate laws and regulations for your government.

POWERFUL ANALYSIS: RAWLS VS. NOZICK

Compare and contrast the views of Rawls and Nozick on Justice. Which, if any, seems to have a more reasonable notion?

Rawls believes that if you did not know if you were a man, a woman, or a minority, you would not create laws that benefit one social group at the expense of another—since you are ignorant of your social status and position. Given that you do not know your race or your economic class, Rawls thinks that a reasonable person in such a situation would adapt his strategy of maximizing the situation of those in the least advantageous social position. It is Rawls' view that if one were to engage in such a thought experiment, then you could develop the most fair and just social principles and laws.

Powerful Thinkers: Karl Marx

Karl Marx (1818–1883) employs a dialectical analysis of history to argue that because of the exploitation of the workers by the capitalist will lead to a revolution of the workers, to socialism where the proletariat's interests and welfare will be guaranteed by the state; and eventually to communism, where the necessity for the state will disappear along with alienation of labor from life. Simply put, according to Marx's analysis of society, it is not fair that the owners of business make all the money and profit, when the workers are the ones actually doing the work.

This notion is captured by his **theory of surplus value**. In this theory, the harder you work for something, the more value it has. In his mammoth 1863 *Theories of Surplus Value*, intended as a fourth volume of his revolutionary *Capital*, the value in question is the difference between what it costs to have a worker create a product with his labor and what price the capitalist who owns the means of production can get for whatever the worker creates. In Marx's view, the owners of the means of production do little but reap the rewards, and he proposes that those actually performing the labor should earn the money.

An anti-Marxist objection would suggest that Marx never spent any time in a middle management position. There is no question that day laborers work very hard, but perhaps the owner and manager have some say in a business's success. Furthermore, the saying "work smarter not harder" may call this theory into question from a reactionary point of view. You could work very hard and struggle to climb a tree and pick a coconut, whereas someone else could use a pole and knock the coconut out of the tree with little effort, but at the end of the day, it is just a coconut—it has limited value. The value of objects does not vary in accordance with how hard you worked to get or create the object in most cases. Marx's point remains, however, that whoever owns the coconut gets to eat or sell it for a profit—whether he or she picked it or not.

It is important to note that Marx's philosophy has little to do with the way his views were put to revolutionary use after his death. His early works In particular, from his 1841 doctoral dissertation on Democritus (460–370 BCE) and Epicurus (341–270 BCE) through *The German Ideology* (1845), *The Poverty of Philosophy* (1847), and the *Communist Manifesto* (1848)—excerpted in this chapter—are primarily philosophical works that are far from the so-called "scientific materialism" of later developments in Marxism. Marx was not a materialist, though his views are certainly ambiguous on this crucial ontological issue. Marx's later writings, which focus on the philosophical foundations of political action, did provide Vladimir Illych Lenin (1870–1924) the philosophical trappings of a practical plan for what would prove to be tragic and ruthlessly opportunistic perversions of Marx's own humanistic philosophy.

Criticism of what Marxism became after the Russian Revolution has been strong and pointed, from philosophers as diverse as Rosa Luxemburg (1871–1919) in *Leninism or Marxism?* Georg Lukacs (1885–1975) in the visionary *History and Class Consciousness*; Herbert Marcuse (1898–1979) in *Reason and Revolution* and *One-Dimensional Man*, and Jean-Paul Sartre (1905–1980) in *The Ghost of Stalin* and especially in his posthumously published masterpiece of political philosophy *Critique of Dialectical Reason*.

Making full use of Georg Wilhelm Friedrich Hegel's (1770–1831) dialectic method and his vision of the human being constantly making and remaking himself, Marx in fact anticipated much of today's humanism in his own dialectical philosophy. What Sartre called humanism in action is at the heart of Marx's vision, as the French philosopher explained in his celebrated preface to Franz Fanon's (1925–1961) 1961 *The Wretched of the Earth*: "The demands of the least favored members of society express the truth of a society," Sartre writes, "not least because their interests are often in clear contradiction with the values espoused by that society itself."

nadi555/Shutterstock.com

Marx ultimately believes in an egalitarian society, where everyone is equal in social status. This type of humanism/egalitarianism in action has yet to happen.

"We work for the betterment of mankind, not material gain."

— *Captain Jean-Luc Picard, Star Trek: First Contact*

It should be pointed out that Marxist socialist views of the role of the state in guaranteeing the welfare of all citizens have become the current state of affairs in many, if not most, developed democracies: guaranteed free health care, guaranteed retirement with dignity, free education for everyone, a lessening rather than widening gap in overall income, and heavy taxing of capitalist interests in order to pay for these social guarantees are more often the rule, not the exception, in post-World War II Western Europe. If anything, Lenin's Russian revolution of 1917, held back the cause of Marxism as Marx himself envisioned it, and the fall of the Soviet Empire in 1989 is leading to a re-examination of Marx's ideas in the twenty-first century.

Without doubt, socialism as Marx envisioned it has never been realized under the tyrannies of self-described Marxist societies, as Alan Ryan notes in "Socialisms" at the end of this chapter. From the Soviet Union's murderously influential Marxism–Leninism and China's Maoism with its bizarre transformation into a state-capitalist hybrid, right through Cuba's *Castrismo* and Venezuela's *Chavismo* during and after the Chávez dictatorship, human rights, freedom, and life with dignity are not valued in any of these governments any more than well-planned economic development or general happiness.

Perhaps humanism in action, that elusive egalitarian society for which Karl Marx made the blueprint, has only been epitomized in *Star Trek: First Contact,* where Captain Picard once said, "We work for the betterment of mankind, not material gain."

Ultimately, it is unfortunate but true that there is no agreement regarding the structure, nature, and purpose of government. History may be the ultimate judge of which systems work. It may be the case that certain systems can thrive at certain times and under certain social or cultural conditions.

Nasjonalmuseet for kunst, arkitektur og design/The National Museum of Art, Architecture and Design

So What Do You Do Now?

We are not alone here, and none of us lives in a perfect society. No question is posed in a vacuum, and few answers are perfectly clear when it comes to how to live and what to do. We don't in fact all work for the betterment of mankind, as Captain Picard would want us to in *Star Trek*. If we think about it, there is not a lot we can be sure of. In the meantime, we live, here and now, always with others. It is no accident that philosophy and democracy grew up side by side, that ethics in ancient Athens was from the beginning discussed in the *polis*, always leading to politics. These are not just theoretical questions that philosophy is posing; these are powerful ideas that can point our way. Philosophy matters, particularly amid the balkanization of disciplines and fragmentation of learning that are all too common. These are powerful ideas that lead us away from isolation and toward the immense diversity all around us.

So, what now? There is so much we don't know. Philosophy as the first learning discipline began with a thirst for knowledge. Philosophy began by asking what life means, and that is still an open question. It can be such a confusing and also fuzzy question that some philosophers shy away from asking it. Still, it seems like a perfectly good question, and it is your life after all that you are asking about.

Perhaps you find meaning in believing in another life after this one. Or not. Perhaps life has no meaning, as Albert Camus and Jean-Paul Sartre have suggested, except whatever meaning we create for ourselves. But, since we will all be dead in a hundred years, what does it matter anyway?

> "It is better for a private citizen to live on equal terms with his fellows,
> and not to cringe and grovel or to hold his head too high, and in public
> affairs to support peaceful and honorable policies"
>
> —*Cicero*

POWERFUL IDEAS BOX: THE MEANING AND PURPOSE OF LIFE?

Is there a bucket list of things you'd like to do before you die? Do you expect to get to all of them? Does it matter?

Maybe the meaning of life matters because we're still here living it. If a desire for immortality makes no sense to you, maybe the meaning of life lies in a higher purpose, in living and working with others, in loving. In being part of a family, of a nation, and of humanity.

Aristotle suggested that the purpose of human life is in fact happiness, *eudaemonia*, not any quick-fix passing pleasure but rather true happiness over an entire life. The post-Aristotelians proposed more modest goals, such as Epicurus's concept of *ataraxia*, that is, freedom from worry. Concentrate on what really matters to you and just relax.

> "Accustom yourself to believing that death is nothing to us, for good and evil imply the capacity for sensation, and death is the privation of all sentience; therefore a correct understanding that death is nothing to us makes the mortality of life enjoyable, not by adding to life a limitless time, but by taking away the yearning after immortality"
>
> —*Epicurus*

Still, what Marx called material conditions always have been undeniable, and these conditions in fact place brutal limits on your possibilities. Political philosophy can only guide you a bit in affecting your situation in the here and now. What Marx called material conditions always have been undeniable, and these conditions in fact place brutal limits on your possibilities.

And what about suffering? According to both Buddhists and existentialists, life is suffering. For the Buddhists, suffering emerges from desire, so eliminating unnecessary desire may put us on the right path to happiness. For existentialists, suffering and anguish are the flip side of blind faith. If indeed we are alone here—alone with other people, that is—in a world that will not give us any answers, then our situation is absurd. What meaning can we find in that?

POWERFUL ANALYSIS: LIFE'S PURPOSE?

Do you think life has a point? Does it have to?

Powerful Ideas

Perhaps we can find meaning amid all the absurdity. All this philosophy seemingly has not led to clear answers so far. All these big abstract questions about what is real and how we know that, about how to love and what to do—none of these ever lead to answers that are as clear as $2 + 2 + 4$. Philosophy may not give us clear answers, but isn't it a great travel companion for this life journey?

"There is no shame in choosing joy"

—*Albert Camus*

Powerful ideas for centuries, for millennia, have set us on an intensely personal journey of discovery. "There is only one serious philosophical question," wrote Albert Camus, "and that is suicide. Whether life is worth living or not amounts to answering the fundamental question of philosophy." Start with that one and keep going.

As Camus describes the human condition in his *Myth of Sisyphus*, we are all condemned to roll a rock uphill ceaselessly and constantly, then we die. The catch here, and it's a good one, is that we can choose our attitude. We can choose to be happy. No, we are not alone here. And it's on us to make that happen.

READINGS

Jean-Jacques Rousseau was born on June 28, 1712 in Geneva and died on July 2, 1778 in Ermenonville, France. He was one of the most important philosophers of the French enlightenment. He had many jobs before he became a writer and philosopher including working as an engraver, teacher, and secretary. In 1750, he wrote his first major philosophical work, and in 1754, he wrote the Discourse on Inequality.

A Dissertation on the Origin and Foundation of the Inequality of Mankind

It is of man that I have to speak; and the question I am investigating shows me that it is to men that I must address myself: for questions of this sort are not asked by those who are afraid to honor truth. I shall then confidently uphold the cause of humanity before the wise men who invite me to do so, and shall not be dissatisfied if I acquit myself in a manner worthy of my subject and of my judges.

I conceive that there are two kinds of inequality among the human species; one, which I call natural or physical, because it is established by nature, and consists in a difference of age, health, bodily strength, and the qualities of the mind or of the soul: and another, which may be called moral or political inequality, because it depends on a kind of convention, and is established, or at least authorized by the consent of men. This latter consists of the different privileges, which some men enjoy to the prejudice of others; such as that of being more rich, more honored, more powerful or even in a position to exact obedience.

It is useless to ask what is the source of natural inequality, because that question is answered by the simple definition of the word. Again, it is still more useless to inquire whether there is any essential connection between the two inequalities; for this would be only asking, in other words, whether those who command are necessarily better than those who obey, and if strength of body or of mind, wisdom or virtue are always found in particular individuals, in proportion to their power or wealth: a question fit perhaps to be discussed by slaves in the hearing of their masters, but highly unbecoming to reasonable and free men in search of the truth.

The subject of the present discourse, therefore, is more precisely this. To mark, in the progress of things, the moment at which right took the place of violence and nature became subject to law, and to explain by what sequence of miracles the strong came to submit to serve the weak, and the people to purchase imaginary repose at the expense of real felicity.

The philosophers, who have inquired into the foundations of society, have all felt the necessity of going back to a state of nature; but not one of them has got there. Some of them have not hesitated to ascribe to man, in such a state, the idea of just and unjust, without troubling themselves to show that he must be possessed of such an idea, or that it could be of any use to him. Others have spoken of the natural right of every man to keep what belongs to him, without explaining what they meant by *belongs*. Others again, beginning by giving the strong authority over the weak, proceeded directly to the birth of government, without regard to the time that must have elapsed before the meaning of the words authority and government could have existed among men. Every one of them, in short, constantly dwelling on wants, avidity, oppression, desires and pride, has transferred to the state of nature ideas which were acquired in society; so that, in speaking of the savage, they described the social man. It has not even entered into the heads of most of our writers to doubt whether the state of nature ever existed; but it is clear from the Holy Scriptures that the first man, having received his understanding and commandments immediately from God, was not himself in such a state; and that, if we give such credit to the writings of Moses as every Christian philosopher ought to give, we must deny that, even before the deluge, men were ever in the pure state of nature; unless, indeed, they fell back into it from some very extraordinary circumstance; a paradox which it would be very embarrassing to defend, and quite impossible to prove.

Let us begin then by laying facts aside, as they do not affect the question. The investigations we may enter into, in treating this subject, must not be considered as historical truths, but only as mere conditional and hypothetical reasoning, rather calculated to explain the nature of things, than to ascertain their actual origin; just like the hypotheses which our physicists daily form respecting the formation of the world. Religion commands us to believe that, God Himself having taken men out of a state of nature immediately after the creation, they are unequal only because it is His will they should be so: but it does not forbid us to form conjectures based solely on the nature of man, and the beings around him, concerning what might have become of the human race, if it had been left to itself. This then is the question asked me, and that which I propose to discuss in the following discourse. As my subject interests mankind in general, I shall endeavor to make use of a style adapted to all nations, or rather, forgetting time and place, to attend only to men to whom I am speaking. I shall suppose myself in the Lyceum of Athens, repeating the lessons of my masters, with Plato and Xenocrates for judges, and the whole human race for audience.

O man, of whatever country you are, and whatever your opinions may be, behold your history, such as I have thought to read it, not in books written by your fellow-creatures, who are liars, but in nature, which never lies. All that comes from her will be true; nor will you meet with anything false, unless I have involuntarily put in something of my own. The times of which I am going to speak are very remote: how much are you changed from what you once were! It is, so to speak, the life of your species which I am going to write, after the qualities which you have received, which your education and habits may have depraved, but cannot have entirely destroyed. There is, I feel, an age at which the individual man would wish to stop: you are about to inquire about the age at which you would have liked your whole species to stand still. Discontented with your present state, for reasons which threaten your unfortunate descendants with still greater discontent, you will perhaps wish it were in your power to go back; and this feeling should be a panegyric on your first ancestors, a criticism of your contemporaries, and a terror to the unfortunates who will come after you.

The First Part

Important as it may be, in order to judge rightly of the natural state of man, to consider him from his origin, and to examine him, as it were, in the embryo of his species; I shall not follow his organization through its successive developments, nor shall I stay to inquire what his animal system must have been at the beginning, in order to become at length what it actually is. I shall not ask whether his long nails were at first, as Aristotle supposes, only crooked talons; whether his whole body, like that of a bear, was not covered with hair; or whether the fact that he walked upon all fours, with his looks directed toward the earth, confined to a horizon of a few paces, did not at once point out the nature and limits of his ideas. On this subject I could form none but vague and almost imaginary conjectures. Comparative anatomy has as yet made too little progress, and the observations of naturalists are too uncertain to afford an adequate basis for any solid reasoning. So that, without having recourse to the supernatural information given us on this head, or paying any regard to the changes which must have taken place in the internal, as well as the external, conformation of man, as he applied his limbs to new uses, and fed himself on new kinds of food, I shall suppose his conformation to have been at all times what it appears to us at this day; that he always walked on two legs, made use of his hands as we do, directed his looks over all nature, and measured with his eyes the vast expanse of Heaven.

If we strip this being, thus constituted, of all the supernatural gifts he may have received, and all the artificial faculties he can have acquired only by a long process; if we consider him, in a word, just as he must have come from the hands of nature, we behold in him an animal weaker than some, and less agile than others; but, taking him all round, the most advantageously organized of any. I see him satisfying his hunger at the first oak, and slaking his thirst at the first brook; finding his bed at the foot of the tree which afforded him a repast; and, with that, all his wants supplied.

While the earth was left to its natural fertility and covered with immense forests, whose trees were never mutilated by the axe, it would present on every side both sustenance and shelter for every species of animal. Men, dispersed up and down among the rest, would observe and imitate their industry, and thus attain even to the instinct of the beasts, with the advantage that, whereas every species of brutes was confined to one particular instinct, man, who perhaps has not any one peculiar to himself, would appropriate them all, and live upon most of those different foods which other animals shared among themselves; and thus would find his subsistence much more easily than any of the rest.

Accustomed from their infancy to the harshness of the weather and the rigor of the seasons, inured to fatigue, and forced, naked and unarmed, to defend themselves and their prey from other ferocious animals, or to escape them by flight, men would acquire a robust and almost unalterable constitution. The children, bringing with them into the world the excellent constitution of their parents, and fortifying it by the very exercises which first produced it, would thus acquire all the vigor of which the human frame is capable. Nature in this case treats them exactly as Sparta treated the children of her citizens: those who come well formed into the world she renders strong and robust, and all the rest she destroys; differing in this respect from our modern communities, in which the State, by making children a burden to their parents, kills them indiscriminately before they are born.

The body of a savage man being the only instrument he understands, he uses it for various purposes, of which ours, for want of practice, are incapable: for our industry deprives us of that force and agility, which necessity obliges him to acquire. If he had had an axe, would he have been able with his naked arm to break so large a branch from a tree? If he had had a sling, would he have been able to throw a stone with so great velocity? If he had had a ladder, would he have been so nimble in climbing a tree? If he had had a horse, would he have been himself so swift of foot? Give civilized man time to gather all his machines about him, and he will no doubt easily beat the savage; but if you would see a still more unequal contest, set them together naked and unarmed, and you will soon see the advantage of having all our forces constantly at our disposal, of being always prepared for every event, and of carrying one's self, as it were, perpetually whole and entire about one.

Hobbes contends that man is naturally intrepid, and is intent only upon attacking and fighting. Another illustrious philosopher holds the opposite, and Cumberland and Puffendorf also affirm that nothing is more timid and fearful than man in the state of nature; that he is always in a tremble, and ready to fly at the least noise or the slightest movement. This may be true of things he does not know; and I do not doubt his being terrified by every novelty that presents itself, when he neither knows the physical good or evil he may expect from it, nor can make a comparison between his own strength and the dangers he is about to encounter. Such circumstances, however, rarely occur in a state of nature, in which all things proceed in a uniform manner, and the face of the earth is not subject to those sudden and continual changes which arise from the passions and caprices of bodies of men living together. But savage man, living dispersed among other animals, and finding himself betimes in a situation to measure his strength with theirs, soon comes to compare himself with them; and, perceiving that he surpasses them more in adroitness than they surpass him in strength, learns to be no longer afraid of them. Set a bear, or a wolf, against a robust, agile, and resolute savage, as they all are, armed with stones and a good cudgel, and you will see that the danger will be at least on both sides, and that, after a few trials of this kind, wild beasts, which are not fond of attacking each other, will not be at all ready to attack man, whom they will have found to be as wild and ferocious as themselves. With regard to such animals as have really more strength than man has adroitness, he is in the same situation as all weaker animals, which notwithstanding are still able to subsist; except indeed that he has the advantage that, being equally swift of foot, and finding an almost certain place of refuge in every tree, he is at liberty to take or leave it at every encounter, and thus to fight or fly, as he chooses. Add to this that it does not appear that any animal naturally makes war on man, except in case of self-defense or excessive hunger, or betrays any of those violent antipathies, which seem to indicate that one species is intended by nature for the food of another....

The Second Part

The first man who, having enclosed a piece of ground, bethought himself of saying *This is mine*, and found people simple enough to believe him, was the real founder of civil society. From how many crimes, wars and murders, from how many horrors and misfortunes might not any one have saved mankind, by pulling up the stakes, or filling up the ditch, and crying to his fellows, "Beware of listening to this impostor; you are undone if you once forget that the fruits of the earth belong to us all, and the earth itself to nobody." But there is great probability that things had then already come to such a pitch, that they could no longer continue as they were; for the idea of property depends on many prior ideas, which could only be acquired successively, and cannot have been formed all at once in the human mind. Mankind must have made very considerable progress, and acquired considerable knowledge and industry which they must also have transmitted and increased from age to age, before they arrived at this last point of the state of nature. Let us then go farther back, and endeavor to unify under a single point of view that slow succession of events and discoveries in the most natural order.

Man's first feeling was that of his own existence, and his first care that of self-preservation. The produce of the earth furnished him with all he needed, and instinct told him how to use it. Hunger and other appetites made him at various times experience various modes of existence; and among these was one which urged him to propagate his species—a blind propensity that, having nothing to do with the heart, produced a merely animal act. The want once gratified, the two sexes knew each other no more; and even the offspring was nothing to its mother, as soon as it could do without her.

Such was the condition of infant man; the life of an animal limited at first to mere sensations, and hardly profiting by the gifts nature bestowed on him, much less capable of entertaining a thought of forcing anything from her. But difficulties soon presented themselves, and it became necessary to learn how to surmount them: the height of the trees, which prevented him from gathering their fruits, the competition of other animals desirous of the same fruits, and the ferocity of those who needed them for their own preservation, all obliged him to apply himself to bodily exercises. He had to be active, swift of foot, and vigorous in fight. Natural weapons, stones and sticks, were easily found: he learnt to surmount the obstacles of nature, to contend in case of necessity with other animals, and to dispute for the means of subsistence even with other men, or to indemnify himself for what he was forced to give up to a stronger. . . .

. . . As soon as men began to value one another, and the idea of consideration had got a footing in the mind, every one put in his claim to it, and it became impossible to refuse it to any with impunity. Hence arose the first obligations of civility even among savages; and every intended injury became an affront; because, besides the hurt which might result from it, the party injured was certain to find in it a contempt for his person, which was often more insupportable than the hurt itself.

Thus, as every man punished the contempt shown him by others, in proportion to his opinion of himself, revenge became terrible, and men bloody and cruel. This is precisely the state reached by most of the savage nations known to us: and it is for want of having made a proper distinction in our ideas, and see how very far they already are from the state of nature, that so many writers have hastily concluded that man is naturally cruel, and requires civil institutions to make him more mild; whereas nothing is more gentle than man in his primitive state, as he is placed by nature at an equal distance from the stupidity of brutes, and the fatal ingenuity of civilized man. Equally confined by instinct and reason to the sole care of guarding himself against the mischief which threaten him, he is restrained by natural compassion from doing any injury to others, and is not led to do such a thing even in return for injuries received. For, according to the axiom of the wise Locke, *There can be no injury, where there is no property.*

But it must be remarked that the society thus formed, and the relations thus established among men, required of them qualities different from those which they possessed from their primitive constitution. Morality began to appear in human actions, and every one, before the institution of law, was the only judge and avenger of the injuries done him, so that the goodness which was suitable in the pure state of nature was no longer proper in the new-born state of society. Punishments had to be made more severe, as opportunities of offending became more frequent, and the dread of vengeance had to take the place of the rigor of the law. Thus, though men had become less patient, and their natural compassion had already suffered some diminution, this period of expansion of the human faculties, keeping a just mean between the indolence of the primitive state and the petulant activity of our egoism, must have been the happiest and most stable of epochs. The more we reflect on it, the more we shall find that this state was the least subject to revolutions, and altogether the very best man could experience; so that he can have departed from it only through some fatal accident, which, for the public good, should never have happened. The example of savages, most of whom have been found in this state, seems to prove that men were meant to remain in it, that it is the real youth of the world, and that all subsequent advances have been apparently so many steps towards the perfection of the individual, but in reality towards the decrepitude of the species...

... Politicians indulge in the same sophistry about the love of liberty as philosophers about the state of nature. They judge, by what they see, of very different things, which they have not seen; and attribute to man a natural propensity to servitude, because the slaves within their observation are seen to bear the yoke with patience; they fail to reflect that it is with liberty as with innocence and virtue; the value is known only to those who possess them, and the taste for them is forfeited when they are forfeited themselves. "I know the charms of your country," said Brasidas to a satrap, who was comparing the life at Sparta with that at Persepolis, "but you cannot know the pleasures of mine."...

... I have endeavored to trace the origin and progress of inequality, and the institution and abuse of political societies, as far as these are capable of being deduced from the nature of man merely by the light of reason, and independently of those sacred dogmas which give the sanction of divine right to sovereign authority. It follows from this survey that, as there is hardly any inequality in the state of nature, all the inequality which now prevails owes its strength and growth to the development of our faculties and the advance of the human mind, and becomes at last permanent and legitimate by the establishment of property and laws. Secondly, it follows that moral inequality, authorized by positive right alone, clashes with natural right, whenever it is not proportionate to physical inequality; a distinction which sufficiently determines what we ought to think of that species of inequality which prevails in all civilized, countries; since it is plainly contrary to the law of nature, however defined, that children should command old men, fools wise men, and that the privileged few should gorge themselves with superfluities, while the starving multitude are in want of the bare necessities of life.

Locke wrote his major political work, *Two Treatises of Civil Government* in the 1680s, but in a time of political turmoil and upheaval in England, the ideas the work expressed were thought to be revolutionary and contrary to royal authority. Locke had to flee into exile in Holland during this period in his life. The work was finally published in 1690. In the works, he puts forth his theory of natural law and natural rights in which he makes a distinction between legitimate and illegitimate civil governments.

John Locke Two Treatises on Government

Chapter I.

Sec. 3. POLITICAL POWER, then, I take to be a RIGHT of making laws with penalties of death, and consequently all less penalties, for the regulating and preserving of property, and of employing the force of the community, in the execution of such laws, and in the defense of the common-wealth from foreign injury; and all this only for the public good.

Chapter II.

Of the State of Nature.

***

Sec. 4. To understand political power right, and derive it from its original, we must consider, what state all men are naturally in, and that is, a state of perfect freedom to order their actions, and dispose of their possessions and persons, as they think fit, within the bounds of the law of nature, without asking leave, or depending upon the will of any other man.

A state also of equality, wherein all the power and jurisdiction is reciprocal, no one having more than another; there being nothing more evident, than that creatures of the same species and rank, promiscuously born to all the same advantages of nature, and the use of the same faculties, should also be equal one amongst another without subordination or subjection, unless the lord and master of them all should, by any manifest declaration of his will, set one above another, and confer on him, by an evident and clear appointment, an undoubted right to dominion and sovereignty.

Sec. 5. This equality of men by nature, the judicious Hooker looks upon as so evident in itself, and beyond all question, that he makes it the foundation of that obligation to mutual love amongst men, on which he builds the duties they owe one another, and from whence he derives the great maxims of justice and charity. His words are,

"The like natural inducement hath brought men to know that it is no less their duty, to love others than themselves; for seeing those things which are equal, must needs all have one measure; if I cannot but wish to receive good, even as much at every man's hands, as any man can wish unto his own soul, how should I look to have any part of my desire herein satisfied, unless myself be careful to satisfy the like desire, which is undoubtedly in other men, being of one and the same nature? To have anything offered them repugnant to this desire, must needs in all respects grieve them as much as me; so that if I do harm, I must look to suffer, there being no reason that others should show greater measure of love to me, than they have by me showed unto them: my desire therefore to be loved of my equals in nature as much as possible may be, imposed upon me a natural duty of bearing to them-ward fully the like affection; from which relation of equality between ourselves and them that are as ourselves, what several rules and canons natural reason hath drawn, for direction of life, no man is ignorant, Eccl. Pol. Lib. 1."

Sec. 6. But though this be a state of liberty, yet it is not a state of license: though man in that state have an uncontrollable liberty to dispose of his person or possessions, yet he has not liberty to destroy himself, or so much as any creature in his possession, but where some nobler use than its bare preservation calls for it. The state of nature has a law of nature to govern it, which obliges every one: and reason, which is that law, teaches all mankind, who will but consult it, that being all equal and independent, no one ought to harm another in his life, health, liberty, or possessions: for men being all the workmanship of one omnipotent, and infinitely wise maker; all the servants of one sovereign master, sent into the world by his order, and about his business; they are his property, whose workmanship they are, made to last during his, not one another's pleasure: and being furnished with like faculties, sharing all in one community of nature, there cannot be supposed any such subordination among us, that may authorize us to destroy one another, as if we were made for one another's uses, as the inferior ranks of creatures are for our use. Everyone, as he is bound to preserve himself, and not to quit his station willfully, so by the like reason, when his own preservation comes not in competition, ought he, as much as he can, to preserve the rest of mankind, and may not, unless it be to do justice on an offender, take away, or impair the life, or what tends to the preservation of the life, the liberty, health, limb, or goods of another.

Sec. 7. And that all men may be restrained from invading others rights, and from doing hurt to one another, and the law of nature be observed, which will the peace and preservation of all mankind, the execution of the law of nature is, in that state, put into every man's hands, whereby everyone has a right to punish the transgressors of that law to such a degree, as may hinder its violation: for the law of nature would, as all other laws that concern men in this world 'be in vain, if there were no body that in the state of nature had a power to execute that law, and thereby preserve the innocent and restrain offenders. And if anyone in the state of nature may punish another for any evil he has done, every one may do so: for in that state of perfect equality, where naturally there is no superiority or jurisdiction of one over another, what any may do in prosecution of that law, everyone must have a right to do.

Sec. 8. And thus, in the state of nature, one man comes by a power over another; but yet no absolute or arbitrary power, to use a criminal, when he has got him in his hands, according to the passionate heats, or boundless extravagancy of his own will; but only to take retribution, so far as calm reason and conscience dictate, what is proportionate to his transgression, which is so much as may serve for reparation and restraint: for these two are the only reasons, why one man may lawfully do harm to another, which is that we call punishment. In transgressing the law of nature, the offender declares himself to live by another rule than that of reason and common equity, which is that measure God has set to the actions of men, for their mutual security; and so he becomes dangerous to mankind, the tie, which is to secure them from injury and violence, being slighted and broken by him. Which being a trespass against the whole species, and the peace and safety of it, provided for by the law of nature, every man upon this score, by the right he hath to preserve mankind in general, may restrain, or where it is necessary, destroy things noxious to them, and so may bring such evil on any one, who hath transgressed that law, as may make him repent the doing of it, and thereby deter him, and by his example others, from doing the like mischief. And in the case, and upon this ground, EVERY MAN HATH A RIGHT TO PUNISH THE OFFENDER, AND BE EXECUTIONER OF THE LAW OF NATURE.

***

Sec. 11. From these two distinct rights, the one of punishing the crime for restraint, and preventing the like offence, which right of punishing is in everybody; the other of taking reparation, which belongs only to the injured party, comes it to pass that the magistrate, who by being magistrate hath the common right of punishing put into his hands, can often, where the public good demands not the execution of the law, remit the punishment of criminal offences by his own authority, but yet cannot remit the satisfaction due to any private man for the damage he has received. That, he who has suffered the damage has a right to demand in his own name, and he alone can remit: the damned person has this power of appropriating to himself the goods or service of the offender, by right of self-preservation, as every man has a power to punish the crime, to prevent its being committed again, by the right he has of preserving all mankind, and doing all reasonable things he can in order to that end: and thus it is, that every man, in the state of nature, has a power to kill a murderer, both to deter others from doing the like injury, which no reparation can compensate, by the example of the punishment that attends it from everybody, and also to secure men from the attempts of a criminal, who having renounced reason, the common rule and measure God hath given to mankind, hath, by the unjust violence and slaughter he hath committed upon one, declared war against all mankind, and therefore may be destroyed as a lion or a tiger, one of those wild savage beasts, with whom men can have no society nor security: and upon this is grounded that great law of nature, Whoso sheds man's blood, by man shall his blood be shed. And Cain was so fully convinced, that everyone had a right to destroy such a criminal, that after the murder of his brother, he cries out, Everyone that find me, shall slay me; so plain was it writ in the hearts of all mankind.

***

Sec. 13. . . . I easily grant, that civil government is the proper remedy for the inconveniencies of the state of nature, which must certainly be great, where men may be judges in their own case, since it is easy to be imagined, that he who was so unjust as to do his brother an injury, will scarce be so just as to condemn himself for it: but I shall desire those who make this objection, to remember, that absolute monarchs are but men; and if government is to be the remedy of those evils, which necessarily follow from men's being judges in their own cases, and the state of nature is therefore not to be endured, I desire to know what kind of government that is, and how much better it is than the state of nature, where one man, commanding a multitude, has the liberty to be judge in his own case, and may do to all his subjects whatever he pleases, without the least liberty to anyone to question or control those who execute his pleasure and in whatsoever he doth, whether led by reason, mistake or passion, must be submitted to. Much better it is in the state of nature, wherein men are not bound to submit to the unjust will of another. And if he that judges, judges amiss in his own, or any other case, he is answerable for it to the rest of mankind.

***

CHAP. III.

Of the State of War.

Sec. 16. THE state of war is a state of enmity and destruction: and therefore declaring by word or action, not a passionate and hasty, but a sedate settled design upon another man's life, puts him in a state of war with him against whom he has declared such an intention, and so has exposed his life to the other's power to be taken away by him, or any one that joins with him in his defense, and espouses his quarrel; it being reasonable and just, I should have a right to destroy that which threatens me with destruction: for, by the fundamental law of nature, man being to be preserved as much as possible, when all cannot be preserved, the safety of the innocent is to be preferred: and one may destroy a man who makes war upon him, or has discovered an enmity to his being, for the same reason that he may kill a wolf or a lion; because such men are not under the ties of the common law of reason, have no other rule, but that of force and violence, and so may be treated as beasts of prey, those dangerous and noxious creatures, that will be sure to destroy him whenever he falls into their power.

CHAP. IV.

Of Slavery.

Sec. 22. THE natural liberty of man is to be free from any superior power on earth, and not to be under the will or legislative authority of man, but to have only the law of nature for his rule. The liberty of man, in society, is to be under no other legislative power, but that established, by consent, in the commonwealth; nor under the dominion of any will, or restraint of any law, but what that legislative shall enact, according to the trust put in it. Freedom then is not what Sir Robert Filmer tells us, Observations, A. 55. a liberty for everyone to do what he lists, to live as he pleases, and not to be tied by any laws: but freedom of men under government is, to have a standing rule to live by, common to every one of that society, and made by the legislative power erected in it; a liberty to follow my own will in all things, where the rule prescribes not; and not to be subject to the inconstant, uncertain, unknown, arbitrary will of another man: as freedom of nature is, to be under no other restraint but the law of nature.

Sec. 23. This freedom from absolute, arbitrary power, is so necessary to, and closely joined with a man's preservation, that he cannot part with it, but by what forfeits his preservation and life together: for a man, not having the power of his own life, cannot, by compact, or his own consent, enslave himself to any one, nor put himself under the absolute, arbitrary power of another, to take away his life, when he pleases. Nobody can give more power than he has himself; and he that cannot take away his own life, cannot give another power over it. Indeed, having by his fault forfeited his own life, by some act that deserves death; he, to whom he has forfeited it, may (when he has him in his power) delay to take it, and make use of him to his own service, and he does him no injury by it: for, whenever he finds the hardship of his slavery outweigh the value of his life, it is in his power, by resisting the will of his master, to draw on himself the death he desires.

Sec. 24. This is the perfect condition of slavery, which is nothing else, but the state of war continued, between a lawful conqueror and a captive: for, if once compact enter between them, and make an agreement for a limited power on the one side, and obedience on the other, the state of war and slavery ceases, as long as the compact endures: for, as has been said, no man can, by agreement, pass over to another that which he hath not in himself, a power over his own life. I confess, we find among the Jews, as well as other nations, that men did sell themselves; but, it is plain, this was only to drudgery, not to slavery: for, it is evident, the person sold was not under an absolute, arbitrary, despotical power: for the master could not have power to kill him, at any time, whom, at a certain time, he was obliged to let go free out of his service; and the master of such a servant was so far from having an arbitrary power over his life, that he could not, at pleasure, so much as maim him, but the loss of an eye, or tooth, set him free, Exod. xxi.

CHAP. V.

Of Property.

***

Sec. 27. Though the earth, and all inferior creatures, be common to all men, yet every man has a property in his own person: this nobody has any right to but himself. The labor of his body, and the work of his hands, we may say, are properly his. Whatsoever then he removes out of the state that nature hath provided, and left it in, he hath mixed his labor with, and joined to it something that is his own, and thereby makes it his property. It being by him removed from the common state nature hath placed it in, it hath by this labor something annexed to it, that excludes the common right of other men: for this labor being the unquestionable property of the laborer, no man but he can have a right to what that is once joined to, at least where there is enough, and as good, left in common for others.

Sec. 28. He that is nourished by the acorns he picked up under an oak, or the apples he gathered from the trees in the wood, has certainly appropriated them to himself. Nobody can deny but the nourishment is his. I ask then, when did they begin to be his? When he digested? Or when he eats? Or when he boiled? Or when he brought them home? Or when he picked them up? And it is plain, if the first gathering made them not his, nothing else could. That labor put a distinction between them and common: that added something to them more than nature, the common mother of all, had done; and so they became his private right. And will anyone say, he had no right to those acorns or apples, he thus appropriated, because he had not the consent of all mankind to make them his? Was it a robbery thus to assume to himself what belonged to all in common? If such consent as that was necessary, man had starved, notwithstanding the plenty God had given him. We see in commons, which remain so by compact, that it is the taking any part of what is common, and removing it out of the state nature leaves it in, which begins the property; without which the common is of no use. And the taking of this or that part does not depend on the express consent of all the commoners. Thus the grass my horse has bit; the turfs my servant has cut; and the ore I have dug in any place, where I have a right to them in common with others, become my property, without the assignation or consent of any body. The labor that was mine, removing them out of that common state they were in, hath fixed my property in them.

***

CHAP. VII.

Of Political or Civil Society.

***

Sec. 94. But whatever flatterers may talk to amuse people's understandings, it hinders not men from feeling; and when they perceive, that any man, in what station whatsoever, is out of the bounds of the civil society which they are of, and that they have no appeal on earth against any harm, they may receive from him, they are apt to think themselves in the state of nature, in respect of him whom they find to be so; and to take care, as soon as they can, to have that safety and security in civil society, for which it was first instituted, and for which only they entered into it. And therefore, though perhaps at first , (as shall be showed more at large hereafter in the following part of this discourse) someone good and excellent man having got a pre -eminency amongst the rest, had this deference paid to his goodness and virtue, as to a kind of natural authority, that the chief rule, with arbitration of their differences, by a tacit consent devolved into his hands, without any other caution, but the assurance they had of his uprightness and wisdom; yet when time, giving authority, and (as some men would persuade us) sacredness of customs, which the negligent, and unforeseen innocence of the first ages began, had brought in successors of another stamp, the people finding their properties not secure under the government, as then it was, (whereas government has no other end but the preservation of property) could never be safe nor at rest, nor think themselves in civil society, till the legislature was placed in collective bodies of men, call them senate, parliament, or what you please.

By which means every single person became subject, equally with other the meanest men, to those laws, which he himself, as part of the legislative, had established; nor could anyone, by his own authority; avoid the force of the law, when once made; nor by any pretence of superiority plead exemption, thereby to license his own, or the miscarriages of any of his dependents.

No man in civil society can be exempted from the laws of it: for if any man may do what he thinks fit, and there be no appeal on earth, for redress or security against any harm he shall do; I ask, whether he be not perfectly still in the state of nature, and so can be no part or member of that civil society; unless any one will say, the state of nature and civil society are one and the same thing, which I have never yet found any one so great a patron of anarchy as to affirm.

Karl Marx's *Communist Manifesto* (1848), edited by his close friend and collaborator Friedrich Engels, gives Marx's earliest and most accessible analysis of class relations and of the accumulation of capital at the expense of workers. Marx exhorts the working class to take political action as "everything solid melts into air," with the famous closing lines "Workers of the world, unite! You have nothing to lose but your chains." Though Marx's philosophy has been radically interpreted and misinterpreted in the twentieth and twenty-first centuries, the questions Marx asked and the way he examined them continue to pose philosophical and political challenges with the development of what the French economist Thomas Piketty calls a "patrimonial capitalism," which is at once global and more concentrated on ever fewer, richer capitalists owning more and more of the means of production.

Karl Marx and Friedrich Engels, Communist Manifesto

The history of all hitherto existing societies is the history of class struggles.

Freeman and slave, patrician and plebeian, lord and serf, guild-master and journeyman, in a word, oppressor and oppressed, stood in constant opposition to one another, carried on an uninterrupted, now hidden, now open fight, a fight that each time ended, either in a revolutionary re-constitution of society at large, or in the common ruin of the contending classes.

In the earlier epochs of history, we find almost everywhere a complicated arrangement of society into various orders, a manifold gradation of social rank. In ancient Rome we have patricians, knights, plebeians, slaves; in the Middle Ages, feudal lords, vassals, guild-masters, journeymen, apprentices, serfs; in almost all of these classes, again, subordinate gradations.

The modern bourgeois society that has sprouted from the ruins of feudal society has not done away with class antagonisms. It has but established new classes, new conditions of oppression, new forms of struggle in place of the old ones. Our epoch, the epoch of the bourgeoisie, possesses, however, this distinctive feature: it has simplified the class antagonisms. Society as a whole is more and more splitting up into two great hostile camps, into two great classes, directly facing each other: Bourgeoisie and Proletariat.

From the serfs of the Middle Ages sprang the chartered burghers of the earliest towns. From these burgesses the first elements of the bourgeoisie were developed.

The discovery of America, the rounding of the Cape, opened up fresh ground for the rising bourgeoisie. The East-Indian and Chinese markets, the colonization of America, trade with the colonies, the increase in the means of exchange and in commodities generally, gave to commerce, to navigation, to industry, an impulse never before known, and thereby, to the revolutionary element in the tottering feudal society, a rapid development.

The feudal system of industry, under which industrial production was monopolized by closed guilds, now no longer sufficed for the growing wants of the new markets. The manufacturing system took its place. The guild-masters were pushed on one side by the manufacturing middle class; division of labor between the different corporate guilds vanished in the face of division of labor in each single workshop. Meantime, the markets kept ever growing, the demand ever rising. Even manufacture no longer sufficed. Thereupon, steam and machinery revolutionized industrial production. The place of manufacture was taken by the giant, Modern Industry, the place of the industrial middle class, by industrial millionaires, the leaders of whole industrial armies, the modern bourgeois.

Modern industry has established the world-market, This market has given an immense development to commerce, to navigation, to communication by land. This development has, in its time, reacted on the extension of industry; and in proportion as industry, commerce, navigation, railways extended, in the same proportion the bourgeoisie developed, increased its capital, and pushed into the background every class handed down from the Middle Ages. We see, therefore, how the modern bourgeoisie is itself the product of a long course of development, of a series of revolutions in the modes of production and of exchange.

Each step in the development of the bourgeoisie was accompanied by a corresponding political advance of that class. The executive of the modern State is but a committee for managing the common affairs of the whole bourgeoisie. The bourgeoisie, historically, has played a most revolutionary part. The bourgeoisie, wherever it has got the upper hand, has put an end to all feudal, patriarchal, idyllic relations. It has pitilessly torn asunder the motley feudal ties that bound man to his "natural superiors," and has left remaining no other nexus between man and man than naked self-interest, than callous "cash payment." It has drowned the most heavenly ecstasies of religious fervor, of chivalrous enthusiasm, of philistine sentimentalism, in the icy water of egotistical calculation. It has resolved personal worth into exchange value. In one word, exploitation, veiled by religious and political illusions, naked, shameless, direct, brutal exploitation. The bourgeoisie has stripped of its halo every occupation hitherto honored and looked up to with reverent awe. It has converted the physician, the lawyer, the priest, the poet, the man of science, into its paid wage laborers.

The bourgeoisie has torn away from the family its sentimental veil, and has reduced the family relation to a mere money relation.

The bourgeoisie cannot exist without constantly revolutionizing the instruments of production, and thereby the relations of production, and with them the whole relations of society. Conservation of the old modes of production in unaltered form, was, on the contrary, the first condition of existence for all earlier industrial classes. Constant revolutionizing of production, uninterrupted disturbance of all social conditions, everlasting uncertainty and agitation distinguish the bourgeois epoch from all earlier ones. All fixed, fast-frozen relations, with their train of ancient and venerable prejudices and opinions, are swept away, all new-formed ones become antiquated before they can ossify. All that is solid melts into air, all that is holy is profaned, and man is at last compelled to face with sober senses, his real conditions of life, and his relations with his kind.

The need of a constantly expanding market for its products chases the bourgeoisie over the whole surface of the globe. It must nestle everywhere, settle everywhere, establish connections everywhere.

The bourgeoisie has through its exploitation of the world-market given a cosmopolitan character to production and consumption in every country. All old-established national industries have been destroyed or are daily being destroyed. In place of the old wants, satisfied by the productions of the country, we find new wants, requiring for their satisfaction the products of distant lands and climes.

The bourgeoisie, by the rapid improvement of all instruments of production, by the immensely facilitated means of communication, draws all, even the most barbarian, nations into civilization. It compels all nations, on pain of extinction, to adopt the bourgeois mode of production; it compels them to introduce what it calls civilization into their midst, that is, to become bourgeois themselves. In one word, it creates a world after its own image.

We see then: the means of production and of exchange, on whose foundation the bourgeoisie built itself up, were generated in feudal society. At a certain stage in the development of these means of production and of exchange, the conditions under which feudal society produced and exchanged, the feudal organization of agriculture and manufacturing industry, in one word, the feudal relations of property became no longer compatible with the already developed productive forces; they became so many fetters. They had to be burst asunder; they were burst asunder. Society suddenly finds itself put back into a state of momentary barbarism. The productive forces at the disposal of society no longer tend to further the development of the conditions of bourgeois property; on the contrary, they have become too powerful for these conditions, by which they are fettered, and so soon as they overcome these fetters, they bring disorder into the whole of bourgeois society, endanger the existence of bourgeois property.

The weapons with which the bourgeoisie felled feudalism to the ground are now turned against the bourgeoisie itself.

But not only has the bourgeoisie forged the weapons that bring death to itself; it has also called into existence the men who are to wield those weapons—the modern working class—the proletarians.

In proportion as the bourgeoisie, capital is developed, in the same proportion is the proletariat, the modern working class, developed—a class of laborers, who live only so long as they find work, and who find work only so long as their labor increases capital. These laborers, who must sell themselves piece-meal, are a commodity, like every other article of commerce, and are consequently exposed to all the vicissitudes of competition, to all the fluctuations of the market.

Owing to the extensive use of machinery and to division of labor, the work of the proletarians has lost all individual character, and consequently, all charm for the workman. He becomes an appendage of the machine, and it is only the most simple, most monotonous, and most easily acquired knack, that is required of him. Hence, the cost of production of a workman is restricted, almost entirely, to the means of subsistence that he requires for his maintenance. But the price of a commodity, and therefore also of labor, is equal to its cost of production. In proportion therefore, as the repulsiveness of the work increases, the wage decreases.

Modern industry has converted the little workshop of the patriarchal master into the great factory of the industrial capitalist. Masses of laborers, crowded into the factory, are organized like soldiers. Not only are they slaves of the bourgeois class, and of the bourgeois State; they are daily and hourly enslaved by the machine, by the over-looker, and, above all, by the individual bourgeois manufacturer himself. The more openly this despotism proclaims gain to be its end and aim, the more petty, the more hateful and the more embittering it is.

The proletariat goes through various stages of development. With its birth begins its struggle with the bourgeoisie. But with the development of industry the proletariat not only increases in number; it becomes concentrated in greater masses, its strength grows, and it feels that strength more. The growing competition among the bourgeois, and the resulting commercial crises, make the wages of the workers ever more fluctuating. The unceasing improvement of machinery, ever more rapidly developing, makes their livelihood more and more precarious; the collisions between individual workmen and individual bourgeois take more and more the character of collisions between two classes. Thereupon the workers begin to form combinations, trade unions, against the bourgeois.

The bourgeoisie finds itself involved in a constant battle. At first with the aristocracy; later on, with those portions of the bourgeoisie itself, whose interests have become antagonistic to the progress of industry; at all times, with the bourgeoisie of foreign countries. In all these battles it sees itself compelled to appeal to the proletariat, to ask for its help, and thus, to drag it into the political arena. The bourgeoisie itself, therefore, supplies the proletariat with its own instruments of political and general education, in other words, it furnishes the proletariat with weapons for fighting the bourgeoisie.

Of all the classes that stand face to face with the bourgeoisie today, the proletariat alone is a really revolutionary class. The other classes decay and finally disappear in the face of Modern Industry; the proletariat is its special and essential product. The lower middle class, the small manufacturer, the shopkeeper, the artisan, the peasant, all these fight against the bourgeoisie, to save from extinction their existence as fractions of the middle class. They are therefore not revolutionary, but conservative. More than that, they are reactionary, for they try to roll back the wheel of history. If by chance they are revolutionary, they are so only in view of their impending transfer into the proletariat, they thus defend not their present, but their future interests, they desert their own standpoint to place themselves at that of the proletariat.

The proletarian is without property; his relation to his wife and children has no longer anything in common with the bourgeois family-relations; modern industrial labor, modern subjection to capital has stripped him of every trace of national character. Law, morality, religion, are to him so many bourgeois prejudices, behind which lurk in ambush just as many bourgeois interests.

All previous historical movements were movements of minorities, or in the interests of minorities. The proletarian movement is the self-conscious, independent movement of the immense majority, in the interests of the immense majority. The proletariat, the lowest stratum of our present society, cannot stir, cannot raise itself up, without the whole superincumbent strata of official society being sprung into the air.

Hitherto, every form of society has been based, as we have already seen, on the antagonism of oppressing and oppressed classes. But in order to oppress a class, certain conditions must be assured to it under which it can, at least, continue its slavish existence. The serf, in the period of serfdom, raised himself to membership in the commune, just as the petty bourgeois, under the yoke of feudal absolutism, managed to develop into a bourgeois. The modern laborer, on the contrary, instead of rising with the progress of industry, sinks deeper and deeper below the conditions of existence of his own class. And here it becomes evident, that the bourgeoisie is unfit any longer to be the ruling class in society, and to impose its conditions of existence upon society as an over-riding law. It is unfit to rule because it is incompetent to assure an existence to its slave within his slavery, because it cannot help letting him sink into such a state, that it has to feed him, instead of being fed by him. Society can no longer live under this bourgeoisie, in other words, its existence is no longer compatible with society.

The essential condition for the existence, and for the sway of the bourgeois class, is the formation and augmentation of capital; the condition for capital is wage-labor. Wage-labor rests exclusively on competition between the laborers.

The development of Modern Industry, therefore, cuts from under its feet the very foundation on which the bourgeoisie produces and appropriates products. What the bourgeoisie, therefore, produces, above all, is its own grave-diggers.

The bourgeois sees in his wife a mere instrument of production. He hears that the instruments of production are to be exploited in common, and, naturally, can come to no other conclusion than that the lot of being common to all will likewise fall to the women. He has not even a suspicion that the real point is to do away with the status of women as mere instruments of production. The workers have no country. We cannot take from them what they have not got. When the ancient world was in its last throes, the ancient religions were overcome by Christianity. When Christian ideas succumbed in the 18th century to rationalist ideas, feudalsociety fought its death battle with the then revolutionary bourgeoisie. The ideas of religious liberty and freedom of conscience merely gave expression to the sway of free competition within the domain of knowledge. The history of all past society has consisted in the development of class antagonisms, antagonisms that assumed different forms at different epochs.

But whatever form they may have taken, one fact is common to all past ages, the exploitation of one part of society by the other.

The Communists everywhere support every revolutionary movement against the existing social and political order of things. In all these movements they bring to the front, as the leading question in each, the property question, no matter what its degree of development at the time. Finally, they labor everywhere for the union and agreement of the democratic parties of all countries.

Let the ruling classes tremble at a communist revolution. Workers have nothing to lose but their chains. They have a world to win.

WORKERS OF ALL COUNTRIES, UNITE!

In this short selection from his magisterial *On Politics*, Alan Ryan analyzes the tragic devolutions of Marxism after Marx, pointing out what he calls the impossibility of socialism, tracing the transformation of Marxism to Leninism and Stalinism, and noting that "Marxism is a doctrine in tension with itself."

THE TRIUMPH OF NATIONALISM over proletarian internationalism is not surprising. It is more surprising that the religious attachments that socialism was to eliminate have so effectively resisted the secularizing pressures of industrialization and urbanization. Not only national and ethnic but also confessional solidarity is more visible than proletarian solidarity. There remains a paradox. It is universally agreed that proletarian democracy and the withering away of the state are no longer live options; capitalist liberal democracy is the only game in town.[1] Yet successful modern states are expected to ensure the welfare of their citizens from cradle to grave in ways that nineteenth-century observers would unhesitatingly have described as socialist. Today the publicly funded social insurance system that constitutes the welfare state is seen as a step toward full-blown socialism only by particularly unbalanced conservative critics. The right to vote has been vastly expanded, equality of opportunity is an unchallengeable ideal, barriers of race, class, and gender to participation in politics at the highest level have been abolished; but whatever else modern liberal democracies are, they are not the dictatorship of the proletariat or heading toward the abolition of the coercive state as both Marx and the "utopian socialists" hoped.

. . . As a matter of history, socialism sprang out of the dislocations and unhappinesses created by early industrialization. It is not surprising that socialism appealed to the first generations of industrial workers, who had been swept off the land and into the disgusting conditions of the first industrial towns. Objectively, as regards nutrition and health, they were on average no worse off than they had been; the hideous impression the early industrial towns made on observers owed much to the fact that they crammed so many poor people together. Subjectively, the new working class was angry, disoriented, and readier to be recruited for revolution than it later became. Marx and many others believed the reverse of the truth: they thought that the developed and self-conscious proletariat would make a socialist revolution, but only the uprooted first generation has ever been ready to attempt it. Moreover, the social stratum that supplied revolutionary recruits was skilled artisans such as clockmakers who were threatened economically and psychologically by changes that made their skills obsolete and their old social ties harder to sustain. They were in a nonabusive sense reactionary, reacting against loss. The leading thinkers, as distinct

Ryan, Alan. From *On Politics: A History of Political Thought: From Herodotus to the Present* by Alan Ryan. Copyright © 2012 by Alan Ryan. Used by permission of Liveright Publishing Corporation.

from the insurrectionists themselves, were mostly writers who, by the time that they put pen to paper, were intellectuals or engaged in work of a highly intellectual kind—in Mill's case, the administration of India. Exception must be made for Marx, who was supported by Engels's reluctant employment in his family's thread mill.

The outrage caused by the squalor and brutality of early industrialization was not felt only by socialists. In *The Communist Manifesto*, Marx described what he called "feudal socialism"; and thinkers such as Thomas Carlyle and John Ruskin are often thought to be socialists. They were opponents of Victorian laissez-faire, admirers of cohesive and coherent societies, disdainful of moneymaking, and preachers of the gospel of work. Nonetheless, it is stretching the envelope to call them socialists: Carlyle admired Frederick the Great of Prussia, and Ruskin described himself as "a violent Tory of the old type," in the same breath as he described himself as a communist of the reddest stripe. One reason to exclude them is that they believed in hierarchy, and their social models were avowedly backward looking. The first reason is not quite conclusive: Saint-Simon and Edward Bellamy believed in a hierarchical system of administration. The second is more nearly so. Ruskin loathed industrialization; Carlyle's image of a morally acceptable economic order was drawn from Abbot Samson's thirteenth-century abbey of Bury St. Edmund. Most socialist theorists wanted economic progress; they saw industrialization as the key to emancipating working people from backbreaking toil and wanted technological advance harnessed to something other than the exploitation of the poor and the indulgences of the rich. Many skilled workers, on the other hand, viewed technological change with well-justified fear. Because almost the only unequivocal element in socialism is its emphasis on the idea of production for *social* purposes, little is essential to socialism beyond hostility to the unbridled reign of profit-seeking private property; but for most socialists the remedy lies in heightened industrialization, not in its repudiation.

Marx backed up his attack on capitalism with the extraordinary image of capital as a vampire sucking the lifeblood out of the worker; but all socialists thought that a world where people were allowed to accumulate all they could legally contrive, dispose of it however they wished, and were entitled to manage the labor of others, not in virtue of skill or public spirit but merely in virtue of their ownership of capital, needed reform. Not everyone was as concerned as Marx with what he called the anarchy of production: the unpredictable cycle of boom and slump. Mill deplored the division of producers into workers and managers, as did later writers in the guild socialist tradition and cooperativists generally; Morris wanted men to have fulfilling work. It was not until the last quarter of the twentieth century that the deep intractability of central planning for a complex modern economy was universally understood.

... To the two vexed questions of how a socialist society will be governed, and by what route socialism will be achieved, there are no agreed answers. Almost all socialists have disliked the state, especially as manifested in bureaucracies, police forces, armies, and the coercive apparatus of the

... "Welfarism" poses two interesting questions. These were raised by the humanist Marxist movement of the 1950s and 1960s, as well as by radical liberals and neoconservative or neoliberal critics of the postwar welfare state. They were also raised by political thinkers influenced by Hannah Arendt, and as hard to place on the political spectrum as she. The first question is whether the welfare state has taken the politics out of politics; the second, whether new forms of political association might revive political life or reinvigorate communal life in ways that amount to new forms of political life.

These questions coincide in a focus on the idea of civil society. Marx, as we saw, borrowed from Hegel the thought that the state—the coercive, lawmaking, rule-setting mechanism—could be contrasted with civil society—the economic and social relationships that gave society its vitality. The young Marx imagined the state being absorbed by civil society in such a way that social and economic relationships would be spontaneously and noncoercively self-governing. Nothing is more obvious or more painful to an admirer of the young Marx than the extent to which the Communist parties of the Soviet bloc were bureaucratic, corrupt, conservative, and a joke in execrable taste against Marx's youthful dreams. The "humanist" strain in Marx's early writings was known to scholars in the 1920s and 1930s when his unpublished and partly published writings were edited by David Riazanov in Moscow. This Hegelian, philosophical, and speculative work was hard enough to square with Marx's own later writings, but it was quite impossible to square with the Stalinist view that Marx had produced a historical science—historical materialism—and a methodological system valid in all realms of thought—dialectical materialism. Marx would have thought this pretentious nonsense; Stalin would have murdered Marx.

In the 1960s, and in the West, it was the sense that "things drive men" that was uppermost in the minds of critics who despised the state socialism of the communist bloc but despised capitalism too. It also attracted writers who had moved away from Marx's concern with the irrationality of the economic system as a whole to the particular miseries of everyday working life: the tedium of white-collar work and the mind-sapping boredom of work on an assembly line. Philosophically adept critics such as Herbert Marcuse held on to Marx's central insight, and taught a generation of student radicals to denounce the System. We were governed by It.

The difficulty was the absence of a plausible politics to go with the social analysis. Marcuse briefly imagined an alliance of students, intel-lectuals, ethnic minorities, and Third World revolutionaries leading us into transcendence, but this was only an intoxicating image; it bore no relation to Marx's view that capitalism itself would create its own gravediggers by building up an industrial proletariat able and willing to build socialism. What ended wishful thinking and abortive attempts to bring imagination to power was not a serious argument against such hankerings but two decades of high inflation, industrial unrest, and a widespread resentment of the levels of taxation required to sustain the modern welfare state. The return of low inflation and a period of economic growth did much to take discontent off the boil, but nothing to build a better understanding of the social contract on which the welfare state was based, and nothing to revive the old hankerings after new forms of social cooperation and industrial management.

Two things ensured that the socialist dream remains just that. The first is the implosion of the Soviet bloc during the late 1980s. The critics who had said for many years that a failure to build the institutions of civil society within the communist carapace would bring about the collapse of the communist regimes of Eastern Europe turned out to be right. Attempts to build socialism with a human face were suppressed by Soviet tanks in 1956 and 1968; and regimes that had depended for their legitimacy on the memory of liberation by the Red Army at the end of World War II found their legitimacy eroded as official corruption disillusioned everyone who encountered it, while West Germany emerged as a byword for prosperity and good government. The Marxian ideal of bottom-up self-government was more obviously at home in the American Midwest than in the exploitative top-down bureaucracy of a failed state such as Ceaușescu's Romania. The extraordinary thing was that the final implosion of "actually existing socialism" was virtually bloodless. It was less surprising that there was no sudden surge of prosperity, no sudden leap into pluralist democracy. The theorists of civil society who had said that democracy required a social infrastructure that would inculcate the habits—Tocqueville's *moeurs*—that sustained cooperative relations, the rule of law, and the like were right. Conversely, skeptics who thought the theorists of civil society underestimated the need for an effective state to make those habits worth acquiring could point to the way in which the collapse of socialist states too often led to kleptocracy and cronyism rather than capitalist liberal democracy. True though it is that efficient and accountable government respectful of its citizens' rights and a heavily regulated market economy are the only basis of a secure twenty-first-century future, not everyone understands this, and not everyone's short-term self-interest is neatly aligned with the long-term welfare of her or his society. A banker who knows full well that his bank will go under in eighteen months' time may know equally well that he can extract many millions of dollars from it before it does. In states such as Russia, seventy-five years of a combination of state terrorism and individual selfishness led naturally enough to the rise of a kleptocracy. One may believe devoutly in the truth of *après moi le deluge*, but the crucial words are "after me."

What Marx thought of as "unproductive labor," which did not directly result in the production of usable objects, which has always played a prominent role in the economy, now plays a more prominent role than directly productive labor. Marx could not imagine that capitalists and their political helpers would decide that it was in their own interests to reduce the amount of grinding toil that workers endured. He focused on the grinding toil. The most moving pages of *Capital* describe the horrors of overwork across the board, from seamstresses in sweatshops to signalmen working dangerously long shifts on the railroads. Such work is not repulsive if it is not excessive in amount and allows those who do it a degree of autonomy in determining how and at what pace to do it; Marx assumed that neither condition could be met under capitalism. There is plenty of drudgery still, but it is not universal and is a lot less repulsive in a white-collar setting. Working in a call center is no fun, but much office work is interesting in itself and provides social interaction; conversely, long-distance truck driving removes those who dislike too much social interaction from its burdens, but the work is interesting and affords more autonomy than many grander occupations. In short, the idea that *travail attractif* is a utopian aspiration in the abusive sense of the term is false, but so is the idea that a change in the ownership of the means of production is essential to its achievement. Technological change, the leeway allowed by improvements in productivity, the success of trade unions in making management behave more or less humanely, and the varied tastes prevalent in different societies and sections of society make more difference than the ownership of capital.

We should end on a cautious note. Human beings are historical creatures, moved by reminiscence as much as by hopes for a far future. To announce as aggressively as this chapter has done that one of those hopes must be abandoned invites refutation in much the way that commentators invited refutation when they wrote about the inevitability of secularization immediately before large parts of the world embarked on the desecularization of politics. Still, one set of socialist aspirations has run its course: the belief that public ownership of the means of production and distribution was indispensable to prosperity, and the first step toward making the workplace humane and interesting, is no longer tenable. This does not mean that capitalism In Its present-day European, Chinese, or American form constitutes the end of history; we should hope devoutly that it does not.

... That Marxism became the creed of a totalitarian state was not inevitable. To say that the Stalinist state was created by Lenin with contributions in both theory and practice from Trotsky is not to say that they wished to create it but that they laid its foundations in ways that were neither wholly within nor wholly outside the Marxist tradition. Vladimir Ilyich Ulanov, always known as V.I. Lenin, was the second son of a minor official; he was born in 1870 and died prematurely in 1924—he had been wounded two years earlier by a would-be assassin and never regained his health. His great achievement was the invention of the revolutionary party, something Marx had never fully conceptualized. He became a revolutionary when his older brother, implicated in a plot to assassinate Alexander III, was executed in 1887. Russian revolutionaries were at the time not much influenced by Marxism; they were more often populists than socialists, and aimed to achieve their goals by acts of terror against the government, in the belief that an unsettled government would be replaced by a populist government on the back of an uprising by peasants and urban workers.

Lenin was not an insurrectionist, though he became a professional revolutionary. By 1895 he was a fluent Marxist, and became visible enough to the czarist government to be exiled; he left Russia in 1902, returned during the 1905 revolution, and went into exile again when the Second Duma was dissolved in 1907. It was not until 1917 that he returned to Russia, allowed safe passage across Germany by the German military authorities who rightly thought that he would undermine the Russian war effort. His intransigent insistence that a socialist revolution could be launched against the centrist government of Alexander Kerensky was decisive in bringing about the revolution; and after a humiliating peace treaty with Germany, civil war, famine, and innumerable economic missteps, his unflinching leadership established the Soviet Union as it remained until its collapse at the end of the 1980s. He died shortly after the Soviet Union was formally instituted; he was, for good and ill, one of the great nation builders of history; one wonders what Machiavelli would have made of him.

Lenin's great invention was the idea of the revolutionary party. This needs explanation, and the explanation involves two other crucial elements in Lenin's Marxism. The first we have seen already: Lenin's insistence on locating what happened in Russia in the context of global capitalism. Lenin's analysis in *Imperialism, the Highest Stage of Capitalism* allowed him to imagine that Russia might take the lead in overthrowing world capitalism by "breaking the weakest link in the capitalist chain." Events showed how dangerous the thought was. It was also heretical. By the 1890s orthodox Marxism was dictated by Engels and Karl Kautsky; they shared a house in London and were the custodians of Marx's papers and reputation, as well as the organization of the Second International. They held rigid views about what Marx had discovered, and one of the most rigid was the view that the most developed country would make the socialist revolution first. If England, Holland, and the United States grasped their opportunity, they might make an almost bloodless, perhaps even an almost silent, revolution as the workers used parliamentary means to seize real power. Things would be different in Germany, where liberalism and parliamentary democracy had made less headway. The German autocracy would almost certainly meet its end in a less tranquil takeover from below. They were certain that there would be a *revolution*; how violent was another matter. The reformism of Eduard Bernstein, who saw that the German socialist party had become a reformist party interested in promoting workers' rights and a welfare state, and was prospering because of it, was anathema to Kautsky. Bernstein's "gradualism" was indistinguishable from the reformism of the New Liberals in Britain and was treated with contempt by orthodox Marxists. Lenin sided with Kautsky against the revisionists, but took his own line on the prospects of revolution in Russia.

Because capitalism was global, the health of capitalism in the West depended on its profitability in foreign ventures. A successful revolution in Russia would ripple backward through Europe. As to why Russia was a plausible place to launch a revolution, Lenin was politically perceptive but economically naïve: the Russian state lacked legitimacy; the population was kept obedient by fear, not by affection for the czar or belief in the authority of his regime. Lenin also thought that because Russia came late to industrialization, and its workers worked in more modern conditions—in larger plants and with more modern machinery—they were more likely to be class-conscious and ripe for revolution. The implausibility of this view was that worker discontent is always greatest in the early days of capitalism. Lenin was right about the revolutionary potential of the Russian workers, and wrong about the cause; it was the sudden shift into an urban workplace that rendered them discontented, not the technology they encountered. American labor relations at the same period were strikingly violent for much the same reasons.

Lenin thought he saw an advanced revolutionary consciousness, but he probably saw a conservative dislike of change. Even so, the political point was valid; he could make a Russian revolution that *might* lead to something global. It would be a narrowly political revolution, it would be impossible to institute a socialist society in Russia by the unaided efforts of the Russian revolutionaries, and Lenin had no thought of creating "socialism in one country." An orthodox Marxist thought such a project made no sense. What was possible was to make a political revolution whose economic ramifications would bring about revolutions elsewhere, which would ensure that socialism was made not in one country but as an international enterprise.

. . . He ended by accepting the possibility of creating socialism in one country because he had no alternative; he had gained and kept power where everyone else had failed, and the only intellectual framework in which he could explain his success made it inexplicable. Something must give, and what gave was the doctrine that socialism must be international. The question is why Lenin was successful, and what he bequeathed by being so. The doctrine of the party is central. Lenin wrote a pamphlet in 1903 that had an enormous influence on party organization all over the world. This was *What Is to Be Done?* The answer to the question was that a cadre of revolutionary activists had to form a revolutionary party capable of uniting the workers and peasants; it became the canonical recipe for national liberation movements in colonial settings, and for all Communist parties, whether overt or clandestine. The party had to adopt the policy of democratic centralism, whereby leaders of the party at every level were democratically elected, but policy was devised at the center, and all members were instructed in it and followed it. The cell structure of Bolshevism was common to all clandestine organizations then and now, but democratic centralism is a distinctively Bolshevik doctrine.

It presupposed what Marx had accepted but others had flinched from, the division of the working class into the revolutionary vanguard and the rest. The party was to be the vanguard, agitating and propagandizing among the masses, and waiting for the moment to lead an actual revolution. This view was anathema to many democratic socialists, who wanted a broad-based party that would embark on a long educative process until there was an overwhelming mass base. Although he eventually accepted Lenin's vanguardist vision, Trotsky was initially deeply hostile. He thought it threatened what he called "substitutism," in which the party substituted for a missing working class, and he accurately predicted what would happen if democratic centralism came to power: the central committee would substitute for the party, and the first secretary would eventually substitute for the central committee. In short, Stalin.

To treat Marxism as a doctrine in the same intellectual category as the creeds of religious radicals like John of Leiden need not be an unfriendly act. Russell's treatment of Marxism in *German Social Democracy* is admiring; but as early as 1896, when he published the book, he took Marx to be more impressive as a prophet than as an economist, and Marxism to be closer to religion than to science.

Marxism is a doctrine in tension with itself; because it offers itself as science but a science of revolution, it simultaneously demands a deep respect for the intransigence of things as they really are and a deep confidence in the ability of the radicalized working class to change them. Marx emphasized the latter when young and the former later in life. His caution about the likely outcome of the Paris Commune, expressed in *The Civil War in France* and even more in the letters he wrote before the actual uprising, was exemplary. There is no virtue in the workers' sacrificing themselves when they have no prospects of making a successful revolution. Whether Marx in his later life would ever have thought the time was ripe for revolution is hard to guess; he would certainly have thought Lenin's gamble doomed to fail.

Any Marxist would have thought that the disaster was that means became ends; an ideologically monolithic party backed by a secret police monopolized politics, then that party fell into the hands of Stalin, whose capacity for mastering the details of what was happening in his vast empire was astonishing, and whose lack of inhibition in securing his position by murder both retail and wholesale was equally astonishing. The details of his crimes against the Russian people are not our subject, but if anyone wanted total control over every detail of his subjects' lives, he did; and if anyone regarded everyone else as expendable, he did. There have been many rulers with similar ambitions; our interest is in whether Marxism lent itself to misuse by Stalin. Utopianism, a lack of scruple, a tendency to think only in terms of class struggle, which led to the bizarre situation in which the party made war against its own supporters, all played their part. There was one other feature of the Stalinist autocracy that distinguished it from older autocracies, and also from the autocracies of the right that came to power in interwar Europe. This was its curiously theological quality. Autocracies of the right were interested in holding power, and cared less for doctrinal unity than for unity behind the leader of the day. Whether it was Stalin's early training as a seminarian or simply his obsession with detail, it is impossible to say, but his obsession with laying down a correct party line on matters remote from practical politics seems in retrospect bizarre. Stalin's role was papal; once he had pronounced, the matter was closed, and although he never declared himself infallible, he was treated as if he were. Nor was it merely a matter of establishing that, for instance, reformist social democrats were social fascists in the early 1930s, then allies in a popular front in the later 1930s; doctrinal correctness extended to the making of films and the writing of operas, as Eisenstein and Shostakovich discovered.

Lenin had sown the seed. He had no time for dissent; he held not only the reasonable view that a revolutionary party must preserve a high degree of unity to be effective but also the much less reasonable view that because Marxism was a science, there was no more room for freedom of speech in Marxism than in chemistry. It goes without saying that there is a great deal of freedom of speech in chemistry and that scientific theories are not protected from criticism by putting a bullet in the back of dissenters' heads. The difficulty in saying more than this lies in two obvious facts. The first is that Lenin's success in November 1917 was astonishing and gave his ideas a standing among Marxists everywhere that made them hard to challenge. Marxists might find novel ways of being Leninist, but not ways of being a non-Leninist. Forms of discipline appropriate to clandestine, revolutionary parties were imposed on Communist parties everywhere, along with the attendant machinery of purges, instant changes in party lines that adherents were supposed to accept *de fide*, and a cult of the leader. Once Stalin's dictatorship was firmly established, Stalinist models of leadership became canonical in all parties affiliated to the Comintern. Patterns of control varied, as did the level of violence, the degree of cruelty, and the prevalence of general gangsterism; but the combination of Soviet "imperial" influence and the quasi-theology of "Marxism-Leninism-Stalinism" gave all communist regimes, other than Tito's Yugoslav breakaway regime, a distinctive and all but totalitarian character—not that Tito's regime could have been mistaken for a liberal democracy.

Aristotle suggested *eudemonia*, happiness over a lifetime, as the guiding goal of life. Epicurus (341–270 BCE), proposed a simpler goal to reach happiness: *ataraxia*, a clear state of mind characterized both by tranquility and by freedom from fear of death. In this excerpt, from his *Letter to Menoeceus*, he believes this can be reached through developing a habit of guiding our lives by wisdom.

Epicurus

Life: A User's Manual

Let no one be slow to seek wisdom when he is young nor weary in the search of it when he has grown old. For no age is too early or too late for the health of the soul. And to say that the season for studying philosophy has not yet come, or that it is past and gone, is like saying that the season for happiness is not yet or that it is now no more. Therefore, both old and young alike ought to seek wisdom.

Accustom yourself to believing that death is nothing to us, for good and evil imply the capacity for sensation, and death is the privation of all sentience; therefore a correct understanding that death is nothing to us makes the mortality of life enjoyable, not by adding to life a limitless time, but by taking away the yearning after immortality. For life has no terrors for him who has thoroughly understood that there are no terrors for him in ceasing to live. Foolish, therefore, is the man who says that he fears death, not because it will pain when it comes, but because it pains in the prospect. Whatever causes no annoyance when it is present, causes only a groundless pain in the expectation. Death, therefore, the most awful of evils, is nothing to us, seeing that, when we are, death is not come, and, when death is come, we are not. It is nothing, then, either to the living or to the dead, for with the living it is not and the dead exist no longer.

But in the world, at one time men shun death as the greatest of all evils, and at another time choose it as a respite from the evils in life. The wise man does not deprecate life nor does he fear the cessation of life. The thought of life is no offense to him, nor is the cessation of life regarded as an evil. And even as men choose of food not merely and simply the larger portion, but the more pleasant, so the wise seek to enjoy the time which is most pleasant and not merely that which is longest. And he who admonishes the young to live well and the old to make a good end speaks foolishly, not merely because of the desirability of life, but because the same exercise at once teaches to live well and to die well.

KEY TERMS

Ataraxia is freedom from worry and from fear of death according to Epicurus.

Bourgeoisie is Karl Marx's term for what today is usually called the middle class, allied with the interests of capitalism against the proletariat and in fact usually voting against their own interests in democratic elections.

Direct democracy is the notion that each citizen has an active role in the government and has an equal say and role in the creation of laws.

Eudaemonia is happiness, the goal of life according to Aristotle.

General will is the opinion people will reach, if they consider a matter objectively and determine what is best for society as a whole (and are not swayed by their personal interest).

Harm principle states that the sole end for which mankind are warranted, individually or collectively, in interfering with the liberty of action of any of their number, is self-protection.

Labor theory of property states that if you work for something, and it is not already owned by someone, then you acquire ownership of it.

Libertarians argue for a limited government, one that has as its sole purpose, protection.

Natural rights are rights people have without a government. They are rights that we have in virtue of our humanity.

Original position is a hypothetical situation discussed by John Rawls where there is no government. Persons in the original position are under the veil or ignorance and no nothing of their own social class, gender, race, or status. The goal is to develop principles of justice.

Positive rights are rights created by an act of legislation by the government. The government makes a law, and a right is created.

Representative democracy is a system where the citizens vote for representatives who represent their political interest.

Theory of surplus value elaborated in Karl Marx's *Theories of Surplus Value* (1863), refers to the difference between the cost of what a worker produces with his labor and the amount that the capitalist who owns the means of production can profit from that product.

Proletariat is Karl Marx's term for the labor class who do not own the means of productions and work for capitalists who own those means and profit from the surplus value of the workers' labor.

State of nature is a hypothetical situation where mankind is living without any government.

Veil of ignorance is a hypothetical thought experiment where one is to imagine oneself as a representative of the populous as a whole. Under the veil you will be looking for guiding principles of justice and begin to stipulate laws and regulations for your government.

Will of all is simply the will of the majority, considering only their self-interest—not what is best for society.

QUESTIONS FOR DISCUSSION AND REVIEW

1. Compare and contrast various views of Hobbes and Locke on the state of nature and natural rights.
2. Explain and evaluate Rousseau's criticism of both Hobbes and Locke regarding the state of nature.
3. Explain the difference between the labor theory of property and labor theory of value.
4. Explain and evaluate Karl Marx's analysis of class struggle as presented in his *Communist Manifesto.*
5. Explain the views of Nozick and Hospers regarding legitimate laws and the role of government.
6. Compare and contrast Rawls and Nozick on justice.
7. Critically analyze Karl Marx's views on workers' rights and how to get them, as suggested in his Communist Manifesto.
8. The creation of workers' unions had a violent beginning in the United States, but that movement led to much we take for granted today including the five-day work week, overtime pay, sick leave, and child labor laws. Attitudes and laws regarding unions vary from state to state. Should workers have a right to unionize?
9. Where do your political ideas come from? Do race, ethnicity, economic status and culture determine your politics?
10. Is Epicurus right that we are likelier to be happy if we do not fear death? Explain.

SUGGESTED READINGS

Camus, A. (1955). *The Myth of Sisyphus.*

Cicero, M. T. (1951). *The Basic Works of Cicero.*

Dupré, L. (1966). *The Philosophical Foundations of Marxism.*

Dworkin, R. (1978). *Taking Rights Seriously.*

Epicurus. *Letter to Menoeceus.* Available from http://classics.mit.edu/Epicurus/menoec.html. Oates, W. (1940). *The Stoic and Epicurean Philosophers.*

Hart, H. (1963). *Law Liberty and Morality.*

Hart, H. (1961). *The Concept of Law.*

Hobbes, T. (1651). *Leviathan.*

Internet Encyclopedia of Philosophy. A peer-reviewed academic resource. Available from http://www.iep.utm.edu/

Locke, J. (1690). *Two Treatises of Civil Government.*

Marx, Karl, (1977). *Selected Works*, 3 vols. Marx, K. & Engels, F. (1888). *Communist manifesto.*

Piketty, T. (2014). *Capital in the 21st century.* Rawls, J. (1971). *A Theory of Justice.*

Russell, B. (2015). *"The Value of Philosophy.* In *The Problems of Philosophy.*

Ryan, A. (2012). *On politics.*

Sartre, J-P. (1956). *"I am the Self Which I will Be".* In *Being and Nothingness* .

Sartre, J-P. (2006). *Critique of Dialectical Reason.* Vols. 1 and 2. (Sheridan-Smith, A. and Hoare, Q. transl.).

Stanford Encyclopedia of Philosophy. Available from http://plato.stanford.edu/